THE BOOK OF ODDS

THE BOOK OF ODDS

FROM LIGHTNING STRIKES TO LOVE AT FIRST SIGHT,
THE ODDS OF
EVERYDAY LIFE

AMRAM SHAPIRO

LOUISE FIRTH CAMPBELL

ROSALIND WRIGHT

Alison Caverly, Contributing Editor

Zachary Turpin, Jon Sobel, Contributing Writers

wm

WILLIAM MORROW

An Imprint of HarperCollins*Publishers*

HarperCollins books may be purchased for educational, business, or sales promotional use. For information please e-mail the Special Markets Department at SPsales@harpercollins.com.

FIRST EDITION

Designed by Walter Zekanoski, WZ DESIGN

Library of Congress Cataloging-in-Publication Data has been applied for.

ISBN 978-0-06-206085-3

14 15 16 17 18 ID/SCP 10 9 8 7 6 5 4 3 2 1

To Those Who Count

To those who sample us randomly
and collect their numbers humbly
and confess how wrong they may be honestly
and report what they see whether it is
what they wished for or not
and share what they find with all of us
so we may learn something
we did not know of ourselves

CONTENTS

INTRODUCTION

This book is a numerical snapshot of the United States. Like a photograph its subject is stopped for a moment and set in context. It can be looked at so closely you can count the people in the bleachers and the buttons on their shirts. The photograph is not an Instagram but a panorama or 360-degree image. It addresses the destinies of people, from health and happiness to accidents and loss. It covers the cycle of life from conception to birth to childhood to schooling to adult life to aging and decline. It covers the everyday and holidays, the serious concerns of life and its comic turns.

"What are the odds of that?" We ask this when something strikes us as unlikely. We don't expect a reply since the question is rhetorical, an exclamation of surprise.

This book answers those questions in subject areas that tickle our curiosity or touch our anxieties and fears. Sometimes the odds surprise us. Sometimes they appall. Sometimes they amuse.

One thing the odds have in common in commonality. They are clear and simple. Every odds statement was created the same way and followed the same rules and conventions, the way entries in a dictionary do.

We look for the most fundamental units of activities or events to count, things just as we see them instead of more sophisticated, explanatory, but invisible measures. The likelihood of a batter hitting a single in a plate appearance is counted instead of his OPS (On-base Plus Slugging), or the odds a person owns blue jeans, rather than his propensity to spend.

Why? By concentrating on the experiences of normal existence, we have been able to develop a way of expressing the likelihood of these experiences. And we are able to compare likelihoods across a wide section of American life—something we call *calibration*. All of us already have an ability to calibrate, whether we recognize it or not. Think about how you automatically compare prices from one store to the next—you not only have a grasp of what things should cost; you also have a sense of the "reasonableness" of a price. Or how about the morning weather forecast? Without thinking you know if a projected temperature suggests the need for a coat. You not only understand the number in context; you understand the implications it has for your daily life.

The odds in this book can help us calibrate all kinds of possibilities in the same kind of way. We can judge risk or likelihood in a way we have never been able to do before. For example, the odds are **1 in 8.0** a woman will receive a diagnosis of breast cancer in her lifetime, about the odds a person lives in California, the most populous state.[1] For men the odds are **1 in 769**,[2] about the same odds a Major League Baseball game will be a no-hitter (**1 in 725**).[3] And speaking of baseball, one story became iconic during the three years we were developing the Book of Odds database. In those days our researchers met weekly to review their work with one another. We often had visitors. On this day our visitor was a college student, the daughter of a close friend. The presentations she saw were really varied: one researcher had just completed work on the odds associated with contraception; another one had compiled the odds of baseball.

1. N Howlader, AM Noone, M Krapcho, N Neyman, R Aminou, SF Altekruse, CL Kosary, J Ruhl, Z Tatalovich, H Cho, A Mariotto, MP Eisner, DR Lewis, HS Chen, EJ Feuer, KA Cronin, eds., *SEER Cancer Statistics Review, 1975–2009 (Vintage 2009 Populations)*. Bethesda, MD: National Cancer Institute, http://seer.cancer.gov/csr/1975_2009_pops09/, based on November 2011 SEER data submission, posted to the SEER website, April 2012.

2. US Census Bureau, "State & County Quick Facts," http://quickfacts.census.gov/qfd/states/06000.html.

3. Using the data from 1875 to present excluding those for the National Association, www.baseballreference.com.

The odds of a woman becoming pregnant after relying on one form or other of contraception were displayed. Starting with the population of women in 2002 who were of child-bearing years (15–44), the presentation identified the odds that one of these women was sexually active, the odds that she relied on condoms for contraception, and the odds that she would stop relying on condoms because she was pregnant. Each step of this "thread" of probabilities (as we term such chains) had independent odds. When put together, the odds that a woman in that original group would end up having given up condoms because there was no longer any point—she had become pregnant despite the contraceptive measure—were **1 in 142**.[4]

Next came the baseball presentation, and as it happened, our visitor was a baseball fan. She seemed captivated as the Book of Odds' Major League Baseball statistics were summarized. They were different from those she was used to on the sports pages. What will happen next on average, independent of who's pitching and who's batting? Viewed this way, the odds that the next batter will hit a triple are **1 in 144**.[5]

Later that day I received a call from my friend, the college student's mother. Her daughter had returned home on a mission. She had immediately called her boyfriend, and her mother overheard her daughter's part of the conversation. "She asked her boyfriend if he knew the odds of a couple conceiving a child if they were relying solely on condoms," my friend said. "She informed him that the odds were **1 in 142**."

---

4. Book of Odds calculation of thread of contingent probabilities based on "Use of Contraception and Use of Family Planning Services in the United States: 1982–2002," *Advance Data from Vital and Health Statistics* 350, 2002, and A Chandra, GM Martinez, WD Mosher, JC Abma, J Jones, "Fertility, Family Planning, and Reproductive Health of U.S. Women: Data from the 2002 National Survey of Family Growth," *Vital and Health Statistics* 23(25), 2005.

5. Book of Odds estimate based on MLB statistics for triples and plate appearances (not at bats). Strategic Baseball simulator has it at 1 in 132: http://sbs-baseball.com/theory.txt.

Then she asked if he knew the odds of the next batter in a Major League Baseball game hitting a triple. Again, he didn't know.

"It's **1 in 144**," she told him. And then she added, jabbing her finger for emphasis, "And I've seen triples."

We could go on and on: the odds a death will include HIV on the death certificate are becoming rarer and are **1 in 21,774**[6]—this says an HIV death is less likely than that a visit to the ER is due to an accident involving a golf cart in a year: **1 in 22,325**.[7] Multiply by 10 and you have the approximate odds a person visiting the Grand Canyon will die during the trip: **1 in 232,100**.[8] Multiply by 10 again and you have the odds a person will die from chronic constipation: **1 in 2,215,900**.[9] For those working on murder mysteries: the odds of being murdered during a trip to the Grand Canyon: **1 in 8,156,000**. Of dying in a Grand Canyon flash flood? **1 in 14,270,000**.[10]

As I said, we could go on and on, which is why we wrote a book. Enjoy!

---

6. WK Adih, RM Selik, X Hu, "Trends in Diseases Reported on US Death Certificates That Mentioned HIV Infection, 1996–2006," *Journal of the International Association of Physicians in AIDS Care* 10(1), January/February 2011: 5–11.

7. Book of Odds calculation based on US Consumer Product Safety Commission, *National Electronic Injury Surveillance System (NEISS) Data Highlights—2010*, http://www.cpsc.gov/LIBRARY/neiss.html.

8. Books of Odds estimate based on data in MP Ghiglieri, TM Myers, *Over the Edge: Death in Grand Canyon,* 1st ed., 13th revision (Flagstaff, AZ: Puma Press, 2006).

9. Book of Odds estimate based on Centers for Disease Control and Prevention, *Compressed Mortality File, 1979–2005,* http://wonder.cdc.gov/mortsql.html.

10. Book of Odds estimate based on Ghiglieri and Myers, *Over the Edge.*

METHOD

This book is constructed on a considerable foundation. We began with a rigorous methodology, creating conventions and holding ourselves to the same standards as any reference source. Only then did we begin to assemble what has become a formidable database.

The very first database had only 450 odds but already vividly demonstrated how comparing disparate subjects with similar odds could both shock and inform. Take this example: "The odds a female who is raped is under 12 are **1 in 3.4**."[1] That is shocking in and of itself, but it is made more vividly awful when one looks for other odds in the same range. "The odds a person 99–100 will die in a year are **1 in 3.3**."[2] The odds a female rape victim is under 12 are about the same as a 99-year-old man dying in the next 12 months.

From there we went to work on growing the database and making it accessible for Internet use. We needed a way to classify the subjects we would cover and created a taxonomy that aided us later in employing semantic tools. More than fifty person-years went into creating more than 400,000 odds. Each one can be compared to any other, and thus each part enriches the whole.

But what do we mean when we talk about odds? When we say, "My doctor says the odds are one in ten that the test will be positive," we're expressing *probability*. In mathematical terms, statements like these put fractions into words. When we say, "the odds are one in ten," think of a fraction, with the first, lower number as the numerator, or top number in the fraction, and the second, larger number as the denominator, or bottom number. So, "one in ten" literally means *one-tenth*, or a *10 percent chance*. Each odds in *The Book of Odds* expresses the probability that a specific occurrence will take place, given the number of situations in which that occurrence might take place. Since it is past experience that provides a basis for expecting what will take place, odds are based entirely on past counts or on rare occasions actuarial forecasts.

---

1. DG Kilpatrick, "From the Mouths of Victims: What Victimization Surveys Tell Us About Sexual Assault and Sex Offenders," paper presented at the Association for the Treatment of Sexual Abusers Meeting, November 1996, Chicago, Illinois.

2. Book of Odds estimate based on Centers for Disease Control and Prevention, *Compressed Mortality File, 1979–2005,* http://wonder.cdc.gov/mortsql.html.

Each statement in *The Book of Odds* contains certain required components. Consider the example, "The odds a person will be struck by lightning in a year are **1 in 1,101,000** (US)."[3] First, we have to know what will happen, in this case, a lightning strike. Second, we have to know to whom it will happen—a person, any person. As we narrow that definition (a farmer, a golfer) the odds will change. Next, the statement tells us the parameters, or limitations, of the calculation. In this case, there are parameters of time (a single year), data span (annual data from 2008–2012), and of place (US). In this book **all odds are US odds,** so we have left the geography off and the data spans are usually evident in the sources cited. Any change to these parameters, as well as the time frame used to collect data, may change the odds. Some odds, such as those about the ideal fair coin toss coming up heads or tails, have no such parameters, and are considered true everywhere and any time because they are defined that way.

Odds, Probability, and Chances

At Book of Odds we treat these terms as synonymous. Odds are statements of probability. So, "The odds of . . ." should be interpreted mathematically as "The chances of . . . ," or "The probability of . . . ," or, the ratio of favorable outcomes to total outcomes. This is a subtle but important convention to be aware of when using the odds in this book. Its purpose is to be simple, accessible, and consistent with conversational English.

Traditionally, the term "odds" refers to the ratio of favorable to nonfavorable outcomes. So, a gambler might say, "A horse that is expected to win 25 percent of the races it enters has **3 to 1 (3:1)** odds against or **1 to 3 (1:3)** odds to win." This is a great tool for a bettor who is attempting to calculate the expected

---

3. Book of Odds estimates based on 2008–2012 data from StruckByLightning.org.

value of a gamble. However, this form can be troublesome for ordinary people trying to understand complex statistics. "1 in 4" is easier to grasp in your mind's eye than "3 to 1 against." You can picture it, can't you? This is also the way we humans commonly think and speak when discussing uncertainty.

That brings us to the question, why do we include what we do? We purposely focus on the events of everyday life, things that all or most of us will have experienced firsthand. This is vital for the exercise of calibration— understanding odds in a larger context. We also include those things we may not have experienced but whose likelihood we may worry about: misfortune, illness, death . . . We have broken the odds of human experience into three large sets: destiny, actions, and the cycle of life. Destiny is what happens to us. Actions are what we do. And cycle of life is a way of looking at the odds associated with the stages of our existence: conception, birth, childhood, schooling, adult life, work, retirement, aging, and death.

All the odds won't be relevant or of interest to everyone, but each will be relevant or interesting to someone. We aim to present data and information objectively and without bias, but we readily acknowledge that decisions about what to include inevitably involve some subjective judgment and are subject to certain parameters: for example, we must work with the terms the data collectors have chosen to use. Our principles of selection, however, are not knowingly biased to support one position or another. And when we address controversial subjects, we seek to maintain a neutral perspective, shedding light, but not heat, on politically charged issues.

In every case we have searched for the most authoritative and reliable source for our data, but we are transparent about the fact that quality varies. For all sources we ask the same questions: who collected information from whom, in what manner, and for what purpose. Some are straightforward, actual counts like the US Census. For survey data and experimental trials, we evaluate the underlying hypothesis or research questions, study design, sample frame, and size, and make a judgment about whether it accurately reflects the population under study, as well as assess the methodology of analysis, fairness of presentation of the data, explanations of variables and limitations, reproducibility of results, and quality of peer review. Further, we examine the sponsoring body and those executing the study, looking to see if they have a vision or mission or mandate that might have had even a subtle influence on the findings. We don't dismiss any source with an expected point of view out of hand, but we make every attempt to be mindful. There is a wealth of wonderful sources, but there are also many of limited or no value and applicability. These are either left out or, if used at all, presented with appropriate caveats attached.

Timeliness also matters, and within the time boundaries publishing affords we have updated most odds statements. Even so, some measurements are irregularly collected, and even those with regular measurements, such as economic data and annual crime and cancer statistics, have their quirks, since they rely on human input. One year New York City failed to provide crime data to the FBI, for example. And some subjects are studied sporadically. Sex, for example, is one of these, with a Kinsey Report or equivalent sometimes released only once a decade.

In addition to our internal controls, we seek independent external reviews of our sources. We consult book reviews and commentary and reviews in academic journals. We also contact relevant and appropriate specialists, including authors of related academic work, industry or research specialists, editors of and contributors to relevant journals, and any and all credible experts uncovered in our own investigations.

Tense Conventions

At its heart, the invention of a reference work is really the invention of a set of conventions followed by their application with relentless consistency. This is the work that Dr. Samuel Johnson, defining "lexicographer" in his own dictionary, called that of "a harmless drudge."

The most subtle and important of our conventions relate to tenses. Odds naming past dates or historical events such as wars are in the past tense. Odds describing an outer or inner state of being or using the predicate nominative use the present tense. Most odds use the future tense, however, despite being based on past counts. This practice has the advantage of placing our readers and users into the condition we experience at all times, that of being about to learn what the future holds. Our internal methods document explains it this way:

> We assume in virtually all of our odds that we are viewing the events and actions to be described from the time before their count began. From this perspective what is in the sentence is what a perfectly prescient forecast would have yielded. This we term the "future implicative." From this perspective, the sentence becomes lively. It invites the reader to imagine standing poised at the beginning of the reference period, wondering perhaps what will happen next.

Caveats

Odds are based on recorded past occurrences among a large group of people. They do not pretend to describe the specific risk to a particular individual, and as such cannot be used to make personal predictions. For example, if a person learns that there is a quantifiable probability of a cure for a specific disease, those statistics cannot take into account this person's personal genetic disposition or medical history, unique environmental factors, the experience of the treating physician, the accuracy of tests performed, the development of new treatments, and so on.

The past is the perch on which we must stand to look toward the future. Still, the view can be clouded, and the past does not always provide reliable guidance about the future. There is always the possibility "a black swan" will appear—an unexpected event with an outsize impact. Complexity theory, which is the latest way of attacking modeling and large data sets, has a great deal to say about the impact of the increasing number of "agents" in our world systems, and what this means about predictability and new sources of risk.

Statistics is divided into two camps, the frequentist camp and the Bayesians. The former puts much reliance on past distributions, the latter on learning from new information. We are both. We like counts as something factual to start with, but we accept the Bayesian view that new insight may trump old data. All our odds may be thought of as potential "priors."

If our work helps people gain a feel for probability because the presentation is fun, easy to understand, and touches on subjects of real interest, we will be very pleased with our efforts.

CHAPTER 1

SEX

Liar, Liar

The odds a man has lied about the number of sex partners he's had in order to protect his ego:

1 in 7.1

SOURCE: AskMen.com, "Part I: Dating & Sex," *The Great Male Survey, 2011 Edition,* http://www.askmen.com/specials/2011_great_male_survey.

SEX PARTNERS:
How High Can You Count?

When it comes to sex, most people think experience is a good thing—but they also think there can be too much of a good thing.

The largest group of women, **1 in 3.2**, feels comfortable with a man who has had no more than 5 previous sexual partners, but the more the number exceeds what can be counted on one hand, the less comfortable many women feel. Up to two hands? **1 in 3.6** women chooses 10 as the maximum number of former partners she's okay with, but just **1 in 5** women feels relaxed about a tally that is no more than 20. A man who fesses up to a maximum of 50 previous partners really limits his options: only **1 in 12.5** women feels comfortable with that number, and if his count is up to twice that, only **1 in 25** women is willing to join his parade.

The double standard still exists, but with a twist. Only **1 in 50** men will report being comfortable if his partner has had a maximum of 50 sexual partners—but if her number maxes out at 100, a larger group of men (**1 in 33.3**) reports they are okay with that. **1 in 8.3** men is at ease with a maximum of 20 predecessors; a far larger group feels okay if there were no more than 10 (**1 in 2.8**). And like women, the largest group of men (**1 in 2.5**) feels comfortable if she's had no more than 5.

But both genders value some experience over none at all. Only **1 in 11.1** women feels most comfortable if her partner has had no sexual partners before her, and for men the odds are even lower—just **1 in 12.5** will feel comfortable if he's the first.

SOURCES: AskMen.com, "Part I: Dating & Sex," *The Great Female Survey, 2009 Edition*, www.askmen.com/specials/yahoo_shine_great_female_survey/part1.html. ⟋ AskMen.com, "Part I: Dating & Sex," *The Great Male Survey, 2009 Edition*, http://www.askmen.com/specials/2009_great_male_survey.

Age at First Time	Odds (1 in)	
	Men	Women
Younger than 14	7.7	25
Between 14 and 15	6.3	7.7
Between 16 and 17	3.7	3.2
Between 18 and 19	4.4	3.6
20+	5.9	4.4

SOURCE: "The American Sex Survey: A Peek Beneath the Sheets," *ABC News Primetime Live Poll*, October 21, 2004, http://abcnews.go.com/images/Politics/959a1AmericanSexSurvey.pdf.

Belief About First Time	%		Odds (1 in)	
	Men	Women	Men	Women
Too young	37	50	2.7	2.0
Just right	57	49	1.8	2.0
Too old	6	1	16.7	100

SOURCE: "The American Sex Survey:" A Peek Beneath the Sheets, *ABC News Primetime Live Poll*, October 21, 2004, http://abcnews.go.com/images/Politics/959a1AmericanSexSurvey.pdf.

ODDS COUPLE

The Age of Love
1 in 5.9

The odds a man who has had sex first did so when he was 20 or older are the same odds as an adult 45 or older in a relationship will cheat.

SOURCES: "The American Sex Survey: A Peek Beneath the Sheets," *ABC News Primetime Live Poll*, October 21, 2004, http://abcnews.go.com/images/Politics/959a1AmericanSexSurvey.pdf ⟋ LL Fisher, *Sex, Romance, and Relationships, AARP Survey of Midlife and Older Adults*, American Association of Retired Persons, April 2010.

Swearing Off Sex— Before It Happens

The odds a person has taken a formal pledge to remain a virgin until marriage:

- Female 15–19: 1 in 5.8
- Male 15–19: 1 in 9.3
- Female 20–24: 1 in 9.7
- Male 20–24: 1 in 12.4

SOURCE: Estimated by Book of Odds from *National Survey of Family Growth 2006–08 Public Use Data Files*, Centers for Disease Control and Prevention.

The odds a man 25–44 has had no female sexual partners in his lifetime:

1 in 43.5

The odds a woman 25–44 has had no male sexual partners in her lifetime:

1 in 62.5

SOURCE: A Chandra, WD Mosher, C Copen, C Sionean, "Sexual Behavior, Sexual Attraction, and Sexual Identity in the United States: Data from the 2006–2008 National Survey of Family Growth," *National Health Statistics Report* 36, Centers for Disease Control and Prevention, March 2011.

1 in 4.4

The odds a male has lied about not being a virgin.

SOURCE: S Jayson, "Truth about Sex," *USA Today,* January 26, 2010.

When the Guy Is Older

Among women 18–24 who first had sex before age 20, **13%** whose first sexual experience was with a partner three or more years older say the intercourse was **not voluntary**.

This compares to **4%** of those who first had sex with a partner their own age or younger.

SOURCE: JC Abma, GM Martinez, CE Copen, "Teenagers in the United States: Sexual Activity, Contraceptive Use, and Childbearing, National Survey of Family Growth 2006–2008," *Vital and Health Statistics* 23(30), June 2010.

"My parents are going to be out of town all weekend."

Most Americans **lose their virginity** in their high school years.

The odds a twelfth grade **male** has had sex are **1 in 1.7**.

The odds a twelfth grade **female** has had sex are **1 in 1.5**.

SOURCE: DK Eaton, L Kann, S Kinchen, S Shanklin, J Ross, J Hawkins, et al., "Youth Risk Behavior Surveillance—United States, 2009," *Morbidity and Mortality Weekly Report* 59(SS-5), June 4, 2010.

Premarital Sex—Most Everyone Has Done It

A number of older adults are preaching "Do as I say, not as I did." According to a report written by Lawrence Finer of the Guttmacher Institute, rates of premarital sex have remained fairly constant since 1960, and about **90%** of women born as far back as the 1940s did the dirty before tying the knot (if they've tied it at all). What has changed dramatically over the past several decades is the way Americans view premarital sex. A 2004 survey found that only **1 in 3.3** people born before 1940 believe premarital sex is okay. The odds increase dramatically to **1 in 1.7** for those born between 1940 and 1954. And they increase further to **1 in 1.4** for people born between 1975 and 1986.

SOURCES: L Finer, "Trends in Premarital Sex in the United States, 1954–2003," *Public Health Report,* 122(1), Jan–Feb 2007: 73–78. ↗ "The American Sex Survey: A Peek Beneath the Sheets," *ABC News Primetime Live Poll,* October 21, 2004, http://abcnews.go.com/images/Politics/959a1AmericanSexSurvey.pdf.

DID YOU know?

Out of all women 18–24 who shed their virginity before 20, **1 in 2.1** said she had mixed feelings about it at the time, compared to **1 in 3** men.

SOURCE: JC Abma, GM Martinez, CE Copen, "Teenagers in the United States: Sexual Activity, Contraceptive Use, and Childbearing, National Survey of Family Growth 2006–2008." *Vital and Health Statistics* 23 (30), June 2010.

in the Past Year

Number of Sex Partners

(ages 15–44 years)

The odds a male has had **a female sexual partner** but **not** in the past year are **1 in 15.6**.
The odds a female has had **a male sexual partner** but **not** in the past year are **1 in 16.4**.

The odds a male has had **1 female sexual partner** in the past year are **1 in 1.6**.
The odds a female has had **1 male sexual partner** in the past year are **1 in 1.4**.

The odds a male has had **2 female sexual partners** in the past year are **1 in 11.6**.
The odds a female has had **2 male sexual partners** in the past year are **1 in 13.2**.

The odds a male has had **3 female sexual partners** in the past year are **1 in 25.6**.
The odds a female has had **3 male sexual partners** in the past year are **1 in 40**.

The odds a male has had **4 or more female sexual partners** in the past year are **1 in 16.7**.
The odds a female has had **4 or more male sexual partners** in the past year are **1 in 34.5**.

PAST YEAR opposite sex partners

Partners	Males	Females
	%	
0	6	6
1	63	69
2	9	8
3	4	3
4+	6	3

SOURCE: A Chandra, WD Mosher, C Copen, C Sionean, "Sexual Behavior, Sexual Attraction, and Sexual Identity in the United States: Data from the 2006–2008 National Survey of Family Growth," *National Health Statistics Report* 36, Centers for Disease Control and Prevention, March 2011.

 **GENDER WARS**

Slightly more men than women admit to lying about the number of sex partners they've had: **1 in 2.1** vs. **1 in 2.2**

SOURCES: Book of Odds estimate based on data from Askmen.com, "Part I: Dating & Sex," *The Great Male Survey, 2010 Edition,* http://www.askmen.com/specials/2010_ great_male_survey/. ✗ Book of Odds estimate based on data from Askmen.com, "Part I: Dating & Sex," *The Great Female Survey, 2009 Edition,* http://www.askmen .com/specials/yahoo_shine_great_female_ survey/part1.html

1 + 2 = Threesomes

1 in 7.4 adults has had a threesome. An adult is more than twice as likely to have had a threesome than to have four older siblings.

Threesome odds diverge sharply by gender: While more than 18% (1 in 5.4) of men say they've had one, only 1 in 12.9 women, or about 8%, reports having participated in one.

SOURCES: "The American Sex Survey: A Peek Beneath the Sheets," *ABC News Primetime Live Poll,* October 21, 2004. http://abcnews .go.com/images/Politics/959a1AmericanSexSurvey. ✗ Book of Odds estimate based on data from *General Social Survey 1972–2008.* Cumulative Datafile, NORC, University of Chicago.

LØVE Hurts

The odds a man has experienced physical pain during sex for at least a few months in the past year: **1 in 33.3**

The odds for a woman: **1 in 6.9**

SOURCE: EO Laumann, JH Gagnon, RT Michael, S Michaels, *The Social Organization of Sexuality: Sexual Practices in the United States,* Chicago: University of Chicago Press, 1994.

in a Lifetime

The odds a male has had **1 female sexual partner** are **1 in 6.7**.
The odds a female has had **1 male sexual partner** are **1 in 4.5**.

The odds a male has had **2 female sexual partners** are **1 in 13.2**.
The odds a female has had **2 male sexual partners** are **1 in 9.3**.

The odds a male has had **3–6 female sexual partners** are **1 in 3.8**.
The odds a female has had **3–6 male sexual partners** are **1 in 3.2**.

The odds a male has had **7–14 female sexual partners** are **1 in 5.5**.
The odds a female has had **7–14 male sexual partners** are **1 in 6.3**.

The odds a male has had **15 or more female sexual partners** are **1 in 4.7**.
The odds a female has had **15 or more male sexual partners** are **1 in 12**.

Number of Sex Partners

(ages 15–44 years)

SOURCE: A Chandra, WD Mosher, C Copen, C Sionean, "Sexual Behavior, Sexual Attraction, and Sexual Identity in the United States: Data from the 2006–2008 National Survey of Family Growth," *National Health Statistics Report* 36, Centers for Disease Control and Prevention, March 2011.

LIFETIME opposite sex partners

Partners	Males	Females
	%	
0	11	11
1	15	22
2	8	11
3 to 6	27	32
7 to 14	18	16
15+	21	8

Sex:
THE COMPLICATIONS

The odds a man does not enjoy sex at all are **1 in 50**.

The odds a woman does not enjoy sex at all are **1 in 14.3**.

The odds a man usually spends 15 minutes or less having sex are **1 in 12.5**.

The odds a woman hardly ever or never orgasms during sex are **1 in 14.3**.

The odds a man 18–59 climaxed too early for at least a few months in the past year are **1 in 3.5**.

The odds a woman 18–59 climaxed too early for at least a few months in the past year are **1 in 9.8**.

The odds a man 18–59 felt anxious about his sexual performance for at least a few months in the past year are **1 in 5.9**.

The odds a woman 18–59 felt anxious about her sexual performance for at least a few months in the past year are **1 in 8.7**.

The odds a man will exaggerate sex stories he tells his friends are **1 in 1.3**.

The odds a woman will exaggerate her sex stories to her friends are **1 in 12.5**.

The odds a woman will gives oral sex but does not like doing it are **1 in 5.3**.

The odds a woman does not like receiving oral sex are **1 in 10**.

The odds a man would change the size of his partner's breasts if he could are **1 in 2.8**.

The odds a man has suggested his partner get breast enlargements are **1 in 12.7**.

The odds a woman 18–65 will hide her breasts during sex are **1 in 11.1**.

The odds a man 18–65 considers his penis size to be small are **1 in 8.3**.

The odds a woman 18–65 considers her partner's penis size to be small are **1 in 16.7**.

The odds a man prefers to have sex with the lights on are **1 in 3.5**.

The odds a woman prefers to have sex with the lights on are **1 in 7.1**.

The odds a man prefers to have sex with the lights off are **1 in 3.7**.

The odds a woman prefers to have sex with the lights off are **1 in 2**.

The odds a man has insincerely told a woman he loves her to get sex are **1 in 5.6**.

The odds a woman has withheld sex until a partner said he loves her are **1 in 8.3**.

SOURCES: "The American Sex Survey: A Peek Beneath the Sheets," *ABC News Primetime Live Poll,* October 21, 2004, http://abcnews.go.com/images/Politics/959a1AmericanSexSurvey.pdf. ✗ EO Laumann, JH Gagnon, RT Michael, S Michaels, *The Social Organization of Sexuality: Sexual Practices in the United States,* Chicago: University of Chicago Press, 1994. ✗ AskMen.com, "Part I: Dating & Sex," *The Great Male Survey, 2009 Edition,* www.askmen.com/specials/2009_great_male_survey. ✗ "What Are the Rules of Attraction?" *Elle/MSNBC.com Sex and Beauty Survey, Elle* magazine, 2004. ✗ DA Frederick, A Peplau, J Lever, "The Barbie Mystique," *International Journal of Sexual Health* 20(3), March 2008: 200–212. ✗ J Lever, DA Frederick, A Peplau, "Does Size Matter? Men's and Women's Views on Penis Size Across the Lifespan," *Psychology of Men and Masculinity* 7(3), March 2006: 129–143.

None of the Above

1 in 25.6 men 18–44 and **1 in 26.3** women 18–44 will report being something other than heterosexual, homosexual, or bisexual.

SOURCE: WD Mosher, A Chandra, J Jones, "Sexual Behavior and Selected Health Measures: Men and Women 15–44 Years of Age, United States 2002," *Advance Data from Vital and Health Statistics* 362, September 15, 2005.

1 in 43.5 men 18–44 reports being homosexual vs. **1 in 76.9** women, but many more women 18–44 than men report being bisexual: **1 in 35.7** vs. **1 in 55.6**.

SOURCE: WD Mosher, A Chandra, J Jones, "Sexual Behavior and Selected Health Measures: Men and Women 15–44 Years of Age, United States 2002," *Advance Data from Vital and Health Statistics* 362, September 15, 2005.

 1 in 250 The odds a man 18–44 married to a woman is gay.

SOURCE: WD Mosher, A Chandra, J Jones, "Sexual Behavior and Selected Health Measures: Men and Women 15–44 Years of Age, United States 2002," *Advance Data from Vital and Health Statistics* 362, September 15, 2005.

The odds a man 18–44 who has ever had same-sex sexual contact will report being heterosexual: **1 in 2**

The odds a woman 18–44 who has ever had same-sex sexual contact will report being heterosexual: **1 in 1.5**

SOURCE: WD Mosher, A Chandra, J Jones, "Sexual Behavior and Selected Health Measures: Men and Women 15–44 Years of Age, United States 2002," *Advance Data from Vital and Health Statistics* 362, September 15, 2005.

 ODDS COUPLE **"Somewhat"**

1 in 4: The odds a woman enjoys sex only somewhat.
1 in 4: The odds an employed adult is somewhat satisfied with his or her boss.

SOURCES: "The American Sex Survey: A Peek Beneath the Sheets," *ABC News Primetime Live Poll*, October 21, 2004, http://abcnews.go.com/imagesPolitics959a1AmericanSexSurvey.pdf. ✎ Book of Odds estimate based on data from L Saad, "Job Security Slips in the US, Worker Satisfaction Rankings," Gallup News Service, August 27, 2009. http://www.gallup.com/poll/122531/Job-Security-Slips-Worker-Satisfaction-Rankings.aspx.

GENDER WARS

The odds a person has had sex on a first date are **1 in 2.4** for a man vs. **1 in 6.1** for a woman.

SOURCE: "The American Sex Survey: A Peek Beneath the Sheets," *ABC News Primetime Live Poll*, October 21, 2004." http://abcnews.go.com/images/Politics/959a1AmericanSexSurvey.pdf.

Love Itches

The odds an adult has had sex outdoors or in a public place: **1 in 1.8**

SOURCE: "The American Sex Survey: A Peek Beneath the Sheets," *ABC News Primetime Live Poll*, October 21, 2004, http://abcnews.go.com/images/Politics/959a1AmericanSexSurvey.pdf.

30 Rock with No Commercials

Most adults usually spend 30 minutes or more having a sexual encounter.

15 minutes or less	1 in 11.1	◗ -
16–30 minutes	1 in 3.3	◗ +
31–59 minutes	1 in 9.1	◗◗ +
Between 1 and 2 hours	1 in 3.6	● +
2 hours or more	1 in 7.1	●● +

SOURCE: "The American Sex Survey: A Peek Beneath the Sheets," *ABC News Primetime Live Poll*, October 21, 2004, http://abcnews.go.com/imagesPolitics959a1AmericanSexSurvey.pdf.

WHAT EXACTLY IS SEX?

In a 2010 issue of *Sexual Health*, researchers from the Kinsey Institute describe conducting a randomly dialed telephone survey of Indianans, in which nearly 500 people answered questions on what they believe constitutes "sex." All questions began with the same carefully neutral clause (in italics) followed by one of fourteen variants of four major sexual acts, for example, "*Would you say you 'had sex' with someone if the most intimate behavior you engaged in was* [fill in the blank]." The result: though men and women answer similarly, the team found that "there was no universal agreement as to what behaviors constituted having 'had sex.'"

Manual-genital intercourse: Of all the methods of intercourse run by these 486 residents of Indiana—you can almost see them getting up from dinner to answer the phone—manual stimulation ends up being the least likely to be considered sex—but the "direction" matters: when it is received, **1 in 2.1** adults considers manual-genital intercourse to be sex, and when it is given, slightly fewer adults, **1 in 2.2**, consider it to be sex.

Oral-genital intercourse: Almost 30% do not consider oral contact with genitals as having sex, either giving or receiving. **1 in 3.5** adults does not consider performing oral intercourse on their partner to be sex, and **1 in 3.7** does not consider receiving it from a partner to be sex—a sort of Clintonesque way of looking at it.

Penile-anal intercourse: As with the others, this act falls on a semantic divide in American minds. **1 in 5.3** does not consider it to be sex, although there is strong generational variation. Younger men are significantly likelier to consider penile-anal intercourse to be sex than older men: about 77% of 18- to 29-year-old men consider it to be sex, compared to just 50% of those 65 and older.

Penile-vaginal intercourse: While an expected overwhelming majority considers penile-vaginal intercourse to be sex—**1 in 1.1**, or 95%—that still leaves 5% who disagree.

It's a free country.

SOURCE: S Sanders, B Hill, W Yarber, C Graham, R Crosby, R Milhausen, "Misclassification Bias: Diversity in Conceptualisations about Having 'Had Sex,'" *Sexual Health* 7(1), 2010: 31–34.

The odds a woman 18–59 has experienced a lack of interest in sex for at least a few months in the past year are **1 in 3**.

SOURCE: EO Lauman, JH Gagnon, RT Michael, S Michaels, *The Social Organization of Sexuality: Sexual Practices in the United States*, Chicago: University of Chicago Press, 1994.

1 in 100

The odds a man or a woman 45–49 has sought help from a sex therapist.

SOURCE: "Sexuality at Midlife and Beyond, 2004 Update of Attitudes and Behaviors," *AARP The Magazine*, May 2005.

For Women It Gets Better and Better...

Up to a Point

The odds by age a woman considers her partner to be a skillful lover:

45–49: **1 in 2.8**

50–59: **1 in 2.6**

60–69: **1 in 2.1**

70+: **1 in 4**

SOURCE: LL Fisher, *Sex, Romance, and Relationships Survey*, AARP Survey of Midlife and Older Adults, American Association of Retired Persons, April 2010.

 **ODDS COUPLES**

Hot and Sweaty

The odds a sexually active adult has sex every day are **1 in 16.7**.

The odds a state has recorded a temperature of more than 120 degrees Fahrenheit in August are **1 in 16.7**.

SOURCES: "The American Sex Survey: A Peek Beneath the Sheets," *ABC News Primetime Live Poll*, October 21, 2004. http://abcnews.go.com/imagesPolitics959a1American SexSurvey.pdf. ✗ Book of Odds estimate based on Temperature Extremes NCDC, http://www.ncdc.noaa .gov/oa/climate/severeweather/temperatures.html. Table Maximum Temperatures, Appendix Monthly Extremes.

Cold and Unenjoyable

The odds a sexually active adult will describe his or her sex life as not at all exciting are **1 in 25**.

The odds an adult considers winter weather to be the least enjoyable part of the holiday season are **1 in 25**.

SOURCES: "The American Sex Survey: A Peek Beneath the Sheets," *ABC News Primetime Live Poll,* October 21, 2004, http://abcnews.go.com/ imagesPolitics959a1AmericanSexSurvey.pdf. ✗ Book of Odds estimate based on L Saad, "Americans Relish Time with Loved Ones During Holidays, Not Gifts," Gallup News Service, December 22, 2006, http://www.gallup.com.

No Offense Taken

The odds a man will report he would not be offended if a woman faked an orgasm during intercourse with him are **1 in 5**.

The odds an adult is not bothered by adult language on TV shows are **1 in 4.6**.

SOURCES: AskMen.com, "Part I: Dating & Sex," *The Great Male Survey, 2010 Edition,* http://www.askmen.com/specials/2010_ great_male_survey. ✗ Pew Research Center for the People and the Press, *Support for Tougher Indecency Measures, But Worries About Government Intrusiveness,* April 19, 2005.

GENDER WARS

The odds a **man** has had **revenge** sex are **1 in 10.2**.

The odds a **woman** has had **revenge** sex are **1 in 11.5**.

The odds a **man** has had **rebound** sex are **1 in 4.4**.

The odds a **woman** has had **rebound** sex are **1 in 5.2**.

%

Have you ever had:	Men	Women		
Revenge sex	10	9		
Rebound sex	23	19		

SOURCE: "The American Sex Survey: A Peek Beneath the Sheets," *ABC News Primetime Live Poll,* October 21, 2004, http://abcnews.go.com/imagesPolitics959a1American SexSurvey.pdf.

Erectile Dysfunction

The odds a man 40–49 will be diagnosed with erectile dysfunction are **1 in 80.6**.

The odds a man 50–59 will be diagnosed with erectile dysfunction are **1 in 33.6**.

The odds a man 60–69 will be diagnosed with erectile dysfunction are **1 in 21.6**.

SOURCE: CB Johannes, AB Araujo, HA Feldman, CA Derby, KP Kleinman, JB McKindlay, "Incidence of Erectile Dysfunction in Men 40 to 69 Years Old: Longitudinal Results from the Massachusetts Male Aging Study," *Journal of Urology* 163(2), February 2000: 460–463.

Treatment for Erectile Dysfunction

by Age

THE ODDS...

a man 50–59

has ever used a penile implant to treat erectile dysfunction are **1 in 1,000**.
has ever used vacuum suction to treat erectile dysfunction are **1 in 500**.
has ever used testosterone to treat erectile dysfunction are **1 in 200**.
has ever used oral medication to treat erectile dysfunction are **1 in 25.6**.
has ever used a urethral suppository to treat erectile dysfunction are **1 in 333**.

a man 60–69

has ever used a penile implant to treat erectile dysfunction are **1 in 333**.
has ever used vacuum suction to treat erectile dysfunction are **1 in 100**.
has ever used testosterone to treat erectile dysfunction are **1 in 100**.
has ever used oral medication to treat erectile dysfunction are **1 in 13.3**.
has ever used a urethral suppository to treat erectile dysfunction are **1 in 111**.

a man 70–79

has ever used a penile implant to treat erectile dysfunction are **1 in 125**.
has ever used vacuum suction to treat erectile dysfunction are **1 in 38.5**.
has ever used testosterone to treat erectile dysfunction are **1 in 83.3**.
has ever used oral medication to treat erectile dysfunction are **1 in 13**.
has ever used a urethral suppository to treat erectile dysfunction are **1 in 90.9**.

SOURCE:
CG Bacon, MA Mittleman, I Kawachi, E Giovannucci, DB Glaser, EB Rimm, "Sexual Function in Men Older Than 50 Years of Age: Results from the Health Professionals Follow-up Study," *Annals of Internal Medicine* 139(3), August 5, 2003: 161–169.

a man 80 or older

has ever used a penile implant to treat erectile dysfunction are **1 in 111**.
has ever used vacuum suction to treat erectile dysfunction are **1 in 43.5**.
has ever used testosterone to treat erectile dysfunction are **1 in 167**.
has ever used oral medication to treat erectile dysfunction are **1 in 29.4**.
has ever used a urethral suppository to treat erectile dysfunction are **1 in 167**.

Who's Having More Fun?

1 in 2.3 men thinks about sex at least once a day, and when he gets it, he likes it—**1 in 1.2** men reports enjoying sex a great deal. Only **1 in 7.7** women thinks about sex on a daily basis, and **1 in 1.7** really enjoys herself when she gets it. In fact, the odds a woman doesn't enjoy sex at all are **1 in 14.3,** compared to only **1 in 50** men who feels that way.

SOURCE: "The American Sex Survey: A Peek Beneath the Sheets," *ABC News Primetime Live Poll,* October 21, 2004, http://abcnews.go.com/images Politics959a1AmericanSexSurvey.pdf.

 **Numbers Tell the Story**

Oh Negative

1 in 3.3 adults has faked an orgasm.
That's **1 in 2.1** women and **1 in 9.1** men.

Why?

To please a partner ....1 in 3.9
To hurry up and finish ....1 in 4.6
Tired out ....1 in 11.1
Sex was not satisfying ....1 in 14.3
Bored ....1 in 33.3
Not in the mood ....1 in 50

SOURCE: "The American Sex Survey: A Peek Beneath the Sheets," *ABC News Primetime Live Poll,* October 21, 2004, http://abcnews.go.com/ imagesPolitics959a1AmericanSexSurvey.pdf.

 **ODDS COUPLE**

Not Tonight, Darling,
I Have to Tweet

The odds an adult uses the Internet before going to bed: **1 in 3.6**

The odds an adult has sex before going to bed: **1 in 3.7**

SOURCE: *2009 Sleep in America Poll, Summary of Findings,* National Sleep Foundation.

The odds a woman will report she won't have sex early in a relationship if she hasn't shaved her legs and armpits: **1 in 1.3**

 **DID YOU know?**

SOURCE: J Weaver, "What Are Our Dating Pet Peeves?" *Elle/MSNBC.com Sex and Beauty Survey,* May 5, 2005, http://www.msnbc.msn.com/id/7736649/.

GENDER WARS

The odds a man has had sex in the workplace: **1 in 5.9**

The odds a woman has had sex in the workplace: **1 in 12.5**

SOURCE: "The American Sex Survey: A Peek Beneath the Sheets," *ABC News Primetime Live Poll,* October 21, 2004, http://abcnews.go.com/imagesPolitics959a1AmericanSexSurvey.pdf.

The odds a sexually active adult usually has sex in the morning are **1 in 9.1**.

The odds a sexually active adult usually has sex in the afternoon are **1 in 33.3**.

The odds a sexually active adult usually has sex in the evening are **1 in 4.4**.

The odds a sexually active adult usually has sex **late at night** are **1 in 2.3**.

	%
Morning	11
Afternoon	3
Evening	23
Late night	44

SOURCE: "The American Sex Survey: A Peek Beneath the Sheets," *ABC News Primetime Live Poll*, October 21, 2004, http://abcnews.go.com/imagesPolitics959a1AmericanSexSurvey.pdf.

Teeing Off?

The odds a married retired adult 55–75 will have sex more often after retirement:

1 in 16.7

SOURCE: J Koppen, G Anderson, "Retired Spouses, a National Survey of Adults," *AARP The Magazine,* November 2008.

The odds a female 15–44 has ever had sexual contact with another female.

1 in 8.9   **1 in 16.7**

The odds a male 15–44 has ever had sexual contact with another male.

SOURCE: WD Mosher, A Chandra, J Jones, "Sexual Behavior and Selected Health Measures: Men and Women 15–44 Years of Age, United States 2002," *Advance Data from Vital and Health Statistics* 362, September 15, 2005.

How Does Your Sex Life Stack Up?

The odds a person 18–59 will not have sex in a year are **1 in 8.4**.

The odds a person 18–59 will have sex a few times a year are **1 in 6**.

The odds a person 18–59 will have sex a few times a month are **1 in 2.7**.

The odds a person 18–59 will have sex 2–3 times a week are **1 in 3.6**.

The odds a person 18–59 will have sex 4 or more times a week are **1 in 14**.

Sex Frequency	%
Less than once a year	12
A few times a year	17
A few times a month	37
2–3 times a week	28
4+ times a week	7

SOURCE: EO Laumann, JH Gagnon, RT Michael, S Michaels, *The Social Organization of Sexuality: Sexual Practices in the United States,* Chicago: University of Chicago Press, 1994.

The odds a man 45 or older has not had intercourse in the past 6 months are **1 in 2.7**.

The odds a woman 45 or older has not had intercourse in the past 6 months are **1 in 1.7**.

SOURCE: LL Fisher, *Sex, Romance, and Relationships Survey, AARP Survey of Midlife and Older Adults,* American Association of Retired Persons, April 2010.

GENDER WARS

The odds a man with a sexually traditional partner would like more adventure in the bedroom: **1 in 2.1**. For women: **1 in 3**.

SOURCE: "The American Sex Survey: A Peek Beneath the Sheets," *ABC News Primetime Live Poll*, October 21, 2004, http://abcnews.go.com/images/Politics/959a1AmericanSex Survey.pdf.

But Male Satisfaction Gets
Harder to Come By

The odds a man 45 or older who is less sexually satisfied than he was 10 years ago will report it's because:

Too stressed. . . . . **1 in 3**

Worsening health . . . . **1 in 3.1**

Worsening health of a partner . . . . **1 in 3.2**

Weight gain . . . . **1 in 4.6**

Worse financial situation . . . . **1 in 4.6**

Retirement . . . . **1 in 7.7**

Divorce or separation . . . . **1 in 7.7**

Death of partner . . . . **1 in 8.3**

Change in partners . . . . **1 in 9.1**

Too much free time . . . . **1 in 11.1**

Children moving back home. . . . . **1 in 16.7**

Change in sexual orientation . . . . **1 in 33.3**

Loss of interest . . . . **1 in 50**

More medications. . . . . **1 in 50**

Factor	%
Too stressed	33
Worsening health	32
Worsening health of a partner	31
Weight gain	22
Worse financial situation	22
Retirement	13
Divorce or separation	13
Death of a partner	12
Change in partners	11
Too much free time	9
Children moving back home	6
Change in sexual orientation	3
Loss of interest	2
More medications	2

SOURCE: LL Fisher, Sex, *Romance, and Relationships Survey, AARP Survey of Midlife and Older Adults*, American Association of Retired Persons, April 2010.

Numbers Tell the Story

A Very Bad Night on the Town

Go to a bar, looking to meet someone:
The odds an adult will go to a bar or nightclub in a year are 1 in 5.

Drink a little too much:
The odds a person 18–25 will binge drink alcohol in a month are 1 in 2.4.

Start to dance:
The odds an adult will go dancing in a year are 1 in 9.9.

One thing leads to another:
The odds an adult has had an unexpected sexual encounter with someone new are 1 in 3.8.

No condom:
The odds a never-married and noncohabitating male 15–44 didn't use a condom during his last sexual encounter are 1 in 2.9.

Start to feel weird:
Only 1 in 7 people 14–49 who have genital herpes know they have it.

Get tested:
The odds a female 15–44 has been tested for HIV and other STDs in the past year are 1 in 10.5.

The odds a male 15–44 has been tested for HIV and other STDs in the past year are 1 in 14.1.

The results:
The odds a female 14–49 has genital herpes are 1 in 4.3.

The odds a male 14–49 has genital herpes are 1 in 8.9.

SOURCES: US Census Bureau, "Adult Participation in Selected Leisure Activities by Frequency, 2009," *Statistical Abstract of the United States 2011*, January 2011. ✗ Substance Abuse and Mental Health Services Administration, *Results from the 2009 National Survey on Drug Use and Health, Volume I: Summary of National Findings,* Office of Applied Studies, NSDUH Series H-38A, HHS Publication No. SMA 10-4586 Findings, 2010. http://www.oas.samhsa.gov. ✗ "The American Sex Survey: A Peek Beneath the Sheets," *ABC News Primetime Live Poll*, October 21, 2004, http://abcnews.go.com/images/Politics/959a1AmericanSexSurvey. ✗ WD Mosher, A Chandra, J Jones, "Sexual Behavior and Selected Health Measures: Men and Women 15–44 Years of Age, United States 2002," *Advance Data from Vital and Health Statistics* 362, September 15, 2005. ✗ DK Carlson, "Over Half of Americans Believe in Love at First Sight," Gallup News Service, February 14, 2001. ✗ SM Berman, BJ Kottiri, K Lee, et al., "Trends in Herpes Simplex Virus Type 1 and Type 2 Seroprevalence in the United States," *JAMA*, 296(8), August 23, 2006: 964–973.

Birth Control

Over Time

1982

The odds a female 15–44 uses **any** form of contraception . . . . **1 in 1.8**

The odds a female 15–44 is on the **pill** . . . . **1 in 6.4**

The odds a female 15–44 is **surgically sterile** for contraceptive reasons. . . . . **1 in 7.8**

The odds a female 15–44 uses **condoms** for contraceptive purposes . . . . **1 in 14.9**

The odds a female 15–44 uses an **intrauterine device** for contraceptive purposes . . . . **1 in 25**

The odds a female 15–44 uses a **calendar rhythm** for contraceptive purposes . . . . **1 in 55.6**

The odds a female 15–44 uses **withdrawal** for contraceptive purposes . . . . **1 in 90.9**

The odds a female 15–44 uses **natural family planning** for contraceptive purposes . . . . . **1 in 333**

2008

The odds a female 15–44 uses **any** form of contraception . . . . **1 in 1.6**

The odds a female 15–44 is on the **pill** . . . . **1 in 5.8**

The odds a female 15–44 is **surgically** sterile for contraceptive reasons . . . . **1 in 6**

The odds a female 15–44 uses **condoms** for contraceptive purposes . . . . **1 in 10**

The odds a female 15–44 uses an **intrauterine device** for contraceptive purposes . . . . . . **1 in 29.4**

The odds a female 15–44 uses **withdrawal** for contraceptive purposes . . . . **1 in 31.3**

The odds a female 15–44 uses a **contraceptive ring** . . . . **1 in 66.7**

The odds a female 15–44 uses a **calendar rhythm** for contraceptive purposes . . . . **1 in 200**

The odds a female 15–44 uses **natural family planning** for contraceptive purposes . . . . **1 in 1,000**

	%	
Birth Control Method	**2008**	**1982**
Any form of contraception	62	56
The pill	17	16
Surgically sterile for contraceptive reasons	17	13
Condom	10	7
Intrauterine device	3	4
Contraceptive ring	1	Not available
Withdrawal	3	1
Calendar rhythm	1	2
Natural family planning	0.1	0.3

SOURCE: WD Mosher, J Jones, "Use of Contraception in the United States: 1982–2008," *Vital and Health Statistics* 23(29), 2010.

Popping Pills

Birth control pills are often called campus candy. The odds a woman in her early 20s is on the pill are **1 in 3.8**.

But it's not just young, single women who punch a pill through the foil casing each day. The odds any sexually active female between the ages of 15 and 44 has ever taken the pill for contraceptive reasons are **1 in 1.2**. Condom use declines as women get older, and **1 in 6.1** married women uses birth control pills to prevent unwanted pregnancies.

SOURCE: WD Mosher, J Jones, "Use of Contraception in the United States: 1982–2008," *Vital and Health Statistics* 23(29), 2010.

How's That Fit?

The odds a never-married and noncohabitating male put on a condom during his last sexual encounter are **1 in 1.5**. But did he leave it on? According to the February 2010 issue of *Sexually Transmitted Infections*, men saddled with an ill-fitting condom are twice as likely to yank it off in the middle of having sex as men who have the right fit. That can have unfortunate consequences, but sometimes it's hard to recall them during the act. An insightful study, titled "Bikinis Instigate Generalized Impatience in Intertemporal Choice," set out to determine if men "exposed to sexual cues" make choices based on immediate gratification, rather than longer-term reward. Turns out they do.

1 in 1.5

SOURCES: WD Mosher, A Chandra, J Jones, "Sexual Behavior and Selected Health Measures: Men and Women 15–44 Years of Age, United States 2002," *Advance Data from Vital and Health Statistics* 362, September 15, 2005. ↗ RA Crosby, WL Yarber, CA Graham, SA Sanders, et al., "Does It Fit Okay? Problems with Condom Use as a Function of Self-Reported Poor Fit," *Sexually Transmitted Infections* 86, 2010: 36–39. ↗ B Van den Bergh, S Dewitte, L Warlop, "Bikinis Instigate Generalized Impatience in Intertemporal Choice," *Journal of Consumer Research,* June 2008.

"Pick Up Prescription"

The odds a man will report that he would take a male birth control pill if it were available:

1 in 1.4

SOURCE: AskMen.com, "Part I: Dating & Sex," *The Great Male Survey, 2011 Edition,* http://www.askmen.com/specials/2011_great_male_survey.

The odds a female 15–44 has had sex using condoms as contraception but discontinued because she got pregnant:

1 in 222

SOURCE: WD Mosher, J Jones, "Use of Contraception in the United States: 1982–2008." *Vital and Health Statistics* 23(29), 2010.

The Odds of
Internet
Porn

The odds a website will **contain pornography** are **1 in 8.3**.

The odds a visitor to a **pornographic** website is **male** are **1 in 1.4**.
The odds a visitor to a **pornographic** website is **female** are **1 in 3.6**.

The odds an Internet search request for **"sex"** will be made by a **male** are **1 in 2**.
The odds an Internet search request for **"sex"** will be made by a **female** are **1 in 2**.

The odds an Internet search request for **"free porn"** will be made by a **male** are **1 in 1.03**.
The odds an Internet search request for **"free porn"** will be made by a **female** are **1 in 3**.

The odds an Internet search request for **"porn"** will be made by a **male** are **1 in 1.04**.
The odds an Internet search request for **"porn"** will be made by a **female** are **1 in 25**.

The odds an Internet search request for **"playboy"** will be made by a **male** are **1 in 1.2**.
The odds an Internet search request for **"playboy"** will be made by a **female** are **1 in 7.1**.

The odds an Internet search request for **"teen porn"** will be made by a **male** are **1 in 1.2**.
The odds an Internet search request for **"teen porn"** will be made by a **female** are **1 in 5.6**.

The odds an Internet search request for **"anal sex"** will be made by a **male** are **1 in 1.5**.
The odds an Internet search request for **"anal sex"** will be made by a **female** are **1 in 3**.

The odds an Internet search request for **"XXX"** will be made by a **male** are **1 in 2**.
The odds an Internet search request for **"XXX"** will be made by a **female** are **1 in 2**.

The odds an Internet search request for **"group sex"** will be made by a **male** are **1 in 2**.
The odds an Internet search request for **"group sex"** will be made by a **female** are **1 in 2**.

The odds an Internet search request for **"cyber sex"** will be made by a **male** are **1 in 2.4**.
The odds an Internet search request for **"cyber sex"** will be made by a **female** are **1 in 1.7**.

The odds an Internet search request for **"adult dating"** will be made by a **male** are **1 in 2.8**.
The odds an Internet search request for **"adult dating"** will be made by a **female** are **1 in 1.6**.

 ODDS COUPLE

FW: Debbie Does Dallas: 1 in 12.5

The odds an email will contain pornography.

The odds a person lives in Texas.

SOURCES: J Ropelator, "Internet Pornography Statistics, Internet Software Filter Review, Top Ten Reviews," http://internet-filter-review.toptenreviews.com/internet-pornography-statistics.html. ✎ Population Estimates Program [Internet]. US Census Bureau, http://www.census.gov/popest/estimates.php

 ODDS COUPLE

Pretty Darn Common: 1 in 1.1

The odds a child 8–16 has ever viewed pornography online.

The odds a person is right-handed.

SOURCES: J Ropelator, "Internet Pornography Statistics, Internet Software Filter Review, Top Ten Reviews," http://internet-filter-review.toptenreviews.com/internet-pornography-statistics.html. ✎ "The History and Geography of Human Handedness," in *Language Lateralization and Psychosis*, eds. IEC Sommer, RS Kahn, Cambridge: Cambridge University Press, 2009.

Search Term	% Men	Women
Sex	50	50
Free porn	97	3
Porn	96	4
Playboy	86	14
Teen porn	82	18

Search Term	% Men	Women
Anal sex	67	33
XXX	50	50
Group sex	50	50
Cyber sex	41	59
Adult dating	38	64

Half of American men, **1 in 2.2**, say it is never okay to pay for sex—yet **1 in 6.7** men who have had sex have paid for it at least once and **1 in 4.4** hasn't but says he would consider it. The vast majority of women, **1 in 1.2**, report they have never been paid for sex and would never entertain the idea. And the odds a woman who has had sex has ever paid for it are **1 in 100**.

SOURCES: AskMen.com, "Part I: Dating & Sex," *The Great Male Survey, 2011 Edition*, http://www.askmen.com/specials/2011_great_male_survey. ⚡ "The American Sex Survey: A Peek Beneath the Sheets," *ABC News Primetime Live Poll*, October 21, 2004, http://abcnews.go.com/images/Politics/959a1AmericanSexSurvey.pdf ⚡ AskMen.com, "Part I: Dating & Sex," *The Great Male Survey, 2009 Edition*, http://www.askmen.com/specials/2009_great_male_survey. ⚡ AskMen.com, "Part I: Dating & Sex," *The Great Female Survey, 2009 Edition*, www.askmen.com/specials/yahoo_shine_great_female_survey/part1.html.

The Odds an Adult Who Visits
Pornographic Websites:

has an annual income of **less than $15,000** . . . . **1 in 16.1**

has an annual income of **$15,000–$25,000** . . . . **1 in 15.2**

has an annual income of **$25,000–$35,000** . . . . **1 in 10.5**

has an annual income of **$35,000–$50,000** . . . . **1 in 6**

has an annual income of **$50,000–$75,000** . . . . **1 in 3.9**

has an annual income of **more than $75,000** . . . . **1 in 2.8**

The odds an employee with Internet access has visited a porn site **at work** . . . . **1 in 8.3**

The odds an adult who visited a pornographic website **at work** claims it was an **accident** . . . . **1 in 1.1**

SOURCES: J Ropelator, "Internet Pornography Statistics, Internet Software Filter Review, Top Ten Reviews," http://internet-filter-review.toptenreviews.com/internet-pornography-statistics.html. ⚡ Websense, *Web @Work Survey 2006*, http://www.websense.com.

 **ODDS COUPLE**

PROSTITUTION
1 in 12.7

{

Sometimes There Is a Price to Pay

The odds an adult has ever paid for or been paid for sex.

The odds a man has suggested his partner get breast enlargements.

SOURCES: JA Davis, TW Smith, PV Marsden, *General Social Surveys, 1972–2008* [CUMULATIVE FILE] [Computer file]. ICPSR04697–v1. Chicago: National Opinion Research Center, [producer] 2009. Storrs, CT: Roper Center for Public Opinion Research, University of Connecticut/Ann Arbor, MI: Inter-university Consortium for Political and Social Research [distributors]. ⚡ "What Are the Rules of Attraction?" *Elle/MSNBC.com Sex and Beauty Survey, Elle* magazine, 2004.

AIDS
in America
by Age

The odds that a person will be diagnosed with AIDS in a year are **1 in 5,747**. But this risk varies dramatically with age. For children younger than 13, the risk is **1 in 250,000**, reflecting the fact that most persons in this group are not sexually active and are only likely to have been exposed if their mother was HIV-positive during pregnancy. The odds rise sharply once Americans become sexually active: for people age 20–24, for example, the risk is **1 in 2,710**. The next highest likelihood occurs between ages 25 and 29, at which the odds of being diagnosed with AIDS are **1 in 2,841**. After this age the risk decreases, falling to **1 in 43,498** for a person 65 or older.

SOURCE: Centers for Disease Control and Prevention, *HIV Surveillance Report, 2009,* vol. 21 (February 2011), http://www.cdc.gov/hiv/topics/surveillance/resources/reports/.

STD Cases
per Year, by Gender

The odds a man will be diagnosed with **chlamydia** are **1 in 472**.
The odds a woman will be diagnosed with **chlamydia** are **1 in 171**.

The odds a man will be diagnosed with **gonorrhea** are **1 in 973**.
The odds a woman will be diagnosed with **gonorrhea** are **1 in 843**.

The odds a man 13 or older will be diagnosed with **AIDS** are **1 in 3,058**.
The odds a woman 13 or older will be diagnosed with **AIDS** are **1 in 10,204**.

The odds a man will be diagnosed with primary or secondary **syphilis** are **1 in 13,160**.
The odds a woman will be diagnosed with primary or secondary **syphilis** are **1 in 66,670**.

STD	Men Rate/1000	Women Rate/1000
Chlamydia	210	580
Gonorrhea	100	120
AIDS (13+)	30	10
Syphilis	10	1

SOURCES: Centers for Disease Control and Prevention, *Sexually Transmitted Disease Surveillance, 2008.* Atlanta, GA: US Department of Health and Human Services; November 2009. ✗ Centers for Disease Control and Prevention, *HIV Surveillance Report, 2009,* vol. 21 (February 2011), http://www.cdc.gov/hiv/topics/surveillance/resources/reports/.

When It Comes to STDs, Who Tells the Truth?

The odds a male 15–44 has ever been tested for HIV are **1 in 1.7**; for a female, **1 in 2.4**.

Now, what about honestly reporting the results of STD tests to your partner? In a 2008 survey of 75,000 men by AskMen.com, **2%** of respondents admitted they have lied about their sexual health. But before you decree this as proof that men are pigs, consider that an accompanying survey of 10,000 women got the same result.

SOURCES: Book of Odds estimate based on Centers for Disease Control and Prevention, *National Survey of Family Growth 2006–08 Public Use Data Files.* ✗ AskMen.com, "Men's Dating Trends," *The Great Male Survey, 2008 Edition,* http://static.askmen.com/specials/2008_great_male_survey/2008_dating_survey.html.

The Odds of Having
Genital Herpes

The odds a person 14–49 who has had no sexual partners in his or her lifetime has genital herpes . . . . .1 in 38.5

The odds a person 14–49 who has had 1 sexual partner in his or her lifetime has genital herpes . . . . .1 in 26.3

The odds a person 14–49 who has had 2–4 sexual partners in his or her lifetime has genital herpes . . . . .1 in 7.5

The odds a person 14–49 who has had 5–9 sexual partners in his or her lifetime has genital herpes . . . . .1 in 4.8

The odds a person 14–49 who has had 10–49 sexual partners in his or her lifetime has genital herpes . . . . . . .1 in 3.7

The odds a person 14–49 who has had 50 or more sexual partners in his or her lifetime has genital herpes. . . . . .1 in 2.5

Number of Lifetime Sexual Partners	%
0	3
1	4
2–4	13
5–9	21
10–49	27
50+	40

SOURCE: SM Berman, BJ Kottiri, K Lee, et al., "Trends in Herpes Simplex Virus Type 1 and Type 2 Seroprevalence in the United States," *JAMA* 296(8), August 23, 2006.

Genital Herpes Infection by Age

The odds that...

a teenage boy 14–19 has genital herpes: **1 in 111**

a man 20–29 has genital herpes: **1 in 17.9**

a man 30–39 has genital herpes: **1 in 6.9**

a man 40–49 has genital herpes: **1 in 5.4**

a teenage girl 14–19 has genital herpes: **1 in 43.5**

a woman 20–29 has genital herpes: **1 in 6.4**

a woman 30–39 has genital herpes: **1 in 3.4**

a woman 40–49 has genital herpes: **1 in 3**

Age	%	
	Male	Female
14–19	1	2
20–29	6	16
30–39	15	30
40–49	19	34

SOURCE: SM Berman, BJ Kottiri, K Lee, et al., "Trends in Herpes Simplex Virus Type 1 and Type 2 Seroprevalence in the United States," *JAMA* 296(8), August 23, 2006: 964–973.

Fantasy Land

The odds a **man** 45 or older who has sexual thoughts, fantasies, or erotic dreams has fantasized about having sex:

with a stranger: **1 in 2.2**

with more than one person at the same time: **1 in 3.3**

with a celebrity: **1 in 5**

in public: **1 in 7.7**

with someone of the same sex: **1 in 11.1**

The odds a **woman** 45 or older who has sexual thoughts, fantasies, or erotic dreams has fantasized about having sex:

with a stranger: **1 in 3.6**

with more than one person at the same time: **1 in 10**

with a celebrity: **1 in 5.9**

in public: **1 in 11.1**

with someone of the same sex: **1 in 12.5**

SOURCE: LL Fisher, *Sex, Romance, Relationships, AARP Survey of Midlife and Older Adults,* American Association of Retired Persons, April 2010.

Masturbation

The odds a never-married and noncohabitating man will masturbate at least once a week are **1 in 2.4**—and even **married men are more frequent masturbators than single women:** the odds a married man 18–59 will masturbate at least once a week are **1 in 6.1**, as compared with **1 in 8.1** never-married and noncohabitating women.

Frequency of Masturbation Among Men:

Age	Not in the Past Year		Few Times per Year to Monthly		Few Times per Month to Weekly		2–3 Times per Week		4+ Times per Week	
	%	Odds (1 in)	%	Odds (1 in)	%	Odds (1 in)	%	Odds (1 in)	%	Odds (1 in)
18–24	19	**5.4**	17	**5.9**	25	**4.0**	21	**4.8**	19	**5.3**
25–29	17	**6.1**	16	**6.8**	25	**3.9**	23	**4.3**	20	**5.0**
30–39	20	**5.0**	19	**5.3**	27	**3.7**	21	**4.9**	14	**7.4**
40–49	24	**4.2**	20	**5.1**	25	**4.0**	17	**6**	14	**6.9**
50–59	28	**3.6**	24	**4.1**	24	**4.2**	18	**5.7**	6	**15.6**
60–69	39	**2.6**	29	**3.4**	18	**5.6**	10	**9.9**	4	**26.3**
70+	54	**1.9**	24	**4.3**	14	**7.1**	7	**13.7**	2	**58.8**

SOURCES: EO Laumann, JH Gagnon, RT Michael, S Michaels, *The Social Organization of Sexuality: Sexual Practices in the United States,* Chicago: University of Chicago Press, 1994. ✔ M Reece, D Herbenick, V Schick, SA Sanders, B Dodge, JD Fortenberry, "Sexual Behaviors, Relationships, and Perceived Health Among Adult Men in the United States: Results from a National Probability Sample," *Journal of Sexual Medicine* 7(S 5), 2010: 291–304.

Big Man, Little Man

The odds a man 18–65 who is 5'2" to 5'4" tall considers his penis size to be large are **1 in 8.3**.

The odds a man 18–65 who is 5'5" to 5'8" tall considers his penis size to be large are **1 in 6.7**.

The odds a man 18–65 who is 5'9" to 5'11" tall considers his penis size to be large are **1 in 5**.

The odds a man 18–65 who is 6' to 6'3" tall considers his penis size to be large are **1 in 3.9**.

The odds a man 18–65 who is 6'4" to 6'6" tall considers his penis size to be large are **1 in 2.8**.

SOURCE: J Lever, DA Frederick, A Peplau, "Does Size Matter? Men's and Women's Views on Penis Size Across the Lifespan," *Psychology of Men and Masculinity* 7(3), March 2006: 129–143.

Satisfaction and Penis Size

Odds a woman 18–65 who considers her partner's penis size to be large is very satisfied . . . . **1 in 1.1**

If she considers it average, odds she is very satisfied . . . . **1 in 1.2**

If she thinks it's on the small side but is very satisfied . . . . **1 in 3.1**

SOURCE: J Lever, DA Frederick, A Peplau, "Does Size Matter? Men's and Women's Views on Penis Size Across the Lifespan," *Psychology of Men and Masculinity* 7(3), March 2006: 129–143.

Men's Cup Size Preferences

The odds a man will report that he prefers for a woman to have a C cup breast size are **1 in 1.9**. The odds a man will report that he has no breast size preference are **1 in 5**. The odds a man will report that he prefers for a woman to have a B cup breast size are **1 in 6.7**. The odds a man will report that he prefers for a woman to have a D cup or bigger breast size are **1 in 8.3**. The odds a man will report that he prefers for a woman to have an A cup breast size are **1 in 100**.

Cup size	%
A	1
B	15
C	52
D+	12
No preference	20

SOURCE: AskMen.com, "Part I: Dating & Sex," *The Great Male Survey, 2010 Edition,* http://www.askmen.com/specials/2010_great_male_survey.

DID YOU know?

The majority—**1 in 1.6**—of married women 18–59 will not masturbate in a year.

SOURCE: EO Laumann, JH Gagnon, RT Michael, S Michaels, *The Social Organization of Sexuality: Sexual Practices in the United States,* Chicago: University of Chicago Press, 1994.

ODDS COUPLE

1 in 2.2 Men

The odds a man 18–65 wants his penis size to be larger.

The odds a man has a Facebook or MySpace account.

SOURCES: J Lever, DA Frederick, A Peplau, "Does Size Matter? Men's and Women's Views on Penis Size Across the Lifespan," *Psychology of Men and Masculinity* 7(3), March 2006: 129–143. ✔ Harris Interactive, "Just Under Half of Americans Have a Facebook or MySpace Account," April 6, 2009. http://www.harrisinteractive.com/harris_poll/pubs/Harris_Poll_2009_04_16.pdf.

1 in 4.8

The odds a man 70 or older will have sexual thoughts, fantasies, or erotic dreams two or more times a day.

SOURCE: LL Fisher, Sex, Romance, Relationships, *AARP Survey of Midlife and Older Adults,* American Association of Retired Persons, April 2010.

CHAPTER 2

SINGLES AND DATING

What Fun?

The odds an adult thinks it is more enjoyable to be single and dating than to be married:

1 in 5.6

SOURCE: "The American Sex Survey: A Peek Beneath the Sheets," *ABC News Primetime Live Poll*, October 21, 2004, http://abcnews.go.com/images/Politics/959a1AmericanSexSurvey.pdf.

Experienced Daters Are
Discriminating

Match.com reports that **1 in 5** of its members is 50 or older—this demographic is the site's fastest-growing segment.

Experienced daters know what they want and don't want. Among unmarried adults 40–69 who date, **1 in 1.6** is comfortable dating outside his or her faith, but other things are real deal breakers. HIV and AIDS pose the biggest stop sign: just **1 in 33.3** unmarried adults in this age group would date someone with HIV or AIDS. More would date someone who is married (**1 in 16.7**) or who has a criminal record (**1 in 10**).

And women age 40–69 are even pickier than their male counterparts.

Odds (1 in)

Men	Women	Would Date Someone
1 in 1.4	1 in 2	who is less educated.
1 in 1.9	1 in 2.4	who is of a different race or ethnicity.
1 in 1.9	1 in 2.6	who is raising children.
1 in 1.4	1 in 2.9	who has less money.
1 in 1.8	1 in 6.7	who is unemployed.
1 in 5.9	1 in 16.7	who has ever paid for sex.
1 in 7.7	1 in 50	who has been paid for sex.
1 in 9.1	1 in 50	who is married.

SOURCES: Match.com, "Member Demographics," March 2011, http://match.mediaroom.com/index.php?s=41. ✕ XP Montenegro, "Lifestyles, Dating, and Romance: A Study of Midlife Singles," *AARP The Magazine,* September 2003.

Numbers Tell the Story

The odds an unmarried man 40–69 who dates is looking for someone at least...

15 years younger	1 in 5.9
10–14 years younger	1 in 4.8
5–9 years younger	1 in 3.9
1–4 years younger	1 in 6.3
His own age	1 in 33.3

SOURCE: XP Montenegro, "Lifestyles, Dating, and Romance: A Study of Midlife Singles," *AARP The Magazine,* September 2003.

The odds a women says she won't date a man who is too short are
1 in 2.

SOURCE: J Weaver, "What Are Our Dating Pet Peeves?," *Elle/ MSNBC.com Sex and Beauty Survey,* MSNBC.com, May 5, 2005, http://www.nbcnews .com/id/7736649.

1 in 4.5 men vs. **1 in 10** women ranks intelligence as "the most important trait" in deciding if a person is "relationship material."

The odds are **1 in 1.3** a man will report he is *not* dating a woman with a bigger brain than his, but he *would.*

SOURCES: AskMen.com, "Part I: Dating & Sex," *The Great Male Survey, 2011 Edition,* http://www .askmen.com/specials/2011_great_ male_survey. ✕ AskMen.com, "Q1," *The Great Female Survey, 2011 Edition,* http://www.askmen.com/ specials/great_female_survey. ✕ AskMen.com, "Men's Dating Trends," *The Great Male Sex Survey, 2008 Edition,* http://static.askmen .com/specials/2008_great_male_ survey/2008_dating_survey.html.

ODDS COUPLE

The Shallow End

The odds an unmarried adult looks mostly for physical appearance in a potential date are **1 in 4.6**.

The odds an adult 65 or older does not know how to swim are **1 in 4.6**.

SOURCES: Yahoo! Personals, "Singles' Voice Survey, 2005," http://personals.yahoo.com. ✗ *Water Safety Poll*, the American Red Cross, March 31, 2009.

What Does a Woman Want?

The odds a woman considers **family orientation** or **closeness** as the most important in a significant other . . . . **1 in 2.3**

The odds a woman considers **religious orientation** as the most important in a significant other . . . . **1 in 5.9**

The odds a woman considers **social life** as the most important in a significant other . . . . **1 in 6.3**

The odds a woman considers **work or life habits** as the most important in a significant other . . . . **1 in 9.1**

The odds a woman considers **age** as the most important in a significant other . . . . **1 in 20**

The odds a woman considers **ethnicity** as the most important in a significant other . . . . **1 in 33.3**

The odds a woman considers **profession** as the most important in a significant other . . . . **1 in 50**

The odds a woman considers **political views** as the most important in a significant other . . . . **1 in 100**

The odds a woman considers **income** as the most important in a significant other . . . . **1 in 100**

SOURCE: Yahoo! Personals and TheKnot.com, "Dating Survey: Women on Finding 'The One.'"

You Have No New Messages

The odds an adult who is "single and looking" has not been on a date in the past 3 months:

1 in 2.8

SOURCE: Pew Internet and American Life Project, "September 2005 Daily Tracking Survey/Online Dating Extension," 2005.

Where and How People Met

	% of People Dating			
	Men	**Women**	**Gay Men**	**Gay Women**
Through friends	33	38	20	26
Through family	14	15	0.1	8
As coworkers	11	15	13	23
At a bar, club, or restaurant	16	18	27	11
Online	14	10	27	24
Through work as a client	8	10	2	4
In primary or secondary school	9	8	0	7
In college	6	7	9	11
Through church	3	3	2	1
In a nonchurch social group	7	7	13	17
In the neighborhood	6	12	11	5
On a blind date	3	3	5	1
At a private party	14	10	12	13
In a public place	14	10	6	5

	Odds (1 in) for People Dating			
	Men	**Women**	**Gay Men**	**Gay Women**
Through friends	3.0	2.6	5.1	3.9
Through family	7.1	6.7	1000	13.0
As coworkers	8.9	6.5	7.9	4.4
At a bar, club, or restaurant	6.4	5.6	3.8	8.8
Online	7.3	10.0	3.7	4.2
Through work as a client	13.2	9.6	47.6	25.0
In primary or secondary school	11.5	12.8	0.0	15.4
In college	17.9	14.3	11.0	9.2
Through church	34.5	38.5	66.7	76.9
In a nonchurch social group	14.7	14.7	7.6	6.0
In the neighborhood	17.5	8.3	9.2	21.3
On a blind date	34.5	34.5	20.4	200
At a private party	7.1	10.5	8.6	7.8
In a public place	7.0	9.8	17.0	21.3

SOURCE: MA Rosenfeld, RJ Thomas, "Table 5: How Americans Met Their Spouses and Current Partners," *How Couples Meet and Stay Together, Waves I and II*, Public Version 2.04 [Computer file]. Stanford, CA: Stanford University Libraries, 2011–January 2012.

The Odds of Meeting Your Partner on a Blind Date:

1 in 34.5

Things as likely...

- Meeting your partner through church
- A man has bipolar disorder
- A death row inmate is widowed
- A male college athlete is a pathological gambler

SOURCES: MA Rosenfeld, RJ Thomas, "Table 5: How Americans Met Their Spouses and Current Partners," *How Couples Meet and Stay Together, Waves I and II,* Public Version 2.04 [Computer file]. Stanford, CA: Stanford University Libraries, 2011–January 2012. ✗ Harvard School of Medicine, "National Comorbidity Survey (NCS-R) Appendix Tables," July 19, 2007. ✗ Bureau of Justice Statistics, "Capital Punishment, 2008–Statistical Tables," 2009–2008. ✗ National Collegiate Athletic Association, "NCAA Study on Collegiate Wagering," November 13, 2009.

It's the Alcohol

The odds an adult in a relationship met his or her partner at a New Year's Eve party: **1 in 465**.

SOURCE: Harris Interactive and eHarmony.com, "Relationship Status," *Valentine Poll 2006,* Table 1.

Maybe Opposites Don't Attract

The odds a woman will report she is similar to her partner in:

age:
1 in 1.1

income:
1 in 1.4

ethnicity:
1 in 1.2

social life:
1 in 1.1

political views:
1 in 1.2

work or life habits:
1 in 1.2

religious orientation:
1 in 1.2

SOURCE: Yahoo! Personals and TheKnot.com, "Dating Survey: Women on Finding 'The One.'"

What's Your Main Weapon?

The odds a man thinks his main weapon to attract women is his...

sense of humor	**1 in 2.9**
charm	**1 in 5.3**
confidence	**1 in 7.1**
intelligence	**1 in 7.7**
conversational skills	**1 in 11.1**
looks	**1 in 12.5**
money	**1 in 100**
talent	**1 in 100**

SOURCE: AskMen.com, "Part I: Dating & Sex," *The Great Male Survey, 2009 Edition,* http://www.askmen.com/specials/2009_great_male_survey.

GENDER WARS

1 in 12.5

women will consider the person she is dating to be her boyfriend or girlfriend after 3–5 dates. Men are twice as likely to make that leap.

SOURCE: Yahoo! Personals, "What Does America Think About Breakups," July 2006.

Dating the Boss

In a given year, **1 in 17.5** full-time employed adults will date the boss.

SOURCE: Book of Odds estimate based on *Annual CareerBuilder .com Valentine's Day Survey, February 2009,* http://www.careerbuilder .com/share/aboutus/ pressreleasesdetail.aspx.

Online Lies

Many people stretch the truth in their online dating profiles, and when it comes to lies about body size, men and women are almost equal offenders. The odds an online dater will lie about weight on his or her profile are about the same for each sex: about **1 in 1.7**.

Singles frequently misrepresent their height as well, and in this case men are more likely than women to lie—**1 in 1.8** vs. **1 in 1.9**. There's a good reason for this. A study of online dating by Duke University found that tall men have such an advantage when it comes to attracting women that in order to match the dating success of a man one inch taller, a 5'9" man would have to make $35,000–$40,000 a year more.

As for telling the truth about age, in one study only **1 in 7.6** women lied about it, while nearly a quarter (**1 in 4.3**) of the men did. But the study found most people who stretch the truth do so by small amounts, on average "adjusting" their weight by only 5.5%, and their height and age by even less.

But some lies are potentially more hurtful and harder to detect upon meeting. The odds an adult Internet user thinks people on online dating sites often lie about being married are **1 in 1.8**.

SOURCES: CL Toma, JT Hancock, NB Ellison, "Separating Fact from Fiction: An Examination of Deceptive Self-Presentation in Online Dating Profiles," *Personality and Social Psychology Bulletin* 34(8), August 2008: 1023–1036. ✦ Pew Internet and American Life Project, "September 2005 Daily Tracking Survey/Online Dating Extension," 2005. ✦ E Frazier, "Online Love Life: World's Just Not Fair," *Charlotte Observer*, February 13, 2010.

Is Love Really a Click Away?

eHarmony has claimed in television or online ads in the US, UK, and Australia that it's responsible for 2% of all new US marriages, based on a twelve-month survey that concluded in March 2007. A 2010 study sponsored by **Match.com** also has some intriguing numbers.

The study surveyed people who had married during the previous five-year period, and **1 in 5.9** people had met his or her spouse through an online dating site—making these sites the third most common way people meet future partners, just after work/school and family/friends. Happily for the corporate sponsor, twice as many couples had met through **Match.com** as the nearest competitor. And the numbers had been consistent over a three-year period and been performed by independent research organizations. The bar and club scene is proving less successful. Over the three-year period surveyed, the percentage of married couples who found each other through "bars/clubs/other social events" dropped from 11% to 8%.

SOURCES: C Bialik, "Marriage-Maker Claims Are Tied in Knots," The Numbers Guy, *Wall Street Journal*, July 29, 2009. ✦ Match.com and Chadwick Martin Bailey, "Marriage Survey," *Recent Trends: Online Dating*, http://cp.match.com/cppp/media/CMB_Study.pdf.

Why There Was No Second Date

The odds a woman will become uninterested if a first date says "you remind me of my ex" are **1 in 1.5**.

The odds a woman will be bothered if a man expects her to help pay for a date are **1 in 2.2**.

The odds a man believes good hygiene is necessary before a man can be considered handsome are **1 in 4.4**.

The odds a woman will report that she has dumped a man because of his body odor are **1 in 7.1**.

The odds an unmarried adult is dating for casual sex are **1 in 33.3**.

SOURCES: Yahoo! Personals, "What Does America Think About Breakups?," July 2006. ✦ JA Persch, "It's Complicated: Who Pays on Dates," Personal Finance, MSNBC.com, March 8, 2008, htttp://msnbc.msn.com/id/23244363/ns/business-personal_finance. ✦ Synovate, "Synovate Global Male Beauty Survey Uncovers Attitudes and Perceptions Towards Appearances and Male Beauty Products," press release, December 2008. ✦ J Weaver, "What Are Our Dating Pet Peeves?," *Elle/MSNBC.com Sex and Beauty Survey*, MSNBC.com, May 5, 2005, http://www.nbcnews.com/id/7736649. ✦ Harris Interactive, *Chemistry.com Relationship Survey* by 2007, http://www.chemistry.com/relationshipcentral/rcfacts.aspx.

Interracial Dating

In 2010 about 15% of American marriages were interracial or cross-ethnic—twice the rate of 1980. Today the odds a person "would be fine with it" if a member of his or her family were to marry someone outside his or her racial or ethnic group are 1 in 1.6, a dramatic change since 1986, when only 1 in 3 people viewed intermarriage as okay for everyone. In fact, 1 in 2.9 people now has a close relative married to someone of a different race.

When it comes to interracial dating, young adults are twice as likely to approve of it as their grandparents. The odds an adult between the ages of 18 and 29 approves of a mixed-race (black and white) couple are 1 in 1.1, compared to 1 in 2.2 among adults 65 or older. The odds a person has dated someone of a different racial background are 1 in 2.1.

However, some lingering prejudice can still be found among adults when it comes to which gender should be black and which one should be white. The odds an adult disapproves of a black man dating a white woman dating are 1 in 4.6, compared to 1 in 5.3 odds that an adult disapproves of a white man dating a black woman.

Despite the general public's preference, nuptials generally go the other way. Of all black male newlyweds in 2010, 1 in 4.2 married outside their race, compared with just 1 in 11.9 of black female newlyweds.

SOURCES: JM Jones, "Most Americans Approve of Interracial Dating," Gallup News Service, October 7, 2005. ∕ W Wang, "The Rise of Intermarriage: Rates Characteristics Vary by Race and Gender," *Social & Demographic Trends,* Pew Research Center, February 16, 2012.

Who Pays for the Date—and Who Cares?

The odds a woman will...

offer to pay for a date . . . . 1 in 1.8

be bothered if a man accepts her offer to pay for a date . . . . 1 in 2.9

be bothered if a man refuses to accept her offer to pay for a date . . . . 1 in 2.2

Who pays belief	Men %	Men Odds	Women %	Women Odds
The man should not pay for more dates than the woman	16	1 in 6.3	36	1 in 2.8
The man should pay for most of the dates until the relationship is established	42	1 in 2.4	34	1 in 2.9
The man should pay for the majority of dates for the duration of the relationship	24	1 in 4.2	19	1 in 5.3
The man should pay for all dates	1	1 in 7.7	5	1 in 20

SOURCES: JA Persch, "It's Complicated: Who Pays on Dates," Personal Finance, MSNBC.com, March 8, 2008, http://www.msnbc.msn.com/id/23244363/ns/business-personal_finance// ∕ AskMen.com, "Part I: Dating and Sex," *The Great Female Survey, 2011 Edition,* http://www.askmen.com/specials/yahoo_shine_great_female_survey/part1.html. ∕ AskMen.com, "Part I: Dating & Sex," *The Great Male Survey, 2011 Edition,* http://www.askmen.com/specials/2011_great_male_survey.

"Wife/ Husband"

The odds a man thinks it's important for his girlfriend to have **"wife potential,"** and won't bother pursuing a relationship with a woman who doesn't have it: **1 in 2.9**.

The odds a woman believes it is important for a boyfriend to have **"husband potential"** and won't bother pursuing a relationship with a man who doesn't have it: **1 in 2.6**.

SOURCES: AskMen.com, "Part I: Dating & Sex," *The Great Male Survey, 2011 Edition,* http://www.askmen.com/specials/2011_great_male_survey. ∕ AskMen.com, "Q1," *The Great Female Survey, 2011 Edition,* http://www.askmen.com/specials/great_female_survey.

ODDS COUPLE

Do We Need to Get Out More?

The odds a male massively multiplayer online role-playing game (MMORPG) player has ever dated someone he met through an MMORPG are **1 in 6.4**.

The odds a man 45–49 has never been married are **1 in 6.1**.

SOURCES: N Yee, "The Psychology of MMORPGs: Emotional Investment, Motivations, Relationship Formation, and Problematic Usage," in *Avatars at Work and Play: Collaboration and Interaction in Shared Virtual Environments,* eds. R Schroeder and A Axelsson, (London: Springer-Verlag, 2006, 187–207. http://www.nickyee.com/index-papers.html. ∕ US Census Bureau, *Current Population Survey, 2010, Annual Social and Economic Supplement.*

Interview with William Cane, Author of
THE ART OF KISSING

Why do we kiss?

The main reason is to express our affection. Another reason is cultural—we're surrounded by TV shows and movies where kissing is extremely important in a romantic context, so we learn through a kind of osmosis. And the third reason is, as Freud pointed out, we all go through various stages of development, the first of which is the oral stage, and so, certainly it's still a part of our pleasure drive—oral contact is a lot of fun.

You say that the lips have a lot of nerve endings.

The tip of the tongue has more nerve endings than any other part of the body. It's extremely sensitive. And most people don't realize the lips themselves have taste sensors so it's not only the tongue but the inner part of the lips that can taste things; so when you kiss you're actually tasting your partner.

You list statistics in The Art of Kissing—for example, 67% of men don't mind if a woman's wearing lipstick when kissing, 53% of women prefer a clean-shaven man, and 33% of people open their eyes while kissing. Do you have favorite statistics?

Women's favorite spot to be kissed, other than the mouth, is the neck. 96% of women reported that they like neck kisses, while only about 10% of men do, so a guy will not even *believe* that a girl likes being kissed on the neck because it doesn't really do anything for him. So I tell guys to move or slide off the lips occasionally down to the neck, and that will produce big results. And women like being kissed on the ears much more than men do.

So the odds a neck kiss will succeed on a woman are 1 in 1.04. What about men?

Men often respond most to the French kiss, whereas women often respond to a *romantic* kiss. Guys will say they're not really getting excited unless there is some tongue contact, while girls will often say if you're passionate and loving, a lip kiss is good enough. You don't have to rush in and, you know, trigger the gag reflex with the tongue. The number one mistake girls make in kissing is not opening their mouths wide enough—probably because the guy is trying to initiate a French kiss.

SOURCES: Book of Odds interview with William Cane, 2010. ✗ W Cane, *The Art of Kissing*, rev. ed., New York, St. Martin's Press, 1995.

The first kiss is notoriously nerve-racking—and for good reason. A research survey from the University of Albany found that **59%** of men and **66%** of women lost their attraction for someone after kissing them for the first time.

SOURCE: R Alleyne, "AAAS First Kiss is Screening Process for Potential Mates," *The Telegraph*, February 13, 2009, http://www.telegraph.co.uk/science/science-news/4611149/AAAS-First-kiss-is-screening-process-for-potential-mates.html.

ODDS COUPLE

Owning First Base

The odds a woman kissed her partner on their first date: **1 in 1.9**

The odds an MLB game will be won by the home team: **1 in 1.9**

SOURCES: Yahoo! Personals and TheKnot.com, "Dating Survey: Women on Finding 'The One.'" ✗ Book of Odds estimate based on data from: Game Logs, Retrosheet, Table Retrosheet Game Logs 2000, 2001, 2002, 2003, 2004, 2005, 2006.

The odds that an undergraduate student 18 or older has kissed at least 20 members of the opposite sex: **1 in 4.3**

SOURCE: Book of Odds estimate based on data from SM Hughes, MA Harrison, GG Gallup, "Sex Differences in Romantic Kissing Among College Students: An Evolutionary Perspective," *Evolutionary Psychology* 5(3), 2007: 12–631.

The odds a homosexual or bisexual man is in a steady relationship with a man and they live together: **1 in 5**

The odds he is in a steady relationship with a woman and lives with her: **1 in 2.4**

SOURCE: JA Davis, TW Smith, PV Marsden, *General Social Surveys, 1972–2008* [CUMULATIVE FILE] [Computer file] ICPSR04697 v. 1., Chicago: National Opinion Research Center [producer], 2009; Storrs, CT: Roper Center for Public Opinion Research, University of Connecticut/Ann Arbor, MI: Inter-university Consortium for Political and Social Research [distributors].

1 in 40

The odds a traditional Sweethearts candy says "FIRST KISS."

SOURCE: Book of Odds estimate based on production data provided by Aimee Scott, brand manager, New England Confectionery Company.

If I Had One Wish

1 in 3.3 men would change his partner's **attitude or moodiness** vs. **1 in 6.7** women.

1 in 4 men would change **nothing** about his partner vs. **1 in 5.6** women.

1 in 5.1 men would change his partner's **lack of sexual appetite** vs. **1 in 25** women.

1 in 11.2 men would change his partner's **looks** vs. **1 in 33.3** women.

1 in 18.7 men would change his partner's **domestic skills** vs. **1 in 33.3** women.

1 in 56 men would change his partner's **intelligence** vs. **1 in 100** women.

	Men/%	Women/%
Attitude or moodiness	30	15
Nothing	25	18
Lack of sexual appetite	20	4
Looks	9	3
Domestic skills	5	3
Intelligence	2	1

SOURCES: AskMen.com, "Part I: Dating & Sex," *The Great Male Survey, 2011 Edition,* http://www.askmen.com/specials/2011_great_male_survey. ✗ AskMen.com, "Q7," *The Great Female Survey, 2011 Edition,* http://www.askmen.com/specials/great_female_survey.

Women Want Other Changes, Too

1 in 16.7 women would change her partner's **laziness**.

1 in 16.7 women would change her partner's **level of ambition**.

1 in 20 women would change her partner's **income**.

1 in 33.3 women would change her partner's **jealousy**.

SOURCE: AskMen.com, "Q7," *The Great Female Survey, 2011 Edition,* http://www.askmen.com/specials/great_female_survey.

GENDER WARS

The odds an unmarried man 40–69 who dates thinks it's okay to have sex on the first date: **1 in 5**

The odds an unmarried woman 40–69 who dates thinks it's okay: **1 in 50**

SOURCES: AskMen.com, "Q10," *The Great Female Survey, 2011 Edition,* http://www.askmen.com/specials/great_female_survey.

The odds an unmarried man 40–69 is gay: **1 in 14.3**

The odds an unmarried woman 40–69 is gay: **1 in 33.3**

SOURCE: XP Montenegro, "Lifestyles, Dating, and Romance: A Study of Midlife Singles," *AARP The Magazine,* September 2003.

I Can't Believe You Said That!

The odds a man will report that he has suggested his partner **lose weight**:

1 in 2.4

The odds a man will report that he has suggested his partner get **plastic surgery**:

1 in 8

The odds a man will report that he has suggested his partner get **breast enlargements**:

1 in 12.7

The odds a man will report that he has suggested his partner get **liposuction**:

1 in 50

The odds a man will report that he has suggested his partner get **breast reductions**:

1 in 66.7

SOURCE: J Weaver, "What Are Our Dating Pet Peeves?," *Elle/MSNBC.com Sex and Beauty Survey*, MSNBC.com, May 5, 2005, http://www.nbcnews.com/id/7736649.

1 in 5 women and **1 in 2.1** men report they would dump a partner who became fat.

SOURCES: AskMen.com, "Part I: Dating and Sex," *The Great Female Survey, 2011 Edition*, http://www.askmen.com/specials/yahoo_shine_ great_female_survey/part1.html. ✎ AskMen.com, "Part I: Dating & Sex," *The Great Male Survey, 2011 Edition*, http://www.askmen.com/ specials/2011_great_male_survey.

Numbers Tell the Story

She suspects:
The odds a woman will report she is not comfortable with her boyfriend "friending" his exes on Facebook: **1 in 3**

The odds a woman will report she has never read her boyfriend's email or instant messages but would if she suspected he was up to something: **1 in 6.7**

She asks him to stop:
The odds a man will report that if he could change one thing about his partner he would change her nagging: **1 in 11.2**

He spends an evening on the town flirting with her best friend:
The odds a man has ever fantasized about his partner's friend: **1 in 1.5**

The last straw—an out-of-town trip with his sexy colleague:
The odds a man has never had sex with a coworker but would if the opportunity arose: **1 in 1.9**

She hacks into his email:
The odds a woman will report she has read her boyfriend's email or electronic messages by breaking into his email or messaging account: **1 in 8.3**

It's over—or maybe not:
The odds a stalker is a former lover: **1 in 7.6**

SOURCES: AskMen.com, "Part I: Dating and Sex," *The Great Female Survey, 2011 Edition*, http://www.askmen.com/specials/ yahoo_shine_great_female_survey/part1.html. ✎ AskMen.com, "Part I: Dating & Sex," *The Great Male Survey, 2011 Edition*, http:// www.askmen.com/specials/2011_great_male_survey. ✎ K Baum, S Catalano, M Rand, *Stalking Victimization in the United States*, National Crime Victimization Survey, Bureau of Justice Statistics Special Report, January 13, 2009.

The Kiss Is the Cutoff

The point at which a man considers his girlfriend to be cheating:

Kissed someone . . . . **1 in 1.9**

Slept with someone . . . . **1 in 5**

Danced suggestively with someone . . . . **1 in 7.7**

Flirted with someone . . . . **1 in 12.5**

Fantasized about someone. **1 in 20**

SOURCE: AskMen.com, "Men's Dating Trends," *The Great Male Sex Survey, 2008 Edition,* http://static.askmen.com/specials/2008_great_male_survey/2008_dating_survey.html.

GENDER WARS

The odds a woman says she would cheat on her partner if there was no way he could find out but would feel guilty about it: **1 in 10**

For a man: **1 in 5.3**

SOURCES: AskMen.com, "Part I: Dating and Sex," *The Great Female Survey, 2011 Edition,* http://www.askmen.com/specials/yahoo_shine_great_female_survey/part1.html. ✎ AskMen.com, "Part I: Dating & Sex," *The Great Male Survey, 2011 Edition,* http://www.askmen.com/specials/2011_great_male_survey.

$how Me the Money

F i n a n c i a l   W o r t h

The odds a man believes women put too much value on a man's financial worth, but men put a lot of value on women's looks so it balances out are **1 in 1.9**.

The odds a man believes women put too much value on a man's financial worth, and it bothers him that women are so shallow are **1 in 4.3**.

The odds a man believes women put too much value on a man's financial worth, and it works to his advantage are **1 in 25**.

SOURCE: AskMen.com, "Part I: Dating & Sex," *The Great Male Survey, 2011 Edition,* http://www.askmen.com/specials/2011_great_male_survey.

ODDS COUPLE

"Just Friends"

The odds a man will report that he is not comfortable with a partner "friending" her exes on Facebook: **1 in 3.4**

The odds a man will report he knows someone who has used the Internet to facilitate cheating: **1 in 3**

SOURCE: AskMen.com, "Part I: Dating & Sex," *The Great Male Survey, 2011 Edition,* http://www.askmen.com/specials/2011_great_male_survey.

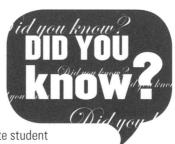

The odds an undergraduate student has ever broken up and gotten back together with the same person: **1 in 1.6**

SOURCE: Book of Odds estimate based on RM Dailey, A Pfiester, B Jin, G Beck, G Clark, "On-Again/Off-Again Dating Relationships: How Are They Different from Other Dating Relationships?" *Personal Relationships,* 16(1), March 2009: 23–47.

Why the Breakup?

his or her last relationship ended because of physical distance: **1 in 5.4**

his or her last relationship ended because of unbalanced needs or expectations: **1 in 6.5**

his or her last relationship ended because of a third party or external sources: **1 in 7**

his or her last relationship ended because of communication problems: **1 in 7.4**

his or her last relationship ended because of negative behavior: **1 in 8.6**

his or her last relationship ended because of a desire to explore other options: **1 in 9.9**

his or her last relationship ended because of a negative change in the relationship: **1 in 10.2**

his or her last relationship ended because of a need for independence: **1 in 12.2**

his or her last relationship ended because of cheating: **1 in 13.7**

his or her last relationship ended because of trust issues: **1 in 28.6**

his or her last relationship ended because of lying: **1 in 62.5**

Leaving Your Lover

Whose idea was it?

The odds an undergraduate student in a relationship will report...

his or her last relationship ended by a direct dissolution by one partner: **1 in 4.1**

his or her last relationship ended with an explanation or justification: **1 in 4.1**

his or her last relationship ended mutually: **1 in 6.1**

his or her last relationship ended by agreeing to take a break: **1 in 11.5**

his or her last relationship ended in conflict from both partners blaming each other: **1 in 14.5**

his or her last relationship ended with one partner withdrawing from the relationship: **1 in 16.1**

his or her last relationship ended with one partner suggesting that they both date other people: **1 in 25**

his or her last relationship ended by both partners drifting apart: **1 in 40**

The odds a man will report that he is usually the one to initiate a breakup: **1 in 2.5**

The odds a man will report that his breakups are usually a mutual decision: **1 in 2.6**

The odds a man will report that his girlfriends are usually the ones to dump him: **1 in 4.6**

How was it done?

The odds an undergraduate student in a relationship will report his or her last relationship ended using manipulation, bullying, or third parties: **1 in 111**

The odds a woman 18–34 who uses social media will report having used Facebook as a way to break up: **1 in 11.1**

The odds a man 18–34 who uses social media will report having used Facebook as a way to break up: **1 in 4.2**

The odds a woman 18–34 who uses social media will report having used texting as a way to break up: **1 in 7.1**

The odds a man 18–34 who uses social media will report having used texting as a way to break up: **1 in 3.2**

Not on my birthday!

The odds a person 18 or older believes the worst time for a breakup is a birthday: **1 in 2.9**

The odds a person 18 or older believes the worst time for a breakup is the holiday season: **1 in 3.3**

Worst Way

Ouch

The odds a person 18 or older believes the worst way to break up with someone is through an email at work are **1 in 3.2**.

The odds a person 18 or older believes the worst way to break up with someone is through a family member or friend are **1 in 3.7**.

SOURCES: RM Dailey, A Pfiester, B Jin, G Beck, G Clark, "On-Again/Off-Again Dating Relationships: How Are They Different from Other Dating Relationships?" *Personal Relationships* 16(1), March 2009:23–47. ✎ AskMen.com, "Men's Dating Trends," *The Great Male Sex Survey, 2008 Edition,* http://static.askmen.com/specials/2008_great_male_survey/2008_dating_survey.html. ✎ Oxygen Media Insights Group, "The United States of Facebook," 2010. ✎ Yahoo! Personals, "What Does America Think About Breakups?," July 2008.

An international survey conducted by the market research company Synovate found that **1 in 8.3** cell phone owners had dumped someone via text message. Another survey by SNAP Interactive, makers of an iPhone dating app, surveyed a thousand Facebook users and found that almost **1 in 4** has learned his or her relationship was terminated by seeing the news posted on the social networking site.

SOURCES: K LaCapria, "More Relationships Are Ending Via Facebook, Survey Finds," *SNAP Interactive Survey Results,* June 15, 2010, http://www.inquisitr.com/75923/facebook-breakup-survey/. ✎ Synovate, "Global Survey Shows Cell Phone is 'Remote Control' for Life: 42% of Americans 'Can't Live Without It' and Almost Half Sleep with It Nearby," *Global Cell Phone Survey Results,* September 17, 2009, http://www.synovate.com/news/article/2009/09/global-survey-shows-cell-phone-is-remote-control-for-life-42–of-americans-can-t-live-without-it-and-almost-half-sleep-with-it-nearby.html.

Man Up

The odds a man most recently broke up with someone in person:
. . . . **1 in 1.8**

The odds a man has never broken up with someone . . . . **1 in 4.8**

The odds a man most recently broke up with someone on the phone
. . . . **1 in 6.3**

The odds a man most recently broke up with someone via text message
. . . . **1 in 14.3**

The odds a man most recently broke up with someone via Facebook message
. . . . **1 in 100**

SOURCE: AskMen.com, "Part III: Men in 2011," *The Great Male Survey, 2011 Edition,* http://www.askmen.com/specials/2011_great_male_survey.

Getting Over Her

To get over a breakup, the odds a man:

Distracts himself with exercise or hobbies . . . . . . **1 in 1.9**

Parties and drinks . . . . . . **1 in 4**

Has rebound sex . . . . **1 in 4.4**

Sleeps with someone else . . **1 in 7.7**

Mopes around the house . . **1 in 11.1**

SOURCE: AskMen.com, "Men's Dating Trends," *The Great Male Sex Survey, 2008 Edition,* http://static.askmen.com/specials/2008_great_male_survey/2008_dating_survey.html.

And Here Come the Tears

The odds a man will report that he has shed tears over a woman when he was alone
. . . . **1 in 2.8**

The odds a man will report that he has shed tears over a woman in front of her
. . . . **1 in 3.1**

SOURCE: Social Issues Research Centre, *The Kleenex for Men Crying Report: A Study of Men and Crying,* September 30, 2004.

CHAPTER 3

LOVE, MARRIAGE, AND DIVORCE

Love at First Sight

The odds an adult believes in love at first sight:

1 in 1.9

SOURCE: DK Carlson, "Over Half of Americans Believe in Love at First Sight," Gallup Poll, February 14, 2001, *2000*, http://www .gallup.com/poll/2017/ Over-Half-Americans- Believe-Love-First- Sight.aspx.

ODDS OF BEING married, single, widowed, or divorced

by race/ethnicity

The odds a **white** adult...

is **married** . . . . 1 in 1.8
is **divorced** . . . . 1 in 9.6
is **widowed** . . . . 1 in 15.8
is **separated** . . . . 1 in 47.1
has **never married** . . . . 1 in 4.1

The odds a **black** adult...

is **married** . . . . 1 in 2.9
is **divorced** . . . . 1 in 8.5
is **widowed** . . . . 1 in 15
is **separated** . . . . 1 in 22.6
has **never married** . . . . 1 in 2.3

The odds an **Asian** adult...

is **married** . . . . 1 in 1.6
is **divorced** . . . . 1 in 22.4
is **widowed** . . . . 1 in 20.5
is **separated** . . . . 1 in 75.8
has **never married** . . . . 1 in 4

The odds a **Hispanic** adult...

is **married** . . . . 1 in 2
is **divorced** . . . . 1 in 12.2
is **widowed** . . . . 1 in 26.6
is **separated** . . . . 1 in 22.8
has **never married** . . . . 1 in 2.9

SOURCE: US Census Bureau, *Current Population Survey Annual Social and Economic Supplement,* November 2010.

In 1980, the odds a couple were from different races or ethnicities, no matter when they married, were **1 in 31.3**.

In 2010 the odds a couple were from different races or ethnicities, no matter when they married, were **1 in 11.9**.

SOURCE: W Wang "The Rise of Intermarriage, Rates Characteristics Vary by Race and Gender," Social & Demographic Trend, Pew Research Center, February 16, 2012.

The odds a woman believes her relationship is the result of fate: **1 in 1.3**

The odds she believes it was pure chance: **1 in 4.6**

SOURCE: Yahoo! Personals and TheKnot.com, "Dating Survey: Women on Finding 'The One.'"

The Power of Love

If there is a measure of love's power it is perhaps altruism. The odds an adult 30–49 will report he or she would rather suffer than let his or her loved one suffer are **1 in 1.1**—that's 90%. Almost as many would "endure all things" for the sake of the one he or she loves: **1 in 1.3**. Even younger people (age 18–29), whom we might expect to be more self-focused, come in at **1 in 1.3** in this extreme measure of devotion. We wouldn't just endure pain for someone we love—we'd also give up our own heart's desires. The odds an adult 30–49 will report he or she is willing to sacrifice his or her wishes for his or her loved one's are **1 in 1.2**. Folks 65 and up are even more willing to do so, at **1 in 1.1**. Perhaps they've grown even more giving. Or maybe they just have fewer dreams left unfulfilled.

SOURCE: JA Davis, TW Smith, PV Marsden, *General Social Surveys, 1972–2008* [CUMULATIVE FILE] [Computer file] ICPSR04697 v. 1., Chicago: National Opinion Research Center [producer], 2009; Storrs, CT: Roper Center for Public Opinion Research, University of Connecticut/Ann Arbor, MI: Inter-university Consortium for Political and Social Research [distributors].

 Numbers Tell the Story

Odds of Finding Prince Charming by 30

Almost a Sure Thing?

The odds a woman is married by 30 are **1 in 1.4**.

The odds are the same that . . .

- A female high school graduate will go to college within a year of graduation
- An adult living in North Carolina is a registered voter
- An NBA team will score at least 90 points in a game
- A divorced female 15–44 will remarry within ten years of the divorce

Maybe Not

The odds a woman is not married by 30 are **1 in 3.5**.

The odds are the same that...

- A woman has ever suggested her partner lose weight
- A person shares his or her last name with 9,999–99,998 people
- A person is younger than 21
- A female high school student will be the passenger of a drunk driver in a month

SOURCES: Book of Odds estimate based on Centers for Disease Control and Prevention, *National Survey of Family Growth 2006–2008*, Public Use Data Files. ✔ National Center for Education Statistics, Institute of Education Sciences, U.S. Department of Education. *Digest of Education Statistics, 2009.* ✔ US Census Bureau, "Voting and Registration in the Election of November 2008," http://www.census.gov/population/www/socdemo/voting/cps2008.html. ✔ Basketball Reference [Internet]. Sports Reference LLC. http://www.basketball -reference.com/. ✔ J Weaver, "What Are Our Dating Pet Peeves?," *Elle/MSNBC.com Sex and Beauty Survey*, MSNBC.com, May 5, 2005, http://www.nbcnews.com/id/7736649. ✔ US Census Bureau, "Top 1,000 Names." ✔ Book of Odds estimate based on US Census Bureau, Population Estimates Program, http://www.census.gov/popest/estimates.php. ✔ DK Eaton, L Kann, S Kinchen, S Shanklin, J Ross, J Hawkins, et al., "Youth Risk Behavior Surveillance—United States, 2009," *Morbidity and Mortality Weekly Report* 59(SS-5), June 4, 2010.

GENDER WARS

The odds a romance novel reader is female: **1 in 1.1**

The odds a romance novel reader is male: **1 in 10.5**

SOURCE: Romance Writers of America, "Romance Literature Statistics," 2009 *RWA Readers Survey*, May 2009.

Soul Mates?

Can you fall in love with any number of people?

1 in 4.2 adults thinks so—compared to **1 in 1.4** who believes we each have no more than one true love.

SOURCE: DK Carlson, "Over Half of Americans Believe in Love at First Sight," Gallup Poll, February 14, 2001, http://www.gallup.com/poll/2017/Over-Half -Americans-Believe-Love -First-Sight.aspx.

Objectum Sexuality

It can be a steam locomotive, an archer's bow, even the Eiffel Tower—the object of one's affections can literally be an object, as cherished as any person. Just ask Erika Eiffel, one of the 71% of married adults who report their marriage has lasted because of deep love. We know her spouse as the Eiffel Tower.

Ms. Eiffel is an objectum-sexual, one of a small group of people who love and are attracted to things.

The idea of sincerely loving an object in an emotional and/or physical way has been around for a long time, although it didn't always have a name. For centuries, schoolchildren have been taught the legend of Pygmalion, an ancient Greek sculptor who fell madly in love with a female figure he'd carved from ivory. He loved her so singularly, the myth goes, and prayed so fervently that the goddess Aphrodite eventually took pity on him and made her flesh. They immediately tied the knot.

Not all objectum-sexuals are interested in matrimony—or having material transformed into flesh. Most find objects sexy *as objects*; there is hardly any talk of wishing they were human, because many objectophiles are not attracted to humans.

The term "objectum-sexual" (OS) was first coined by Eija-Riitta Eklöf Berliner-Mauer, who may be the first self-declared objectum-sexual of modern times. In 1979, she and the Berlin Wall were "wed," and her last name reflects her part of the commitment: in German, *Berliner-Mauer* means "Berlin-Wall."

Many of us find comfort in taming the unusual by naming it. Some psychologists with this obsession classify OS as an obsession turned paraphilia, defined in the *DSM-IV* as a sexual feeling/behavior that involves nonhuman or nonconsenting sexual partners. By this criterion, objectum sexuality is a mental disorder—in the same category as pedophilia or bestiality.

Others consider it more of an independent orientation—independent of heterosexuality and homosexuality alike. While there are theories as to how objectum sexuality originates in the psyche (e.g., in autism or childhood abuse), objectophiles simply cast themselves in with the **1 in 1.4** adults who report being in love, regardless of whom—or what—they love.

SOURCES: "The Truth About American Marriage," *Parade Magazine*, September 15, 2008. ✗ Objectum Sexuality International!, http://objectum-sexuality.org/. ✗ F Thadeusz, "Falling in Love with Things," *Spiegel Online International*, May 11, 2007, http://www.spiegel.de/international/spiegel/0,1518,482192,00.html. ✗ A Frances, H Pincus, M First, *DSM-IV-TR Guidebook*, Arlington, VA: American Psychiatric Publishing, 2004. ✗ Book of Odds calculation based on data from L Saad, "Romance to Break Out Nationwide This Weekend," Gallup Poll, February 13, 2004, http://www.gallup.com/poll/10609/romance-break-nationwide-weekend .aspx.

About That Ring

The odds a person will get engaged in a year:

1 in 66.7

The same odds that...

- An adult will report having told eight lies in the past day
- A woman 25–29 will report being gay
- A boy 6–11 drinks coffee at least once a day
- An adult who has a costume in mind for Halloween will be Batman

SOURCES: Book of Odds estimate based on Robbins Brothers, *Valentine's Day Engagement and Proposal Survey Results.* ✗ KB Serota, TR Levine, FJ Boster, "The Prevalence of Lying in America: Three Studies of Self-Reported Lies," *Human Communication Research* 36, 2010: 2–25. ✗ US Department of Agriculture, "Nationwide Food Consumption Survey: Food and Nutrient Intakes by Individuals in the United States, 1 Day, 1987–88." ✗ National Retail Federation, *Consumer Intentions Survey*, September 2010.

A TINY BOX

Under the Tree

The odds a person will get engaged in December: **1 in 416**

SOURCE: "The Knot Unveils 2009 Real Wedding Survey Results," February 17, 2010, http://www.xogroupinc.com/press-releases-home/2010-press-releases/2010-02-17-real-weddings-survey-results-2009.aspx.

DID YOU know?

The odds an engaged woman proposed to her groom: **1 in 100**

SOURCE: Nast Bridal Group, "American Wedding Study 2006," http://www.bridalgroup .com/0710/index.cfm.

Living Together? What Are the Odds You'll Get Married?

It turns out that cohabitation is, more often than not, a straight shot to the altar. Half of all cohabitating couples marry within three years, and even more (**1 in 1.5**), do so within five years. But do they stay married?

Maybe Not

Whether they lived together prior to marriage seems relevant. A study based on the National Survey of Family Growth found a small gap in marriage success rates between those who cohabitate premarriage and those who don't.

1 in 1.6 men who cohabitated before marriage stayed married for at least ten years; that's less than the **1 in 1.5** who moved in after the wedding. For women, the gap was smaller. **1 in 1.7** cohabitating women were likely to stay married for at least ten years, compared to **1 in 1.5** noncohabitating women. Whether a couple was engaged matters, too: those who were engaged *before* moving in together were just as likely to see their tenth anniversary as those who did *not* live together before marriage.

SOURCE: Romance Writers of America, "Romance Literature Statistics," *2009 RWA Readers Survey,* May 2009.

Hard to Pin Down

The odds a man 30–34 has lived with at least three different significant others without being married:

1 in 9.1

For a man 35–39 the odds increase to

1 in 6.9

SOURCE: Romance Writers of America, "Romance Literature Statistics," *2009 RWA Readers Survey,* May 2009.

How and Where Married People Met

	%		Odds (1 in)	
	Married Men	**Married Women**	**Married Men**	**Married Women**
Through friends	37	36	**2.7**	**2.8**
At a bar, club, or restaurant	21	17	**4.8**	**6.0**
As coworkers	19	16	**5.2**	**6.2**
Through family	17	22	**5.8**	**4.6**
In primary or secondary school	14	14	**7.4**	**7.4**
At a private party	14	11	**7.4**	**9.0**
Through work as a client	10	8	**10.5**	**11.9**
In the neighborhood	10	11	**10.4**	**9.1**
In college	9	10	**11.6**	**10.3**
Through church	7	10	**14.3**	**10.5**
In a public place	6	9	**17.0**	**11.0**
In a nonchurch social group	5	5	**18.9**	**20.4**
Online	5	4	**22.2**	**27.8**
On a blind date	4	4	**23.3**	**26.3**

SOURCE: MA Rosenfeld, RJ Thomas, "Table 5: How Americans Met Their Spouses and Current Partners," *How Couples Meet and Stay Together, Waves I and II,* Public Version 2.04 [Computer file]. Stanford, CA: Stanford University Libraries, 2011–January 2012.

DID YOU know?

The odds a "very religious" female 15–44 has lived with a significant other without being married:

1 in 2.3

The odds a "very religious" man from the same age group has done so:

1 in 2.3

SOURCE: Romance Writers of America, "Romance Literature Statistics," *2009 RWA Readers Survey,* May 2009.

Teens at the ALTAR

The odds a teenager 15–17 is married are **1 in 127**, about the same odds a tourist in the United States will visit Minneapolis–St. Paul, Minnesota.

The heyday of teen marriage was the mid-twentieth century, when the median marrying age for women was just 20.3 (22.8 for men). Rates fell sharply after that, and the median marrying age for women reached 26 in 2007.

The birth rate for 15- to 19-year-olds declined steadily from 1991 to 2005. In both 2006 and 2007, the birth rates *increased* for this group.

How do teens compare to the whole population? The overall rate is declining but the teen rate is still higher. In 2008, the number of US births declined about 2% from the 2007 peak, along with a decline in overall fertility. The birth rate for females 15–19 also declined to 41.5 per 1,000, but is still above the 40.5 per 1,000 for 2005.

Many teen marriages designed to beat the stork do not have a happy ending. A National Bureau of Economic Research study found that a woman who marries before age 16 is 31% more likely to live in poverty later in life. High divorce rates are largely to blame: couples who marry before the age of 18 are at least twice as likely as couples who marry at 25 or later to divorce within 10 years, and divorced or separated women often suffer significant economic consequences.

SOURCES: US Census Bureau, *Current Population Survey Annual Social and Economic Supplement,* November 2010. ✔ R Baedeker, "America's 30 Most Visited Cities," ForbesTraveler.com, July 27, 2008, http://www.forbestraveler.com/best-lists/most-visited-us-cities-story.html. ✔ National Center for Chronic Disease Prevention and Health Promotion, Division of Reproductive Health, "Teen Birth Rates Rose Again in 2007, Declined in 2008," May 5, 2010, http://www.cdc.gov/Features/dsTeenPregnancy/. ✔ BE Hamilton, JA Martin, SJ Ventura, "Births: Preliminary Data for 2008," *National Vital Statistics Report* 58(16), April 6, 2010. ✔ G Dahl, "Early Teen Marriage and Future Poverty," NBER Working Paper No. 11328, National Bureau of Economic Research (NBER), March 2009.

Has Marriage Always Been in the Plans?

The odds a **female** high school senior thinks she will most likely get married:

1 in 1.2

The odds a **male** high school senior thinks he will most likely get married:

1 in 1.3

SOURCE: LD Johnston, JG Bachman, PM O'Malley, *Monitoring the Future: Questionnaire Responses from the Nation's High School Seniors 2009,* University of Michigan, 2010.

Nearly 10%
(**1 in 9.8**) of brides are pregnant on their wedding day.

SOURCE: Centers for Disease Control and Prevention, *National Survey of Family Growth 2006–2008,* Public Use Data Files.

ODDS COUPLE

Who's Scrooge?

The odds a bride will intend to sign a prenuptial agreement:

1 in 33.3

The odds an adult will spend less than $100 on Christmas gifts in a year:

1 in 33.3

SOURCES: About.com, "Wedding & Honeymoon Statistics," http://honeymoons.about.com/cs/eurogen1/a/weddingstats.htm. ✔ Book of Odds calculation based on data from L Saad, "Americans' Christmas Budget Falls $200 Below Last Year's," Gallup Poll, 2008, http://www.gallup.com.

♂♀ Why Get Married?

The odds a married man will report he married...

♥ for **love** . . . . **1 in 1.2**

🕐 because it was the **right time in his life** . . . . **1 in 2.2**

☹ because he **did not want to be alone** . . . . **1 in 4.4**

☂ for **practical reasons** . . . . **1 in 5.6**

⧗ because he **wanted to have children** . . . . **1 in 6.3**

💣 because it **got him out of a bad situation** . . . . **1 in 50**

The odds a married woman will report she married...

♥ for **love** . . . . **1 in 1.2**

🕐 because it was the **right time in her life** . . . . **1 in 2.5**

☹ because she **did not want to be alone** . . . . **1 in 5.6**

⧗ because she **wanted to have children** . . . . **1 in 6.3**

☂ for **practical reasons** . . . . **1 in 7.7**

💣 because it **got her out of a bad situation** . . . . **1 in 25**

SOURCE: "The Truth About American Marriage," *Parade Magazine*, September 15, 2008.

Do I or Don't I?

Reasons Men Give for Not Sealing the Deal

Fear of commitment: **1 in 2**

Might pick the wrong person: **1 in 4**

Don't want to give up freedom and independence: **1 in 5.6**

Don't want to have sex with same person forever: **1 in 33.3**

SOURCE: AskMen.com, "Men's Dating Trends," *The Great Male Sex Survey, 2008 Edition,* http://static.askmen.com/specials/2008_great_male_survey/2008_dating_survey.html.

1 in 5

The odds a single adult has broken an engagement in the past three years.

SOURCE: P Paul, "Calling It Off," *Time,* October 6, 2003, http://www.time.com/time/magazine/article/0,9171,1005857,00.html.

ODDS COUPLE

I Did It for the Cash

The odds a married woman or a married man will report she/he got married for money: **1 in 100**

The odds a spy will receive $1,000,000 or more as payment: **1 in 100**

SOURCES: "The Truth About American Marriage," *Parade Magazine,* September 15, 2008. ✒ KL Herbig, *Changes in Espionage by Americans: 1947–2007,* Northrop Grumman, March 2008.

What's Your Lawyer Doing Here?

The odds a woman reports she would never sign a prenuptial agreement and wouldn't marry a man who didn't trust her enough not to need one: **1 in 1.6**

The odds a man believes it is somewhat or very important for his future wife to sign a prenuptial agreement: **1 in 3.4**

SOURCES: AskMen.com, "Part I: Dating & Sex," *The Great Female Survey, 2009 Edition,* www.askmen.com/specials/yahoo_shine_great_female_survey/part1.html. ✒ AskMen.com, "Part I: Dating & Sex," *The Great Male Survey, 2009 Edition,* http://www.askmen.com/specials/2009_great_male_survey.

Age at First Marriage

The odds a **man** will enter his first marriage by the age of…

20	**1 in 21.7**
25	**1 in 3.2**
30	**1 in 1.7**
35	**1 in 1.3**

The odds a **woman** will enter her first marriage by the age of…

20	**1 in 7.6**
25	**1 in 2.1**
30	**1 in 1.4**
35	**1 in 1.2**

SOURCE: Book of Odds estimate based on Centers for Disease Control and Prevention, *National Survey of Family Growth 2006–2008*, Public Use Data Files.

The odds a man believes a man should be married by the age of 25 are **1 in 11.1**. The odds a man believes a man should be married by 30 are **1 in 2.9**. Those are the same odds that a woman in a relationship will report it is unlikely she will marry her current partner.

SOURCES: AskMen.com, "Men's Dating Trends," *The Great Male Sex Survey, 2008 Edition,* http://static.askmen.com/specials/2008_great_male_survey/2008_dating_survey.html. ✔ JA Davis, TW Smith, PV Marsden, *General Social Surveys, 1972–2008* [CUMULATIVE FILE] [Computer file] ICPSR04697 v. 1., Chicago, IL: National Opinion Research Center [producer], 2009; Storrs, CT: Roper Center for Public Opinion Research, University of Connecticut/Ann Arbor, MI: Inter-university Consortium for Political and Social Research [distributors].

Wedding Day

The odds a wedding will be a **formal or black-tie** affair are **1 in 5**.

The odds a wedding will be a **semiformal** affair are **1 in 1.6**.

The odds a wedding will be a **casual-dress** affair are **1 in 8.3**.

The odds a wedding will have a **buffet** are **1 in 2.6**.

The odds a wedding will have a **sit-down dinner** are **1 in 2.9**.

The odds a wedding will have **only cake and punch** are **1 in 3.6**.

The odds a wedding will have a **vanilla- or chocolate-flavored cake** are **1 in 2**.

The odds a wedding will have a **lemon-flavored cake** are **1 in 7.7**.

The odds a wedding will have a **cream cheese cake** are **1 in 10**.

The odds a wedding will have a **red velvet cake** are **1 in 10**.

The odds a wedding will have a **DJ** for the wedding reception are **1 in 1.5**.

The odds a wedding will have a **band** for the wedding reception are **1 in 5.9**.

SOURCES: "The Knot Unveils 2009 Real Wedding Survey Results," February 17, 2010, http://www.xogroupinc.com/press-releases-home/2010-press-releases/2010-02-17-real-weddings-survey-results-2009.aspx. ✔ "The Knot Unveils 2008 Real Wedding Survey Results," April 8, 2009, http://www.xogroupinc.com/press-releases-home/2009-press-releases/2009-04-08-real-wedding-survey.aspx. ✔ All the Right Tunes, "Wedding Statistics," www.alltherighttunes.com.

Who Pays for the Wedding?

Glass-breaking, cake-cutting, bouquet-throwing, "something old, something new, something borrowed, something blue"—the list of such wedding traditions goes on and on. The odds a couple that gets married will have a large, traditional wedding are **1 in 1.3**.

And most of us adhere to another custom—brides' families are still footing the biggest chunk of the bill. According to wedding site The Knot, the average budget for a US wedding in 2009 was $28,385—although the odds are **1 in 1.9** a bride *will plan* for her wedding to cost less than $25,000. On average, the bride's parents pay 46% of the final bill—and the bride and groom kick in most of the rest (40%). Memo to the groom's folks: better make the rehearsal dinner something special. Their contribution to the big day is 12% on average.

SOURCES: Brides.com, "*Brides* Magazine Releases Survey Results; Defines the 'New American Wedding,'" press release, December 7, 2009. ✔ David's Bridal, "Bridal Authority's 'What's On Brides' Minds' Survey Reveals Couples Tying the Knot Still Cutting Costs," press release, January 25, 2010.

⚔ GENDER WARS

The odds a wedding is not the first for a groom . . . . **1 in 9.1**

The odds it's not the first for a bride . . . . **1 in 12.5**

SOURCE: Bridal Association of America, *The Wedding Report*, http://www.bridalassociationofamerica.com.

The odds an unmarried adult is looking for a gay partnership, marriage, or civil union . . . . **1 in 100**

SOURCE: Harris Interactive, "Chemistry.com Relationship Survey," 2007, http://www.chemistry.com/relationshipcentral/rcfacts.aspx.

1 in 5.3

The odds a bride will hire a wedding planner.

SOURCE: "The Knot Unveils 2009 Real Wedding Survey Results," February 17, 2010, http://www.xogroupinc.com/press-releases-home/2010-press-releases/2010-02-17-real-weddings-survey-results-2009.aspx.

"Aunt Martha Called—She's Coming"

Odds a wedding has at least 200 guests. . . . . **1 in 2.5**

SOURCE: AmericanBridal.com, "AmericanBridal.com Announces Results of 2008 Wedding Survey," press release, December 13, 2008.

Warm Weddings

In 2009, June and July were equally popular months for a wedding (the odds were **1 in 9.6** for each). The least popular month was January—the odds of a January marriage were **1 in 16.9**.

SOURCE: "Births, Marriages, Divorces, and Deaths: Provisional Data for 2009," *National Vital Statistics Reports* 58(25), August 2010.

The odds an engaged couple will plan to create a wedding website: **1 in 1.8**

SOURCE: Condé Nast Bridal Media, "Bridal Redefined, Results of the American Wedding Study 2007," 2008.

⚔ GENDER WARS

1 in 11.1 men admits to having cried at a wedding vs. **1 in 2.5** women.

SOURCE: Social Issues Research Centre, *The Kleenex for Men Crying Report: A Study of Men and Crying*, September 30, 2004.

The odds a bride will not plan to take her new husband's name . . . . **1 in 8.3**

SOURCE: WeddingChannel.com, "Will You Be My Bridesman? WeddingChannel.com Announces New Wedding Traditions," press release, April 28, 2008.

1 in 7.6

The odds a bride is a virgin or first had sex the same month as her wedding.

SOURCE: Book of Odds estimate based on Centers for Disease Control and Prevention, *National Survey of Family Growth 2006–2008*, Public Use Data Files.

Saying Yes to the Dress

1 in 1.2 brides will wear a long white dress.

SOURCE: Romance Writers of America, "Romance Literature Statistics," *2009 RWA Readers Survey*, May 2009.

Want Your Wedding in the *Times*?
Let's See Your Degree

Do you dream of having your wedding featured in the *New York Times*? Here's a tip: get yourself a degree from Columbia University—or marry someone who has one. If Columbia won't take you, Harvard, or even Yale, will do.

It is a matter of note that the who's who of the wedding pages has undergone a transformation in recent decades, moving away from featuring the offspring of privilege. In the words of Robert Woletz, the paper's Society editor, "We're looking for people who have achievements."

There's no doubt that when it comes to getting into the Ivies nowadays, Miss A+ increasingly gets the nod over Mr. A+. But it's also true that if the right family name once multiplied the odds your marriage vows would be in "the paper of record," the names Harvard, Yale, Princeton, Columbia, Dartmouth, University of Pennsylvania, Cornell, and Brown *significantly* up your chances today.

The analysis of "Weddings/Celebrations," from June 14, 2009, to June 6, 2010, revealed that Ivy League affiliations accounted for **49.2%** of all wedding announcements in the *Times*. Indeed, the odds at least one member of the happy couple is affiliated with an Ivy League school, either as an undergrad or grad student (or both), were **1 in 2**.

Columbia University is not only the most frequently appearing Ivy, it is the most frequently appearing *school* in "Weddings/Celebrations": **16%** of all wedding announcements include Columbia somewhere in a couple's educational history. The next most frequently appearing Ivies in the study were Harvard with 182 (**15%**), Yale with 128 (**10%**), and UPenn with 123 (**10%**).

The *Times*' hometown favorite, New York University made a big showing with 172 (**14%**). The "West Coast" Ivy, Stanford, showed up only 48 times out of 1,223 announcements, as did the "Southern Ivy," Duke, also with 48. MIT came in third at 47.

The least frequently appearing Ivy was the smallest, Dartmouth, appearing in 39 couples' announcements (**3%**), but that's still a very impressive showing when you consider that Rutgers University, a school almost ten times as large, boasting approximately 50,000 undergraduate and graduate students spread over three campuses (all of which are much closer to the backyard of the *Times* than Dartmouth), appeared only 24 times. By contrast Cornell appeared 91 times and Princeton 66. Brown had 41 mentions.

SOURCES: Book of Odds estimates based on an analysis of *New York Times* wedding announcements from June 14, 2009, to June 7, 2010. ✒ C Hoyt, "Love and Marriage, *New York Times* Style," *New York Times*, July 12, 2009.

Making an Entrance

The odds a bride will arrive at her wedding in a stretch limo:
1 in 3.7

The odds she will arrive in a vintage or specialty car:
1 in 7.1

Horse and carriage?
1 in 50

SOURCE: TheKnot.com and Wedding Channel, "The Knot Unveils 2008 Real Wedding Survey Results," April 8, 2009, http://www.xogroupinc.com/press-releases-home/2009-press-releases/2009-04-08-real-wedding-survey.aspx.

DID YOU know?

The odds a groom will be involved in the planning of the honeymoon: **1 in 1.8**

SOURCE: David's Bridal, "Bridal Authority's 'What's On Brides' Minds' Survey Reveals Couples Tying the Knot Still Cutting Costs," press release, January 25, 2010.

Wedding Time of Day

The odds a wedding will take place in the afternoon are **1 in 1.9**.

The odds a wedding will take place in the evening are **1 in 3.2**.

The odds a wedding will take place in the morning are **1 in 6.3**.

Time of day	%
Afternoon	53
Evening	31
Morning	16

SOURCE: Wedding Statistics, "All the Right Tunes," www.alltherighttunes.com.

Where Weddings Take Place

The odds a wedding will take place at a church are **1 in 1.9**.

The odds a wedding will take place outdoors are **1 in 2.9**.

The odds a wedding will take place out of town are **1 in 5**.

The odds a wedding will be a destination wedding are **1 in 10**.

Ceremony	%
At a church	53
Outdoors	35
Out of town	20
Destination wedding	10

Where Receptions Take Place

The odds a wedding reception will take place at a banquet hall are **1 in 2.8**.

The odds a wedding reception will take place at a hotel ballroom are **1 in 5.9**.

The odds a wedding reception will take place at a country club are **1 in 6.3**.

The odds a wedding reception will take place at a historic building are **1 in 9.1**.

The odds a wedding reception will take place at a restaurant are **1 in 11.1**.

Receptions	%
Banquet hall	36
Hotel ballroom	17
Country club	16
Historic building	11
Restaurant	9

SOURCE: Bridal Association of America, *The Wedding Report*, http://www.bridalassociationofamerica.com. ✗
"The Knot Unveils 2008 Real Wedding Survey Results," April 8, 2009, http://www.xogroupinc.com/press-releases
-home/2009-press-releases/2009-04-08-real-wedding-survey.aspx.

Getting Harder to Stay Married

Men and women who say "I do" today are less likely to reach significant anniversaries than couples from previous generations. The odds that a woman first married between 1955 and 1959 reached a tenth wedding anniversary are **1 in 1.2**. For women first married in the 1990s, however, the likelihood dropped to **1 in 1.5**.

Husbands and wives hoping to toast to twenty-five years of marriage face tougher odds. While **1 in 1.5** women first married between 1955 and 1959 reached a twenty-fifth anniversary, the odds for women first married between 1975 and 1979 were **1 in 2.2**. And with marriage rates in the United States declining (**1 in 133** total population in 2006 down from **1 in 102** in 1990), couples standing the test of time have all the more cause for celebration.

SOURCE: US Census Bureau, "Detailed Tables—Number, Timing and Duration of Marriages and Divorces: 2004," http://www.census.gov/population/www/socdemo/marr-div/2004detailed_tables.html.

Honeymoon Dreams

Honeymoons still fulfill their traditional function of giving newlyweds a chance to flee the scene of their vows and spend a few days concentrating on having fun and getting used to being Mr. and Mrs. Newlyweds. Most trips are 5 to 7 days (**1 in 2.6** couples choose this length) and cost between $3,000 and $4,999 (**1 in 2.7**).

If you've got your heart set on a Hawaiian honeymoon, better put down a deposit. Many brides-to-be (**1 in 2.3**) do their vacation planning between 3 and 6 months in advance, and nearly the same number (**1 in 2.5**) say Hawaii is their dream destination.

An article in the *Journal of Family History* reviewed articles on honeymoon destinations published in the popular press from 1880 to 1995. According to the authors, by the end of the twentieth century, a preference for primitive accommodations in the midst of natural grandeur (think a Niagara Falls motel or a cabin in Yosemite) had evolved to an emphasis on the luxurious and exotic. That means not only Maui and Kauai, but also Tahiti and Bora Bora—and **1 in 3.3** women says a few days in the South Pacific is exactly her notion of nuptial nirvana.

1 in 2.7 honeymooners opts for a domestic destination, but more (**1 in 1.6**) go abroad. Indeed, the romantic standby from the Gilded Age, the European bridal tour, still exerts a strong pull. There are still plenty of brides who dream of opening the curtains the morning after their wedding to see the canals of Venice (**1 in 4.2** favors Italy), the columns of the Acropolis (**1 in 5.8** settles on Greece), or the plazas of Madrid (**1 in 31.3** opts for Spain). And for that matter, is there anything more romantic than a stroll through Paris? If you ask women headed for the altar and then the airport, **1 in 23.3** plan for a honeymoon in Paris.

Cocktail Dress, Bikini, Sunblock, Passport

DID YOU know?

The odds a newly married couple will go on a cruise for their honeymoon are **1 in 10**.

SOURCE: Wedding & Honeymoon Statistics [Internet]. About.com. [accessed May 18, 2010]. Available from: http://honeymoons.about.com/cs/eurogen1.

The odds a woman first married between 1955 and 1959 reached her 40th anniversary are **1 in 1.8**. For women married during the next five-year period, the odds their union would last that long declined to **1 in 2.2**.

SOURCE: US Census Bureau, Detailed Tables-Number, Timing and Duration of Marriages and Divorces: 2004, http://www.census.gov/population/www/socdemo/marrdiv/2004detailed_tables.html.

SOURCES: K Bulcroft, R Bulcroft, L Smeins, H Cranage, "The Social Construction of the North American Honeymoon, 1880–1995," *Journal of Family History* 2(4), October 1997: 462–490. ✗ MacNair Travel and Cruises, *MacNair Travel & Cruises Honeymoon Trends Survey*, Compiled Results, July 2006. ✗ About.com, "Wedding & Honeymoon Statistics," http://honeymoons.about.com/cs/eurogen1/a/weddingstats.htm.

Why People Stay Married

The odds a married adult will report his or her marriage has lasted...

because of companionship: **1 in 1.4**

because of deep love: **1 in 1.4**

because both spouses want to live up to their commitment: **1 in 1.6**

because of the children: **1 in 2.3**

because of good sex: **1 in 2.4**

because of religious beliefs: **1 in 3.3**

for financial reasons: **1 in 5.9**

because it is too much trouble to end the marriage: **1 in 8.3**

Reasons	Married Adults %
Companionship	73
Deep love	71
Both spouses want to live up to their commitment	61
The children	44
Good sex	41
Religious beliefs	30
Financial reasons	17
It is too much trouble to end the marriage	12

SOURCE: "The Truth About American Marriage," *Parade Magazine*, September 15, 2008.

Same-Sex Couples

The odds a same-sex couple lives in a state...

performing same-sex marriage[1]: **1 in 14.1**

performing same-sex marriage and reports his/her partner as a spouse: **1 in 2.4**

performing same-sex marriage and reports his/her partner as an unmarried partner: **1 in 1.7**

recognizing domestic partnerships or civil unions[2]: **1 in 3.5**

recognizing domestic partnerships or civil unions and reports his/her partner as a spouse: **1 in 3.5**

recognizing domestic partnerships or civil unions and reports his/her partner as an unmarried partner: **1 in 1.4**

SOURCE: D Lofquist, "Same-Sex Couple Households," *American Community Survey Briefs*, ACSBR/10–03, US Census Bureau, September 2011.

[1]Connecticut, Iowa, Massachusetts, New Hampshire, Vermont, and the District of Columbia

[2]California, Colorado, Delaware, Hawaii, Maine, Nevada, New Jersey, Oregon, Washington, and Wisconsin (California performed same-sex marriages from June to November 2008.)

1 in 6.6 The odds a same-sex couple lives in **California**.

1 in 3.1 The odds a same-sex couple living in **California** reports his/her partner as a spouse.

1 in 1.5 The odds a same-sex couple living in **California** reports his/her partner as an unmarried partner.

BUT THE SEX CAN GO
DOWNHILL

The odds a man 45–49 will report that his partner is imaginative about sex are **1 in 3.3**.

The odds a man 70 or older will report that his partner is imaginative about sex are **1 in 6.3**.

Most people prefer marriage over the supposedly sexier single life (the odds are **1 in 1.3** compared to **1 in 5.6**), but adults responding to an ABC poll reported that the quality of their sex lives does correlate negatively with the length of time they've been married. The odds a couple has sex at least several times a week worsen from **1 in 1.4** if they've been married for less than three years to **1 in 3.1** if they've been married for ten or more years. The odds they would label their sex lives as "very exciting" decrease from **1 in 1.7** to **1 in 3.5**. There is some extrapolation in these assumptions—an expectation that those who report low sex rates are expressing low sex satisfaction as well. The responses, however, may alternatively reflect an equal tapering off of sex drives or already-low libidos for both partners.

SOURCES: LL Fisher, *Sex, Romance, Relationships, AARP Survey of Midlife and Older Adults,* American Association of Retired Persons, April 2010. ✎ "The American Sex Survey: A Peek Beneath the Sheets," *ABC News Primetime Live Poll,* October 21, 2004, http://abcnews.go.com/images/Politics/959a1AmericanSexSurvey.pdf.

Vaginal Intercourse Frequency	Age	%
4 or more times a week	18–24	21
4 or more times a week	25–29	6
4 or more times a week	30–39	6
4 or more times a week	40–49	4
4 or more times a week	50–59	1
4 or more times a week	60–69	0.8
4 or more times a week	70+	0.8
2 or 3 times a week	18–24	46
2 or 3 times a week	25–29	37
2 or 3 times a week	30–39	27
2 or 3 times a week	40–49	20
2 or 3 times a week	50–59	15
2 or 3 times a week	60–69	10
2 or 3 times a week	70+	6
A few times a month to weekly	18–24	17
A few times a month to weekly	25–29	46
A few times a month to weekly	30–39	47
A few times a month to weekly	40–49	51
A few times a month to weekly	50–59	38
A few times a month to weekly	60–69	35
A few times a month to weekly	70+	15
A few times a year to monthly	18–24	13
A few times a year to monthly	25–29	9
A few times a year to monthly	30–39	16
A few times a year to monthly	40–49	16
A few times a year to monthly	50–59	25
A few times a year to monthly	60–69	21
A few times a year to monthly	70+	24
Not at all	18–24	4
Not at all	25–29	2
Not at all	30–39	5
Not at all	40–49	9
Not at all	50–59	21
Not at all	60–69	34
Not at all	70+	54

Sex **Frequency** in Marriage

The odds a married man 18–24 has vaginal intercourse 4 or more times per week are **1 in 4.8**.

The odds a married man 25–29 has vaginal intercourse 4 or more times per week are **1 in 16.9**.

The odds a married man 30–39 has vaginal intercourse 4 or more times per week are **1 in 17.2**.

The odds a married man 40–49 has vaginal intercourse 4 or more times per week are **1 in 27**.

The odds a married man 50–59 has vaginal intercourse 4 or more times per week are **1 in 90.9**.

The odds a married man 60–69 has vaginal intercourse 4 or more times per week are **1 in 100**.

The odds a married man 70–79 has vaginal intercourse 4 or more times per week are **1 in 125**.

The odds a married man 18–24 has vaginal intercourse 2 or 3 times per week are **1 in 2.2**.

The odds a married man 25–29 has vaginal intercourse 2 or 3 times per week are **1 in 2.7**.

The odds a married man 30–39 has vaginal intercourse 2 or 3 times per week are **1 in 3.7**.

The odds a married man 40–49 has vaginal intercourse 2 or 3 times per week are **1 in 5**.

The odds a married man 50–59 has vaginal intercourse 2 or 3 times per week are **1 in 6.7**.

The odds a married man 60–69 has vaginal intercourse 2 or 3 times per week are **1 in 10.5**.

The odds a married man 70–79 has vaginal intercourse 2 or 3 times per week are **1 in 17.2**.

The odds a married man 18–24 has vaginal intercourse a few times per month to weekly are **1 in 6**.

The odds a married man 25–29 has vaginal intercourse a few times per month to weekly are **1 in 2.2**.

The odds a married man 30–39 has vaginal intercourse a few times per month to weekly are **1 in 2.1**.

The odds a married man 40–49 has vaginal intercourse a few times per month to weekly are **1 in 2**.

The odds a married man 50–59 has vaginal intercourse a few times per month to weekly are **1 in 2.6**.

The odds a married man 60–69 has vaginal intercourse a few times per month to weekly are **1 in 2.8**.

The odds a married man 70–79 has vaginal intercourse a few times per month to weekly are **1 in 6.7**.

The odds a married man 18–24 has vaginal intercourse a few times a year to monthly are **1 in 8**.

The odds a married man 25–29 has vaginal intercourse a few times a year to monthly are **1 in 10.8**.

The odds a married man 30–39 has vaginal intercourse a few times a year to monthly are **1 in 6.4**.

The odds a married man 40–49 has vaginal intercourse a few times a year to monthly are **1 in 6.2**.

The odds a married man 50–59 has vaginal intercourse a few times a year to monthly are **1 in 4**.

The odds a married man 60–69 has vaginal intercourse a few times a year to monthly are **1 in 4.7**.

The odds a married man 70–79 has vaginal intercourse a few times a year to monthly are **1 in 4.1**.

The odds a married man 18–24 has not had vaginal intercourse in the past year are **1 in 23.8**.

The odds a married man 25–29 has not had vaginal intercourse in the past year are **1 in 62.5**.

The odds a married man 30–39 has not had vaginal intercourse in the past year are **1 in 22.2**.

The odds a married man 40–49 has not had vaginal intercourse in the past year are **1 in 11**.

The odds a married man 50–59 has not had vaginal intercourse in the past year are **1 in 4.9**.

The odds a married man 60–69 has not had vaginal intercourse in the past year are **1 in 2.9**.

The odds a married man 70–79 has not had vaginal intercourse in the past year are **1 in 1.8**.

SOURCE: Book of Odds estimate based on M Reece, D Herbenick, V Shick, SA Sanders, B Dodge, JD Fortenberry, "Sexual Behaviors, Relationships, and Perceived Health Among Adult Men in the United States: Results from a National Probability Sample," *Journal of Sexual Medicine* 7(Suppl 5), 2010: 291–304.

Taking a
Young Husband?

He Could Be
the Death of You.

The average bride is 2.3 years younger than her husband. This number jibes with a number of studies demonstrating that, on average, men prefer partners who are around three years younger than they are, and women prefer their men to be about three years older.

Currently, **1 in 1.7** married men is older than his spouse, compared to **1 in 5** women who are older. The odds are especially slim that a woman will marry a man *significantly* younger; only **1 in 43.5** married women is seven or more years older than her spouse, compared to **1 in 11.6** men.

And that could be a good thing. Few major studies have been done on the effect of age differences on mortality, but one relatively recent one published in the journal *Demography* used data from almost two million Danish couples over a fifteen-year period. Women who marry a man seven to nine years their junior increase their mortality risk in a year by 20% compared to women coupled with men the same age as they are. In fact, the study found that women who have any age difference from their mates, either younger or older, face a shortened life expectancy, although the degree is less dramatic for those who are younger than their husbands.

Here's the topper: men who marry women seven to nine years younger than themselves *decrease* their own mortality risk by 11%.

SOURCES: PY Goodwin, WD Mosher, A Chandra, "Marriage and Cohabitation in the United States: A Statistical Portrait Based on Cycle 6 (2002) of the National Survey of Family Growth," *Vital and Health Statistics* 23(28), 2010. ✔ US Census Bureau, *America's Families and Living Arrangements: 2009*, http://www.census .gov/population/www/socdemo/hh-fam/cps2009.html. ✔ Max Planck Institute for Demographic Research, "Marriage and Life Expectancy." ✔ Drefahl S, "How Does the Age Gap Between Partners Affect Their Survival?," *Demography*, 47(2), May 2010: 313.

The odds a female victim of nonfatal partner violence was raped: **1 in 13.9**

SOURCE: S Catalano, *Intimate Partner Violence in the United States*, Bureau of Justice Statistics, December 19, 2007.

Women Thinking of
Leaving Husbands

The odds a married woman **never** thinks about leaving her husband . . . . 1 in 1.8

The odds a married woman **occasionally** thinks about leaving her husband. . . . . 1 in 3.3

The odds a married woman **often** thinks about leaving her husband . . . . 1 in 10

The odds a married woman thinks about leaving her husband **every day** . . . . 1 in 25

Frequency	%
Never	56
Occasionally	30
Often	10
Every day	4

SOURCE: "The Truth About American Marriage," *Parade Magazine*, September 15, 2008.

Who's the Guilty Party?

The odds an ever-married or cohabitating adult who cheated during the relationship did so with:

A friend . . . . 1 in 1.5

A neighbor . . . . 1 in 6.7

SOURCE: "The American Sex Survey: A Peek Beneath the Sheets," *ABC News Primetime Live Poll*, October 21, 2004, http://abcnews.go.com/images/Politics/ 959a1AmericanSexSurvey.pdf.

 **Numbers Tell the Story**

Midlife Crisis

A man, 45 or older, had an extracurricular sexual relationship. Through his own sense of guilt (or her private detective) the truth is revealed.

What happened next:

No effect on relationship . . . . 1 in 2.5

Tension but the relationship is okay. . . . . 1 in 3.3

Lasting problems and lack of trust in the relationship . . . . 1 in 12.5

It ended the relationship or marriage . . . . 1 in 14.3

The relationship is stronger than ever. . . . . 1 in 20

A woman, 45 or older, cheats on her partner. She is forced by her conscience (or his insistent suspicions) to confess.

What happened next:

No effect on relationship . . . . 1 in 4.2

Tension but the relationship is okay. . . . . 1 in 2.5

Lasting problems and lack of trust in the relationship . . . . 1 in 4.6

It ended the relationship or marriage . . . . 1 in 25

The relationship is stronger than ever. . . . . 1 in 10

SOURCE: LL Fisher, *Sex, Romance, Relationships, AARP Survey of Midlife and Older Adults,* American Association of Retired Persons, April 2010.

Domestic Abuse

Comparison of Odds by Gender for Mistreatment by Partner

	Men		Women	
Abuse Type	**%**	**Odds (1 in)**	**%**	**Odds (1 in)**
Called bad names	29	**3.5**	33	**3.0**
Pushed, slapped, choked, or hit	14	**7.1**	27	**3.7**
Publicly humiliated	15	**6.7**	22	**4.6**
Kept away from friends and family	9	**11.1**	17	**5.9**
Threatened	6	**16.7**	14	**7.1**

SOURCE: Harris Interactive, "Over Thirty Million Adults Claim to Be Victims of Domestic Violence," June 16, 2006.

Your Cheating Heart

The odds an ever-married or cohabiting adult who has not cheated during the relationship fantasizes about cheating: **1 in 3.3**

The odds an ever-married or cohabiting man has cheated during the relationship: **1 in 4.8**

The odds an ever-married or cohabiting woman has cheated during the relationship: **1 in 9.1**

SOURCE: "The American Sex Survey: A Peek Beneath the Sheets," *ABC News Primetime Live Poll,* October 21, 2004, http://abcnews.go.com/images/Politics/959a1AmericanSexSurvey.pdf.

The odds a woman 65 or older is widowed: **1 in 2.4**

The odds a man 65 or older is widowed: **1 in 7.8**

SOURCE: US Census Bureau, *America's Families and Living Arrangements: 2009,* http://www.census.gov/population/www/socdemo/hh-fam/cps2009.html.

The odds a separated female 15–44 will divorce within 1 year of the separation: **1 in 1.9**

SOURCE: MD Bramlett, WD Mosher, "Cohabitation, Marriage, Divorce, and Remarriage in the United States," *Vital and Health Statistics* 23(22), 2002.

Is Divorce a Socially Transmitted Disease?

Under "relationship status," a Facebook user whose marriage has recently ended has three options: *Widowed, It's Complicated,* and *Single.* Why no *Divorced?* Maybe users prefer the ambiguity and fresh sound of "single." But the site itself is hesitant to offer the label, after a 2009 study found that divorce tends to spread within a social network "like a contagion."

Of course, "social network" means more than an electronic arrangement of profiles. It is a person's total group of friends and family, as well as *their* friends' friends and families. The authors of *Breaking Up Is Hard to Do, Unless Everyone Else Is Doing It Too,* Rose McDermott, James Fowler, and Nicholas Christakis, found that a couple who are divorcing sets an example, which can inspire others to follow. And divorce is infectious not only at one degree of removal, among your friends and relatives, but also at two degrees—among your friends' friends and relatives.

1 in 1.9 people 15 or older is married (also the odds that a woman has a Facebook or MySpace account). Of those married individuals, **1 in 50.7** will divorce in a year.

SOURCES: R McDermott, JH Fowler, NA Christakis, *Breaking Up Is Hard to Do, Unless Everyone Else Is Doing It Too: Social Network Effects on Divorce in a Longitudinal Sample Followed for 32 Years*; Monograph 10.1.1.169.5075. ✎ Book of Odds estimate based on data from US Census Bureau, *American Community Survey, 2008.* ✎ Harris Interactive, "Just Under Half of Americans Have a Facebook or MySpace Account," April 2009.

Her vs. Him

The odds a woman thinks men and women get fair and equal treatment in divorce court: **1 in 2.3**; the odds a man thinks so: **1 in 6.3**.

The odds a woman thinks men get screwed by divorce courts: **1 in 2.5**; the odds a man thinks so: **1 in 1.2**.

The odds a woman doesn't think men get screwed by divorce courts and that if anything women get screwed: **1 in 6.3**; the odds a man thinks so: **1 in 50**.

SOURCES: AskMen.com, "Part I: Dating & Sex," *The Great Male Survey, 2010 Edition,* http://www.askmen.com/specials/2010_great_male_survey. ✎ AskMen.com, "Part I: Dating & Sex," *The Great Female Survey, 2009 Edition,* www.askmen.com/specials/yahoo_shine_great_female_survey/part1.html.

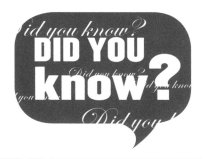

The odds a divorced woman will remarry within 1 year of the divorce: **1 in 5.7**

3 years: **1 in 2.6**

5 years: **1 in 1.9**

10 years: **1 in 1.4**

SOURCE: Book of Odds estimate based on Centers for Disease Control and Prevention, *National Survey of Family Growth 2006–2008,* Public Use Data Files.

⚧ GENDER WARS

The odds a man 40–44 has been married at least three times: **1 in 11.8**

The odds a woman 40–44 has been married at least three times: **1 in 14.1**

SOURCE: PY Goodwin, WD Mosher, A Chandra, "Marriage and Cohabitation in the United States: A Statistical Portrait Based on Cycle 6 (2002) of the National Survey of Family Growth," *Vital and Health Statistics* 23(28), 2010.

Strike TWO

The odds a remarried female 15–44 will have her second marriage end within 10 years: **1 in 2.7**

SOURCE: Book of Odds estimate based on Centers for Disease Control and Prevention, *National Survey of Family Growth 2006–2008,* Public Use Data Files.

CHAPTER 4

PREGNANCY AND BIRTH

Birth

The odds a female 15–44 will give birth in a year:

1 in 15

SOURCE: JA Martin, BE Hamilton, SJ Ventura, MJK Osterman, S Kirmeyer, TJ Mathews, EC Wilson, "Births: Final Data for 2009," *National Vital Statistics Reports* 60(1), November 3, 2011.

You've Been Born!
What Are the Odds You'll Live to 100?

With life expectancy in the United States at an all-time high of 77.9 years, people topping 100 years are the fastest-growing age segment. The number of centenarians is expected to increase from 75,000 to more than 600,000 by 2050 as the children of baby boomers outdo their parents.

Here's a happy way to think about getting older: every birthday you reach statistically improves your odds of reaching the next one. For example, the predicted odds a 1-year-old will live to be at least 100 years old are **1 in 57.2**. Making it through the perilous teen years raises the odds only slightly; the predicted odds a 21-year-old will live to at least 100 are **1 in 56.8**. But once those candles start piling up in middle age, your chance of living a long life is looking better and better. At 50, your odds improve to **1 in 54**, jumping to **1 in 31.2** once you reach 80. Before you know it, you'll be 90 years old, with **1 in 12** odds of making it to the century mark.

As in all things related to longevity, women have an advantage over men in reaching the century mark. Not only do women live longer in general, but they increase their staying power toward the end. At 40, a woman's life expectancy is 11% higher than a man's, 41.7 additional years compared to 37.6 additional years for men. At 80, the gap has grown to 19%. Out of every 100,000 women, just over 2,460 will live to 100. Among 100,000 men, only 850 are likely to live that long.

SOURCES: "100-Year-Olds' Club Is Starting to Get Crowded," Associated Press, July 20, 2009, http://www.msnbc.msn.com/id/32009767/ns/health -aging. ✏ Book of Odds estimates based on E Arias, "United States Life Tables, 2007," *National Vital Statistics Reports* 59(9), September 28, 2011.

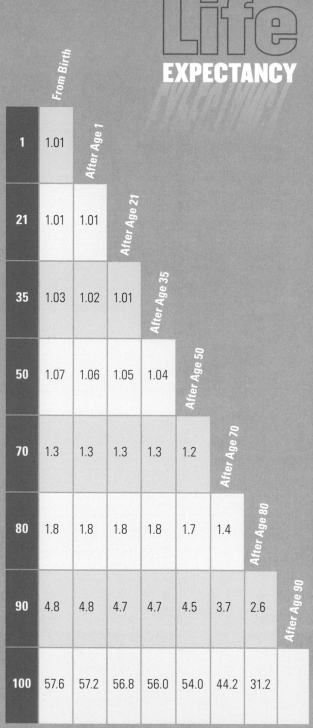

Life EXPECTANCY

	From Birth	After Age 1	After Age 21	After Age 35	After Age 50	After Age 70	After Age 80	After Age 90
1	1.01							
21	1.01	1.01						
35	1.03	1.02	1.01					
50	1.07	1.06	1.05	1.04				
70	1.3	1.3	1.3	1.3	1.2			
80	1.8	1.8	1.8	1.8	1.7	1.4		
90	4.8	4.8	4.7	4.7	4.5	3.7	2.6	
100	57.6	57.2	56.8	56.0	54.0	44.2	31.2	

SOURCE: Book of Odds estimates based on E Arias, "United States Life Tables, 2007," *National Vital Statistics Reports* 59(9), September 28, 2011.

The Odds a Woman
Has Never Been Pregnant
by Age Bracket

A teenage girl 15–19	**1 in 1.2**
A woman 20–24	**1 in 1.7**
A woman 25–29	**1 in 3.2**
A woman 30–34	**1 in 5.6**
A woman 35–39	**1 in 9.7**
A woman 40–44	**1 in 10.6**

SOURCE: A Chandra, GM Martinez, WD Mosher, JC Abma, J Jones, "Fertility, Family Planning, and Reproductive Health of U.S. Women: Data from the 2002 National Survey of Family Growth," *Vital and Health Statistics* 23(25), 2005.

The odds a man with a biological child fathered his first child when he was 20–24 are **1 in 2.8**, compared to **1 in 3.5** for men 25–29 and **1 in 4.8** for men 30–44.

SOURCE: Book of Odds estimates based on Centers for Disease Control and Prevention, *National Survey of Family Growth 2006–2008*, Public Use Data Files.

The Odds a Female Who Gives Birth Will **Not** Be Married, **by Age:**

Younger than 15	1 in 1.01
15–19	1 in 1.1
20–24	1 in 1.6
25–29	1 in 3
30–34	1 in 4.8
35–39	1 in 5.5
40 +	1 in 4.8

Age	%
Younger than 15	99
15–19	87
20–24	62
25–29	34
30–34	21
35–39	19
40+	21

SOURCE: JA Martin, BE Hamilton, SJ Ventura, MJK Osterman, S Kirmeyer, TJ Mathews, EC Wilson, "Births: Final Data for 2009," *National Vital Statistics Reports* 60(1), November 3, 2011.

What's the Guy **Thinking?**

The odds a man believes a man should have children by age:

25: **1 in 16.7**

30: **1 in 4.2**

35: **1 in 2.8**

40: **1 in 7.7**

Age	%
25	6
30	24
35	36
40	13

SOURCE: AskMen.com, "Men's Dating Trends," *The Great Male Sex Survey, 2008 Edition*, http://static.askmen.com/specials/2008_great_male_survey/2008_dating_survey.html.

GENDER WARS

The odds a man 40–44 intends to have a child in the future: **1 in 7.2**; vs. **1 in 19.3** for a woman 40–44.

SOURCE: Book of Odds estimates based on Centers for Disease Control and Prevention, *National Survey of Family Growth 2006–2008*, Public Use Data Files.

The odds a man 15–44 will report never having fathered a biological child: **1 in 1.8**

SOURCE: Book of Odds estimates based on Centers for Disease Control and Prevention, *National Survey of Family Growth 2006–2008*, Public Use Data Files.

Who Reads the Instructions?

Condoms are highly effective in lab tests, but when people actually use them the results are less than perfect. Incredibly, not even sterilization (tubal ligation for women and vasectomies for men) is foolproof; some couples using these methods have unintended and profoundly unexpected pregnancies.

The real-life odds—the odds in a year—that condoms and other forms of contraception will fail are as follows:

Spermicide . . . . **1 in 3.4**

Periodic abstinence . . . . **1 in 4**

Withdrawal . . . . **1 in 5.4**

Male condom . . . . **1 in 5.7**

The pill . . . . **1 in 11.5**

Injectable contraception . . . . . **1 in 14.9**

There is a more personal and precise way of looking at these odds from a human perspective. We call it a "thread" and it is a sequence of conditional probabilities. Think of it like the nursery rhyme "There Was an Old Lady Who Swallowed a Fly":

There was an old lady who swallowed a fly

I don't know why she swallowed a fly, perhaps she'll die!

There was an old lady who swallowed a spider,

That wriggled and wiggled and tickled inside her;

She swallowed the spider to catch the fly;

I don't know why she swallowed a fly, perhaps she'll die!

After a while the odds that the old lady will die increase with each new snack, until she swallows a horse and what rhymes with horse?

She's dead, of course!

In the case of contraception the odds of being in each group multiply against each other so that in the end **1 in 225** of women between 14 and 55 will experience the whole chain. Here is the whole sentence, hungry old-lady style: The odds a person is female aged 14–44, has had sexual intercourse with a man, has used contraception, ever relied on condoms, and stopped using condoms because she got pregnant are **1 in 225**.

SOURCES: Traditional nursery rhyme heard by authors as children, "There Was an Old Lady Who Swallowed a Fly." ✗ WD Mosher, J Jones, "Use of Contraception in the United States: 1982–2008," *Vital and Health Statistics* 23(29), August 2010.

What Are Your Odds?

The odds a couple trying to become pregnant will conceive:

Within 1 cycle: **1 in 5**

Within 3 months: **1 in 2.5**

Within 6 months: **1 in 1.4**

Within 1 year: **1 in 1.2**

SOURCE: BabyMed.com, "Getting Pregnant," http://babymed.com/faq/Content.aspx?13273.

Numbers Tell the Story
Surprise Package

The odds a woman 40–44 will give birth in a year: **1 in 99**

The odds a woman 40–44 at risk for unintended pregnancy does not use contraception: **1 in 13.2**

The odds a woman 40–44 has been pregnant 4 or more times: **1 in 2.9**

The odds a surgically sterile woman 40–44 is so for contraceptive reasons: **1 in 2.6**

SOURCES: JA Martin, BE Hamilton, SJ Ventura, MJK Osterman, S Kirmeyer, TJ Mathews, EC Wilson, "Births: Final Data for 2009," *National Vital Statistics Reports* 60(1), November 3, 2011. ✗ US Census Bureau, *America's Families and Living Arrangements: 2010,* Current Population Survey. ✗ WD Mosher, J Jones, "Use of Contraception in the United States: 1982–2008," *Vital and Health Statistics* 23(29), August 2010. ✗ Book of Odds estimate based on Centers for Disease Control and Prevention, *National Survey of Family Growth 2006–2008,* Public Use Data Files. ✗ A Chandra, GM Martinez, WD Mosher, JC Abma, J Jones, "Fertility, Family Planning, and Reproductive Health of U.S. Women: Data from the 2002 National Survey of Family Growth," *Vital Health Statistics* 23(25), December 2005.

Condoms: Do They Work?

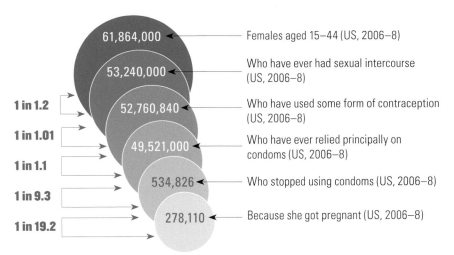

61,864,000 — Females aged 15–44 (US, 2006–8)

53,240,000 — Who have ever had sexual intercourse (US, 2006–8)

52,760,840 — Who have used some form of contraception (US, 2006–8)

49,521,000 — Who have ever relied principally on condoms (US, 2006–8)

534,826 — Who stopped using condoms (US, 2006–8)

278,110 — Because she got pregnant (US, 2006–8)

1 in 1.2

1 in 1.01

1 in 1.1

1 in 9.3

1 in 19.2

The odds a female aged 14–44 who has ever principally relied on condoms for contraception discontinued their use because she became pregnant (US, 2006–8): **1 in 225**

"Pick Up Pregnancy Test"

The odds a sexually experienced teenage girl 15–19 has used withdrawal for contraceptive reasons:

1 in 1.7

SOURCE: WD Mosher, J Jones, "Use of Contraception in the United States: 1982–2008," *Vital and Health Statistics*, 23(29), August 2010.

Trying for a Baby

The odds a woman is not using contraception because she is trying to get pregnant by age:

15–19 . . . . **1 in 111**

20–24 . . . . **1 in 23.3**

25–29 . . . . **1 in 15.9**

30–34 . . . . **1 in 17**

35–39 . . . . **1 in 19.7**

40–44 . . . . **1 in 40**

SOURCE: WD Mosher, J Jones, "Use of Contraception in the United States: 1982–2008," *Vital and Health Statistics* 23(29), August 2010.

...and Not: Contraceptive Methods for Married Women

Contraceptive Method	Odds (1 in)
Surgically sterile/contraceptive	4.2
The pill	6.1
Condoms	8.6
An intrauterine device	18.9
Withdrawal	22.2
The three-month injectable Depo-Provera	71.4
A contraceptive ring	100.0
A calendar rhythm	100.0
The Norplant implant, one-month injectable Lunelle, or a contraceptive patch	143.0
Surgically sterile/noncontraceptive	333.3
Natural family planning	500.0

SOURCE: WD Mosher, J Jones, "Use of Contraception in the United States: 1982–2008," *Vital and Health Statistics* 23(29), August 2010.

How Accidents Happen

The odds a teenage girl 15–19 at risk for unintended pregnancy does not use contraception:

1 in 5.4

The odds for other age brackets:

20–24: **1 in 7**
25–29: **1 in 8.4**
30–34: **1 in 14.3**
35–39: **1 in 10.3**

SOURCE: WD Mosher, J Jones, "Use of Contraception in the United States: 1982–2008," *Vital and Health Statistics* 23(29), August 2010.

Oops

What Should We Name the
Quintuplets, Dear?

Considering how important the imperative to "be fruitful and multiply" is to humankind, the modern language of fertility is awfully dull and lacking in playfulness or passion. It doesn't have to remain that way, since the English language has a knack for naming collective nouns inventively.

Such nouns are called "terms of venery" by James Lipton, whose book *An Exaltation of Larks, or The Venereal Game* revived the practice by terms authentically used by English speakers in the fifteenth century. Many of these, such as a *swarm* of bees or a *pride* of lions, are still in use. Other terms—such as a *bouquet* of pheasants, an *ostentation* of peacocks, or a *parliament* of owls—were the correct usage then and knowing the correct terms of venery was a necessary social grace. Given that *venery* is derived from Venus, goddess of love, and *veneri* is rooted in the word "to hunt" but also "to desire," it seems a shame that this naming game has not yet been applied to the product of love.

Why not redress the dull reliance on "sets" as the standard terms for all multiples? A set of octuplets sounds awfully pedestrian for such a gathering. If ever terms of venery were needed it is for the collectives of multiple births. Here is our list. Note that the first is common usage so we do not seek to alter it. What follows is a lark, yes, and also—we hope—an exultation:

A pair of twins	👤👤
A triumph of triplets	👤👤👤
A quandary of quadruplets	👤👤👤👤
A dionne of quintuplets	👤👤👤👤👤
A seminary of sextuplets	👤👤👤👤👤👤
A swaddling of septuplets	👤👤👤👤👤👤👤
An oratorio of octuplets	👤👤👤👤👤👤👤👤
A bafflement of nonuplets	👤👤👤👤👤👤👤👤👤
A guillotine of decaplets	👤👤👤👤👤👤👤👤👤👤

SOURCE: J Lipton, *An Exaltation of Larks, or The Venereal Game,* 1st ed., New York: Grossman Publishers, 1968.

ODDS COUPLE
Unlikely Beginnings, Untimely Ends

The odds a woman 50–54 will give birth in a year:
1 in 20,250

The odds a person will be murdered in a year:
1 in 20,140

SOURCES: JA Martin, BE Hamilton, PD Sutton, S Ventura, TJ Matthews, MJK Osterman, "Births: Final Data for 2008," *National Vital Statistics Reports* 59(1), December 2010. ✔ US Department of Justice, Federal Bureau of Investigation, *Crime in the United States, 2009*, http://www2.fbi.gov/cius2009/index.html.

1 in 5.31
pregnancies is aborted.

SOURCE: SJ Ventura, JC Abma, WD Mosher, SK Henshaw, "Estimated Pregnancy Rates for the United States, 1990–2005: An Update," *National Vital Statistics Reports* 58(4), October 14, 2009.

⚔ GENDER WARS

The odds a woman 15–44 has ever had problems conceiving or carrying a child to term:
1 in 9.4

The odds a man 15–44 has ever had an infertility problem:
1 in 84.8

SOURCE: Book of Odds estimates based on Centers for Disease Control and Prevention, *National Survey of Family Growth 2006–2008*, Public Use Data Files.

When Babies Come in Pairs...
or Bafflements!

The odds a baby born in the United States will be part of a multiple delivery are **1 in 28.8**. Of the 4.1 million total recorded births in 2009, 143,560 were multiple births.

Multiple births are most likely to be twins, and the rates dwindle as the number of babies at a birth rises—from 139,000 twin births (or 278,000 twins born) in 2008 all the way down to 345 quadruplet births and only 46 sets of five or more. The odds a baby will be part of a twin birth are **1 in 30.1**; a triplet birth, **1 in 723**; a quadruplet birth, **1 in 12,310**; and a birth of quintuplets or more, **1 in 92,340**. This is similar to the odds a person will die from exposure to smoke or fire in a year, **1 in 92,720**.

But not all women who get pregnant face the same odds. Because follicle-stimulating hormones and numerous implanted embryos may be involved, the chances of having a multiple birth jump if a woman had medical help to conceive. Book of Odds estimates about 67% of babies born as triplets or more were due to in vitro fertilization.

The likelihood a woman will have more than one baby at a time rises as she ages because older ovaries are more likely to release more than one egg at ovulation. The combination of more older women conceiving, and more women seeking infertility treatment, contributed to a rise in multiple-birth rates over the past several decades.

The odds go up again if a woman has a family history of fraternal twins and multiple births. (A predisposition for fraternal multiples, which happen when ovaries release multiple eggs, can be inherited; identical multiples, which happen when a single fertilized egg spontaneously splits, haven't been linked to genetics.) Similarly, a woman who's had one multiple birth is more likely to have another.

SOURCES: JA Martin, BE Hamilton, SJ Ventura, MJK Osterman, S Kirmeyer, TJ Mathews, EC Wilson, "Births: Final Data for 2009," *National Vital Statistics Reports* 60(1), November 3, 2011. ✔ JA Martin, BE Hamilton, PD Sutton, S Ventura, TJ Matthews, MJK Osterman, "Births: Final Data for 2008," *National Vital Statistics Reports* 59(1), December 2010. ✔ Book of Odds estimate based on Centers for Disease Control and Prevention, *Compressed Mortality File, 1979–2005,* http://wonder.cdc.gov/mortsql.html. ✔ Book of Odds estimate based on Centers for Disease Control and Prevention, American Society for Reproductive Medicine, Society for Assisted Reproductive Technology, *2008 Assisted Reproductive Technology Success Rates: National Summary and Fertility Clinic Reports,* Atlanta: US Department of Health and Human Services, 2010.

Fertility Treatments

The odds a female 15–44 has been treated for infertility are **1 in 8.3**, and **1 in 90.9** women has used artificial insemination. The odds a woman will be treated for infertility to conceive increases with age. For women 40–44, **1 in 49.5** has used artificial insemination.

But the effectiveness of fertility treatments declines as a woman ages. For in vitro fertilization using a woman's own, unfrozen eggs, the success rates are:

Before Age 35:
48% pregnancy success, **41%** live birth success

Age 35–37:
38% pregnancy success, **31%** live birth success

Age 38–40:
30% pregnancy success, **22%** live birth success

Age 41–42:
20% pregnancy success, **12%** live birth success

Age 43–44:
11% pregnancy success, **5%** live birth success

SOURCES: Book of Odds estimate based on Centers for Disease Control and Prevention, *National Survey of Family Growth 2006–2008,* Public Use Data Files. ✔ Centers for Disease Control and Prevention, American Society for Reproductive Medicine, Society for Assisted Reproductive Technology, *2008 Assisted Reproductive Technology Success Rates: National Summary and Fertility Clinic Reports,* Atlanta: US Department of Health and Human Services, 2010.

Pregnancy Outcomes by Maternal Age

Pregnancy Outcomes

The odds a pregnancy will result in a live birth:

1 in 1.6

The odds a pregnancy will result in an induced abortion:

1 in 5.3

The odds a pregnancy will result in fetal loss:

1 in 6

SOURCE: SJ Ventura, JC Abma, WD Mosher, "Estimated Pregnancy Rates for the United States, 1990–2005: An Update," *National Vital Statistics Reports* 58(4), October 14, 2009.

The odds the pregnancy of a girl younger than 15 will result in a live birth are **1 in 2.3**.

The odds the pregnancy of a teenage girl 15–17 will result in a live birth are **1 in 1.9**.

The odds the pregnancy of a woman 18–19 will result in a live birth are **1 in 1.7**.

The odds the pregnancy of a woman 20–24 will result in a live birth are **1 in 1.6**.

The odds the pregnancy of a woman 25–29 will result in a live birth are **1 in 1.5**.

The odds the pregnancy of a woman 30–34 will result in a live birth are **1 in 1.4**.

The odds the pregnancy of a woman 35–39 will result in a live birth are **1 in 1.7**.

The odds the pregnancy of a woman 40 or older will result in a live birth are **1 in 1.8**.

The odds the pregnancy of a girl younger than 15 will result in an abortion are **1 in 2.3**.

The odds the pregnancy of a teenage girl 15–17 will result in an abortion are **1 in 3.5**.

The odds the pregnancy of a woman 18–19 will result in an abortion are **1 in 3.8**.

The odds the pregnancy of a woman 20–24 will result in an abortion are **1 in 4.2**.

The odds the pregnancy of a woman 25–29 will result in an abortion are **1 in 5.8**.

The odds the pregnancy of a woman 30–34 will result in an abortion are **1 in 7.5**.

The odds the pregnancy of a woman 35–39 will result in an abortion are **1 in 7.8**.

The odds the pregnancy of a woman 40 or older will result in an abortion are **1 in 5.3**.

The odds the pregnancy of a girl younger than 15 will result in fetal loss are **1 in 8**.

The odds the pregnancy of a teenage girl 15–17 will result in fetal loss are **1 in 5.4**.

The odds the pregnancy of a woman 18–19 will result in fetal loss are **1 in 7.1**.

The odds the pregnancy of a woman 20–24 will result in fetal loss are **1 in 7.4**.

The odds the pregnancy of a woman 25–29 will result in fetal loss are **1 in 7.1**.

The odds the pregnancy of a woman 30–34 will result in fetal loss are **1 in 6.2**.

The odds the pregnancy of a woman 35–39 will result in fetal loss are **1 in 3.7**.

The odds the pregnancy of a woman 40 or older will result in fetal loss are **1 in 3.9**.

Age of Mother	Live Birth %	Abortion %	Fetal Loss %
Younger than 15	44	44	13
15–17	53	28	18
18–19	59	26	14
20–24	63	24	14
25–29	69	17	14
30–34	71	13	16
35–40	60	13	27
40+	56	19	26

SOURCE: SJ Ventura, JC Abma, WD Mosher, "Estimated Pregnancy Rates for the United States, 1990–2005: An Update," *National Vital Statistics Reports* 58(4), October 14, 2009.

Odds of Having Had an Abortion by Age

The odds a teenage girl 15–19 has had 1 or more induced abortions are **1 in 72.2**.

The odds a woman 20–24 has had 1 or more induced abortions are **1 in 11.9**.

The odds a woman 25–29 has had 1 or more induced abortions are **1 in 8.9**.

The odds a woman 30–34 has had 1 or more induced abortions are **1 in 6.7**.

The odds a woman 35–39 has had 1 or more induced abortions are **1 in 5.4**.

The odds a woman 40–44 has had 1 or more induced abortions are **1 in 6**.

Having Had an Abortion by Age	%
15–19	1
20–24	8
25–29	11
30–34	15
35–39	19
40–44	17

SOURCE: Book of Odds estimates based on Centers for Disease Control and Prevention, *National Survey of Family Growth 2006–2008*, Public Use Data Files.

The odds a woman who has given birth received amniocentesis during her most recent pregnancy: **1 in 72.5**

SOURCE: JA Martin, BE Hamilton , PD Sutton, SJ Ventura, F Menacker, S Kirmeyer, ML Munson, "Births: Final Data for 2005," *National Vital Statistics Reports* 56(6), December 5, 2007.

Abortions by Number

The odds a female 15–44 has never had an induced abortion are **1 in 1.1**.

The odds a female 15–44 has had 1 induced abortion are **1 in 11.7**.

The odds a female 15–44 has had 2 induced abortions are **1 in 44.3**.

The odds a female 15–44 has had 3 or more induced abortions are **1 in 91.6**.

Age 15–44	%
No abortions	88
1 abortion	9
2 abortions	2
3 or more	1

SOURCE: Book of Odds estimates based on Centers for Disease Control and Prevention, *National Survey of Family Growth 2006–2008*, Public Use Data Files.

"Dr. Jackson 555-797-3905"

The odds a female who gives birth:

will first receive prenatal care within three months of conception:

1 in 1.4

will receive little or late (third trimester only) prenatal care:

1 in 14.1

SOURCE: JA Martin, BE Hamilton, PD Sutton, SJ Ventura, TJ Mathews, S Kirmeyer, MJK Osterman, "Births: Final Data for 2007," *National Vital Statistics Reports* 58(24), August 2010.

Hop on the Scale:
Pregnancy Weight Gain

The odds a pregnant female will gain:

less than 11 pounds:

1 in 12.5

11–20 pounds	**1 in 6.1**
21–30 pounds	**1 in 3.4**
31–40 pounds	**1 in 3.9**
41–98 pounds	**1 in 4.8**

SOURCE: JA Martin, BE Hamilton, TJ Mathews, SJ Ventura, MJK Osterman, S Kirmeyer, et al., "Births: Final Data for 2009," *National Vital Statistics Reports* 60(1), November 3, 2011.

Will It Be a
Boy or a Girl?

Achild's gender is determined when a sperm fertilizes an egg. Normally the baby inherits one sex chromosome from each parent. The egg carries one of the mother's two X (female) chromosomes; men have two sex chromosomes, one X and one Y (male), and each sperm cell carries one or the other. Without technical meddling, the odds are slightly higher that a newborn baby in the United States will be male (**1 in 1.95**) than female (**1 in 2**)—a disparity first demonstrated in London by John Arbuthnot in 1710 and found all around the world ever since.

Will the Third One
Be the Charm?

The odds a woman's first two children will be boys are **1 in 3.8**. The odds a woman's first two children will be girls are **1 in 4.2**. As the streaks lengthen, the difference in gender odds increases.

SOURCES: Book of Odds estimate based on JA Martin, BE Hamilton, PD Sutton, SJ Ventura, TJ Mathews, MJK Osterman, "Births: Final Data for 2008," *National Vital Statistics Reports* 59(1), December 2010. ✎ Arbuthnot, "An Argument for Divine Providence, Taken from the Constant Regularity Observed in the Births of Both Sexes," *Philosophical Transactions of the Royal Society of London* 27, 1710: 186–190.

Odds of Gender
The odds a woman's...

first 2 children will be **boys**. . . . . **1 in 3.8**
first 3 children will be **boys**. . . . . **1 in 7.5**
first 4 children will be **boys**. . . . . **1 in 14.6**
first 5 children will be **boys**. . . . . **1 in 28.5**
first 6 children will be **boys**. . . . . **1 in 55.7**

first 2 children will be **girls**. . . . . **1 in 4.2**
first 3 children will be **girls**. . . . . **1 in 8.6**
first 4 children will be **girls**. . . . . **1 in 17.6**
first 5 children will be **girls**. . . . . **1 in 36**
first 6 children will be **girls**. . . . . **1 in 73.8**

Boys

Streak Length	%
2	26
3	13
4	7
5	4
6	2

Girls

Streak Length	%
2	24
3	12
4	6
5	3
6	1

SOURCE: Book of Odds estimate based on JA Martin, BE Hamilton, PD Sutton, SJ Ventura, F Menacker, S Kirmeyer, "Births: Final Data for 2004," *National Vital Statistics Reports* 55(1), September 29, 2006.

Gestation Duration

The odds a baby will be born before **37 weeks** of gestation are 1 in 8.2.

The odds a baby will be born before **28 weeks** of gestation are 1 in 135.

The odds a baby will be born at **28–31 weeks** of gestation are 1 in 81.6.

The odds a baby will be born at **32–33 weeks** of gestation are 1 in 64.7.

The odds a baby will be born at **34–36 weeks** of gestation are 1 in 11.5.

The odds a baby will be born at **37–41 weeks** of gestation are 1 in 1.2.

The odds a baby will be born at **37–38 weeks** of gestation are 1 in 3.6.

The odds a baby will be born at **39 weeks** of gestation are 1 in 3.6.

The odds a baby will be born at **40–41 weeks** of gestation are 1 in 3.7.

The odds a baby will be born at **42 or more weeks** of gestation are 1 in 18.

Weeks of Gestation	%
Fewer than 37	12
Fewer than 28	1
28–31	1
32–33	2
34–36	9
37–41	82
37–38	28
39	27
40–41	27
42+	6

SOURCE: JA Martin, BE Hamilton, SJ Ventura, MJK Osterman, S Kirmeyer, TJ Mathews, EC Wilson, "Births: Final Data for 2009," *National Vital Statistics Reports* 60(1), November 3, 2011.

Birth Months

Month	%	Odds (1 in)	Month	%	Odds (1 in)
January	8	**12.2**	July	9	**11.2**
February	8	**13.0**	August	9	**11.5**
March	8	**11.9**	September	9	**11.4**
April	8	**12.2**	October	8	**11.9**
May	8	**12.0**	November	8	**12.9**
June	8	**11.9**	December	8	**12.1**

SOURCE: JA Martin, BE Hamilton, SJ Ventura, MJK Osterman, S Kirmeyer, TJ Mathews, EC Wilson, "Births: Final Data for 2009," *National Vital Statistics Reports* 60(1), November 3, 2011.

The odds a person has the same birthday as at least 1 person in a group of 25 people: **1 in 15.1**

SOURCE: Book of Odds estimate based on data from R Hocking, N Schwertman, "An Extension of the Birthday Problem to Exactly k Matches," *College Mathematics Journal* 17(4), September 1, 1986.

Pregnancy Complications

The odds a woman who gives birth will develop a complication during her pregnancy:

Gestational diabetes: **1 in 21**

Pregnancy-associated hypertension: **1 in 24.3**

Placenta previa: **1 in 200**

SOURCES: JA Martin, BE Hamilton, SJ Ventura, MJK Osterman, S Kirmeyer, TJ Mathews, EC Wilson, "Births: Final Data for 2009," *National Vital Statistics Reports* 60(1), November 3, 2011. ✒ PubMed Health, "Placenta Previa," http://www.ncbi.nlm.nih.gov/pubmedhealth/PMH0001902/.

Time Warp

The odds a baby born in 1990 would be born in a clinic or doctor's office: **1 in 3,686**

The odds in 2009: **1 in 10,353**

SOURCES: MF MacDorman, F Menacker, E Declercq, "Trends and Characteristics of Home and Other Out-of-Hospital Births in the United States, 1990–2006," *National Vital Statistics Reports* 58(11), March 3, 2010, rev. August 30, 2010. ✒ JA Martin, BE Hamilton, SJ Ventura, MJK Osterman, S Kirmeyer, TJ Mathews, EC Wilson, "Births: Final Data for 2009," *National Vital Statistics Reports* 60(1), November 3, 2011.

Coming
Too Soon

In 1990, **1 in 9.4** births in the United States occurred prematurely, but by 2009, **1 in 8.2** births were premature. The March of Dimes estimates that rates of prematurity have risen 36% since 1987.

Even the norm of pregnancy duration has decreased. A typical pregnancy now lasts about 39 weeks, as opposed to the previous norm of 40, a gradual change that is estimated to have occurred between 1992 and 2002. The full length of pregnancy is important to give the baby time to develop and mature in the protected environment of the womb; any baby born before 37 weeks of gestation is considered premature or preterm, while babies born before 34 weeks into the pregnancy are considered early preterm.

SOURCES: JA Martin, BE Hamilton, PD Sutton, SJ Ventura, F Menacker, "Births: Final Data for 2005," *National Vital Statistics Reports* 56(6), December 5, 2007. ✎ JA Martin, BE Hamilton, SJ Ventura, MJK Osterman, S Kirmeyer, TJ Mathews, EC Wilson, "Births: Final Data for 2009," *National Vital Statistics Reports* 60(1), November 3, 2011. ✎ March of Dimes, "The Serious Problem of Premature Birth," http://www.marchofdimes.com/mission/prematurity.html.

C-Section Birth Rates by State

The odds a birth in **Alabama** will be by Cesarean delivery are **1 in 2.8**.

The odds a birth in **Alaska** will be by Cesarean delivery are **1 in 4.2**.

The odds a birth in **Arizona** will be by Cesarean delivery are **1 in 3.6**.

The odds a birth in **Arkansas** will be by Cesarean delivery are **1 in 2.9**.

The odds a birth in **California** will be by Cesarean delivery are **1 in 3**.

The odds a birth in **Colorado** will be by Cesarean delivery are **1 in 3.8**.

The odds a birth in **Connecticut** will be by Cesarean delivery are **1 in 2.8**.

The odds a birth in **Delaware** will be by Cesarean delivery are **1 in 2.8**.

The odds a birth in the **District of Columbia** will be by Cesarean delivery are **1 in 3.1**.

The odds a birth in **Florida** will be by Cesarean delivery are **1 in 2.6**.

The odds a birth in **Georgia** will be by Cesarean delivery are **1 in 3**.

The odds a birth in **Hawaii** will be by Cesarean delivery are **1 in 3.7**.

The odds a birth in **Idaho** will be by Cesarean delivery are **1 in 4.1**.

The odds a birth in **Illinois** will be by Cesarean delivery are **1 in 3.2**.

The odds a birth in **Indiana** will be by Cesarean delivery are **1 in 3.3**.

The odds a birth in **Iowa** will be by Cesarean delivery are **1 in 3.3**.

The odds a birth in **Kansas** will be by Cesarean delivery are **1 in 3.3**.

The odds a birth in **Kentucky** will be by Cesarean delivery are **1 in 2.8**.

The odds a birth in **Louisiana** will be by Cesarean delivery are **1 in 2.5**.

The odds a birth in **Maine** will be by Cesarean delivery are **1 in 3.4**.

The odds a birth in **Maryland** will be by Cesarean delivery are **1 in 3**.

The odds a birth in **Massachusetts** will be by Cesarean delivery are **1 in 3**.

The odds a birth in **Michigan** will be by Cesarean delivery are **1 in 3.1**.

The odds a birth in **Minnesota** will be by Cesarean delivery are **1 in 3.6**.

The odds a birth in **Mississippi** will be by Cesarean delivery are **1 in 2.6**.

The odds a birth in **Missouri** will be by Cesarean delivery are **1 in 3.2**.

Changing Times

The United States has seen a dramatic rise in births by Cesarean section. The odds a birth would be by Cesarean delivery in 2009 were **1 in 3.1**. In 1995, the odds a birth would be by Cesarean delivery were **1 in 4.8**.

SOURCES: JA Martin, BE Hamilton, SJ Ventura, MJK Osterman, S Kirmeyer, TJ Mathews, EC Wilson, "Births: Final Data for 2009," *National Vital Statistics Reports* 60(1), November 3, 2011. ✎ JA Martin, BE Hamilton, PD Sutton, SJ Ventura, F Menacher, S Kirmeyer, et al., "Births: Final Data for 2006," *National Vital Statistics Reports* 57(7), January 7, 2009.

The odds a birth in **Montana** will be by Cesarean delivery are **1 in 3.4**.

The odds a birth in **Nebraska** will be by Cesarean delivery are **1 in 3.2**.

The odds a birth in **Nevada** will be by Cesarean delivery are **1 in 3**.

The odds a birth in **New Hampshire** will be by Cesarean delivery are **1 in 3.2**.

The odds a birth in **New Jersey** will be by Cesarean delivery are **1 in 2.5**.

The odds a birth in **New Mexico** will be by Cesarean delivery are **1 in 4.4**.

The odds a birth in **New York** will be by Cesarean delivery are **1 in 2.9**.

The odds a birth in **North Carolina** will be by Cesarean delivery are **1 in 3.2**.

The odds a birth in **North Dakota** will be by Cesarean delivery are **1 in 3.4**.

The odds a birth in **Ohio** will be by Cesarean delivery are **1 in 3.2**.

The odds a birth in **Oklahoma** will be by Cesarean delivery are **1 in 2.9**.

The odds a birth in **Oregon** will be by Cesarean delivery are **1 in 3.4**.

The odds a birth in **Pennsylvania** will be by Cesarean delivery are **1 in 3.1**.

The odds a birth in **Rhode Island** will be by Cesarean delivery are **1 in 3**.

The odds a birth in **South Carolina** will be by Cesarean delivery are **1 in 2.8**.

The odds a birth in **South Dakota** will be by Cesarean delivery are **1 in 4.4**.

The odds a birth in **Tennessee** will be by Cesarean delivery are **1 in 3**.

The odds a birth in **Texas** will be by Cesarean delivery are **1 in 2.8**.

The odds a birth in **Utah** will be by Cesarean delivery are **1 in 4.4**.

The odds a birth in **Vermont** will be by Cesarean delivery are **1 in 3.6**.

The odds a birth in **Virginia** will be by Cesarean delivery are **1 in 2.9**.

The odds a birth in **Washington** will be by Cesarean delivery are **1 in 3.4**.

The odds a birth in **West Virginia** will be by Cesarean delivery are **1 in 2.8**.

The odds a birth in **Wisconsin** will be by Cesarean delivery are **1 in 3.9**.

The odds a birth in **Wyoming** will be by Cesarean delivery are **1 in 3.6**.

SOURCE: JA Martin, BE Hamilton, SJ Ventura, MJK Osterman, S Kirmeyer, TJ Mathews, EC Wilson, "Births: Final Data for 2009," *National Vital Statistics Reports* 60(1), November 3, 2011.

Where Babies Are Born

1 in 1.01	in a hospital
1 in 139	at home
1 in 339	in a freestanding birthing center

SOURCE: JA Martin, BE Hamilton, SJ Ventura, MJK Osterman, S Kirmeyer, TJ Mathews, EC Wilson, "Births: Final Data for 2009," *National Vital Statistics Reports* 60(1), November 3, 2011.

State	%
Alabama	36
Alaska	24
Arizona	27
Arkansas	35
California	33
Colorado	26
Connecticut	36
Delaware	36
District of Columbia	32
Florida	38
Georgia	34
Hawaii	27
Idaho	24
Illinois	31
Indiana	31
Iowa	30
Kansas	30
Kentucky	36
Louisiana	45
Maine	30
Maryland	33
Massachusetts	33
Michigan	32
Minnesota	27
Mississippi	38
Missouri	32
Montana	30
Nebraska	32
Nevada	34
New Hampshire	31
New Jersey	39
New Mexico	23
New York	35
North Carolina	31
North Dakota	28
Ohio	31
Oklahoma	35
Oregon	29
Pennsylvania	32
Rhode Island	33
South Carolina	35
South Dakota	23
Tennessee	34
Texas	35
Utah	23
Vermont	28
Virginia	34
Washington	29
West Virginia	36
Wisconsin	26
Wyoming	28

When's the Baby Coming?
Well, It Depends

C-Section vs. Vaginal Birth by Day of Week

The odds a vaginal birth will occur on a **Sunday** are **1 in 9.5**.

The odds a vaginal birth will occur on a **Monday** are **1 in 6.8**.

The odds a vaginal birth will occur on a **Tuesday** are **1 in 6.2**.

The odds a vaginal birth will occur on a **Wednesday** are **1 in 6.2**.

The odds a vaginal birth will occur on a **Thursday** are **1 in 6.3**.

The odds a vaginal birth will occur on a **Friday** are **1 in 6.7**.

The odds a vaginal birth will occur on a **Saturday** are **1 in 8.5**.

The odds a Cesarean birth will occur on a **Sunday** are **1 in 15.1**.

The odds a Cesarean birth will occur on a **Monday** are **1 in 6.1**.

The odds a Cesarean birth will occur on a **Tuesday** are **1 in 5.6**.

The odds a Cesarean birth will occur on a **Wednesday** are **1 in 5.8**.

The odds a Cesarean birth will occur on a **Thursday** are **1 in 5.9**.

The odds a Cesarean birth will occur on a **Friday** are **1 in 5.9**.

The odds a Cesarean birth will occur on a **Saturday** are **1 in 12.7**.

Day	Vaginal %	Cesarean %
Sunday	10	7
Monday	15	17
Tuesday	16	18
Wednesday	16	17
Thursday	16	17
Friday	15	17
Saturday	12	8

SOURCE: Book of Odds estimate based on JA Martin, BE Hamilton, SJ Ventura, MJK Osterman, S Kirmeyer, TJ Mathews, EC Wilson, "Births: Final Data for 2009," *National Vital Statistics Reports* 60(1), November 3, 2011.

A Good Start in Life

The odds a baby will have an excellent five-minute Apgar score (9 or 10): **1 in 1.1**

SOURCE: JA Martin, BE Hamilton, PD Sutton, SJ Ventura, TJ Mathews, MJK Osterman, "Births: Final Data for 2008," *National Vital Statistics Reports* 59(1), December 2010.

Grab the Forceps

The odds a baby will be breech or malpresented at birth:
1 in 19

SOURCE: JA Martin, BE Hamilton, SJ Ventura, MJK Osterman, S Kirmeyer, TJ Mathews, EC Wilson, "Births: Final Data for 2009," *National Vital Statistics Reports* 60(1), November 3, 2011.

The odds a woman who gives birth will receive an epidural or spinal anesthesia during labor:

1 in 1.7

SOURCE: MJK Osterman, JA Martin, F Menacker, "Expanded Health Data from the New Birth Certificate, 2006," *National Vital Statistics Reports* 58(5), October 28, 2009.

More Babies Are Too Slow than Too Fast

The odds a woman who gives birth will have labor induced: **1 in 4.3**

The odds a woman who gives birth will have precipitous labor: **1 in 42.4**

SOURCE: JA Martin, BE Hamilton, SJ Ventura, MJK Osterman, S Kirmeyer, TJ Mathews, EC Wilson, "Births: Final Data for 2009," *National Vital Statistics Reports* 60(1), November 3, 2011.

DID YOU know? The odds a woman who gives birth will breast-feed her child: **1 in 1.5**

SOURCE: *Health, United States, 2006: With Chartbook on Trends in the Health of Americans*, Hyattsville, MD: National Center for Health Statistics, 2006.

Birth Weights

The odds a baby will have a birth weight of less than 1.1 pounds are **1 in 652**.

The odds a baby will have a birth weight of 1.1–2.2 pounds are **1 in 182**.

The odds a baby will have a birth weight of 2.2–3.3 pounds are **1 in 134**.

The odds a baby will have a birth weight of 3.3–4.4 pounds are **1 in 63**.

The odds a baby will have a birth weight of 4.4–5.5 pounds are **1 in 19.6**.

The odds a baby will have a birth weight of 5.5–6.6 pounds are **1 in 5.4**.

The odds a baby will have a birth weight of 6.6–7.7 pounds are **1 in 2.6**.

The odds a baby will have a birth weight of 7.7–8.8 pounds are **1 in 3.8**.

The odds a baby will have a birth weight of 8.8–9.9 pounds are **1 in 15.2**.

The odds a baby will have a birth weight of 9.9–11 pounds are **1 in 109**.

The odds a baby will have a birth weight of 11 or more pounds are **1 in 970**.

Pounds	%		Pounds	%
Less than 1.1	0.2		6.6–7.7	39
1.1–2.2	0.5		7.7–8.8	26
2.2–3.3	0.7		8.8–9.9	7
3.3–4.4	2		9.9–11	0.9
4.4–5.5	5		11+	0.1
5.5–6.6	19			

SOURCE: JA Martin, BE Hamilton, SJ Ventura, MJK Osterman, S Kirmeyer, TJ Mathews, EC Wilson, "Births: Final Data for 2009," *National Vital Statistics Reports* 60(1), November 3, 2011.

The Odds a Woman Will Breast-Feed for Longer than Three Months, by Age of Mother (First Birth)

ALL AGES: 1 in 2.1

Younger than 20 . . . **1 in 3.1**   25–29 . . . . **1 in 2.2**
20–24 . . . . **1 in 2.4**   30–44 . . . . **1 in 1.6**

SOURCE: *Health, United States, 2006: With Chartbook on Trends in the Health of Americans*, Hyattsville, MD: National Center for Health Statistics, 2006.

The odds a baby born to a woman 20–24 will have Down syndrome: **1 in 3,650**

The odds for a baby born to a woman 40–54: **1 in 295**

SOURCE: JA Martin, BE Hamilton, SJ Ventura, MJK Osterman, S Kirmeyer, TJ Mathews, EC Wilson, "Births: Final Data for 2009," *National Vital Statistics Reports* 60(1), November 3, 2011.

The odds a baby born to a mother younger than 15 will have a very low birth weight: **1 in 8.1**

The odds a baby born to a mother 25–29 will have a very low birth weight: **1 in 13.5**

SOURCE: JA Martin, BE Hamilton, SJ Ventura, MJK Osterman, S Kirmeyer, TJ Mathews, EC Wilson, "Births: Final Data for 2009," *National Vital Statistics Reports* 60(1), November 3, 2011.

Birth Defects

The odds at birth a baby will have:

Klinefelter's syndrome: 1 in 1,085

Cleft lip or palate: 1 in 1,388

An opening or separation in the abdominal wall: 1 in 2,534

Turner syndrome: 1 in 2,710

Meningomyelocele or spina bifida: 1 in 5,582

Vaginal agenesis: 1 in 5,917

Congenital adrenal hyperplasia: 1 in 7,500

Anencephaly: 1 in 8,864

Androgen insensitivity syndrome: 1 in 13,160

Partial androgen insensitivity syndrome: 1 in 131,600

SOURCES: JA Martin, BE Hamilton, SJ Ventura, MJK Osterman, S Kirmeyer, TJ Mathews, EC Wilson, "Births: Final Data for 2009," *National Vital Statistics Reports* 60(1), November 3, 2011. ✎ M Blackless, A Charuvastra, A Derryck, A Fausto-Sterling, K Lauzanne, E Lee, "How Sexually Dimorphic Are We?," *American Journal of Human Biology* 12(2), March 15, 2000: 151–166. ✎ DP Merke, SR Bomstein, "Congenital Adrenal Hyperplasia," *Lancet* 365(9477), June 18, 2005: 2125–2136.

When Tragedy Strikes

The odds a baby will not survive infancy:

1 in 149

SOURCE: SL Murphy, J Xu, KD Kochanek, "Deaths: Preliminary Data for 2010," *National Vital Statistics Report* 60(4), January 11, 2012.

...But Infant Survival Today Is More Likely than in the Past

The odds a baby will not survive infancy are **1 in 34.3** (1950).

The odds a baby will not survive infancy are **1 in 38.5** (1960).

The odds a baby will not survive infancy are **1 in 50** (1970).

The odds a baby will not survive infancy are **1 in 79.4** (1980).

The odds a baby will not survive infancy are **1 in 84** (1981).

The odds a baby will not survive infancy are **1 in 87** (1982).

The odds a baby will not survive infancy are **1 in 89.3** (1983).

The odds a baby will not survive infancy are **1 in 92.6** (1984).

The odds a baby will not survive infancy are **1 in 94.3** (1985).

The odds a baby will not survive infancy are **1 in 96.2** (1986).

The odds a baby will not survive infancy are **1 in 99** (1987).

The odds a baby will not survive infancy are **1 in 100** (1988).

The odds a baby will not survive infancy are **1 in 102** (1989).

The odds a baby will not survive infancy are **1 in 109** (1990).

The odds a baby will not survive infancy are **1 in 112** (1991).

The odds a baby will not survive infancy are **1 in 118** (1992).

The odds a baby will not survive infancy are **1 in 119** (1993).

The odds a baby will not survive infancy are **1 in 125** (1994).

The odds a baby will not survive infancy are **1 in 132** (1995).

The odds a baby will not survive infancy are **1 in 137** (1996).

The odds a baby will not survive infancy are **1 in 139** (1997).

The odds a baby will not survive infancy are **1 in 139** (1998).

The odds a baby will not survive infancy are **1 in 141** (1999).

The odds a baby will not survive infancy are **1 in 145** (2000).

The odds a baby will not survive infancy are **1 in 147** (2001).

The odds a baby will not survive infancy are **1 in 143** (2002).

The odds a baby will not survive infancy are **1 in 145** (2003).

The odds a baby will not survive infancy are **1 in 147** (2004).

The odds a baby will not survive infancy are **1 in 145** (2005).

The odds a baby will not survive infancy are **1 in 149** (2006).

The odds a baby will not survive infancy are **1 in 147** (2007).

The odds a baby will not survive infancy are **1 in 152** (2008).

The odds a baby will not survive infancy are **1 in 156** (2009).

SOURCES: *Health, United States, 2009: With Chartbook on Trends in the Health of Americans,* Hyattsville, MD: National Center for Health Statistics, 2010. ✔ *Health, United States, 2011: With Chartbook on Trends in the Health of Americans,* Hyattsville, MD: National Center for Health Statistics, May 2012. ✔ SL Murphy, J Xu, KD Kochanek, "Deaths: Preliminary Data for 2010," *National Vital Statistics Reports* 60(4), January 11, 2012.

Year	%	Rate/1000 Live Births
1950	3	29.2
1960	3	26.0
1970	2	20.0
1980	1	12.6
1981	1	11.9
1982	1	11.5
1983	1	11.2
1984	1	10.8
1985	1	10.6
1986	1	10.4
1987	1	10.1
1988	1	10.0
1989	1	9.8
1990	1	9.2
1991	1	8.9
1992	1	8.5
1993	1	8.4
1994	1	8.0
1995	1	7.6
1996	1	7.3
1997	1	7.2
1998	1	7.2
1999	1	7.1
2000	1	6.9
2001	1	6.8
2002	1	7.0
2003	1	6.9
2004	1	6.8
2005	1	6.9
2006	1	6.7
2007	1	6.8
2008	1	6.6
2009	1	6.4

SIDS: Has My Baby Stopped Breathing?

There can't be too many parents in the world who haven't had that terrible thought cross their minds. Annually **1 in 1,741** babies dies of sudden infant death syndrome (SIDS). Thankfully, the rate of SIDS has decreased by more than 50% since 1994, when the "Back to Sleep" campaign educated parents on the critical importance of placing infants on their backs at bedtime. Still, about 2,500 babies die of SIDS each year in the United States.

SOURCES: Book of Odds estimate based on *Wonder Database Compressed Mortality File,* Centers for Disease Control and Prevention, 1999–2006 data. ✎ National Institute of Child Health and Human Development, Back to Sleep public education campaign.

Dying from Complications of Pregnancy or Childbirth

The odds a woman will die as a result of her pregnancy in a year: **1 in 150,721**

The odds both mother and baby will die: **1 in 2,217,758**

SOURCE: Book of Odds estimate based on Centers for Disease Control and Prevention, *Wonder Database Compressed Mortality File,* 1999–2006 data.

The Odds a Baby Will Die in Infancy Due to:

Unintentional injury: **1 in 3,732**

Maternal complications of pregnancy: **1 in 1,339**

Disorders related to prematurity and low birth weight: **1 in 788**

SOURCE: Book of Odds estimate based on Centers for Disease Control and Prevention, *Wonder Database Compressed Mortality File,* 1999–2006 data.

Racial Disparities

The odds a baby born to a white mother will not survive infancy . . . . **1 in 193**

The odds a baby born to a black mother will not survive infancy. . . . . **1 in 86**

SOURCE: SL Murphy, J Xu, KD Kochanek, "Deaths: Preliminary Data for 2010," *National Vital Statistics Reports* 60(4), January 11, 2012.

GENDER WARS

1 in 7.1 new mothers will suffer from postpartum depression. **1 in 10** new fathers will experience it as well—the same odds that a person is left-handed.

SOURCES: JF Paulson, S Dauber, JA Leifermann, "Individual and Combined Effects of Postpartum Depression in Mothers and Fathers on Parenting Behavior," *Pediatrics* 118(2), August 31, 2006:12. ✎ AN Gilbert, CJ Wysocki, "Hand Preference and Age in the United States," *Neuropsychologia* (30), 1992: 601–608.

Adoption

In the United States, the odds a child is adopted are

1 in 41.4

The odds a family with children includes adopted children are **1 in 27**. Most (75%) children adopted in the States are born here. The odds an adopted child will be adopted through a domestic private adoption are **1 in 2.6**. The odds an adopted child will be adopted by a relative are **1 in 6.5**.

SOURCES: S Vandivere, K Malm, L Radel, *Adoption USA: A Chartbook Based on the 2007 National Survey of Adoptive Parents,* Washington, D.C.: US Department of Health and Human Services, Office of the Assistant Secretary for Planning and Evaluation, 2009. ✗ US Census Bureau, "Adopted Children and Stepchildren: 2000," *Census 2000 Special Reports,* October 2003.

 ODDS COUPLE: **1 in 1.5**

The odds an employed female 15–44 who gave birth in the past five years took maternity leave, the same odds that . . .

a child lives with 2 married parents.

SOURCES: Book of Odds estimate based on Centers for Disease Control and Prevention, *National Survey of Family Growth 2006–2008,* Public Use Data Files. ✗ US Census Bureau, *America's Families and Living Arrangements: 2009,* http://www.census.gov/population/www/socdemo/hh-fam/cps2009.html.

GENDER WARS
The Kids Are All Right

The odds a married different-sex couple will raise a child: **1 in 2.3**

The odds an unmarried different-sex couple will raise a child: **1 in 2.3**

The odds a married same-sex male couple will raise a child: **1 in 3**

The odds an unmarried same-sex male couple will raise a child: **1 in 13.5**

The odds a married same-sex female couple will raise a child: **1 in 3.6**

The odds an unmarried same-sex female couple will raise a child: **1 in 3.9**

SOURCE: GJ Gates, *Same-Sex Spouses and Unmarried Partners in the American Community Survey, 2008,* Williams Institute, UCLA, October 2009.

"Bris—Sunday 11 a.m. Bring Wine"

The odds a newborn boy will be circumcised: **1 in 1.7**

SOURCE: CJ DeFrances, KA Cullen, LJ Kozak, "National Hospital Discharge Survey: 2005 Annual Summary with Detailed Diagnosis and Procedure Data," *Vital Health Statistics Reports* 13(165), 2007.

 ODDS COUPLE
All by Myself

The odds an adult is an only child: **1 in 20.8**

The odds a person 65–69 has never been married: **1 in 20.9**

SOURCES: JA Davis, TW Smith, PV Marsden, *General Social Surveys, 1972–2008* [CUMULATIVE FILE] [Computer file] ICPSR04697 v. 1., Chicago: National Opinion Research Center [producer], 2009. Storrs, CT: Roper Center for Public Opinion Research, University of Connecticut/Ann Arbor, MI: Inter-university Consortium for Political and Social Research [distributors]. ✗ US Census Bureau, *America's Families and Living Arrangements: 2009,* http://www.census.gov/population/www/socdemo/hh-fam/cps2009.html.

The Angelina Jolie and Brad Pitt Household Book of Odds

The odds a woman 18–29 has adopted a child: **1 in 500**

The odds an adopted child is foreign-born: **1 in 4;** vs. **1 in 1.3** an adopted child is native-born

The odds a household with children contains both biological and adopted children: **1 in 56.3**

The odds of being a movie star: **1 in 1,190,000**

The odds a Best Actress Oscar nominee has changed her name: **1 in 3**

The odds a dollar spent at the box office will be for a movie with Angelina Jolie: **1 in 86.1**

The odds a movie with Angelina Jolie will earn $100,000,000 or more in ticket sales: **1 in 4.5**

The odds a movie with Angelina Jolie will earn $10,000,000–$100,000,000 in ticket sales: **1 in 2.5**

The odds a movie with Angelina Jolie will earn less than 10,000,000 in ticket sales: **1 in 2.7**

The odds a woman is named Angelina: **1 in 2,703**

The odds a man is named Brad: **1 in 1,370**

The odds a dollar spent at the box office will be for a movie with Brad Pitt: **1 in 73.4**

The odds a movie with Brad Pitt will earn $100,000,000 or more in ticket sales: **1 in 4**

The odds a movie with Brad Pitt will earn $10,000,000–$100,000,000 in ticket sales: **1 in 1.8**

The odds a movie with Brad Pitt will earn less than $10,000,000 in ticket sales: **1 in 5.1**

The odds a child 6–11 is adopted: **1 in 38.1**

The odds a child younger than 5 is adopted: **1 in 51.7**

The odds an adopted infant is a girl: **1 in 1.9**

The odds a household with adopted children contains at least 3 adopted children: **1 in 30**

The odds a foreign-born adopted child is from Vietnam: **1 in 46.4**

The odds a foreign-born adopted child is from Africa: **1 in 64**

The odds a birth will be to an unmarried woman: **1 in 2.5**

The odds a woman with the BRCA genetic mutation will develop breast cancer: **1 in 1.7**

The odds a woman 35–39 has ever lived with a significant other without being married: **1 in 1.6**

The odds a woman 35–39 has ever been divorced: **1 in 3.9**

The odds a man 40–49 has ever been divorced: **1 in 3.3**

The odds a married man often thinks about leaving his wife: **1 in 20**

The odds a child lives with at least 5 siblings: **1 in 46.7**

The odds a girl born in 2009 is named Shiloh: **1 in 4,065**

The odds a boy born in 2009 is named Maddox: **1 in 1,003**

SOURCES: J Jones, "Adoption Experiences of Women and Men and Demand for Children to Adopt by Women 18–44 Years of Age in the United States, 2002," *Vital Health Statistics* 23(27), 2008. ✔ S Vandivere, K Malm, L Radel, *Adoption USA: A Chartbook Based on the 2007 National Survey of Adoptive Parents,* US Department of Health and Human Services, Office of the Assistant Secretary for Planning and Evaluation, 2009. ✔ US Census Bureau, "Adopted Children and Stepchildren: 2000," *Census 2000 Special Reports,* October 2003. ✔ Book of Odds estimate based on data from J Ulmer, *James Ulmer's Hollywood Hot List,* 1st ed., New York: St. Martin's Griffin, 2000; http://www.filmsite.org; http://www.imdb.com; http://www.the-numbers.com/market/. ✔ "The American Sex Survey: A Peek Beneath the Sheets," *ABC News Primetime Live Poll,* October 21, 2004, http://abcnews.go.com/images/Politics/959a1AmericanSex Survey.pdf. ✔ Harris Interactive, "Over Thirty Million Adults Claim to Be Victims of Domestic Violence," June 16, 2010. ✔ JA Martin, BE Hamilton, PD Sutton, S Ventura, TJ Matthews, MJK Osterman, "Births: Final Data for 2008," *National Vital Statistics Reports* 59(1), December 2010. ✔ National Cancer Institute, "BRCA1 and BRCA2: Cancer Risk and Genetic Testing," http://www.cancer.gov/cancertopics/factsheet/risk/brca. ✔ Book of Odds estimate based on Centers for Disease Control and Prevention, *National Survey of Family Growth 2006–2008,* Public Use Data Files. ✔ Book of Odds estimate based on data from US Census Bureau, "Number, Timing, and Duration of Marriages and Divorces, 2004." ✔ "The Truth About American Marriage," *Parade Magazine,* September 15, 2008.

Birth Order

A recent Norwegian study has lent some credence to the belief that birth order matters. While controlling for family size, the researchers compared the IQs of nearly 250,000 military conscripts. They found that eldest children exhibit slightly higher levels of intelligence, on the whole, than their younger sibs—and the more elder siblings you have, the lower your IQ is likely to be. Sounds like good news for the **1 in 3.9** adults who are firstborns (and not only children)—and not so good news for those of us who spent our childhoods tagging behind.

A separate survey of its members by Vistage, a CEO peer support organization, found that 43% of respondents were eldest children, compared to 22% youngest and 33% middle children. Other research has shown that firstborns tend to gravitate toward cognitive pursuits, while their younger siblings are more artistic and outdoorsy.

But the most compelling evidence suggests that a child's status within the family as the eldest is what makes the difference rather than actual birth order. The Norwegian study found that oldest children who were not actually born first—in other words, in families whose firstborn child had died—performed on par with natural firstborns.

That parents sometimes devote more attention to their firstborn child is no surprise, nor is the observation that the oldest child in the family may carry the heaviest burden of parental expectations. A large-scale study conducted by a team from Duke University, the University of Maryland, and Johns Hopkins University found that parents are stricter with firstborn children, which could explain why your oldest sibling is the least thrill-seeking (read: less likely to sneak out of the house at 2 a.m.) member of the family. And maybe firstborn children grow up to be leaders, including CEOs, because they've grown up being the head of a pack of siblings and more naturally see themselves in that role.

SOURCES: JA Davis, TW Smith, PV Marsden, *General Social Surveys, 1972–2008* [CUMULATIVE FILE][Computer file] ICPSR04697 v. 1., Chicago: National Opinion Research Center [producer], 2009; Storrs, CT: Roper Center for Public Opinion Research, University of Connecticut/Ann Arbor, MI: Inter-university Consortium for Political and Social Research [distributors]. ⚡ P Kristensen, T Bjerkedal, "Explaining the Relation Between Birth Order and Intelligence," *Science* 316(5832), June 22, 2007: 1717. ⚡ D Jones, "Firstborn Kids Become CEO Material," *USA Today*, September 4, 2007. ⚡ ScienceDaily.com, "Birth Order Affects Career Interests, Study Shows." ⚡ S Shellenbarger, "New Birth Order Study: Parents Spend More Time with First-Borns," The Juggle, WSJ.com, March 31, 2009. ⚡ R Kelley, "Getting Away with It," *Newsweek*, April 30, 2008.

Spacing the Kids Apart

The odds a female 15–44 who has had at least two live births had her second child:

Less than or equal to 12 months after the first: **1 in 24.4**

13–24 months after: **1 in 3.8**

25–36 months after: **1 in 4.2**

37–48 months after: **1 in 6.3**

49 or more months after: **1 in 3.3**

SOURCE: Book of Odds estimates based on A Chandra, GM Martinez, WD Mosher, JC Abma, J Jones, "Fertility, Family Planning, and Reproductive Health of U.S. Women: Data from the 2002 National Survey of Family Growth," *Vital and Health Statistics* 23(25), 2005.

Racial/Ethnic Disparities

The odds a woman 40–55 will experience:

Early Menopause*

Hispanic: **1 in 24.4**

Black: **1 in 27**

White: **1 in 34.5**

Premature Menopause**

Hispanic: **1 in 71.4**

Black: **1 in 71.4**

White: **1 in 100**

*Menopause between ages 40 and 45
**Menopause before age 40

SOURCE: JL Lubrosky, P Meyer, MF Sowers, EB Gold, N Santoro, "Premature Menopause in a Multi-Ethnic Population Study of the Menopause Transition," *Human Reproduction* 18(1), September 3, 2002:199–206.

Baby Name Chart

Odds (1 in)

Born in...	1920	1950	1970	1985	2000	2009
Ashley	‹22,730	‹20,830	1,976	39.3	111.0	259.0
Benjamin	477.0	831.0	485.0	143.0	141.0	162.0
Carol	1,091	67.2	361.0	2,193	6,211	‹7,634
Daniel	282.0	94.8	81.0	49.9	93.6	121.0
Emma	238.0	928.0	3,496	1,972	159.0	113.0
Frank	67.0	157.0	280.0	583.0	1,221	1,859
Gloria	1,220	159.0	899.0	1,855	2,375	3,279
Harold	80.4	253.0	699.0	2,252	5,128	8,000
Isabella	4,926	‹20,830	‹14,710	‹12,000	320.0	90.7
Jacob	1,050	3,906	2,096	157.0	60.6	101.0
Kimberly	‹22,730	3,953	53.7	124.0	381.0	478.0
Logan	14,930	‹37,000	‹28,000	1,942	214.0	146.0
Mary	17.5	26.9	95.4	200.0	323.0	645.0
Noah	4,545	11,900	5,618	1,736	146.0	123.0
Olivia	2,381	2,294	5,263	1,808	155.0	116.0
Patrick	1,253	222.0	162.0	165.0	332.0	656.0
Robert	22.6	21.8	33.3	59.9	152.0	272.0
Susan	1,462	46.3	116.0	694.0	2,967	5,435
Timothy	4,082	173.0	84.9	112.0	288.0	569.0
Ulysses	5,780	10,870	17,240	15,380	9,615	‹10,750
Victor	469	669.0	619.0	578.0	515.0	596.0
Wendy	‹22,730	581.0	165.0	1,035	1,992	3,390
Xavier	‹22,730	28,570	8,621	3,086	573.0	342.0
Yvette	10,200	5,525	892.0	2,710	4,902	‹7,634
Zachary	‹22,730	12,200	3,448	170.0	105.0	263.0

SOURCE: Social Security Administration, *Popular Baby Names.*

Male Sterilization
(and Its Discontents)

Bilateral vasectomy was initially used in the nineteenth century to reduce the incidence of epididymitis in prostatotomy. During the first two decades of the twentieth century, vasectomy was used as an alternative to castration and for limited other purposes. The vasectomy procedure we know of today was invented by Eugen Steinach, a Viennese doctor. It involved cutting a thin tube known as the vas deferens, hence the name we know it by today: the vasectomy. As of 2008, the odds a male 15–44 has had a vasectomy are **1 in 16.7**.

Steinach's procedure was known as the "Steinach vasoligature" and was used to rejuvenate older men. He performed it on himself in 1921. Trying to turn back the clock, the Viennese had intentionally sterilized himself and a great many other men. Both Sigmund Freud and W. B. Yeats are said to have undergone the procedure for "rejuvenation."

It is a classic accidental-invention-of-Silly-Putty story—a discovery meant for one purpose and ultimately used for another. Steinach convinced himself, and hordes of men, that it was a miracle cure: it could cure deafness, he said, increase beard growth, boost energy and strength, and eliminate the need for glasses.

Today, its one simple purpose is to prevent having more children. And the more children a man has had, the likelier he is to have had the quick, out-patient procedure.

The odds a male 15–44 with one child has had a vasectomy are **1 in 16.4**. Two children? **1 in 6.6**; three or more: **1 in 5.7**.

Just **1 in 143** males 15–44 without children has had a vasectomy. Those are the odds a person will report having told nine lies in the past day.

SOURCES: The History of Vasectomy, http://www.vasectomy-information.com/more info/history.htm. ✗ Book of Odds estimate based on data from Centers for Disease Control and Prevention, *National Survey of Family Growth 2006–2008,* Public Use Data Files. ✗ GM Martinez, A Chandra, JC Abma, J Jones, WD Mosher, "Fertility, Contraception, and Fatherhood: Data on Men and Women from Cycle 6 (2002) of the National Survey of Family Growth," *Vital and Health Statistics* 23(26), May 2006. ✗ KB Serota, TR Levine, FJ Boster, "The Prevalence of Lying in America: Three Studies of Self-Reported Lies," *Human Communication Research* 36, 2010: 2–25.

End of Female Fertility

The odds a woman has had a menstrual period in a year:

45–49	1 in 1.5
50–59	1 in 5.6
60–69	1 in 10

SOURCE: *AARP The Magazine,* "Sexuality at Midlife and Beyond, a 2004 Update of Attitudes and Behaviors," May 2005.

CHAPTER 5

INFANCY AND CHILDHOOD

Accident!
The odds
a child 1–4
will die from
an accident
in a year:
1 in 10,120

SOURCE: Book of Odds
estimate based on
Centers for Disease
Control and Prevention,
*Compressed Mortality
File, 1979–2006.*

Racial/Ethnic Makeup

The Odds an American Child Is...

White . . . . **1 in 1.5**

Black . . . . **1 in 6.9**

American Indian or Native Alaskan . . . . **1 in 100**

Asian . . . . **1 in 22.9**

Native Hawaiian or other Pacific Islander . . . . **1 in 500**

Hispanic . . . . **1 in 4.3**

Non-Hispanic . . . . **1 in 1.3**

Race/Ethnicity	%
White	66
Black	14
American Indian or Native Alaskan	1
Asian	4
Native Hawaiian or other Pacific Islander	0.2
Hispanic	23
Non-Hispanic	77

SOURCE: US Census Bureau, *American Community Survey, 2010,* http://www.census.gov/acs/www/.

The Odds a Child Lives with Married or Unmarried Parents

The odds a child in a two-parent household lives with parents who are married: **1 in 1.1**

The odds a child in a two-parent household lives with parents who are unmarried: **1 in 19.1**

Marital Status	%
Married	95
Unmarried	5

SOURCE: Book of Odds estimates based on US Census Bureau, *America's Families and Living Arrangements: 2010,* Current Population Survey.

The odds a child does not live with any siblings:
1 in 4.8

1 sibling . . . . **1 in 2.6**

2 siblings . . . . **1 in 4**

3 siblings . . . . **1 in 10**

4 siblings . . . . **1 in 26.4**

At least 5 siblings . . **1 in 50.5**

SOURCE: US Census Bureau, *America's Families and Living Arrangements: 2010,* Current Population Survey.

1 in 3.3

married same-sex couples, along with **1 in 6** unmarried ones, is raising a child.

SOURCE: GJ Gates, *Same-sex Spouses and Unmarried Partners in the American Community Survey, 2008,* Williams Institute, UCLA, October 2009.

TIMES HAVE CHANGED

1969

The odds a child lived with:

Two parents: **1 in 1.2**

Mother only: **1 in 9.1**

Father only: **1 in 91.9**

Relatives other than parents: **1 in 43.9**

Nonrelatives only: **1 in 202**

2010

The odds a child lived with:

Two parents: **1 in 1.4**

Mother only: **1 in 4.3**

Father only: **1 in 29.1**

Relatives other than parents: **1 in 31.2**

Nonrelatives only: **1 in 113**

SOURCES: US Census Bureau, "Detailed Tables: America's Families and Living Arrangements, 2006," *Current Population Survey, 2006 Annual Social and Economic Supplement.* ↗ Book of Odds estimates based on US Census Bureau, *America's Families and Living Arrangements: 2010,* Current Population Survey.

Where Babies Sleep: From 2 weeks to 12 months

In a bed with their mothers

Age	1+ Nights/Week		3+ Nights/Week		5+ Nights/Week	
	%	Odds (1 in)	%	Odds (1 in)	%	Odds (1 in)
2 weeks	38	2.6	33	3.0	28	3.6
1 month	38	2.7	32	3.1	26	3.8
2 months	32	3.1	27	3.8	23	4.4
3 months	28	3.6	24	4.2	21	4.9
6 months	27	3.8	22	4.6	18	5.6
9 months	24	4.1	20	5.1	16	6.3
12 months	22	4.5	18	5.5	15	6.6

In the same room as their mothers

Age	%	Odds (1 in)
2 weeks	85	1.2
1 month	81	1.2
2 months	71	1.4
3 months	63	1.6
6 months	45	2.2
9 months	34	2.9
12 months	29	3.5

SOURCE: Book of Odds estimate based on F Hauck, C Signore, S Fein, T Raju, "Infant Sleeping Arrangements and Practices During the First Year of Life," *Pediatrics* 122 Supplement(S113–S120), http://pediatrics.aappublications.org/cgi/content/abstract/122/Supplement_2/S113.

By the time we are about two, most of us can walk, even if we can't climb stairs.

Walking, Talking, Thinking

The odds a child 22–25 months:

Possesses problem-solving skills . . . . 1 in 1.01
Can walk skillfully . . . . 1 in 1.1
Can understand words . . . . 1 in 1.2
Has some vocabulary . . . . 1 in 1.6
Has developed fine motor skills . . . . 1 in 1.8
Can climb stairs . . . . 1 in 2.1

SOURCE: GM Mulligan, KD Flanagan, *Age 2: Findings From the 2-Year-Old Follow-up of the Early Childhood Longitudinal Study, Birth Cohort* (ECLS-B) (NCES 2006-043), US Department of Education. Washington, DC: National Center for Education Statistics, 2006.

Saying No
to the Shot

Eighty years ago, when the death toll of pertussis, also known as whooping cough, was at its peak, few would have refused to get their children vaccinated against it. In 1934 alone, 7,518 Americans— **1 in 16,800**—succumbed to it.

In 2010, the odds were much lower that a person will die of whooping cough in a year, just **1 in 33,510,000**, driven by 10 deaths in California. Those odds could increase, largely because of parental concerns over the safety of the vaccine and the failure of many adults to get booster shots themselves. In 2012, Washington State declared a whooping cough epidemic due to a tenfold increase in the number of cases, with 3,000 expected by year end.

SOURCES: ER Stiehm, HD Ochs, JA Winkelstein, *Immunologic Disorders in Infants and Children*, 5th ed., Philadelphia: Elsevier Saunders, 2004. ✓ J Xu, KD Kochanek, SL Murphy, B Tejada-Vera, "Deaths: Final Data for 2007," *National Vital Statistics Reports* 58(10), May 2010. ✓ Book of Odds estimate based on Centers for Disease Control and Prevention, *Wonder Database Compressed Mortality File*, 1999–2006 data. ✓ "Whooping Cough Epidemic Declared in Wash. State," Associated Press, May 12, 2012.

Saying Yes to the Shot

The odds a child younger than 36 months has been vaccinated against:

Diphtheria, tetanus, and whooping cough	**1 in 1.1**
Measles, mumps, and rubella	**1 in 1.1**
Poliovirus	**1 in 1.1**
Haemophilus influenza type B	**1 in 1.2**
Hepatitis B	**1 in 1.1**
Chicken pox	**1 in 1.1**
Haemophilus	**1 in 1.1**

SOURCE: "National, State, and Local Area Vaccination Coverage Among Children Aged 19–35 Months—United States, 2009," *Morbidity and Mortality Weekly Report* 59(36), September 17, 2010.

Who's Watching the Kids?

In the United States, **1 in 1.1** fathers and **1 in 1.7** mothers of children under 6 is employed, either full- or part-time. It comes as no surprise then that only **1 in 2.6** children under 7 is able to be cared for only by his or her parents.

So who else is involved?

1 in 4.5 children under 7 is cared for by relatives.

1 in 7.2 children under 7 is cared for by nonrelatives.

1 in 2.8 spends time in a child-care center.

SOURCE: Federal Interagency Forum on Child and Family Statistics, *America's Children: Key National Indicators of Well-Being, 2007*, Washington, DC: US Government Printing Office.

Taking Chances

The odds a child 19–35 months lives in a home without:

Padding around hard surfaces or sharp edges	**1 in 1.9**
Ipecac syrup on hand for accidental poisoning	**1 in 1.9**
Turned-down hot water thermostat setting	**1 in 2.4**
Baby gates, window guards, or other child safety barriers	**1 in 4.6**
Locks or latches on cabinets that contain cleaners or medicine	**1 in 6.3**
Stoppers or plugs in electric outlets	**1 in 16.7**

SOURCE: N Halfon, L Olson, M Inkelas, et al., "Summary Statistics from the National Survey of Early Childhood Health, 2000," *Vital and Health Statistics* 15(3), 2002.

ODDS COUPLE

The Waiting Game

Some children must wait for a parent to come home from prison. It should come as no surprise that many children grow up with one or more parents behind bars. The United States has a greater percentage of its population in prison than any other country. An appalling milestone was

reached in 2008 when the odds that an adult was incarcerated were **1 in 100**. This has declined to **1 in 104** in 2010 as releases were slightly greater than admissions in that year.

The odds a child under 18 has a parent in prison are **1 in 43.2**.

These are about the same odds as those that an adolescent boy 11–17 on the waiting list for a kidney donation has been there for at least five years: **1 in 43**.

SOURCES: WJ Sabol, HC West, "Bureau of Justice Statistics: Prisoners in 2008." ✎ LE Glaze, "Bureau of Justice Statistics: Correctional Populations in the United States," 2010. ✎ LE Glaze, "Bureau of Justice Statistics: Parents in Prison and Their Minor Children," August 8, 2008. ✎ Organ Procurement and Transplantation Network, "Waiting Time for Organ Transplant as of 8/8/2009," http://OPTN.transplant.hrsa.gov.

"Arrange Sitter for Thursday"

The odds a child younger than 3 will receive only parental care:

1 in 2

SOURCE: Federal Interagency Forum on Child and Family Statistics, *America's Children: Key National Indicators of Well-Being, 2007.* Washington, DC: US Government Printing Office.

The Odds a Parent in a Married Couple with a Child Under Age 6 Is Employed

The odds a married couple with at least 1 child younger than 6 are both employed are **1 in 1.9**.

The odds a married couple with at least 1 child younger than 6 are both unemployed are **1 in 114**.

The odds a married woman with at least 1 child younger than 6 is not in the labor force but her husband is are **1 in 2.8**.

The odds a married man with at least 1 child younger than 6 is not in the labor force but his wife is are **1 in 34.6**.

	Employment Status	%
Married couples with at least 1 child younger than 6	Both employed	52
Married couples with at least 1 child younger than 6	Both unemployed	1
Married women with at least 1 child younger than 6	Not in the labor force but her husband is	36
Married men with at least 1 child younger than 6	Not in the labor force but his wife is	3

Note: To be counted in the labor force, a person must be either employed or actively seeking work; those not employed and not actively seeking work are not included.

SOURCES: US Census Bureau, *America's Families and Living Arrangements: 2010,* Current Population Survey. ✎ Bureau of Labor Statistics, Families Employment Status, Table 5, March 24, 2011

GENDER WARS

1 in 3.7: The odds a married woman with one or more children under 6 is a stay-at-home mom.

1 in 125: The odds a married man with one or more children under 6 is a stay-at-home dad.

SOURCE: Book of Odds estimates based on US Census Bureau, *America's Families and Living Arrangements: 2010,* Current Population Survey.

Grandparents Rule

The odds an adult 50 or older is a grandparent are **1 in 3.5**.

The odds an adult 75 or older is a grandparent are **1 in 2.9**.

Grandparent Spending

The odds a grandparent will purchase a birthday gift for his or her grandchildren in a year are **1 in 1.03**.

The odds a grandparent will purchase a holiday gift for his or her grandchildren in a year are **1 in 1.04**.

The odds a grandparent will spend money to have fun with his or her grandchildren in a year are **1 in 1.1**.

Grandparent Purchases

The odds a grandparent will purchase clothing for his or her grandchildren in a year are **1 in 1.2**.

The odds a grandparent will purchase a book for his or her grandchildren in a year are **1 in 1.3**.

The odds a grandparent will purchase fun food for his or her grandchildren in a year are **1 in 1.3**.

The odds a grandparent will purchase a toy for his or her grandchildren in a year are **1 in 1.3**.

The odds a grandparent will purchase a music CD or tape for his or her grandchildren in a year are **1 in 2.1**.

The odds a grandparent will purchase a video or DVD for his or her grandchildren in a year are **1 in 2.2**.

The odds a grandparent will purchase a video game for his or her grandchildren in a year are **1 in 3.2**.

Grandparent Spending Reasons

The odds a grandparent spends money on his or her grandchildren because he or she enjoys it are **1 in 1.1**.

The odds a grandparent spends money on his or her grandchildren to help with educational expenses are **1 in 1.9**.

The odds a grandparent spends money on his or her grandchildren to help with living expenses are **1 in 2.2**.

The odds a grandparent spends money on his or her grandchildren because requested to are **1 in 3.2**.

The odds a grandparent spends money on his or her grandchildren to help with medical or dental expenses are **1 in 4**.

Grandparent Activities with Grandchildren

The odds a grandparent had his or her grandchildren over for dinner in the past 6 months are **1 in 1.2**.

The odds a grandparent went out to dinner with his or her grandchildren in the past 6 months are **1 in 1.2**.

The odds a grandparent went shopping with his or her grandchildren in the past 6 months are **1 in 1.3**.

The odds a grandparent read with his or her grandchildren in the past 6 months are **1 in 1.3**.

The odds a grandparent cooked with his or her grandchildren in the past 6 months are **1 in 1.5**.

The odds a grandparent went to a park or playground with his or her grandchildren in the past 6 months are **1 in 1.6**.

The odds a grandparent attended a school event for his or her grandchildren in the past 6 months are **1 in 1.8**.

The odds a grandparent exercised or played sports with his or her grandchildren in the past 6 months are **1 in 1.9**.

The odds a grandparent rented a video to watch at home with his or her grandchildren in the past 6 months are **1 in 1.9**.

The odds a grandparent went to a sports event with his or her grandchildren in the past 6 months are **1 in 2**.

The odds a grandparent helped his or her grandchildren with schoolwork in the past 6 months are **1 in 2.4**.

The odds a grandparent went to an amusement park with his or her grandchildren in the past 6 months are **1 in 2.9**.

The odds a grandparent went to a movie with his or her grandchildren in the past 6 months are **1 in 3.1**.

The odds a grandparent provides day care for his or her grandchildren are **1 in 6.7**.

SOURCES: American Association of Retired Persons and Harris Interactive, *AARP Survey on Lifelong Learning,* July 19, 2000, http://assets.aarp.org/rgcenter/general/lifelong .pdf. ✗ C Davies, D Williams, *The Grandparent Study 2002 Report,* American Association of Retired Persons, May 2002, http://assets.aarp.org/rgcenter/general/gp_2002.pdf.

The Odds of Being a Grandparent	%
50+	29
75+	35

Grandparent Spending	%
Birthday gift	91
Holiday gift	96
Having fun	90

Grandparent Purchases	%
Clothing	87
A book	80
Fun food	78
A toy	76
A music CD or tape	48
A video or DVD	45
A video game	31

Spending Reasons	%
Enjoys it	93
To help with educational expenses	52
To help with living expenses	45
Because of requests	31
To help with medical/dental expenses	25

Activities with Grandchildren	%
Hosted dinner	86
Went out to dinner	84
Shopping	75
Reading	75
Cooking	67
Went to a park/playground	63
Attended a school event	57
Exercised or played sports	53
Rented a video	52
Went to a sports event	50
Helped with schoolwork	41
Went to an amusement park	35
Went to a movie	32
Provided day care	15

 **ODDS COUPLE**

Putting Your Money
Where Your Mouth Is

The odds a grandparent will purchase jewelry for his or her grandchildren in a year: **1 in 2.7**

The odds a grandparent believes spoiling grandchildren is the role of a grandparent: **1 in 2.7**

SOURCE: C Davies, D Williams, *The Grandparent Study 2002 Report,* American Association of Retired Persons, May 2002, http://assets. aarp.org/rgcenter/general/gp_2002.pdf.

"Dinner's at Six!"

The odds a child younger than 6 will eat a meal with all the family members in a household:

1–3 days a week	**1 in 6.9**
4–6 days a week	**1 in 4.1**
Every day	**1 in 1.7**

SOURCE: US Department of Health and Human Services, Health Resources and Services Administration, Maternal and Child Health Bureau, *The National Survey of Children's Health 2007*, Rockville, MD: US Department of Health and Human Services, 2009.

DID YOU know?

The odds that every day, for a child younger than 6, a family member will:

Tell stories or sing to the child:
1 in 1.7

Read to the child:
1 in 2.1

Take the child on an outing:
1 in 7.2

SOURCE: US Department of Health and Human Services, Health Resources and Services Administration, Maternal and Child Health Bureau, *The National Survey of Children's Health 2007*, Rockville, MD: US Department of Health and Human Services, 2009.

HOMELESS Families

A growing number of American families are without homes. In 2009, slightly more than 170,000 families were given emergency shelter, a 30% increase in two years. The odds a homeless person is part of a homeless family were **1 in 1.6** in that year.

While a homeless individual seeking shelter is most often a middle-aged adult male, adults seeking emergency housing as part of a family group are overwhelmingly female. The majority are mothers under the age of 31. More than half the children they bring with them are under the age of 6.

Homeless families are more likely than individuals to be offered shelter if they come to the attention of authorities or service agencies, but the odds are still estimated to be **1 in 4.7** that a homeless family will have no place to sleep on a given night. Families that do end up in emergency shelters tend to be there longer than individuals (the 2009 median stay was 36 days for persons in families compared to 17 days for individuals).

SOURCE: US Department of Housing and Urban Development, Office of Community Planning and Development, *The 2009 Annual Homeless Assessment Report to Congress*, June 2010.

Children and Poverty

The odds a child lives in a household with an income less than the poverty level are **1 in 4.7**.

The odds a child lives in a household with an income one to two times the poverty level are **1 in 4.7**.

The odds a child lives in a household with an income more than two times the poverty level are **1 in 1.7**.

The odds a child lives in a household that receives public assistance (excluding food support) are **1 in 24**.

The odds a child lives in a household that receives food stamps are **1 in 5.4**.

The predicted odds a child will receive food stamps in his or her household for at least one year by age 20 are **1 in 2**.

The predicted odds a white child will receive food stamps in his or her household for at least one year by age 20 are **1 in 2.7**.

The predicted odds a black child will receive food stamps in his or her household for at least one year by age 20 are **1 in 1.1**.

Poverty Status	%
<1 times poverty level	21
1–2 times poverty level	21
2+ times poverty level	57
Receives public assistance	4
Receives food stamps	19
Food stamps by age 20, at least one year	49
Food stamps by age 20, at least one year, white	37
Food stamps by age 20, at least one year, black	90

SOURCES: US Census Bureau, *America's Families and Living Arrangements: 2010*, Current Population Survey. ✎ MR Rank, TA Hirschl, "Estimating the Risk of Food Stamp Use and Impoverishment During Childhood," *Archives of Pediatrics and Adolescent Medicine* 163(11), November 2009.

Rich Kids

The odds a family with at least two children younger than 18 is in the top 5% income bracket:

1 in 17.7

SOURCE: US Census Bureau, *Current Population Survey*, 2009.

For Some,
Childhood Is a Time of Neglect and Hurt

The odds the subject of a child maltreatment investigation will be determined to be a victim are **1 in 4.4**.

The odds a child will be the subject of a maltreatment investigation in a year are **1 in 24.8**.

The odds a child will be a victim of neglect in a year are **1 in 137**.

The odds a child will be a victim of physical abuse in a year are **1 in 603**.

The odds a child will be a victim of sexual abuse in a year are **1 in 1,129**.

The odds a child will be a victim of psychological abuse in a year are **1 in 1,388**.

The odds a child will be a victim of medical neglect in a year are **1 in 3,154**.

The odds a victim of child maltreatment will be removed from home by a state child protection agency in a year are **1 in 4.8**.

The odds a child will be removed from home by a state child protection agency due to maltreatment in a year are **1 in 496**.

The odds a child will be removed from home by a state child protection agency due to neglect in a year are **1 in 700**.

The odds a child will be removed from home by a state child protection agency due to physical abuse in a year are **1 in 5,455**.

The odds a child will be removed from home by a state child protection agency due to sexual abuse in a year are **1 in 16,130**.

Foster Care

The odds an infant is in foster care are **1 in 163**.

The odds a child younger than 11 is in foster care are **1 in 161**.

The odds a person younger than 21 is in foster care are **1 in 159**.

The odds a person in foster care has been there for at least 12 months are **1 in 1.6**.

The odds a person in foster care has been there for 3–4 years are **1 in 7.5**.

The odds a person in foster care has been there for at least 5 years are **1 in 6.1**.

The odds a person in foster care is younger than 6 are **1 in 3.5**.

The odds a person in foster care is younger than 11 are **1 in 2**.

The odds a person younger than 21 leaving foster care will exit by reuniting with a parent or primary caretaker are **1 in 1.8**.

The odds a person younger than 21 leaving foster care will exit by being adopted are **1 in 5.6**.

The odds a person younger than 21 leaving foster care will exit by moving in with relatives other than a parent or primary caretaker are **1 in 9.8**.

The odds a person younger than 21 leaving foster care will exit by being emancipated are **1 in 13.9**.

The odds a person younger than 21 leaving foster care will exit by establishing guardianship are **1 in 26**.

The odds a person younger than 21 leaving foster care will exit by transferring to another agency are **1 in 40**.

The odds a person younger than 21 leaving foster care will exit by running away are **1 in 57.6**.

"Arrange Child Protective Services for Thursday"

The odds a child younger than 3 will be a victim of neglect in a year are **1 in 68.6**.

These are the same odds that a man is 50 years old.

SOURCES: Book of Odds estimate based on US Department of Health and Human Services, Administration for Children and Families, Administration on Children, Youth and Families, Children's Bureau, *Child Maltreatment 2009,* http://www.acf.hhs.gov/programs/cb/stats_research/index.htm#can. ✎ US Census Bureau, Population Estimates Program, http://www.census.gov/popest/estimates.php.

ODDS COUPLE
Hard Digs

The odds a sheltered homeless person is younger than 18:
1 in 4.5

The odds an inmate on death row is married:
1 in 4.5

SOURCES: US Department of Housing and Urban Development, Office of Community Planning and Development, *The 2009 Annual Homeless Assessment Report to Congress,* June 2010. ✎ Bureau of Justice Statistics, Capital Punishment, 2008–Statistical Tables.

SOURCES: US Department of Health and Human Services, Administration for Children and Families, Administration on Children, Youth and Families, Children's Bureau, *Child Maltreatment 2005,* http://www.acf.hhs.gov/programs/cb/stats_research/index.htm#can. ✎ US Department of Health and Human Services, Administration for Children and Families, Administration on Children, Youth and Families, Children's Bureau, *Child Maltreatment 2008,* http://www.acf.hhs.gov/programs/cb/stats_research/index.htm#can. ✎ US Department of Health and Human Services, Administration for Children and Families, Administration on Children, Youth and Families, Children's Bureau, *Child Maltreatment 2009,* http://www.acf.hhs.gov/programs/cb/stats_research/index.htm#can. ✎ Book of Odds estimate based on US Department of Health and Human Services, Administration on Children, Youth and Families, *AFCARS Report, Final Estimates for FY 1998 Through FY 2002,* http://www.acf.hhs.gov/programs.

Autism: The Spreading Spectrum

Prior to 1943 there were no diagnoses of autism. It was in that year that psychiatrist D. Leo Kanner coined the term "early infantile autism," based on his observation of fewer than a dozen young children. Asperger's syndrome, a milder variant, was described at the same time. Since then, awareness of and research into autism have increased and tools for evaluating and measuring its prevalence have improved. What was one syndrome in the third edition of the *Diagnostic and Statistical Manual of Mental Disorders* (*DSM-III*) is now a spectrum of five (*DSM-IV-TR*). This spectrum is called Autism Spectrum Disorder (ASD). The measurement of how common autism is is tricky since its cause or causes are not known, but it is clear that there is a strong genetic component. There is overlap among identical twins, and one sibling having it raises the risk of another sibling having it significantly.

With increased attention the measured prevalence has increased:

In 2000, the reported odds of a child having ASD were **1 in 150**.
In 2008, the reported odds of a child having ASD were **1 in 88**.

This is a very large apparent change in a short time. Many people are trying to understand its cause. The US Centers for Disease Control and Prevention, which published these numbers, writes: "We know that some of the increase is probably due to the way children are identified and served in local communities, although exactly how much is due to these factors is unknown. To understand more, we need to keep accelerating our research."

Here are some of the considerations:

- If a disease with so strong a genetic component were epidemic one would expect to find more cases in children than adults, but a British study found otherwise.

- New groups such as blacks and Hispanics are showing large increases, suggesting they were undertested in the past.

- There is some evidence that people who were formerly diagnosed as having "mental retardation" or "speech impairment" are being redefined as autistic, a phenomenon called "diagnostic substitution." Some of this effect seems to be evident in the number of children receiving special education under the Individuals with Disabilities Education Act (IDEA); autism diagnoses have increased while those of mental retardation and learning disabilities have decreased.

SOURCES: National Institute of Mental Health, US Department of Health and Human Services, *Autism Spectrum Disorders, Pervasive Developmental Disorders.* ✎ *Diagnostic and Statistical Manual of Mental Disorders: DSM-IV-TR,* 4th rev. ed., Washington, DC: American Psychiatric Association, 2000. ✎ National Institute of Mental Health, US Department of Health and Human Services, *A Parent's Guide to Autism Spectrum Disorder.* ✎ J Hallmayer, S Cleveland, A Torres, et al., "Genetic Heritability and Shared Environmental Factors Among Twin Pairs with Autism," *Archives of General Psychiatry* 68(11), 2011: 1095–1102. ✎ Autism and Developmental Disabilities Monitoring Network, *Prevalence of Autism Spectrum Disorders (ASDs) Among Multiple Areas of the United States in 2008,* Centers for Disease Control and Prevention, US Department of Health and Human Services, http://www.cdc.gov/ncbddd/autism/documents/ADDM-2012-Community-Report.pdf.

Many Children Face Challenges Early in Life

The odds a child younger than 5 has "activity limitation" due to:

A speech problem:
1 in 63.3

Mental retardation:
1 in 154

A learning disability:
1 in 417

SOURCE: *Health, United States, 2009: With Special Feature on Medical Technology,* Hyattsville, MD: National Center for Health Statistics, 2010.

First Teeth, First Cavities

The odds a child 2–11 has baby teeth cavities are **1 in 2.4**. Those odds jump to **1 in 1.8** for children in families living below the federal poverty level.

SOURCE: BA Dye, S Tan, V Smith, BG Lewis, LK Barker, G Thornton-Evans, et al., "Trends in Oral Health Status: United States, 1988–1994 and 1999–2004," *Vital and Health Statistics* 11(248), 2007.

Identified Prevalence of Autism Spectrum Disorders

Surveillance Year	Birth Year	Number of ADDM Sites Reporting	Prevalence per 1,000 Children (Range)	This Is About 1 in X Children...
2000	1992	6	6.7 (4.5–9.9)	1 in 150
2002	1994	14	6.6 (3.3–10.6)	1 in 150
2004	1996	8	8.0 (4.6–9.8)	1 in 125
2006	1998	11	9.0 (4.2–12.1)	1 in 110
2008	2000	14	11.3 (4.8–21.2)	1 in 88

SOURCE: Centers for Disease Control and Prevention, "Autism Spectrum Disorders, Data and Statistics," http://www.cdc.gov/ncbddd/autism/data.html.

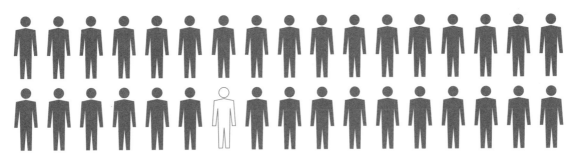

A Sad Toll

Of the approximately 700,000 maltreated children in the United States, 1,770 of them, or **1 in 396**, died from it in 2009.

SOURCE: Book of Odds estimate based on US Department of Health and Human Services, Administration for Children and Families, Administration on Children, Youth and Families, Children's Bureau, *Child Maltreatment 2009*, http://www.acf.hhs.gov/programs/cb/stats_research/index.htm#can.

 ODDS COUPLE

Halfway to Kindergarten! Halfway to Mensa?

The odds a child 22–25 months old will possess counting skills: **1 in 25**

The odds a person will meet the membership criteria for Mensa: **1 in 50**

SOURCES: GM Mulligan, KD Flanagan, *Age 2: Findings from the 2-Year-Old Follow-up of the Early Childhood Longitudinal Study, Birth Cohort* (ECLS–B) (NCES 2006–043), Washington, DC: National Center for Education Statistics, 2006. ↗ Mensa, http://www.mensa.org/.

GENDER WARS

The odds a man 18–65 agrees that "it is sometimes necessary to discipline a child with a good, hard spanking": **1 in 1.3**

The odds a woman 18–65 agrees that "it is sometimes necessary to discipline a child with a good, hard spanking": **1 in 1.4**

SOURCE: Child Trends, *Charting Parenthood: A Statistical Portrait of Fathers and Mothers in America*, 2002, http://fatherhood.hhs.gov/charting02/.

Getting Ready for  SCHOOL

Staying Home to Learn

According to a survey by the National Center for Education Statistics, the number of homeschooled children in the United States increased from an estimated 850,000 students in 1999 to about 1.5 million students in 2007. The survey was conducted three times over the eight-year period, and while the total number has increased by 77.4%, many characteristics of the homeschooled population have remained consistent. The vast majority—between **80%** and **82%**—of homeschooled students receive no instruction from a traditional school. White children make up between **75%** and **77%** of the homeschooled population. A little more than half have two parents, with one parent in the labor force. And **60–62%** of children taught at home live in families with three or more children.

There have also been some interesting changes. More parents of some financial means are choosing to keep their children at home. In 1999, **17%** of homeschooled children lived in households with an income over $75,000; by 2007 the percentage had almost doubled to **33%**. At the same time, fewer black families were making the choice to homeschool; the percentage fell from almost **10%** in 1999 to **4%** in 2007.

SOURCES: National Center for Education Statistics, *Elementary and Secondary School Grades.* ✗ National Center for Education Statistics, National Household Education Surveys Program.

Where Kids Go to School

The odds a student 5–17 attends an assigned public school: **1 in 1.4**

The odds a student 5–17 attends a chosen public school: **1 in 6.7**

The odds a student 5–17 attends a private school: **1 in 8.8**

The odds a student 5–17 is homeschooled: **1 in 34.5**

The odds a student 5–17 attends a chosen charter school: **1 in 50**

SOURCES: TD Snyder, SA Dillow, *Digest of Education Statistics 2009* (NCES 2010-013), Washington, DC: National Center for Education Statistics, 2010. ✗ S Grady, S Bielick, *Trends in the Use of School Choice: 1993 to 2007* (NCES 2010-004), Washington, DC: National Center for Education Statistics, 2010.

⚔ GENDER WARS

The odds a child 3–5 who is not in kindergarten can:

Recognize all the letters in the alphabet: **1 in 3.7** for a girl; **1 in 4.6** for a boy.

Write own name: **1 in 1.8** for a girl; **1 in 2.1** for a boy.

Read or pretend to read a storybook: **1 in 1.3** for a girl; **1 in 1.4** for a boy.

SOURCE: CW Nord, J Lennon, B Liu, K Chandler, "Home Literacy Activities and Signs of Children's Emerging Literacy, 1993 and 1999," *Statistics in Brief*, National Center for Education Statistics, November 1999.

The odds a public elementary school teaches foreign languages: **1 in 6.7**

The odds a private elementary school teaches foreign languages: **1 in 2**

SOURCE: Book of Odds estimate based on NC Rhodes, I Pufah, *Foreign Language Teaching in U.S. Schools*, Washington, DC: Center for Applied Linguistics, 2009.

Report Card: Public vs. Private

The odds a public elementary school student receives mostly As . . . . **1 in 2**

The odds a public elementary school student receives mostly Bs . . . . **1 in 3**

The odds a public elementary school student receives mostly Cs . . . . **1 in 7.5**

The odds a public elementary school student receives mostly Ds or Fs . . . . . **1 in 28.6**

The odds a private elementary school student receives mostly As . . . . **1 in 1.5**

The odds a private elementary school student receives mostly Bs . . . . **1 in 3.8**

The odds a private elementary school student receives mostly Cs . . . . **1 in 15.2**

The odds a private elementary school student receives mostly Ds or Fs . . . . . **1 in 167**

Grade	Public %	Private %
Mostly As	50	66
Mostly Bs	33	27
Mostly Cs	13	7
Mostly Ds or Fs	4	1

SOURCE: TD Snyder, SA Dillow, *Digest of Education Statistics 2009* (NCES 2010-013), Washington, DC: National Center for Education Statistics, 2010.

Getting There:
How Kids Get to School

The odds a child 5–14 will...

usually take a **school bus** to school . . . . . . **1 in 2.5**

usually **walk** to school . . . . **1 in 8.3**

usually **bike** to school . . . . **1 in 100**

Transportation	%
School bus	40
Walk	12
Bike	1

SOURCE: Safe Routes Partnership, "US Travel Data Show Decline in Walking and Bicycling to School Has Stabilized," press release announcing data from the US Department of Transportation *2009 National Travel Survey.*

Preschool

The odds a child is enrolled in a preprimary education program at age:

3: **1 in 2.5**

4: **1 in 1.5**

5: **1 in 1.2**

SOURCE: TD Snyder, SA Dillow, *Digest of Education Statistics 2009* (NCES 2010-013), Washington, DC: National Center for Education Statistics, 2010.

Difficulties in School

The odds a child has been diagnosed with a learning disability:

Age 3–4: **1 in 35.7**

Age 5–11: **1 in 13.2**

Age 12–17: **1 in 9.3**

SOURCE: "Summary Health Statistics for U.S. Children: National Health Interview Survey, 2009," *Vital and Health Statistics* 10(247), August 2010.

GENDER WARS

The odds a male is left-handed:
1 in 7.7

The odds a female is left-handed:
1 in 12.4

SOURCE: C McManus, "Precisely Wrong? The Problems with the Jones and Martin Genetic Model of Sex Differences in Handedness and Language Lateralization," *Cortex,* 2010: 700–702.

1 in 284 employed people 16 or older is a school bus driver.

SOURCE: Bureau of Labor Statistics, *Occupational Employment Statistics, National Cross-Industry Estimates,* 2009.

Turn Off That
(Computer, TV, Cell Phone, Etc.)

A 2008/2009 Kaiser Family Foundation study of 8- to 18-year-olds found that the amount of time young people spend sitting in front of screens of all kinds—from TVs to computers to iPods to cell phones—has dramatically increased. About 79% of people in this age group will watch television in a day, and **1 in 5.9** spends 5 hours or more per day tuned in. As for the Internet, at least **1 in 3** children between 5 and 17 is on it every day. Meanwhile, **1 in 8.3** of those 8 to 18 spends at least 5 hours a day texting on a cell phone and **1 in 6.7** spends 30–60 minutes talking on a cell phone in a day.

For people 8–18, 87% live in a house with a video game console. That number is up from 81% in 1999. 60% of children in this age range will play a video game in a given day. The odds a person 8–18 will spend a half hour to an hour playing video games in a day are **1 in 5.3**; the odds of playing 1–3 hours per day are **1 in 6.3**.

SOURCES: V Rideout, UG Foehr, DF Roberts, *Generation M2: Media in the Lives of 8–18 Year Olds*, Kaiser Foundation Study, March 2005. ✗ *2008 Kids and Family Reading Report*, conducted by Yankelovich for Scholastic. ✗ R Weis, B Cerankosky, "Effects of Video-Game Ownership on Young Boys' Academic and Behavioral Functioning," *Psychological Science*, February 2010.

Good News!

The odds a child 5–17 will read a book not required for school in a week: **1 in 1.7**

SOURCE: *2008 Kids and Family Reading Report,* conducted by Yankelovich for Scholastic.

"Library Books Due Today!"

The odds are **1 in 3.3** a child 5–17 says he or she loves to read vs. **1 in 11.1** says he or she hates to read.

SOURCE: *2008 Kids and Family Reading Report,* conducted by Yankelovich for Scholastic.

Phone Home

The ownership of cell phones by kids has increased dramatically. The odds a child 6–11 owned a cell phone in 2005 were **1 in 8.4** but rose to **1 in 5** by 2009.

The odds a child 6–11 will use a cell phone:

to call his/her parents . . .	**1 in 1.1**
to call friends	**1 in 1.5**
for emergency purposes . .	**1 in 1.8**
to text message	**1 in 1.9**
to play games	**1 in 2**
to take pictures.	**1 in 2.1**
to listen to music	**1 in 2.9**
for picture messaging. . . .	**1 in 4.1**
to download ringtones . . .	**1 in 6.1**

SOURCE: "Kids' Cell Phone Ownership Has Dramatically Increased in Past Five Years," *MRI American Kids Study 2009*, January 4, 2010.

Bring Back Superman

Kids between 5 and 8 are the most likely to have read a comic book in the past week (**1 in 2.5**). The odds drop to **1 in 4.6** for kids 9–11. But once kids reach mid-adolescence, interest in comic books is rekindled. **1 in 3.3** teenagers age 15–17 will read one in a week.

SOURCE: *2008 Kids and Family Reading Report,* conducted by Yankelovich for Scholastic.

GENDER WARS

By the time kids are in their teens, girls are far less likely than boys to be hooked on **video games**: the odds are **1 in 25** a teenage girl 13–17 will typically play them after school compared to **1 in 5.3** for a teenage boy.

SOURCE: L Lyons, "What Teens Are Doing After School," Gallup, April 19, 2005.

Medication

The odds a child took prescription medication regularly for at least 3 months in the past year:

Age 5–17 diagnosed with a learning disability . . . . **1 in 3**

Age 5–17 without a learning disability . . . . **1 in 10.8**

Age 5–17 diagnosed with ADHD . . . . **1 in 2**

Age 5–17 without ADHD . . . . **1 in 11.6**

Condition	%
With learning disability	34
Without learning disability	9
With ADHD	51
Without ADHD	9

SOURCE: GA Simpson, G Scott, RW Manderscheid, MJ Henderson, *Mental Health, United States, 2002,* US Department of Health and Human Services, Center for Mental Health Services, 2002.

Depression and Learning Difficulties

The odds a child 5–17 is unhappy, sad, or depressed: **1 in 27**

The odds a child 5–17 will have contact with a mental health professional: **1 in 15.4**

The odds for a child:
With ADHD: **1 in 6.9**
With a learning disability: **1 in 8.3**

The odds for a child:
With ADHD: **1 in 2.7**
With a learning disability: **1 in 3.7**

SOURCE: GA Simpson, G Scott, RW Manderscheid, MJ Henderson, *Mental Health, United States, 2002,* US Department of Health and Human Services, Center for Mental Health Services, 2002.

"It's not just Kris that's on trial, it's everything he stands for. It's kindness and joy and love and all the other intangibles."

— *From the defense of Santa Claus in* Miracle on 34th Street *(1947)*

The odds an adult believed in Santa Claus as a child are **1 in 1.16**.

The odds a girl 6–11 will hope to receive dolls or doll accessories for the holidays are **1 in 1.83**.

The odds a boy 6–11 will hope to receive sports equipment or outdoor toys for the holidays are **1 in 1.85**.

SOURCES: *Miracle on 34th Street* (1947), Screenplay by George Seaton, 20th Century–Fox. ✎ *Results of AP-AOL News Poll on Angels,* Associated Press, December 23, 2006. ✎ N Zwiers, *State of the Industry: A Kid's Eye View!,* KidzEyes/Funosophy, 2005.

GENDER WARS

The odds a boy 3–17 has been diagnosed with attention deficit hyperactivity disorder (ADHD): **1 in 8.5** vs. **1 in 18.9** for a girl.

SOURCE: "Summary Health Statistics for U.S. Children: National Health Interview Survey, 2009," *Vital and Health Statistics,* 10(247), August 2010.

Go, Team, Go!

The odds a child plays a team sport at:

6: **1 in 2.3**

7: **1 in 1.8**

8: **1 in 1.9**

9: **1 in 1.9**

10: **1 in 1.8**

11: **1 in 1.7**

12: **1 in 1.6**

13: **1 in 1.7**

SOURCE: Sporting Goods Manufacturers Association *Trends in Team Sports 2009,* February 2009.

GENDER WARS

The odds a boy 5–17 will receive special education in a year: **1 in 11.8** vs. **1 in 22.2** for a girl.

SOURCE: GA Simpson, G Scott, RW Manderscheid, MJ Henderson, *Mental Health, United States, 2002,* US Department of Health and Human Services, Center for Mental Health Services, 2002.

Bullied at School: Why They Read *Lord of the Flies*

Over the Course of a Year, Bullying Is Common Across All Grade Levels

Grade	Odds (1 in)	Same Odds That
Sixth	2.3	A person is younger than 31
Seventh	2.8	A person lives in the South
Eighth	2.7	An adult is overweight
Ninth	3.3	A person 15 or older has never been married
Tenth	3.5	An adult sleeps 6 hours or less on average
Eleventh	3.4	A person 15 or older has only a high school diploma
Twelfth	4.3	An adult will watch an NBA game on TV in a year

Associated Events Can Last Long Past Graduation

Between the ages of 13 and 24, the odds are:

1 in 4.2 females who were bullied by other children at age 8 will be treated with antidepressants.

1 in 8.1 females who were bullied by other children at age 8 will be treated with a psychiatric hospital stay.

1 in 8.1 males who were bullied by other children at age 8 will be treated with antidepressants.

1 in 9.6 males who were bullied by other children at age 8 will be treated with a psychiatric hospital stay.

For Some Bullies as Well

Between the ages of 13 and 24, the odds are:

1 in 6.6 males who bullied other children at age 8 will be treated with antidepressants.

1 in 11.6 males who bullied other children at age 8 will be treated with a psychiatric hospital stay.

SOURCES: R Dinkes, J Kemp, K Baum, *Indicators of School Crime and Safety: 2008* (NCES 2009–022/NCJ 226343). National Center for Education Statistics, Institute of Education Sciences, US Department of Education, and Bureau of Justice Statistics, Office of Justice Programs, US Department of Justice, Washington, DC. ✗ Book of Odds estimates based on US Census Bureau, Population Estimates Program, http://www.census.gov/popest/estimates.php. ✗ Centers for Disease Control and Prevention, Behavioral Risk Factor Surveillance System, http://apps.nccd.cdc.gov/brfss/. ✗ US Census Bureau, *Age and Sex in the United States: 2008*, http://www.census.gov/population/www/socdemo/age/age_sex_2009.html. ✗ PF Adams, CA Schoenborn, "Health Behaviors of Adults: United States 2002–04," *Vital and Health Statistics* 10(230), 2006. ✗ National Sporting Goods Association/NSGA and SBRnet. ✗ A Sourander, J Ronning, A Brunstein-Klomeck, D Gyllenberg, K Kumpulainen, S Niemela, et al., "Childhood Bullying Behavior and Later Psychiatric Hospital and Psychopharmacologic Treatment: Findings from the Finnish 1981 Birth Cohort Study," *Archives of General Psychiatry* 66(9), 2009:1005–1012.

 **ODDS COUPLE: Dark Days**

The odds a student 12–18 will be bullied at school in a year . . . . **1 in 3.1**

The odds a February day in Washington, DC, will be rainy. . . . . **1 in 3.1**

SOURCES: R Dinkes, J Kemp, K Baum, *Indicators of School Crime and Safety: 2008* (NCES 2009–022/NCJ 226343). National Center for Education Statistics, Institute of Education Sciences, US Department of Education, and Bureau of Justice Statistics, Office of Justice Programs, US Department of Justice, Washington, DC. ✗ Weatherbase. http://www.weatherbase.com/weather/state.php3?c=US&s=&refer=.

Who Gets Hit at School?

The odds a student will receive corporal punishment at school in a year: **1 in 217**

The odds a student will receive corporal punishment at school in a year differ by race and ethnic background:

Non-Hispanic black male . . . . **1 in 72.8**

Non-Hispanic black female . . . . **1 in 189**

Non-Hispanic white male. . . . . **1 in 144**

Non-Hispanic white female . . . . **1 in 617**

Hispanic male . . . . **1 in 356**

Hispanic female . . . . **1 in 1,111**

Student Race/Ethnic Group	%
Non-Hispanic black male	1
Non-Hispanic black female	1
Non-Hispanic white male	1
Non-Hispanic white female	<0.5
Hispanic male	<0.5
Hispanic female	<0.5

SOURCE: Office For Civil Rights, *2006 Civil Rights Data Collection*, http://ocrdata.ed .gov/Projections_2006.aspx.

Out Sick— or Hurt

The odds a child 5–17 will miss school due to illness or injury in a year:

1–2 days:
1 in 3.6

3–5 days:
1 in 3.5

6–10 days:
1 in 8.6

At least 11 days:
1 in 20.4

A whole year:
1 in 143

SOURCE: EJ Sondik, JH Madans, JF Gentleman, "Summary Health Statistics for US Children: National Health Interview Survey, 2009," *Vital and Health Statistics* 10(247), August 2010.

"Pizza Party at School! — 6 p.m. in the Cafeteria"

The odds a child 5–17 will not stay home from school in a year because of illness or injury:

1 in 3.9

SOURCE: EJ Sondik, JH Madans, JF Gentleman, "Summary Health Statistics for US Children: National Health Interview Survey, 2009," *Vital and Health Statistics* 10(247), August 2010.

Weekly Planner:
Kids, Stress, and After–School Activities

Scout meeting:
1 in 11.9 K–second graders and **1 in 7.9** third–fifth graders participate in Scouts.

Bring doughnuts for Sunday School:
1 in 7.1 K–second graders, **1 in 5.1** third–fifth graders, and **1 in 4.6** sixth–eighth graders participates in after-school religious activities.

Walk for good cause:
1 in 14.3 third–fifth graders and **1 in 7.3** sixth–eighth graders participate in after-school volunteer work or community service.

Drive to medical office:
The odds a child 5–17 will have contact with a mental health professional in a year: **1 in 15.4**

SOURCES: Book of Odds estimates based on data from PR Carver, IU Iruka, *After-School Programs and Activities: 2005* (NCES 2006– 076). Washington, DC: National Center for Education Statistics 2006. ✗ GA Simpson, G Scott, RW Manderscheid, MJ Henderson, *Mental Health, United States, 2002,* US Department of Health and Human Services, Center for Mental Health Services, 2002.

Be Careful at Recess!

The odds a child younger than 15 will visit an emergency room due to an injury involving playground equipment in a year: **1 in 270**

SOURCE: Book of Odds estimates based on US Consumer Product Safety Commission, *National Electronic Injury Surveillance System (NEISS) Data Highlights 2010.*

Dangers Around the House

The odds a child younger than 15 will visit an emergency room due to an accident involving...

stairs, ramps, or landings in a year: **1 in 116**

a bed, mattress, or pillow in a year: **1 in 225**

a chair or sofa in a year: **1 in 265**

toys in a year: **1 in 345**

a table in a year: **1 in 366**

a nonglass door in a year: **1 in 475**

a desk, shelf, cabinet, or rack in a year: **1 in 570**

nursery equipment in a year: **1 in 716**

a bathroom structure or fixtures in a year: **1 in 859**

clothing in a year: **1 in 1,029**

cans or containers in a year: **1 in 1,124**

jewelry in a year: **1 in 1,365**

a carpet or rug in a year: **1 in 1,746**

a glass door, window, or panel in a year: **1 in 1,813**

a television set or stand in a year: **1 in 2,184**

a ladder or stool in a year: **1 in 2,324**

a grooming device in a year: **1 in 3,639**

a cooking range or oven in a year: **1 in 3,881**

an electric lamp or fixture in a year: **1 in 4,213**

a handrail, railing, or banister in a year: **1 in 4,250**

nonsoap cleaning agents in a year: **1 in 4,528**

soaps or detergents in a year: **1 in 5,451**

Household Fixture/Item	%	Rate/100,000	Household Fixture/Item	%	Rate/100,000
Stairs, ramps, or landings	0.8	861.3	Jewelry	0.07	73.3
Bed, mattress, or pillow	0.4	443.6	Carpet or rug	0.06	57.3
Chair or sofa	0.4	377.8	Glass door, window, or panel	0.05	55.1
Toys	0.3	289.5	TV set or stand	0.05	45.8
Table	0.3	298.0	Ladder or stool	0.04	43.0
Nonglass door	0.2	210.7	Grooming device	0.03	27.5
Desk, shelf, cabinet, or rack	0.2	175.6	Cooking range or oven	0.02	25.8
Nursery equipment	0.1	139.6	Electric lamp or fixture	0.02	23.7
Bathroom structure or fixture	0.1	116.4	Handrail, railing, or banister	0.02	23.5
Clothing	0.09	97.2	Nonsoap cleaning agents	0.02	22.1
Cans or containers	0.09	89.0	Soaps or detergents	0.02	18.3

SOURCE: Book of Odds estimates based on US Consumer Product Safety Commission, *National Electronic Injury Surveillance System (NEISS) Data Highlights 2010.*

No Surprise to Parents of Boys

The odds a boy will suffer a fracture in a year . . . . **1 in 12.5**

The odds for a girl. . . . . **1 in 26.3**

The odds a boy will suffer a contusion in a year. . . . . **1 in 33.3**

The odds for a girl. . . . . **1 in 40**

The odds a boy will suffer a dislocation in a year. . . . . **1 in 83.3**

The odds for a girl. . . . . **1 in 167**

However, girls are more likely than boys to have a sprain or strain in a year:
1 in 19.6 vs. **1 in 22.7** for boys.

SOURCE: United States Bone and Joint Decade, *The Burden of Musculoskeletal Diseases in the United States*, Rosemont, IL: American Academy of Orthopedic Surgeons, 2008.

Fatal Car Accidents

The odds a child under 5 will be injured while riding in a car in a year . . **1 in 450**

The odds a child 5–9 will be injured while riding in a car in a year . . . . . **1 in 341**

The odds a child 10–15 will be injured while riding in a car in a year . . . **1 in 250**

The odds a child under 5 will be killed while riding in a car in a year . . . **1 in 49,505**

The odds a child 5–9 will be killed while riding in a car in a year . . . . . . **1 in 54,348**

The odds a child 10–15 will be killed while riding in a car in a year. . . . . **1 in 33,133**

SOURCE: National Highway Traffic Safety Administration, National Center for Statistics and Analysis, *Traffic Safety Facts 2009: A Compilation of Motor Vehicle Crash Data from the Fatality Analysis Reporting System and the General Estimates System.*

Food Allergies in Children Younger than 3

The odds a child younger than 3 is allergic to milk . . . . **1 in 40**

The odds a child younger than 3 is allergic to eggs. . . . . **1 in 76.9**

The odds a child younger than 3 is allergic to peanuts. . . . . **1 in 125**

The odds a child younger than 3 is allergic to tree nuts . . . . **1 in 500**

The odds a child younger than 3 is allergic to fish. . . . . **1 in 1,000**

The odds a child younger than 3 is allergic to shellfish. . . . . **1 in 1,000**

Allergy	%
Milk	2.5
Eggs	1.3
Peanuts	0.8
Tree nuts	0.2
Fish	0.1
Shellfish	0.1

SOURCE: HA Sampson, "Update on Food Allergy," *Journal of Allergy and Clinical Immunology* 113, 2004:805–819.

The odds a child younger than 15 will have his or her tonsils removed in a year: **1 in 114**

SOURCE: KA Cullen, MJ Hall, A Golosinkiy, "National Ambulatory Surgery in the US, 2006," *National Health Statistics Reports* (11), September 4, 2009: 11–28.

The odds a child younger than 15 will be hospitalized for appendicitis in a year: **1 in 997**

SOURCE: JE Everhart, ed. *The Burden of Digestive Diseases in the United States* (NIH Publication No. 09–6443). US Department of Health and Human Services, Public Health Service, National Institutes of Health, National Institute of Diabetes and Digestive and Kidney Diseases. Washington, DC: US Government Printing Office, 2008.

Children and Cancer:
Most Common Forms by Age

Over the past twenty-five years, the incidence of children diagnosed with all forms of invasive cancer has increased from 11.5 cases per 100,000 children in 1975, to 14.8 per 100,000 children in 2004 to an average of 15.4 per 100,000 children 0–14 in 2005 to 2009. Cancer is the leading cause of death by disease for children under 15, but is still relatively rare.

Leukemias (blood cell cancers) and, in particular, acute lymphocytic leukemia as well of cancers of the brain and nervous system, account for about half of new cases. The most common solid tumors are brain tumors such as glomas and medulloblastomas.

The causes of childhood cancers are largely unknown. A small percentage of cases can be explained by chromosomal and genetic abnormalities and ionizing radiation exposure. Environmental causes have been suspected but causality is difficult to establish due to the overall low incidence.

As one can observe in the odds by age, the overall incidence is dependent on the incidence of leukemia, which declines by age, reaching its minimum level at age 9 (**1 in 9,259**). As children get older, other types of cancer increase in importance, causing the overall rate to increase again, and by age 17 the incidence odds are greater than for a 1-year-old (**1 in 4,505** versus **1 in 4,739**).

The Odds a Child Will Be Diagnosed with Cancer in a Year

Age	%	Rate/100,000	Odds (1 in)
1	0.02	21.1	4,739
2	0.02	22.2	4,505
3	0.02	20.5	4,878
4	0.02	17.6	5,682
5	0.01	13.2	7,576
6	0.01	12.6	7,937
7	0.01	11.7	8,547
8	0.01	10.7	9,346
9	0.01	10.8	9,259
10	0.01	11.2	8,929
11	0.01	12.9	7,752
12	0.01	13.1	7,634
13	0.01	14.6	6,849
14	0.02	17.1	5,846
15	0.02	18.9	5,291
16	0.02	20.0	5,000
17	0.02	22.2	4,505

The Odds of Being Overweight or Obese by Age

Gender, Age	Overweight		Obese	
	%	Odds (1 in)	%	Odds (1 in)
All, 2–5	21	4.7	10	9.6
Boys, 2–5	21	4.8	10	10.0
Girls, 2–5	21	4.7	11	9.4
All, 6–11	36	2.8	20	5.1
Boys, 6–11	36	2.8	21	4.7
Girls, 6–11	35	2.8	18	5.6

SOURCE: CC Ogden, MD Carroll, LR Curtin, MM Lamb, KM Flegal, "Prevalence of High Body Mass Index in US Children and Adolescents, 2007–2008." *JAMA*; 303(3), 2010: 242–249.

The Odds of Childhood Cancer by Type

Age 1	%	Rate/100,000	Odds (1 in)
Leukemia	0.01	6.2	**16,129**
Acute lymphocytic leukemia	0.004	4.3	**23,256**
Brain cancer	0.004	4.5	**22,222**
Kidney cancer	0.002	2.2	**45,555**
Soft tissue cancer	0.002	1.8	**55,556**
Cancer of the eye or orbit	0.002	1.5	**66,667**
Age 5			
Leukemia	0.005	4.9	**20,408**
Acute lymphocytic leukemia	0.004	4.3	**23,256**
Brain cancer	0.004	3.7	**27,027**
Kidney cancer	0.001	1.0	**100,000**
Non-Hodgkin lymphoma	0.001	1.1	**100,000**
Soft tissue cancer	0.001	0.7	**142,867**
Age 10			
Leukemia	0.003	3.1	**32,258**
Acute lymphocytic leukemia	0.003	2.3	**43,478**
Brain cancer	0.002	2.4	**41,667**
Non-Hodgkin lymphoma	0.001	1.0	**100,000**
Bone or joint cancer	0.001	1.0	**100,000**
Soft tissue cancer	0.001	0.8	**125,000**
Age 15			
Leukemia	0.003	3.3	**30,303**
Acute lymphocytic leukemia	0.002	2.1	**47,619**
Hodgkin lymphoma	0.003	2.5	**40,000**
Brain cancer	0.002	2.2	**45,455**
Bone or joint cancer	0.002	2.1	**47,619**
Non-Hodgkin lymphoma	0.002	2.0	**50,000**

SOURCES: National Cancer Institute, Childhood Cancers Fact Sheet. ✎ N Howlader, AM Noone, M Krapcho, N Neyman, R Aminou, W Waldron, et al., eds., *SEER Cancer Statistics Review, 1975–2009 (Vintage 2009 Populations)*, based on November 2011 SEER data submission, posted to the SEER website, April 2012, http://seer.cancer.gov/csr/1975_2009_pops09/.

Diabetes: The Odds Rise with Age

At one time the term "juvenile diabetes" referred to Type I diabetes, which results from lack of sufficient production of insulin by the pancreas, and the odds of developing it were low. Type II diabetes, or insulin resistance, typically developed in middle age. Now that being obese and overweight has increased so much among children, Type II diabetes is also increasing:

Younger than 5: **1 in 3,226**   5–9: **1 in 800**   10–14: **1 in 437**   15–19: **1 in 299**

SOURCE: SEARCH for Diabetes in Youth Study Group, "The Burden of Diabetes Mellitus Among US Youth: Prevalence Estimates from the SEARCH for Diabetes in Youth Study," *Pediatrics* 118, 2006: 1510–1518.

CHAPTER 6

HIGH SCHOOL AND COLLEGE

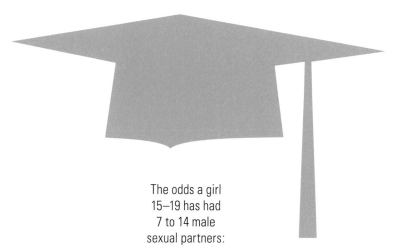

The odds a girl
15–19 has had
7 to 14 male
sexual partners:
1 in 28.4

SOURCE: Book of Odds
estimate based on
Centers for Disease
Control and Prevention,
*National Survey
of Family Growth
2006–2008,* Public Use
Data Files.

High School Means
Spending Most of
Your Time in an
Institution

The odds a person is enrolled in school:

Age 14–15

1 in 1.02

Age 16–17

1 in 1.04

Age 18–19

1 in 1.4

SOURCE: TD Snyder, SA Dillow, *Digest of Education Statistics 2011* (NCES 20121-001). Washington, DC: National Center for Education Statistics, 2012.

Most Kids Go to Public School

The odds a high school student younger than 18 attends an assigned public school . . . .**1 in 1.4**

The odds a high school student younger than 18 attends a chosen public school . . . .**1 in 6.3**

Some Go Private

The odds a high school student younger than 18 attends a private school . . . .**1 in 9.5**

Some Elect Charter

The odds a high school student in ninth–twelfth grades attends a charter school . . . .**1 in 100**

Some Stay Home

The odds a high school student in ninth–twelfth grades is homeschooled. . . . .**1 in 35.7**

SOURCES: TD Snyder, SA Dillow, *Digest of Education Statistics 2009* (NCES 2010–13). Washington, DC: National Center for Education Statistics, 2010. ✔ S Grady, S Bielick, *Trends in the Use of School Choice: 1993 to 2007* (NCES 2010-004). Washington, DC: National Center for Education Statistics, 2010.

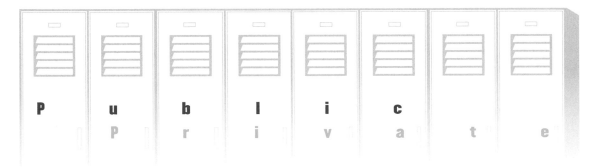

Comparison of Grades for
Public and Private High School Students

The odds a **public** secondary school student receives:

mostly As	**1 in 2.6**
mostly Bs	**1 in 2.6**
mostly Cs	**1 in 5.8**
mostly Ds or Fs	**1 in 19.2**

The odds a private secondary school student receives:

mostly As	1 in 2
mostly Bs	1 in 2.7
mostly Cs	1 in 10.2
mostly Ds or Fs	1 in 83.3

SOURCE: TD Snyder, SA Dillow, *Digest of Education Statistics 2009* (NCES 2010–2013). Washington, DC: National Center for Education Statistics, 2010.

Not Everybody Deserves
A Good Grade

The odds a high school student will copy another student's homework at least once in a year:

Female student: **1 in 1.2**

Male student: **1 in 1.3**

The odds a high school student will cheat on a test in a year:

Female: **1 in 1.7**

Male: **1 in 1.7**

SOURCE: Josephson Institute, *2010 Report Card on the Ethics of American Youth*, 2011.

Not Done
When the Bell Rings

The odds a student 13–17 typically does homework between school and dinnertime:

SOURCE: L Lyons, "What Teens Are Doing After School," Gallup, April 19, 2005.

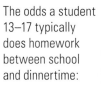

1 in 2.3

School Violence

The odds a school will use **metal detectors** for security:

Type of School	Daily for All Students	Random Checks on Students
Middle school	**1 in 66.7**	**1 in 10.6**
High school	**1 in 20.8**	**1 in 8.3**
Schools with < 300 students	**1 in 111**	**1 in 35.71**
Schools with 300–499 students	**1 in 100**	**1 in 25.6**
Schools with 500–999 students	**1 in 90.9**	**1 in 19.2**
Schools with 1,000 or more students	**1 in 25**	**1 in 7.4**

SOURCE: S Robers, J Zhang, J Truman, T Snyder, *Indicators of School Crime and Safety: 2011* (NCES 2012-002/NCJ 236021). Washington, DC: National Center for Education Statistics/Bureau of Justice Statistics.

Girl-on-Girl Violence Is Up

According to the US Department of Justice, the number of teenage girls arrested for aggravated assault in 2003 was nearly double what it had been in 1980; the arrest rate for simple assault was more than triple. The 2011 report from the Youth Risk Behavior Surveillance System shows that during 2010–2011, **33%** of black female high school students got into a physical fight, as did **27%** of Hispanic and **20%** of white high school girls.

SOURCES: M Zahn, S Brumbaugh, D Steffensmeier, BC Feld, M Morash, M Chesney-Lind, et al., *Violence by Teenage Girls: Trends and Context*, Girls Study Group, Office of Juvenile Justice and Delinquency Prevention, US Department of Justice, May 2008. ✦ DK Eaton, L Kann, S Kinchen, S Shanklin, KH Flint, J Hawkins, et al., "Youth Risk Behavior Surveillance—United States, 2011," *Morbidity and Mortality Weekly Report* 61(4), June 8, 2012.

Fewer Homicides at School

For youth 5–18, the number of homicides at school varies from year to year, but for school years 1992–1993 through 1998–1999, the number ranged from 28 to 34 per year. During the school years 1999–2000 through 2009–2010, the number of homicides ranged from 14 to 30, with an average of 19 per year.

Like airports and courthouses, our schools now have metal detectors (1 in 19.2) and security cameras (1 in 1.6). In a given month, 1 in 6 high school students will carry a weapon into a school, and 1 in 13.5 students will be threatened—or worse, injured—by a weapon brought onto school property. And it is not just students who are at risk. In a given year, 1 in 13.3 teachers will be threatened with injury, and 1 in 25 will be physically attacked by a student.

Have we made things safer, and who is the arbiter of this? These events are rare, variable, but not new. The most devastating school massacre was in 1927, when a mad bomber named Andrew Philip Kehoe killed forty-five people and injured fifty-eight in the Bath Township Consolidated School in Michigan.

SOURCES: S Robers, J Zhang, J Truman, T Snyder, *Indicators of School Crime and Safety: 2011* (NCES 2012-002/NCJ 236021). Washington, DC: National Center for Education Statistics/Bureau of Justice Statistics. ✗ MJ Ellsworth, *The Bath School Disaster*, 1927. ✗ J Barron, "Children Were All Shot Multiple Times with a Semiautomatic, Officials Say," *New York Times*, December 15, 2012.

 Numbers Tell the Story

Party Crashers

The buy:
The odds a high school student who drinks will buy alcohol in a store in a month: 1 in 19.2

The party:
The odds a high school senior will binge drink in a month: 1 in 3.2

The driver:
The odds a twelfth grade male will drive drunk in a month: 1 in 6.3

His buddy rides shotgun:
The odds a high school senior will be the passenger of a drunk driver in a month: 1 in 3.6

A telephone pole:
The odds a male licensed driver 16–20 will be involved in a motor vehicle accident in a year: 1 in 9.2

His buddy is killed:
The odds a person 16–20 will be killed in a motor vehicle accident in a year: 1 in 5,531

He might have been saved:
The odds a passenger 16–20 killed in a motor vehicle accident was not wearing a seat belt: 1 in 1.8

The breathalyzer:
The odds a driver 16–20 involved in a fatal motor vehicle accident had a blood alcohol content of 0.08 or higher: 1 in 5.3

The arrest:
The odds an arrest of a person younger than 18 will be for driving under the influence: 1 in 142

SOURCES: DK Eaton, L Kann, S Kinchen, S Shanklin, J Ross, J Hawkins, et al., "Youth Risk Behavior Surveillance—United States, 2007," *Morbidity and Mortality Weekly Report* 57(SS-4). ✗ DK Eaton, L Kann, S Kinchen, S Shanklin, KH Flint, J Hawkins, et al., "Youth Risk Behavior Surveillance—United States, 2011," *Morbidity and Mortality Weekly Report* 61(4), June 8, 2012. ✗ National Highway Traffic Safety Administration, National Center for Statistics and Analysis, Fatality Analysis Reporting System. ✗ National Highway Traffic Safety Administration, National Center for Statistics and Analysis, US Department of Transportation, *Traffic Safety Facts 2008*. ✗ National Highway Traffic Safety Administration, National Center for Statistics and Analysis, US Department of Transportation, *Traffic Safety Facts 2009*. ✗ Federal Bureau of Investigation, US Department of Justice, *Crime in the United States, 2009*.

Use of Drugs, Alcohol, and Cigarettes

for High School Students by Gender

The odds a female high school student has ever had alcohol . . . . **1 in 1.4**
The odds a male high school student has ever had alcohol . . . . **1 in 1.4**

The odds a female high school student has ever smoked a cigarette . . . . **1 in 2.3**
The odds a male high school student has ever smoked a cigarette . . . . **1 in 2.2**

The odds a female high school student has ever used marijuana . . . . **1 in 2.7**
The odds a male high school student has ever used marijuana . . . . **1 in 2.4**

The odds a female high school student has ever used an inhalant . . . . **1 in 8.1**
The odds a male high school student has ever used an inhalant . . . . **1 in 9.5**

The odds a female high school student has ever used a hallucinogenic drug . . . . . . **1 in 17.0**
The odds a male high school student has ever used a hallucinogenic drug . . . . **1 in 8.8**

The odds a female high school student has ever used ecstasy . . . . **1 in 15.4**
The odds a male high school student has ever used ecstasy . . . . **1 in 10.2**

The odds a female high school student has ever used cocaine . . . . **1 in 17.5**
The odds a male high school student has ever used cocaine . . . . **1 in 12.5**

The odds a female high school student has ever used methamphetamines . . . . **1 in 33.3**
The odds a male high school student has ever used methamphetamines . . . . **1 in 22.2**

The odds a female high school student has ever taken nonprescription steroids . . . . . **1 in 34.5**
The odds a male high school student has ever taken nonprescription steroids . . . . . . **1 in 23.8**

The odds a female high school student has ever used heroin . . . . **1 in 55.6**
The odds a male high school student has ever used heroin . . . . **1 in 25.6**

	Boys	Girls
	%	**%**
Alcohol	71	71
A cigarette	46	43
Marijuana	43	37
An inhalant	11	12
A hallucinogenic drug	11	6
Ecstasy	10	7
Cocaine	6	6
Methamphetamines	5	3
Nonprescription steroids	4	3
Heroin	4	2

SOURCE: DK Eaton, L Kann, S Kinchen, S Shanklin, KH Flint, J Hawkins, et al., "Youth Risk Behavior Surveillance—United States, 2011," *Morbidity and Mortality Weekly Report* 61(4), June 8, 2012.

Teens and Risk
Breaking Loose and Breaking Rules

The odds a high school student will **drink alcohol** on school grounds in a month:

Female:
1 in 21.3
Male:
1 in 18.5

The odds a high school student will **smoke marijuana** on school property in a month:

Female:
1 in 24.4
Male:
1 in 13.3

The odds a high school student has ever **injected an illegal drug**:

Female:
1 in 62.5
Male:
1 in 34.5

SOURCE: DK Eaton, L Kann, S Kinchen, S Shanklin, KH Flint, J Hawkins, et al., "Youth Risk Behavior Surveillance—United States, 2011," *Morbidity and Mortality Weekly Report* 61(4), June 8, 2012.

Mind and Body

Extreme Dieting

According to the National Institute of Mental Health, in their lifetime, an estimated 0.6% of the US population will suffer from anorexia and 1% from bulimia. Teenagers are particularly at risk. The odds of being overweight are similar for both male and female high school students: **1 in 6.6** and **1 in 6.5**, respectively. However, **1 in 3.2** high school boys and **1 in 1.6** high school girls will try to lose weight in a year.

In the course of a month, the odds a male twelfth grader will vomit or take laxatives to lose weight or keep from gaining weight are **1 in 40**; for a male ninth grader, the odds are **1 in 41.7**.

It is not surprising that the numbers are significantly higher for their female counterparts. The odds a female twelfth grader will vomit or take laxatives in a month in order to lose weight or maintain her weight are **1 in 15.6**. For a female ninth grader, the numbers are an alarming **1 in 16.9**.

SOURCE: DK Eaton, L Kann, S Kinchen, S Shanklin, KH Flint, J Hawkins, et al., "Youth Risk Behavior Surveillance—United States, 2011," *Morbidity and Mortality Weekly Report* 61(4), June 8, 2012.

The odds a high school student will be physically active at least 60 minutes a day on 5 or more days a week: **1 in 2.0**

SOURCE: DK Eaton, L Kann, S Kinchen, S Shanklin, KH Flint, J Hawkins, et al., "Youth Risk Behavior Surveillance—United States, 2011," *Morbidity and Mortality Weekly Report*, 61(4), June 8, 2012.

The odds a male high school student is obese: **1 in 6.2**

The odds a female high school student is obese: **1 in 10.2**

Gym Class

The odds a high school student has a physical education class every day: **1 in 3.2**; at least once a week: **1 in 1.9**.

SOURCE: DK Eaton, L Kann, S Kinchen, S Shanklin, KH Flint, J Hawkins, et al., "Youth Risk Behavior Surveillance—United States, 2011," *Morbidity and Mortality Weekly Report* 61(4), June 8, 2012.

In the course of a month, the odds a high school student will fast for at least 24 hours to lose weight or keep from gaining weight: **1 in 13.9** for boys and **1 in 5.7** for girls.

SOURCE: DK Eaton, L Kann, S Kinchen, S Shanklin, KH Flint, J Hawkins, et al., "Youth Risk Behavior Surveillance—United States, 2011," *Morbidity and Mortality Weekly Report* 61(4), June 8, 2012.

Teens and Cosmetic Surgery

During 2009, 209,553 cosmetic procedures were performed on US teenagers. Teens accounted for **1 in 57.5** cosmetic procedures performed that year. Some of the most common procedures were laser hair removal, skin treatments including microdermabrasion and laser skin resurfacing, laser treatment of leg veins, and Botox injections. The odds a cosmetic procedure performed on someone 13–19 will require surgery are **1 in 2.8**.

According to the American Society of Plastic Surgeons, by far the most common surgery (34,994) performed in 2009 on people under the age of 18 was rhinoplasty, a reshaping of the nose, and the second most common was breast reduction (12,908). Third most common was breast augmentation (8,199) and fourth was ear surgery (7,909).

SOURCE: National Clearinghouse of Plastic Surgery Statistics, American Society of Plastic Surgeons, *2010 Report of the 2009 Statistics.*

Teen Suicide

Suicide is the third leading cause of death among kids and young adults between the ages of 10 and 24, according to the CDC. In a given year, **1 in 14,599** teenagers between the ages of 15 and 19 will take his or her own life. Teenage boys are more than four times more likely (**1 in 9,062**) to take their own lives than teenage girls (**1 in 44,220**).

But for every teenager who commits suicide, thousands of others have suicidal thoughts, and many go so far as to make unsuccessful attempts. The odds a high school student will seriously consider attempting suicide in a year are **1 in 6.3**; the odds a high school student will make a suicide plan in a year are **1 in 7.8**; the odds a student will attempt suicide in a year are **1 in 12.8**; and the odds a high school student will attempt suicide and require treatment by a doctor or nurse are **1 in 41.7**.

Although boys are far more likely to succeed in ending their own lives, more girls make the attempt. **1 in 10.2** female high school students try to kill themselves each year compared to **1 in 17.3** of their male peers.

SOURCES: Centers for Disease Control and Prevention, *2007 United States, Suicide Injury Deaths and Rates per 100,000 WISQARS Fatal Injuries: Mortality Reports,* http://webappa.cdc.gov/. ↗ DK Eaton, L Kann, S Kinchen, S Shanklin, KH Flint, J Hawkins, et al., "Youth Risk Behavior Surveillance—United States, 2011," *Morbidity and Mortality Weekly Report* 61(4), June 8, 2012.

The odds a high school student will feel sad or hopeless for two or more weeks in a year: **1 in 3.5**

SOURCE: DK Eaton, L Kann, S Kinchen, S Shanklin, KH Flint, J Hawkins, et al., "Youth Risk Behavior Surveillance—United States, 2011," *Morbidity and Mortality Weekly Report* 61(4), June 8, 2012.

"Limo Comes at Six"

A 2010 Liberty Mutual/Students Against Drunk Driving survey found that 90% of eleventh and twelfth graders believed their friends were more likely to drive drunk on prom night. In a given month the odds are **1 in 8.8** that a junior in high school will drive drunk—and those odds jump to **1 in 6.5** for seniors.

SOURCES: Community Anti-Drug Coalitions of America, "Study Shows 90 Percent of Teens Admit Stronger Likelihood of Drinking and Driving on Prom Night," April 21, 2010, http://www.cadca.org/resources/detail/study-shows-90-percent-teens-admit-stronger-likelihood-drinking-and-driving-prom-night. ↗ DK Eaton, L Kann, S Kinchen, S Shanklin, J Ross, J Hawkins, et al., "Youth Risk Behavior Surveillance—United States, 2009," *Morbidity and Mortality Weekly Report* 59(SS-5), June 4, 2010.

Hard Heads

The odds a female high school student rarely or never wears a seat belt as a passenger: **1 in 15.9**

The odds a male high school student rarely or never wears a seat belt as a passenger: **1 in 11.2**

The odds a high school student who rides a bike rarely or never wears a helmet: **1 in 1.1**

The odds a high school student who rides a motorcycle rarely or never wears a helmet: **1 in 3.1**

SOURCES: DK Eaton, L Kann, S Kinchen, S Shanklin, KH Flint, J Hawkins, et al., "Youth Risk Behavior Surveillance—United States, 2011," *Morbidity and Mortality Weekly Report* 61(4), June 8, 2012. ↗ DK Eaton, L Kann, S Kinchen, S Shanklin, J Ross, J Hawkins, et al., "Youth Risk Behavior Surveillance—United States, 2009," *Morbidity and Mortality Weekly Report* 59(SS-5), June 4, 2010.

Pimples?
Everybody Gets Them

The odds a person 15–24 will have acne vulgaris: **1 in 1.2**

SOURCE: Agency for Healthcare Research and Quality, "Management of Acne: Summary," *Evidence Report/Technology Assessment* 17 (AHRQ Publication No. 01-E018), March 2001, http://www.ahrq.gov/clinic/epcsums/acnesum.htm.

Teens and Sex:

Boys Get Head Start But Girls Catch Up Fast

Ever Had Sex?

The odds a high school student has ever had sexual intercourse:

Ninth Graders: **1 in 2.6** teenage boys vs. **1 in 3.6** teenage girls

Tenth Graders: **1 in 2.2** teenage boys vs. **1 in 2.3** teenage girls

Eleventh Graders: **1 in 1.8** teenage boys vs. **1 in 1.9** teenage girls

Twelfth Graders: **1 in 1.6** teenage boys vs. **1 in 1.6** teenage girls

High School Grade	Teenage Boys Ever Had Sex %	Teenage Girls Ever Had Sex %
Ninth	38	28
Tenth	45	43
Eleventh	55	52
Twelfth	63	64

SOURCE: DK Eaton, L Kann, S Kinchen, S Shanklin, KH Flint, J Hawkins, et al., "Youth Risk Behavior Surveillance—United States, 2011," *Morbidity and Mortality Weekly Report* 61(4), June 8, 2012.

GENDER WARS

The odds a male high school student first had sexual intercourse before age 13 are **1 in 11.1** vs. **1 in 29.4** for a female high school student.

SOURCE: DK Eaton, L Kann, S Kinchen, S Shanklin, KH Flint, J Hawkins, et al., "Youth Risk Behavior Surveillance—United States, 2011," *Morbidity and Mortality Weekly Report* 61(4), June 8, 2012.

Never Been Kissed

The odds a teenage girl 13–17 has never been kissed: **1 in 2.5**

The odds a teenage boy 13–17 has never been kissed: **1 in 2.9**

SOURCE: "The Sex Life of American Teens: A Battle of Restraint vs. Impulse," press release, *ABC News Poll: Teens and Sex*, May 18, 2006.

Going Steady

The odds a teenage boy has a girlfriend or boyfriend:

Age 13–14 . . . . **1 in 2.9**

Age 15–17 . . . . **1 in 2.5**

The odds a teenage girl has a boyfriend or girlfriend:

Age 13–14 . . . . **1 in 3.5**

Age 15–17 . . . . **1 in 2.3**

SOURCE: "The Sex Life of American Teens: A Battle of Restraint vs. Impulse," press release, *ABC News Poll: Teens and Sex*, May 18, 2006.

Sexting Odds by Gender

The odds a teenager 13–19 has ever sent or posted:

	Teenage Boys		Teenage Girls	
	%	Odds (1 in)	%	Odds (1 in)
Sexually suggestive messages	40	**2.5**	37	**2.7**
Nude or seminude pictures or videos of him- or herself	18	**5.6**	22	**4.6**
Sexual content to someone he or she wants to date or hook up with	39	**2.6**	21	**4.8**

SOURCE: The National Campaign to Prevent Teen and Unplanned Pregnancy and Cosmogirl.com, "Sex and Tech: Results from a Survey of Teens and Young Adults," http://www.thenationalcampaign.org/sextech.

The odds a teenage girl 13–19 has ever sent sexually suggestive content to a boyfriend: **1 in 1.4**

The odds a teenage boy 13–19 has ever sent sexually suggestive content to a girlfriend: **1 in 1.5**

SOURCE: The National Campaign to Prevent Teen and Unplanned Pregnancy and Cosmogirl.com, "Sex and Tech: Results from a Survey of Teens and Young Adults," http://www.thenationalcampaign.org/sextech.

Number of Sex Partners
in a Year for Teenagers by Gender, 15–19

The odds a teenage girl 15–19 has never had sex with a male are 1 in 1.7.

The odds a teenage girl 15–19 will have sex with 1 male in a year are 1 in 4.

The odds a teenage girl 15–19 will have sex with 2–3 males in a year are 1 in 9.7.

The odds a teenage girl 15–19 will have sex with 4 or more males in a year are 1 in 30.3.

The odds a teenage boy 15–19 has never had sex with a female are 1 in 1.8.

The odds a teenage boy 15–19 will have sex with 1 female in a year are 1 in 4.8.

The odds a teenage boy 15–19 will have sex with 2–3 females in a year are 1 in 8.3.

The odds a teenage boy 15–19 will have sex with 4 or more females in a year are 1 in 24.4.

Partners	Teenage Boys %	Teenage Girls %
0	57	58
1	22	25
2–3	12	10
4	4	3

SOURCE: JC Abma, GM Martinez, CE Copen, "Teenagers in the United States: Sexual Activity, Contraceptive Use, and Childbearing, National Survey of Family Growth 2006–2008," *Vital and Health Statistics* 23(30), June 2010.

GENDER WARS

The odds a teenage girl 15–19 who has had sex lost her virginity to a male she was going steady with: **1 in 1.4** vs. **1 in 1.8** for a teenage boy 15–19

The odds a teenage girl 15–19 who has had sex lost her virginity to someone she just met or was just friends with: **1 in 7.3** vs **1 in 4** for a teenage boy age 15–19.

SOURCE: JC Abma, GM Martinez, CE Copen, "Teenagers in the United States: Sexual Activity, Contraceptive Use, and Childbearing, National Survey of Family Growth 2006–2008," *Vital and Health Statistics* 23(30), June 2010.

Teens and STDs

Years ago, before anyone without a medical degree had heard of chlamydia, sexually active teens worried about contracting syphilis or gonorrhea. The odds today that a boy 15–19 will be diagnosed with primary or secondary syphilis in a year are 1 in 18,870—and 1 in 33,330 for a girl.

But syphilis is the only STD for which teenage girls face a lower risk than teenage boys. Gonorrhea is far more prevalent, and teenage girls are at a far greater risk. The odds a teenage girl 15–19 will be diagnosed with gonorrhea in a year are 1 in 157 compared to 1 in 359 for teenage boys of the same age. They are also much more likely than teenage boys to have genital herpes: 1 in 43.5 teenage girls 14–19 have it vs. 1 in 111 teenage boys in the same age group. Chlamydia has surged in recent years, with 1.2 million cases reported overall in 2008. The odds of a teenage boy being diagnosed with chlamydia in a year are 1 in 143. The odds for a girl? 1 in 30.5.

The STD most likely to be diagnosed in teenage girls is human papilloma virus (HPV). The odds a teenage girl will be diagnosed with high-risk HPV are 1 in 3.8 and with low-risk HPV, 1 in 4.5.

SOURCES: Centers for Disease Control and Prevention, *Sexually Transmitted Disease Surveillance, 2008*, Atlanta, GA: US Department of Health and Human Services, November 2009. ✎ SM Berman, BJ Kottiri, K Lee, et. al., "Trends in Herpes Simplex Virus Type 1 and Type 2 Seroprevalence in the United States," *JAMA* 296(8), August 23, 2006. ✎ S Hariri, ER Unger, M Sternberg, EF Dunne, D Swan, S Patel, et al., "Prevalence of Genital HPV Among Females in the United States, the National Health and Nutrition Examination Survey, 2003–2006," *Journal of Infectious Diseases*, 204(4), 2011: 566–573.

 **ODDS COUPLE**

Too Many Extracurriculars

The odds a teenage boy 15–19 has had sex with 4 or more females: **1 in 6.4**

The odds an adult has less than a high school diploma: **1 in 6.4**

SOURCES: JC Abma, GM Martinez, CE Copen, "Teenagers in the United States: Sexual Activity, Contraceptive Use, and Childbearing, National Survey of Family Growth 2006–2008," *Vital and Health Statistics* 23(30), June 2010. ✎ Book of Odds estimate based on US Census Bureau, "Table S1501, Educational Attainment by Age," *American Community Survey, 2007.*

GENDER WARS

The odds a female high school student has been tested for HIV: **1 in 6.8** vs. **1 in 8.9** for a male.

SOURCE: DK Eaton, L Kann, S Kinchen, S Shanklin, KH Flint, J Hawkins, et al., "Youth Risk Behavior Surveillance—United States, 2011," *Morbidity and Mortality Weekly Report* 61(4), June 8, 2012.

Contraception Use
Among Sexually Experienced Girls, Age 15–19:

Used a condom: **1 in 1.1**

Withdrawal: **1 in 1.7**

Birth control pills: **1 in 1.8**

Calendar rhythm method: **1 in 6**

Emergency contraception: **1 in 9.4**

SOURCE: JC Abma, GM Martinez, CE Copen, "Teenagers in the United States: Sexual Activity, Contraceptive Use, and Childbearing, National Survey of Family Growth 2006–2008," *Vital and Health Statistics* 23(30), June 2010.

Sexual Maturity

In the 1960s, girls typically entered puberty between ages 10 and 11. Now that age has fallen to between 10 and 10½.

A girl's first menstrual period usually follows the initial signs of puberty by around 2 years. The median age of first menstruation, 12.3 years, has not changed significantly, but the upper range at which it occurs has dropped.

The odds a woman 40–44 reports having her first menstrual period when she was:

15 or older	**1 in 8.2**
15–19.	**1 in 16.4**

SOURCES: A Chandra, GM Martinez, WD Mosher, JC Abma, J Jones, "Fertility, Family Planning, and Reproductive Health of U.S. Women: Data from the 2002 National Survey of Family Growth," *Vital and Health Statistics* 23(25), 2005. ✔ B Kantrowitz, "Coming-of-Age Stories," *Newsweek*, January 28, 2009.

The odds a male 15–22 has had a conversation with his parents about preventing pregnancy: **1 in 1.8**

SOURCE: S Jayson, "Truth About Sex," *USA Today*, January 26, 2010.

ODDS COUPLE
Population Density

The odds a teenage girl 15–19 at risk of unintended pregnancy does not use any form of contraception: **1 in 5.4**

These are the same odds that a person lives in the Northeast

SOURCES: WD Mosher, J Jones, "Use of Contraception in the United States: 1982–2008," *Vital and Health Statistics* 23(29), August 2010. ✔ US Census Bureau, Population Estimates Program, http://www.census.gov/popest/estimates.php.

What Are the Odds My Daughter Will Get
Pregnant on Prom Night?

The odds a female twelfth grade student has ever had sexual intercourse: **1 in 1.6**

Assuming half succumb, the "speculative" odds a teenage girl will have sex on prom night: **1 in 3.1**

The odds she will not use protection: **1 in 4**

The odds she will get pregnant using no protection: **1 in 132**

The odds she will use a condom: **1 in 2.9**

The odds she will get pregnant using a condom: **1 in 3,322**

The odds she's on the pill or other hormonal contraception only: **1 in 5**

The odds she will get pregnant on the pill: **1 in 2,814**

The odds she's on the pill and will use a condom: **1 in 4.8**

The odds she will get pregnant using both the pill and a condom: **1 in 1,019,800**

A nervous parent's speculative odds of a teenage girl getting pregnant when having sex on prom night: **1 in 506**

SOURCES: DK Eaton, L Kann, S Kinchen, S Shanklin, KH Flint, J Hawkins, et al., "Youth Risk Behavior Surveillance—United States, 2011," *Morbidity and Mortality Weekly Report* 61(4), June 8, 2012. ✔ JC Abma, GM Martinez, CE Copen, "Teenagers in the United States: Sexual Activity, Contraceptive Use, and Childbearing, National Survey of Family Growth 2006–2008," *Vital and Health Statistics* 23(30), June 2010. ✔ WD Mosher, J Jones, "Use of Contraception in the United States: 1982–2008," *Vital and Health Statistics* 23(29), August 2010. ✔ K Kost, S Henshaw, L Carlin, *U.S. Teenage Pregnancies, Births and Abortions: National and State Trends and Trends by Race and Ethnicity,* New York: Guttmacher Institute, January 2010. ✔ Book of Odds estimates based on all of the above sources.

The odds a sexually experienced girl 15–19 will become pregnant in a year: **1 in 6.5**

SOURCE: K Kost, S Henshaw, L Carlin, *U.S. Teenage Pregnancies, Births and Abortions: National and State Trends and Trends by Race and Ethnicity*, New York: Guttmacher Institute, January 2010.

Teen Births by State

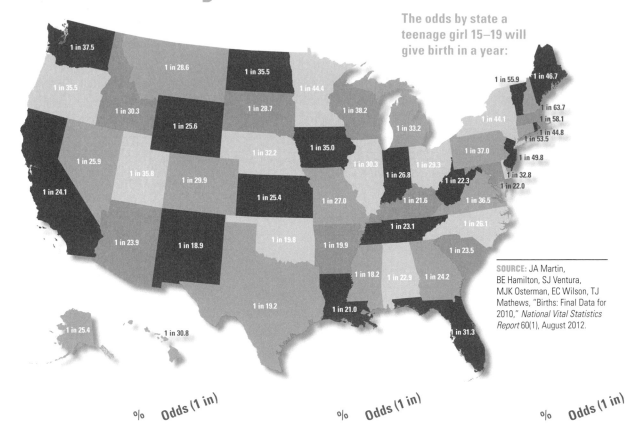

The odds by state a teenage girl 15–19 will give birth in a year:

1 in 37.5
1 in 28.6
1 in 35.5
1 in 44.4
1 in 55.9
1 in 46.7
1 in 35.5
1 in 30.3
1 in 28.7
1 in 38.2
1 in 63.7
1 in 25.6
1 in 33.2
1 in 44.1
1 in 58.1
1 in 25.9
1 in 32.2
1 in 35.0
1 in 30.3
1 in 44.8
1 in 53.5
1 in 35.8
1 in 29.9
1 in 30.3
1 in 29.3
1 in 37.0
1 in 49.8
1 in 24.1
1 in 25.4
1 in 26.8
1 in 22.3
1 in 32.8
1 in 22.0
1 in 27.0
1 in 21.6
1 in 36.5
1 in 23.9
1 in 18.9
1 in 19.8
1 in 19.9
1 in 23.1
1 in 26.1
1 in 23.5
1 in 18.2
1 in 22.9
1 in 24.2
1 in 19.2
1 in 21.0
1 in 31.3
1 in 25.4
1 in 30.8

SOURCE: JA Martin, BE Hamilton, SJ Ventura, MJK Osterman, EC Wilson, TJ Mathews, "Births: Final Data for 2010," *National Vital Statistics Report* 60(1), August 2012.

	%	Odds (1 in)
Alabama	4	22.9
Alaska	4	25.4
Arizona	4	23.9
Arkansas	5	19.9
California	4	24.1
Colorado	3	29.9
Connecticut	2	53.5
Delaware	3	32.8
District of Columbia	5	22.0
Florida	3	31.3
Georgia	4	24.2
Hawaii	3	30.8
Idaho	3	30.3
Illinois	3	30.3
Indiana	4	26.8
Iowa	3	35.0
Kansas	4	25.4

	%	Odds (1 in)
Kentucky	5	21.6
Louisiana	5	21.0
Maine	2	46.7
Maryland	3	36.6
Massachusetts	2	58.1
Michigan	3	33.2
Minnesota	2	44.4
Mississippi	6	18.2
Missouri	4	27.0
Montana	4	28.6
Nebraska	3	32.2
Nevada	4	25.9
New Hampshire	2	63.7
New Jersey	2	49.8
New Mexico	5	18.9
New York	2	44.1
North Carolina	4	26.1

	%	Odds (1 in)
North Dakota	3	35.5
Ohio	4	29.3
Oklahoma	5	19.8
Oregon	3	35.5
Pennsylvania	3	37.0
Rhode Island	2	44.8
South Carolina	4	23.5
South Dakota	3	28.7
Tennessee	4	23.1
Texas	5	19.2
Utah	3	35.8
Vermont	2	55.9
Virginia	3	36.5
Washington	3	37.5
West Virginia	4	22.3
Wisconsin	3	38.2
Wyoming	4	25.6

Teen Attitudes on Pregnancy

The odds a teenage girl 15–17 will report she would be very upset if she got pregnant now are **1 in 1.6**.
The odds a teenage girl 18–19 will report she would be very upset if she got pregnant now are **1 in 1.9**.

The odds a teenage girl 15–17 will report she would be a little upset if she got pregnant now are **1 in 3.4**.
The odds a teenage girl 18–19 will report she would be a little upset if she got pregnant now are **1 in 3.6**.

The odds a teenage girl 15–17 will report she would be a little pleased if she got pregnant now are **1 in 15.4**.
The odds a teenage girl 18–19 will report she would be a little pleased if she got pregnant now are **1 in 8.4**.

The odds a teenage girl 15–17 will report she would be very pleased if she got pregnant now are **1 in 35.7**.
The odds a teenage girl 18–19 will report she would be very pleased if she got pregnant now are **1 in 13.3**.

The odds a teenage boy 15–17 will report he would be very upset if he got a girl pregnant now are **1 in 1.9**.
The odds a teenage boy 18–19 will report he would be very upset if he got a girl pregnant now are **1 in 2.7**.

The odds a teenage boy 15–17 will report he would be a little upset if he got a girl pregnant now are **1 in 3.2**.
The odds a teenage boy 18–19 will report he would be a little upset if he got a girl pregnant now are **1 in 2.6**.

The odds a teenage boy 15–17 will report he would be a little pleased if he got a girl pregnant now are **1 in 9**.
The odds a teenage boy 18–19 will report he would be a little pleased if he got a girl pregnant now are **1 in 5.9**.

The odds a teenage boy 15–17 will report he would be very pleased if he got a girl pregnant now are **1 in 38.5**.
The odds a teenage boy 18–19 will report he would be very pleased if he got a girl pregnant now are **1 in 15.2**.

Feeling	Teenage Boys %	Teenage Girls %
Very Upset		
Age 15–17	54	61
Age 18–19	37	53
A Little Upset		
Age 15–17	31	29
Age 18–19	39	28
A Little Pleased		
Age 15–17	11	7
Age 18–19	17	12
Very Pleased		
Age 15–17	3	3
Age 18–19	7	8

SOURCE: JC Abma, GM Martinez, CE Copen, "Teenagers in the United States: Sexual Activity, Contraceptive Use, and Childbearing, National Survey of Family Growth 2006–2008," *Vital and Health Statistics* 23(30), June 2010.

Strike Up
the Band

Playing an instrument in the school band is a common extracurricular activity. The odds a school musician:

is male: **1 in 1.9**

is female: **1 in 2.1**

plays in a full orchestra: **1 in 1.7**

plays in a marching band: **1 in 3.5**

plays in a jazz band: **1 in 3.8**

plays in a string orchestra: **1 in 9.1**

But school band members engage in other activities as well. The odds a school musician, when not playing his or her instrument, will spend a significant portion of his or her free time:

hanging out with friends: **1 in 1.8**

playing sports: **1 in 2**

watching TV: **1 in 2**

on the computer: **1 in 2.1**

playing video games: **1 in 2.8**

reading: **1 in 4.2**

working a part-time job: **1 in 33.3**

SOURCE: "The 2008 School Musician Survey," *Music Trades Magazine,* July 2008.

The odds a school musician will report that he or she plays an instrument because "it will look good on my college application": **1 in 5**

SOURCE: "The 2008 School Musician Survey," *Music Trades Magazine,* July 2008.

Getting a Job and Getting into College
Education and Income

The odds a family will be in the lowest income 20% if the main breadwinner:

never went to high school: **1 in 2**

has a high school diploma but no higher: **1 in 4.3**

has some college education: **1 in 5.4**

has attained a bachelor's degree or higher: **1 in 16.5**

has a master's degree: **1 in 22.8**

has a professional degree: **1 in 27.5**

has a doctoral degree: **1 in 37.7**

SOURCE: US Census Bureau, *Current Population Survey Annual Social and Economic Supplement,* November 2010.

"GRE exam 9 a.m. Sat."

The odds a family whose main breadwinner has a professional degree is in the highest income quintile: **1 in 1.6**

SOURCE: US Census Bureau, *Current Population Survey Annual Social and Economic Supplement,* November 2010.

Teens Use Cell Phones for Just About Everything—to:

take pictures . . . . **1 in 1.2**

share pictures with others . . . . **1 in 1.6**

play music . . . . **1 in 1.7**

play games . . . . **1 in 2.2**

exchange videos . . . . **1 in 3.1**

exchange instant messages . . . . **1 in 3.2**

go online for general purposes . . . . **1 in 3.7**

access social network sites . . . . **1 in 4.4**

use email . . . . **1 in 4.8**

purchase things . . . . **1 in 9**

SOURCE: A Lenhart, R Ling, S Campbell, K Purcell, *Teens and Mobile Phones,* Pew Internet and American Life Project, Pew Research Center, April 20, 2010.

Full-Time and Part-Time Employment by Age

The odds a teenager age 15 is not in the labor force . . . . **1 in 1.1**

The odds a teenager age 16 is not in the labor force . . . . **1 in 1.2**

The odds a teenager age 17 is not in the labor force . . . . **1 in 1.4**

The odds a teenager age 15 is employed full-time . . . . **1 in 337**

The odds a teenager age 16 is employed full-time . . . . **1 in 116**

The odds a teenager age 17 is employed full-time . . . . **1 in 68.7**

The odds a teenager age 15 is employed part-time . . . . **1 in 31.4**

The odds a teenager age 16 is employed part-time . . . . **1 in 11.7**

The odds a teenager age 17 is employed part-time . . . . **1 in 5.3**

The odds a teenager age 15 looking for work is unemployed. . . . . **1 in 79.3**

The odds a teenager age 16 looking for work is unemployed. . . . . **1 in 20.1**

The odds a teenager age 17 looking for work is unemployed. . . . . **1 in 15.3**

Age	Not in Labor Force %	Employed Full-Time %	Employed Part-Time %	Unemployed %
15	95	0.3	3	1
16	86	1	9	5
17	73	1	19	7

SOURCE: US Census Bureau, *America's Families and Living Arrangements: 2010,* Current Population Survey.

Dating Violence

The odds a female high school student will be a victim of dating violence—that is, "hit, slapped, or physically hurt on purpose"—by a boyfriend or girlfriend in a year are **1 in 10.8**. A male student's odds are slightly higher, at **1 in 10.5**.

Sexual violence, too, often occurs early. The odds a female high school student will be forced to have sex in a year are **1 in 8.5**. That's over 10%—just in a year. For male students, the odds are lower but still substantial at **1 in 22.2**.

SOURCE: DK Eaton, L Kann, S Kinchen, S Shanklin, KH Flint, J Hawkins, et al., "Youth Risk Behavior Surveillance—United States, 2011," *Morbidity and Mortality Weekly Report* 61(4), June 8, 2012.

Victim

What Constitutes Being a Victim?

Teenagers can be victimized by the use of technology by a boyfriend or girlfriend, defined as:

Calling or texting to check up on him/her (e.g., to find out where he/she is or what he/she is doing) between midnight and 5 a.m.

Calling his/her cell phone to check up on him/her 20 or more times per hour.

Texting to check up on him/her more than 40 times per hour.

Sharing or threatening to share private or embarrassing pictures or videos of him/her.

1 in 4.2 high school students has been victimized by the use of technology by a boyfriend or girlfriend.

SOURCE: Family Violence Prevention Fund and Liz Claiborne, *Teen Dating Abuse 2009 Key Topline Findings,* 2009.

Not Everyone Makes It to
Graduation

Some are suspended...

The odds a student in a public primary or secondary school will be suspended in a year: **1 in 14.5**

A few are expelled...

Average overall . . . . **1 in 476**
Males . . . . **1 in 323**
Females . . . . **1 in 909**
Non-Hispanic white . . . . **1 in 714**
Non-Hispanic black . . . . **1 in 213**
Hispanic . . . . **1 in 455**

Others drop out...

dropouts by state

State	%
Alabama	2
Alaska	7
Arizona	7
Arkansas	5
California	5
Colorado	6
Connecticut	3
Delaware	6
District of Columbia	6
Florida	3
Georgia	4
Hawaii	5
Idaho	2
Illinois	5
Indiana	2
Iowa	3

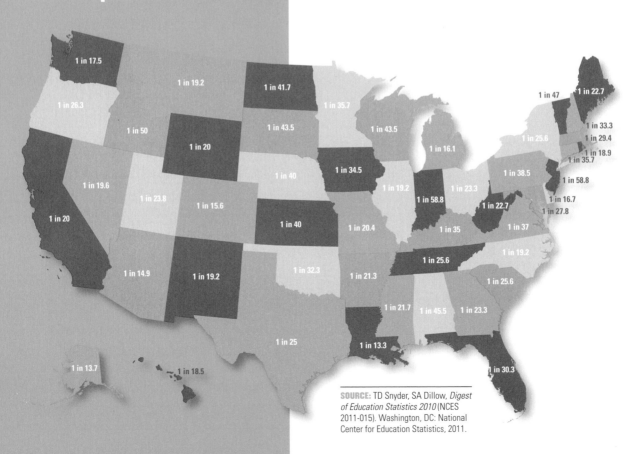

SOURCE: TD Snyder, SA Dillow, *Digest of Education Statistics 2010* (NCES 2011-015). Washington, DC: National Center for Education Statistics, 2011.

State	%
Kansas	3
Kentucky	3
Louisiana	8
Maine	4
Maryland	4
Massachusetts	3
Michigan	6
Minnesota	3
Mississippi	5
Missouri	5
Montana	5
Nebraska	3
Nevada	5
New Hampshire	3
New Jersey	2
New Mexico	5
New York	4

State	%
North Carolina	5
North Dakota	2
Ohio	4
Oklahoma	3
Oregon	4
Pennsylvania	3
Rhode Island	5
South Carolina	4
South Dakota	2
Tennessee	4
Texas	4
Utah	4
Virginia	3
Washington	6
West Virginia	4
Wisconsin	2
Wyoming	5

The odds a student at a public high school will drop out by the end of the school year in:

Alabama . . . . 1 in 45.5	Kentucky . . . . 1 in 35.7	North Dakota . . . . . . 1 in 41.7
Alaska . . . . 1 in 13.7	Louisiana . . . . 1 in 13.3	Ohio . . . . 1 in 23.3
Arizona . . . . 1 in 14.9	Maine . . . . 1 in 22.7	Oklahoma . . . . 1 in 32.3
Arkansas . . . . 1 in 21.3	Maryland . . . . 1 in 27.8	Oregon . . . . 1 in 26.3
California . . . . 1 in 20	Massachusetts . . . . . . 1 in 29.4	Pennsylvania . . . . 1 in 38.5
Colorado . . . . 1 in 15.6	Michigan . . . . 1 in 16.1	Rhode Island . . . . 1 in 18.9
Connecticut . . . . 1 in 35.7	Minnesota . . . . 1 in 35.7	South Carolina . . . . . . 1 in 25.6
Delaware . . . . 1 in 16.7	Mississippi . . . . 1 in 21.7	South Dakota . . . . 1 in 43.5
District of Columbia . . . 1 in 18.2	Missouri . . . . 1 in 20.4	Tennessee . . . . 1 in 25.6
Florida . . . . 1 in 30.3	Montana . . . . 1 in 19.2	Texas . . . . 1 in 25
Georgia . . . . 1 in 23.3	Nebraska . . . . 1 in 40	Utah . . . . 1 in 23.8
Hawaii . . . . 1 in 18.5	Nevada . . . . 1 in 19.6	Virginia . . . . 1 in 37
Idaho . . . . 1 in 50	New Hampshire . . . . . 1 in 33.3	Washington . . . . 1 in 17.5
Illinois . . . . 1 in 19.2	New Jersey . . . . 1 in 58.8	West Virginia . . . . 1 in 22.7
Indiana . . . . 1 in 58.8	New Mexico . . . . 1 in 19.2	Wisconsin . . . . 1 in 43.5
Iowa . . . . 1 in 34.5	New York . . . . 1 in 25.6	Wyoming . . . . 1 in 20
Kansas . . . . 1 in 40	North Carolina . . . . . . 1 in 19.2	

Making It to the
Ivy League: Admittance Rates

The odds an applicant to an **Ivy League** school will be admitted:

1 in 8

School	%	Odds (1 in)
Cornell	19	5.2
UPenn	18	5.7
Dartmouth	13	7.4
Brown	11	9.0
Columbia	11	9.1
Princeton	10	9.9
Yale	9	11.7
Harvard	7	13.9

SOURCE: Book of Odds estimate based on US Department of Education, The Integrated Postsecondary Education Data System, 2009–10.

Guess Your Chances

School	%	Odds (1 in)
Amherst College	16	6.3
California Institute of Technology	15	6.6
Carnegie Mellon University	36	2.8
College of William and Mary	34	3.0
Duke University	22	4.5
Florida State University	61	1.6
Georgetown University	19	5.3
Johns Hopkins University	28	3.6
Massachusetts Institute of Technology	11	9.4
Michigan State University	72	1.3
New York University	38	2.7
Northwestern University	26	3.8

10

The Perfect
Score

The odds a college-bound senior who took the SAT received the top score: **1 in 5,152**

The odds a college-bound senior who took the ACT received the top score: **1 in 2,320**

SOURCES: Communication with Courtney Stevenson, The College Board, September 11, 2009. ✗ Communication with Ed Colby, ACT Media Relations, September 11, 2009.

The odds a high school senior will take an AP test in a year: **1 in 3.5**

The odds a student taking an AP test at any point in high school will receive a score of 3 or higher: **1 in 1.7**

The odds a student taking an AP test at any point in high school will receive a score of 2 or lower: **1 in 2.5**

SOURCE: The College Board, *The 7th Annual AP Report to the Nation,* February 9, 2011.

Chances Continued...

School	%	Odds (1 in)
Stanford University	8	12.5
University of California, Berkeley	21	4.7
University of California, Los Angeles	23	4.4
University of Chicago	27	3.7
University of Florida	43	6.3
University of Michigan, Ann Arbor	50	2.0
University of Southern California	24	4.1
Williams College	20	4.9

SOURCE: US Department of Education, The Integrated Postsecondary Education Data System, 2009–10.

Paying for College
Student Aid

The odds an undergraduate student will receive any student aid are 1 in 1.5.

The odds an undergraduate student will receive grants are 1 in 1.9.

The odds an undergraduate student will receive federal financial aid in an academic year are 1 in 2.1.

The odds an undergraduate student will receive nonfederal financial aid in an academic year are 1 in 2.1.

The odds an undergraduate student will receive student loans are 1 in 2.6.

The odds an undergraduate student will receive nonfederal grants in an academic year are 1 in 2.6.

The odds an undergraduate student will receive federal loans in an academic year are 1 in 2.9.

The odds an undergraduate student will receive federal grants in an academic year are 1 in 3.6.

The odds an undergraduate student will receive nonfederal loans in an academic year are 1 in 6.8.

The odds an undergraduate student will receive work-study are 1 in 13.5.

SOURCE: TD Snyder, SA Dillow, *Digest of Education Statistics 2009* (NCES 2010-013). Washington, DC: National Center for Education Statistics, 2010.

"Send Flowers to Admission Office"

The odds a waitlisted applicant to MIT will be admitted:

1 in 5.8

SOURCE: Massachusetts Institute of Technology, Admissions Statistics, 2009.

Percentage of undergraduate students receiving student aid:

Type of Aid	%
Any	66
Grants	52
Federal aid	48
Nonfederal aid	48
Student loans	39
Nonfederal grants	39
Federal loans	35
Federal grants	28
Nonfederal loans	15
Work-study	7

Does Debt 101 Have a Final?

We've all heard the shocking statistics on personal and household debt leading into the recent financial crisis. Total household debt peaked in late 2008 at $12.7 trillion.

Things have improved. Household debt had declined by about $1.3 trillion by the second quarter of 2012. But there's one area where debt is growing at an alarming rate. As the cost of higher education keeps going up, so do student loans. Over a decade, student loans have grown by $673 billion or 3.8 times. In fact, student loans outstanding are now larger than credit card debt, auto loan debt, and home equity lines of credit! Here is a comparison based on data collected by the Federal Reserve Bank of New York:

Type of Debt	Q1, 2008	Q2, 2012	Change
Mortgage	$9.294 trillion	$8.147 trillion	−$1.147 trillion
Home equity revolving	$692 billion	$589 billion	−$103 billion
Auto loan	$809 billion	$750 billion	−$59 billion
Credit card	$858 billion	$672 billion	−$186 billion
Student loan	$611 billion	$914 billion	+$303 billion

The cost of tuition? For public colleges, tuitions and fees have risen from $4,280 a year in 1996–97 to $8,240 in 2011–12. Even if you deduct grants and scholarships (which the College Board calls "net cost"), the cost has grown from $1,190 to $2,490. And private colleges are far more expensive. Their unadjusted tuition and fees have risen from $18,700 in the 1996–97 school year to $28,500 in 2011–12. After adjusting for grants and scholarships, the annual total is still $12,970, an increase from $10,630.

What makes the situation particularly troubling are the poor job prospects of current and recent graduates. Looking at Labor Department statistics, Northeastern University found that not only were many with bachelor's degrees unemployed; others were underemployed, working at jobs they were overqualified for. In 2012, the total of those unemployed or underemployed with bachelor's degrees and younger than 25 was about 1.5 million, or 1 in 1.9.

It is not surprising that students are finding it hard to pay back these loans. The Federal Reserve has noted that up to 47% of student loan borrowers seem to be in deferral or forbearance periods as of Q3, 2012, and that 21% or 1 in 4.8 of the outstanding student loan balances are delinquent.

As never before, students and their parents must look hard at the decision to borrow. Although an executive order has limited to 10% the amount that can be demanded from salaries to pay down student debt, providing relief to those with lower-paying jobs, student loans are not discharged by bankruptcy. Even people in their 60s, nearing the traditional age of retirement, are finding their Social Security checks tapped to pay back delinquent student loans. It seems hard to believe but as of 2011 there were nearly 2 million borrowers 60 and over owing in the aggregate more than $36.5 billion!

SOURCES: Federal Reserve Bank of New York, Research and Statistic Group, Microeconomic Studies, *Quarterly Report on Household Debt and Credit*, based on data from the FRBNY Consumer Credit Panel, August 2012. ✔ Federal Reserve Bank of New York, "New York Fed Quarterly Report Shows Student Loan Debt Continues to Grow," press release, May 31, 2012. ✔ S Baum, J Ma, "Trends in College Pricing, 2011," College Board Advocacy & Policy Center. ✔ A Sum, I Khatiwada, S Palma, *The Employment Experiences and College Labor Market Job Characteristics of Young Adult Associate Degree and Bachelor Degree Recipients in Massachusetts and the US*, prepared for Massachusetts Department of Higher Education, Research, Planning, and Information Systems, Boston, Massachusetts, February 2012. ✔ A Sum, I Khatiwada, S Palma, *The Employment Experience, Annual Earnings, and Migration Behavior of Young Associate Degree and Bachelor Degree Holders in Massachusetts for Future Workforce Alignment*, prepared for Massachusetts Department of Higher Education, Research, Planning, and Information Systems, Boston, Massachusetts, February 2012. ✔ The White House, Office of the Press Secretary, "We Can't Wait: Obama Administration to Lower Student Loan Payments for Millions of Borrowers," press release, October 25, 2011. ✔ M Brown, A Haughwout, D Lee, W van der Klaauw, "Grading Student Loans," Federal Reserve Bank of New York, using data from FRBNY Consumer Credit Panel/Equifax, March 5, 2012.

The Bills Keep Coming

The cost of college keeps going up—and tuition increases at public universities have even outpaced those of private universities. Some state schools are so strapped for cash they have resorted to charging students hundreds of dollars in extra fees.

- Average student total debt rose nearly 25% between 2004 and 2008, to $24,000.

- Students borrowed $75.1 billion just to get them through 2008–09.

- **39%** of Americans under 35 reported in 2006 that it will take them more than 10 years to pay off their loans—and those predictions have gotten worse.

Many students have been forced to finance their lives while in school the way many Americans finance their lives: on credit. The odds are **1 in 1.2** that an undergrad has a credit card, and **1 in 2** he or she has at least four cards. Today's students carry more cards than ever. They also have record-high balances. Between 1998 and 2008, the average credit card balance of college students increased more than one and a half times, from $1,879 to $3,173. And the balance can be hard to pay off, even with consistent effort.

The odds an undergrad will make more than the minimum payment each month but always carry a balance are **1 in 2.6**.

SOURCES: The Project on Student Debt, *Student Debt and the Class of 2008*, December 2009, http://projectonstudentdebt.org/. ✗ T Lewin, "Burden of College Loans on Graduates Grows," *New York Times*, April 11, 2011. ✗ AM Chaker, "Students Borrow More Than Ever for College," *Wall Street Journal*, September 4, 2009. ✗ *How Undergraduates Use Credit Cards*, Sallie Mae's National Study of Usage Rates and Trends, 2009.

How Families Pay for College

The odds a family will fund an undergraduate student's educational expenses through...

a retirement account loan: **1 in 33.3**

parents' private educational loans: **1 in 25**

a home equity loan or line of credit: **1 in 25**

a student's credit card: **1 in 20**

parents' credit card: **1 in 16.7**

parents' retirement savings withdrawal: **1 in 16.7**

a Federal Parent Plus loan: **1 in 14.3**

federal work-study: **1 in 12.5**

a student's private educational loans: **1 in 7.7**

parents' general savings or investments: **1 in 7.1**

parents' college savings fund: **1 in 6.7**

a student's savings: **1 in 6.7**

relatives or friends: **1 in 6.3**

federal student loans: **1 in 3.5**

grants: **1 in 3.3**

a student's current income: **1 in 3.1**

scholarships: **1 in 2.3**

parents' current income: **1 in 1.8**

Funding Method	%
Retirement account loan	3
Parents' private educational loans	4
Home equity loan or line of credit	4
Student's credit card	5
Parents' credit card	6
Parents' retirement savings withdrawal	6
Federal Parent Plus loan	7
Federal work-study	8
Student's private educational loans	13
Parents' general savings or investments	14
Parents' college savings fund	15
Student's savings	15
Relatives or friends	16
Federal student loans	29
Grants	30
Student's current income	32
Scholarships	43
Parents' current income	57

SOURCE: *How America Pays for College*, Sallie Mae's National Study of College Students and Parents, Gallup, 2010.

College Majors

The odds a student enrolled in a four-year undergraduate institution will major in:

Business, management, or marketing: **1 in 4.9**

Health professions and related sciences: **1 in 10.9**

Education: **1 in 13.8**

Visual and performing arts: **1 in 18.7**

Engineering: **1 in 20.1**

Biological and biomedical sciences: **1 in 21.3**

Psychology: **1 in 22.3**

Liberal arts, sciences, and humanities: **1 in 24.4**

Computer and information sciences: **1 in 28.3**

Communication or journalism: **1 in 28.8**

Security and protective services: **1 in 37**

English language and literature: **1 in 51.5**

Political science and government: **1 in 58.2**

History: **1 in 69.3**

Multi- or interdisciplinary studies: **1 in 71.4**

Physical sciences: **1 in 73**

Parks, recreation, and fitness: **1 in 82.2**

Public administration and social services: **1 in 87.3**

Engineering technologies: **1 in 88.1**

Sociology: **1 in 92.2**

Family and consumer/human sciences: **1 in 102**

Economics: **1 in 104**

Math or statistics: **1 in 136**

Architecture and related services: **1 in 142**

Foreign language and literature: **1 in 148**

Agriculture and related sciences: **1 in 148**

Philosophy and religious studies: **1 in 163**

Legal professions or studies: **1 in 178**

Personal and culinary services: **1 in 213**

Social sciences: **1 in 233**

Natural resources and conservation: **1 in 257**

International relations and affairs: **1 in 279**

Anthropology: **1 in 288**

Theology and religious vocations: **1 in 326**

Transportation and materials movement: **1 in 326**

Criminology: **1 in 376**

Area, ethnic, or gender studies: **1 in 391**

Communications technologies: **1 in 425**

Geography: **1 in 489**

Construction trades: **1 in 652**

Mechanical and repair technologies: **1 in 698**

Science technologies: **1 in 752**

The odds a student enrolled in a four-year undergraduate institution will be undeclared or not in a degree program: **1 in 19.1**

Major	%
Business, management, or marketing	20
Health professions and related sciences	9
Education	7
Visual and performing arts	5
Undeclared or not in a degree program	5
Engineering	5
Biological and biomedical sciences	5
Psychology	4
Liberal arts, sciences, and humanities	4
Computer and information sciences	4
Communication or journalism	3
Security and protective services	3
English language and literature	2
Political science and government	2
History	1
Multi- or interdisciplinary studies	1
Physical sciences	1
Parks, recreation, and fitness	1
Public administration and social services	1
Engineering technologies	1
Sociology	1

Major	%
Family and consumer/human sciences	1
Economics	1
Math or statistics	1
Architecture and related services	1
Foreign language and literature	1
Agriculture and related sciences	1
Philosophy and religious studies	1
Legal professions or studies	1
Personal and culinary services	<0.5
Social sciences	<0.5
Natural resources and conservation	<0.5
International relations and affairs	<0.5
Anthropology	<0.5
Theology and religious vocations	<0.5
Transportation and materials movement	<0.5
Criminology	<0.5
Area, ethnic, or gender studies	<0.5
Communications technologies	<0.5
Geography	<0.5
Construction trades	<0.5
Mechanical and repair technologies	<0.5
Science technologies	<0.5

SOURCE: TD Snyder, SA Dillow, *Digest of Education Statistics 2010* (NCES 2011-015). Washington, DC: National Center for Education Statistics, 2011.

When It's Crunch Time

Packing It On:
The Freshman 15?

The stress of college (not to mention the abundance of alcohol) often leads to weight gain. In two studies on the topic, summarized in the journal *Preventative Medicine*, one study found **77%** of freshmen (**1 in 1.3**) and the other found **70%** of freshmen (**1 in 1.4**) will gain weight during their freshman year.

But even among those who gain weight, the average gain falls far short of fifteen pounds. A 2008 review article found that the average freshman weight gain was five pounds.

SOURCES: EE Lloyd-Richardson, S Bailey, JL Fava, R Wing, "A Prospective Study of Weight Gain During the College Freshman and Sophomore Years," *Preventative Medicine* 48(3), March 2009: 256–261. ✗ C Brown, "The Information Trail of the 'Freshman 15'—a Systematic Review of a Health Myth Within the Research and Popular Literature," *Health Information and Libraries Journal* 25(1), March 2008: 1–12.

Popping Pills

Amphetamines, such as Adderall and Ritalin, prescriptions for attention deficit disorder and hyperactivity, are common on campus, especially around exam time. The odds a person 18–22 enrolled in college full-time will engage in the nonmedical use of Adderall in a year are **1 in 15.6**—twice as high as the odds for a person that age who is not a full-time college student.

SOURCES: Substance Abuse and Mental Health Services Administration, Office of Applied Studies, *The NSDUH Report: Nonmedical Use of Adderall Among Full-Time College Students.* Rockville, MD, April 7, 2009.

My Dog Ate My Calendar

The odds a person 18–22 enrolled in college has made up an excuse to get out of classwork or buy more time:

Personal illness . . . . **1 in 2.7**
Family emergency . . . . **1 in 3.8**
Not understanding assignment . . . . **1 in 4.8**
Computer crashed . . . . **1 in 5.6**
Overslept or alarm clock failed . . . . **1 in 6.4**
"Left my paper in the dorm room" . . . . **1 in 14.6**
Grandparent died . . . . **1 in 31.7**
Best friend died . . . . **1 in 127**

Excuse	%
Personal illness	37
Family emergency	26
Not understanding the assignment	21
Computer crash	18
Oversleeping or alarm clock failure	16
"Left my paper in the dorm room"	7
Grandparent's death	3
Best friend's death	1

SOURCE: M Roig, M Caso, "Lying and Cheating: Fraudulent Excuse Making, Cheating, and Plagiarism," *Journal of Psychology* 139(6), 2005: 485–494.

 ODDS COUPLE

Education Pays Off
in the Long Run

The odds a person 25 or older with a doctoral degree has an income of less than $2,500: **1 in 86.8**

The odds a person 25 or older with some high school education has an income of $100,000 or more: **1 in 204**

SOURCE: US Census Bureau, Current Population Survey, 2009.

College Rituals and Superstitions

The odds an undergraduate student as part of a behavioral ritual or superstition will...

dress up to feel better prepared . . . . **1 in 1.4**	crack his or her knuckles . . . . **1 in 4.8**
knock on wood . . . . **1 in 1.6**	engage in an idiosyncratic routine . . . . **1 in 5.6**
refrain from "jinxing" . . . . **1 in 1.7**	mark his or her shoes or equipment . . . . **1 in 5.8**
visualize success . . . . **1 in 1.8**	eat a particular meal . . . . **1 in 6.2**
cross his or her fingers . . . . **1 in 2**	wear a lucky charm . . . . **1 in 6.2**
participate in a team cheer . . . . **1 in 2.1**	pray in a group . . . . **1 in 6.5**
listen to particular music . . . . **1 in 2.1**	kiss a lucky charm . . . . **1 in 8.5**
pray by him- or herself . . . . **1 in 2.4**	put clothing on in a particular order . . . . **1 in 11.1**
say a particular phrase . . . . **1 in 2.6**	check his or her horoscope . . . . **1 in 15.9**
participate in a pep talk . . . . **1 in 2.6**	refrain from sex . . . . **1 in 15.9**
wear lucky clothing . . . . **1 in 3.3**	refrain from showering . . . . **1 in 22.2**
require silence or seclusion . . . . **1 in 4.6**	dress "sloppily" . . . . **1 in 37**

Superstition	%
Dressing up to feel better prepared	70
Knock on wood	62
Refrain from "jinxing"	60
Visualize success	55
Cross his or her fingers	49
Participate in a team cheer	48
Listen to particular music	47
Pray by him- or herself	42
Say a particular phrase	39

Superstition	%
Participate in a pep talk	38
Wear lucky clothing	31
Require silence or seclusion	22
Crack his or her knuckles	21
Engage in an idiosyncratic routine	18
Mark his or her shoes or equipment	17
Eat a particular meal	16
Wear a lucky charm	16

Superstition	%
Pray in a group	15
Kiss a lucky charm	12
Put clothing on in a particular order	9
Check his or her horoscope	6
Refrain from sex	6
Refrain from showering	5
Dress "sloppily"	3

SOURCE: Book of Odds estimates based on A Edward, JM Rudski, "Malinowski Goes to College: Factors Influencing Students' Use of Ritual and Superstition," *Journal of General Psychology* 134(4), 2007: 389–403.

GENDER WARS

The odds a woman 25–34 has a bachelor's degree or more:

1 in 2.8 vs. 1 in 3.6 for a man

SOURCE: US Census Bureau, *Educational Attainment in the United States: 2009.*

Sex on Campus

Undergrads and Kissing

The odds an undergraduate student 18 or older has kissed…

at least 20 members of the opposite sex . . . . 1 in 4.3

1–2 members of the opposite sex . . . . 1 in 10.7

3–5 members of the opposite sex . . . . 1 in 7.1

6–10 members of the opposite sex . . . . 1 in 4.6

11–20 members of the opposite sex . . . . 1 in 3.9

Has never been kissed . . . . **1 in 208**

# Opposite Sex Kissed	%
0	0.5
1–2	9
3–5	14
6–10	22
11–20	25
20+	23

SOURCE: Book of Odds estimates based on SM Hughes, MA Harrison, GC Gallup, G Gordon, "Sex Differences in Romantic Kissing Among College Students: An Evolutionary Perspective," *Evolutionary Psychology* 5(3), 2007: 612–631.

 **ODDS COUPLE**

"Consistency Is the Hobgoblin…"

The odds a male 15–22 has had unprotected sex: **1 in 1.8**

The odds an adult is not at all concerned about contracting AIDS or an STD: **1 in 1.8**

SOURCES: S Jayson, "Truth About Sex," *USA Today*, January 26, 2010. ✗ "The American Sex Survey: A Peek Beneath the Sheets," *ABC News Primetime Live Poll*, October 21, 2004, http://abcnews.go.com/images/Politics/959a1AmericanSexSurvey.pdf.

The Pressure Is On

The odds a male 15–22 thinks there is "way too much pressure" from society to have sex:

1 in 1.3

SOURCE: S Jayson, "Truth About Sex," *USA Today*, January 26, 2010

Yet Some Guys Apply Their Own Pressure

The odds a male 18–22 enrolled in college has ever talked someone into having sex with him by lying or making false promises:

1 in 4

SOURCE: GJ Fischer, "Deceptive, Verbally Coercive College Males: Attitudinal Predictors and Lies Told," *Archives of Sexual Behavior* 25(5), 1996: 527–533.

GENDER WARS

The odds a male 15–22 believes the more hookups he has the more popular he will be:

1 in 1.9

The odds a male 15–22 believes the more hookups a girl has the less popular she will be:

1 in 1.4

SOURCE: S Jayson, "Truth About Sex," *USA Today*, January 26, 2010.

Reasons for Unwanted Sexual Activity in College

1 in 1.1 male students
1 in 1.03 female students
} has engaged in sexual activity they did not want.

The odds a male college student who engaged in unwanted sexual activity did so because of...

enticement: **1 in 1.1**

inexperience: **1 in 1.5**

intoxication: **1 in 1.8**

peer pressure: **1 in 1.9**

sex-role concerns: **1 in 2.1**

fear of the termination of a relationship: **1 in 2.3**

verbal coercion by his partner: **1 in 3.7**

physical coercion: **1 in 4.3**

a desire to be popular: **1 in 5.5**

a partner threatened self-harm: **1 in 31.2**

The odds a female college student who engaged in unwanted sexual activity did so because of...

enticement: **1 in 1.1**

inexperience: **1 in 1.6**

intoxication: **1 in 1.2**

peer pressure: **1 in 2.2**

sex-role concerns: **1 in 2.1**

fear of the termination of a relationship: **1 in 1.8**

verbal coercion by her partner: **1 in 2.9**

physical coercion: **1 in 3.2**

a desire to be popular: **1 in 7.7**

a partner threatened self-harm: **1 in 58.8**

Reason	Men %	Women %
Enticed	90	93
Inexperienced	66	62
Intoxicated	55	87
Peer pressure	52	45
Sex-role concerns	49	49
Feared the termination of a relationship	43	57
Verbally coerced by partner	27	34
Physically coerced	24	31
To be popular	18	13
Partner threatened self-harm	3	2

SOURCE: CL Muehlenhard, SW Cook, "Men's Self-Reports of Unwanted Sexual Activity," *Journal of Sex Research* 24, 1998: 58–72.

Ouch!

The odds a female college student who has engaged in unwanted sexual activity did so because she was being altruistic are **1 in 1.7**; a male, **1 in 4**.

SOURCE: CL Muehlenhard, SW Cook, "Men's Self-Reports of Unwanted Sexual Activity," *Journal of Sex Research* 24, 1988: 58–72.

Then Comes
Spring Break
Risky Behavior on Spring Break

The odds a male college student 18–25 who went on a spring break vacation reports:

- experimenting sexually on his last break: **1 in 1.4**

- using a condom during sex with someone he just met on his last break: **1 in 1.4**

- getting drunk during his last break: **1 in 2**

- drinking alcohol just prior to having sex during his last break: **1 in 2**

- having sex with someone new the day they met during his last break: **1 in 4.7**

The odds a female college student 18–25 who went on a spring break vacation reports:

- experimenting sexually on her last break: **1 in 4.4**

- using a condom during sex with someone she just met on her last break: **1 in 1.5**

- getting drunk during her last break: **1 in 2.5**

- drinking alcohol just prior to having sex during her last break: **1 in 2.4**

- having sex with someone new the day they met during her last break: **1 in 20.4**

SOURCE: Y Apostolopoulos, S Sonmez, CH Yu, "HIV-Risk Behaviors of American Spring Break Vacationers—a Case of Situational Disinhibition," *International Journal of STD and AIDS* 13, 2002: 733–743.

It Seemed Like a Good Idea at the Time...

The odds a male college student has a tattoo on his...

hand or arm: **1 in 9.1**

back: **1 in 13.3**

shoulder: **1 in 16.7**

foot or leg: **1 in 16.7**

chest: **1 in 33.3**

abdomen: **1 in 90**

The odds a male college student has a pierced...

ear or ears: **1 in 3.8**

tongue: **1 in 55.7**

navel: **1 in 66.7**

nipple: **1 in 90.9**

eyebrow: **1 in 250**

genital area: **1 in 250**

The odds a female college student has a tattoo on her...

back: **1 in 8.3**

foot or leg: **1 in 19.2**

abdomen: **1 in 20.4**

hip or buttock: **1 in 29.4**

hand or arm: **1 in 76.9**

breast or chest: **1 in 76.9**

shoulder: **1 in 125**

neck: **1 in 125**

pubic/genital area: **1 in 125**

face: **1 in 333**

The odds a female college student has a pierced...

navel: **1 in 2.9**

ear or ears: **1 in 3.3**

tongue: **1 in 14.3**

nose: **1 in 16.7**

nipple: **1 in 33.3**

eyebrow: **1 in 125**

pubic/genital area: **1 in 125**

lip: **1 in 200**

SOURCE: LB Mayers, SH Chiffriller, "Body Art (Body Piercing and Tattooing) Among Undergraduate University Students: 'Then and Now,'" *Journal of Adolescent Health* 42(2), February 2008: 201–203.

College Relationships:
"Breaking Up Is Hard to Do"

College Relationship Breakups	%	Odds (1 in)
How It Ended		
Direct dissolution by one partner	25	**4.1**
An explanation or justification	24	**4.1**
Mutually	17	**6.1**
By taking a break	9	**11.5**
Conflict from both partners blaming each other	7	**14.5**
One partner withdrawing from the relationship	6	**16.1**
One partner suggesting to date other people	4	**25.0**
Both partners drifting apart	3	**40.0**
Using manipulation, bullying, or third parties	1	**111.0**
Why It Ended		
Physical distance	18	**5.4**
Unbalanced needs or expectations	16	**6.5**
Third party or external sources	14	**7.0**
Communication problems	14	**7.4**
Negative behavior	12	**8.6**
Desire to explore other options	10	**9.9**
Negative change in the relationship	10	**10.2**
Need for independence	8	**12.2**
Cheating	7	**13.7**
Trust issues	4	**28.6**
Lying	2	**62.5**

Why Why Why Why Why Why Why

SOURCE: RM Dailey, A Pfiester, B Jin, G Beck, G Clark, "On-Again/Off-Again Dating Relationships: How Are They Different from Other Dating Relationships?" *Personal Relationships* 16, 2009: 23–47.

Best Buds

If you haven't done it yourself, you probably know someone who has. The odds a college student has ever had a friend with benefits are **1 in 2**, with men more likely than women to report such arrangements. Among male undergraduates, the odds are **1 in 1.6**, while for women, the number is **1 in 2**.

SOURCE: J Puentes, D Knox, ME Zusman, "Participants in 'Friends with Benefits' Relationships," *College Student Journal* 42(1), March 2008:176–180.

The odds an undergrad will describe him- or herself as a jealous person: **1 in 1.8**

SOURCE: J Puentes, D Knox, ME Zusman, "Participants in 'Friends with Benefits' Relationships," *College Student Journal* 42(1), March 2008: 176–180.

Private Colleges Have Higher Graduation Rates Than Public Colleges

Based on 2009 data, the odds that a student at a four-year public college or university will graduate within four years are **1 in 3.4** vs. **1 in 2** for those attending a private, nonprofit college/university; within six years the public school odds are **1 in 1.8** vs. **1 in 1.6** for those attending a private nonprofit.

However, students attending larger public universities as well as many private colleges/universities beat the average graduation rates.

Six-Year Graduation Rates at Selected Four-Year Private and Public Institutions

Private Universities	%	Odds (1 in)	Public Universities	%	Odds (1 in)
Amherst College	96	1.04	U. Cal–Los Angeles	90	1.1
Stanford University	95	1.1	U. Cal–Berkeley	88	1.1
Notre Dame	95	1.1	U. Michigan (AA)	88	1.1
Williams College	95	1.1	U.N.C., Chapel Hill	83	1.2
Duke	94	1.1	U. Florida	81	1.2
Georgetown	93	1.1	U. Washington	75	1.3
MIT	93	1.1	Michigan State	74	1.4
Northwestern	93	1.1	Ohio State	71	1.4
Boston College	91	1.1	Florida State	69	1.4
College of Wm & Mary	91	1.1	U. South Carolina	63	1.6
Carnegie Mellon U.	87	1.2	U. Minnesota	63	1.6
U. of Southern Cal.	85	1.2	Arizona State	56	1.8
Clemson University	78	1.3	U. Arizona	56	1.8
US Average–Private	65	1.6	US Average–Public	55	1.8

SOURCES: National Center for Education Statistics, *The Condition of Education: Participation in Education, 2008* (NCES 2008-031), US Department of Education. ⚊
US Department of Education, The Integrated Postsecondary Education Data System, 2010 (for the year 2009).

But Sometimes in the Short Run, It's Back to the Bunk Beds
Reasons for Moving In with Parents

Reason	%	Odds (1 in)
No job and cannot afford to live elsewhere	28	3.6
To save money	26	3.9
Was on his or her own but was having a hard time financially	19	5.3
Personal reasons unrelated to finances	19	5.3

SOURCE: Charles Schwab, *Charles Schwab 2009 Young Adults and Money Survey Findings: Insights into Money Attitudes, Behaviors and Concerns of 23- to 28-Year-Olds*, 2009.

DID YOU know?
The odds a first-time student at a four-year private nonprofit college or university will drop out of school during a six-year timeframe: **1 in 10.8**

SOURCE: National Center for Education Statistics, *The Condition of Education: Participation in Education, 2008* (NCES 2008-031), US Department of Education.

CHAPTER 7

HEALTH AND ILLNESS

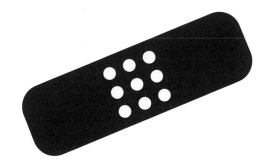

Survivor

The odds a person diagnosed with cancer in 1999 survived at least ten years:

1 in 1.7

SOURCE: N Howlader, AM Noone, M Krapcho, N Neyman, R Aminou, SF Altekruse, et al., eds., *SEER Cancer Statistics Review, 1975–2009 (Vintage 2009 Populations)*. Bethesda, MD: National Cancer Institute, http://seer.cancer.gov/csr/1975_2009_pops09/, based on November 2011 SEER data submission, posted to the SEER website, April 2012.

The
Odds
You
Will
Die
in
a

Year

The Most Common Causes of Death
in a Year

The odds a death will be due to heart disease . . . . **1 in 4.2**

The odds a death will be due to cancer . . . . **1 in 4.4**

The odds a death will be due to chronic lower respiratory diseases . . . . **1 in 17.5**

The odds a death will be due to stroke . . . . **1 in 19.5**

The odds a death will be due to an accident . . . . **1 in 20.5**

The odds a death will be due to Alzheimer's disease . . . . **1 in 29.7**

The odds a death will be due to diabetes mellitus . . . . **1 in 34.3**

The odds a death will be due to influenza or pneumonia . . . . **1 in 46.8**

The odds a death will be due to kidney disease . . . . **1 in 54.9**

The odds a death will be due to intentional self-harm (suicide) . . . . **1 in 65.6**

The odds a death will be due to septicemia . . . . **1 in 70.7**

The odds a death will be due to chronic liver disease or cirrhosis . . . . **1 in 74.9**

The odds a death will be due to essential hypertension . . . . **1 in 91.5**

The odds a death will be due to hypertensive renal disease . . . . **1 in 91.5**

The odds a death will be due to Parkinson's disease . . . . **1 in 109**

The odds a death will be due to pneumonitis due to liquids and solids . . . . **1 in 139**

The odds a person will die in a year:

1 in 135

Those are roughly the odds a male born in 2008 is named David:

1 in 134

SOURCES: DL Hoyert, JQ Xu, "Deaths: Preliminary Data for 2011," *National Vital Statistics Reports* 61(6), October 10, 2012. ✒ Social Security Administration, *Popular Baby Names.*

Cause of Death	%
Heart disease	24
Cancer	23
Chronic lower respiratory diseases	6
Stroke	5
Accident	5
Alzheimer's disease	3
Diabetes mellitus	3
Influenza or pneumonia	2
Kidney disease	2
Intentional self-harm (suicide)	2
Septicemia	1
Chronic liver disease or cirrhosis	1
Hypertensive renal disease	1
Parkinson's disease	1
Pneumonitis due to liquids and solids	1

SOURCE: DL Hoyert, JQ Xu, "Deaths: Preliminary Data for 2011," *National Vital Statistics Reports* 61(6), October 10, 2012.

How Are Health Care Dollars Spent?

The odds a dollar of health expenditures will be spent for:

personal health care: **1 in 1.2**; hospital care: **1 in 3.3**; physician and clinical services: **1 in 5**; prescription drugs: **1 in 10**; net cost of private insurance: **1 in 17.9**; nursing home care and retirement communities: **1 in 18.4**; medical structures and equipment: **1 in 23.5**; dental services: **1 in 25.2**; public health activities: **1 in 31.9**; home health care: **1 in 35.9**; non-MD or clinical professional services: **1 in 36.8**; medical research: **1 in 51.8**; nonprescription drugs and supplies: **1 in 58.2**; durable medical equipment: **1 in 72.4**; public administration: **1 in 78.8**

Type of Health Expenditure	%
Personal health care	84
Hospital care	31
Physician and clinical services	20
Prescription drugs	10
Net cost of private insurance	6
Nursing home care/retirement communities	5
Medical structures and equipment	4
Dental services	4
Public health activities	3
Home health care	3
Non-MD or clinical professional services	3
Medical research	2
Nonprescription drugs and supplies	2
Durable medical equipment	1
Public administration	1

SOURCE: US Centers for Medicare and Medicaid Services, Office of the Actuary, National Health Statistics Group, *National Health Expenditure Projections 2010–2020,* September 2011.

ODDS COUPLE

Lighter Burden

The odds a death will include HIV on the death certificate: **1 in 21,774**

The odds a person will visit an emergency department due to an accident involving a golf cart in a year: **1 in 22,355**

SOURCES: WK Adih, RM Selik, X Hu, "Trends in Diseases Reported on US Death Certificates That Mentioned HIV Infection, 1996–2006," *Journal of the International Association of Physicians in AIDS Care* 10(1), January/February 2011: 5–11. ✔ Book of Odds calculation based on a query of 2010 data in the CPSC NEISS database.

How Much Do We Spend on Health?

The Centers for Medicare and Medicaid Services (CMS) projects health expenditures to grow from **$2.6 trillion** in 2010 to **$2.8 trillion** in 2012 and **$4.6 trillion** by 2020. This means total health expenditures will grow from 17% of gross domestic product in 2010 to just under 20% during that period. The CMS Office of the Actuary's forecast assumes the Affordable Care Act will be implemented as written. Thus, the cost of health care will continue to grow faster than the US economy at least through 2020.

SOURCE: US Centers for Medicare and Medicaid Services, Office of the Actuary, National Health Statistics Group, *National Health Expenditure Projections 2010–2020,* September 2011.

The Odds a Person Will Be
Hospitalized

The odds a person will be hospitalized in a year are **1 in 8.8**.

The odds a child under 15 will be hospitalized in a year are **1 in 31.4**.

The odds a person 15–44 will be hospitalized in a year are **1 in 12.5**.

The odds a person 45–64 will be hospitalized in a year are **1 in 8.5**.

The odds a person 65 or older will be hospitalized in a year are **1 in 3**.

The odds a person will be hospitalized in a year for:

heart disease: **1 in 82.6**

psychosis: **1 in 200**

malignant neoplasms (solid tumor cancers): **1 in 254**

pneumonia: **1 in 273**

bone fracture: **1 in 276**

osteoarthritis and related conditions: **1 in 292**

stroke: **1 in 303**

congestive heart failure: **1 in 305**

septicemia: **1 in 380**

cardiac arrythmia: **1 in 402**

coronary atherosclerosis: **1 in 474**

diabetes: **1 in 485**

chronic bronchitis: **1 in 503**

cellulitis or abscess: **1 in 510**

heart attack: **1 in 518**

urinary tract infection: **1 in 552**

asthma: **1 in 699**

anemia: **1 in 787**

intestinal obstruction: **1 in 800**

benign tumor: **1 in 917**

cholelithiasis (gall bladder, including gallstones): **1 in 917**

enteritis or colitis: **1 in 962**

spinal disc disorders: **1 in 971**

diverticulitis of the intestines: **1 in 1,031**

essential hypertension (high blood pressure): **1 in 1,099**

acute pancreatitis: **1 in 1,111**

appendicitis: **1 in 1,124**

poisoning: **1 in 1,190**

acute bronchitis: **1 in 1,786**

kidney stones: **1 in 1,961**

SOURCE: US Centers for Disease Control and Prevention/National Center for Health Statistics, "Average Length of Stay for Discharges from Short-Stay Hospitals, by First-Listed Diagnosis and Age," *National Hospital Discharge Survey, 2010,* http://www.cdc.gov/nchs/data/nhds/2average/2010ave2_dischargesage.pdf.

DID YOU know?

The odds a person will be hospitalized for complications of surgical or medical care:

1 in 303

SOURCE: US Centers for Disease Control and Prevention/National Center for Health Statistics, "Average Length of Stay for Discharges from Short-Stay Hospitals, by First-Listed Diagnosis and Age," *National Hospital Discharge Survey, 2010,* http://www.cdc.gov/nchs/data/nhds/2average/2010ave2_dischargesage.pdf.

PUSH

The odds a woman will be hospitalized for the delivery of one or more babies:

1 in 23.8

SOURCE: US Centers for Disease Control and Prevention/National Center for Health Statistics, "Average Length of Stay for Discharges from Short-Stay Hospitals, by First-Listed Diagnosis and Age," *National Hospital Discharge Survey, 2010,* http://www.cdc.gov/nchs/data/nhds/2average/2010ave2_dischargesage.pdf.

Physician Visits

Visits to a doctor and related clinical expenditures ranked second in size (over $500 million) and accounted for 20% of total health care expenditures in 2010. The likelihood a person will have one or more physician visits in a year as well as the total number of annual visits increases with age.

The odds, during a year, an adult 18–44 will:

not visit a physician: 1 in 3.9

visit a physician once: 1 in 5.2

visit a physician 2–3 times: 1 in 4

visit a physician 4–9 times: 1 in 5.4

visit a physician 10 or more times: 1 in 8.8

The odds, during a year, an adult 65–74 will:

not visit a physician: 1 in 16.1

visit a physician once: 1 in 9.8

visit a physician 2–3 times: 1 in 3.6

visit a physician 4–9 times: 1 in 2.7

visit a physician 10 or more times: 1 in 5.2

The odds, during a year, an adult 45–64 will:

not visit a physician: 1 in 6.1

visit a physician once: 1 in 6.3

visit a physician 2–3 times: 1 in 3.6

visit a physician 4–9 times: 1 in 4

visit a physician 10 or more times: 1 in 6.7

The odds, during a year, an adult 75 or older will:

not visit a physician: 1 in 23.3

visit a physician once: 1 in 10.3

visit a physician 2–3 times: 1 in 4.4

visit a physician 4–9 times: 1 in 2.4

visit a physician 10 or more times: 1 in 4.6

SOURCE: JR Pleis, BW Ward, JW Lucas, "Summary Health Statistics for US Adults: National Health Interview Survey, 2009," *Vital Health Statistics Reports* 10(249), August 2010.

Complementary and Alternative Medicine

The odds an adult used acupuncture or another form of alternative medicine in 2007: **1 in 2.6**

SOURCE: PM Barnes, B Bloom, RL Nahin, "Complementary and Alternative Medicine Survey of Hospitals," *Health Forum LLC*, 2008.

Prescription Drugs

The third-largest component of health care expenditures is prescription drugs, at 10%. According to a study by the National Center for Health Statistics, the use of prescription drugs continues to increase, doubling in expenditures from 1999 to 2008.

The odds a child 11 or younger will take:

1 prescription drug in a year: **1 in 7.1**

2 prescription drugs in a year: **1 in 21.7**

3–4 prescription drugs in a year: **1 in 37**

5 or more prescription drugs in a year: **1 in 1,111**

The odds an adult 20–59 will take:

1 prescription drug in a year: **1 in 5.1**

2 prescription drugs in a year: **1 in 8.8**

3–4 prescription drugs in a year: **1 in 10.6**

5 or more prescription drugs in a year: **1 in 12.7**

The odds an adolescent 12–19 will take:

1 prescription drug in a year: **1 in 5.8**

2 prescription drugs in a year: **1 in 14.5**

3–4 prescription drugs in a year: **1 in 20.8**

5 or more prescription drugs in a year: **1 in 111**

The odds an adult 60 or older will take:

1 prescription drug in a year: **1 in 8.3**

2 prescription drugs in a year: **1 in 8.1**

3–4 prescription drugs in a year: **1 in 3.7**

5 or more prescription drugs in a year: **1 in 2.7**

SOURCE: Q Gu, CF Dillon, VL Burt, "Prescription Drug Use Continues to Increase: US Prescription Drug Data for 2007–2008," *NDHS Data Brief 42*, September 2010.

Complementary and Alternative Medicine

Although US expenditures on medicine are enormous, the sums accounted for are not complete without considering the many complementary and alternative medicine (CAM) therapies, approaches, healing philosophies, and remedies. These therapies are not usually taught in US medical schools. Historically they were not available in hospitals, but the American Hospital Association reports that the odds that a community hospital will offer a CAM care or service are **1 in 4.8** (2007). How much do we spend on acupuncture, chiropractic care, relaxation techniques, massage therapy, and herbal remedies among the thirty-six CAM therapies and forty-five dietary supplements the NIH tracks in its surveys? In 2007, the total spent out of pocket was $33.9 billion! A decade earlier it had been $27 billion, an annual growth rate of 2.3%.

The odds a person 18 or older used _____ for medical purposes in 2007:

nonvitamin, nonmineral, natural products: **1 in 5.6**

deep breathing exercises: **1 in 7.9**

meditation: **1 in 10.6**

chiropractic or osteopathic manipulation: **1 in 11.6**

massage: **1 in 12**

yoga: **1 in 16.4**

diet-based therapies: **1 in 27.8**

progressive muscle relaxation: **1 in 34.5**

guided imagery: **1 in 43.5**

homeopathic treatment: **1 in 55.6**

movement therapies: **1 in 66.7**

acupuncture: **1 in 71.4**

tai chi: **1 in 100**

naturopathy: **1 in 333**

biofeedback: **1 in 500**

hypnosis: **1 in 500**

SOURCES: JJ Mao, CS Palmer, KE Healy, K Desai, K Amsterdam, "Complementary and Alternative Medicine Use Among Cancer Survivors: A Population-Based Study," *Journal of Cancer Survivorship: Research and Practice* 5(1), 2011: 8–17. ✔ PM Barnes, B Bloom, RL Nahin, "Complementary and Alternative Medicine Use Among Adults and Children: United States, 2007," *National Health Statistics Reports*, December 12, 2008. ✔ S Ananth, "2007 Health Forum/AHA Complementary and Alternative Medicine Survey of Hospitals," *Health Forum LLC*, 2008. ✔ D Eisenberg, R Davis, et al., "Trends in Alternative Medicine Use in the US," *Journal of the American Medical Association* 280(18), November 11, 1998: 1569–1575.

The Number One Killer
Cardiovascular Disease

Cardiovascular disease (heart disease and stroke) kills more people in the United States than cancer, accidents, and HIV combined. The prevalence of cardiovascular disease (CVD) in adults age 20 or older is **1 in 2.8**, and the risk of developing it slowly rises with age.

Why are the odds of an American developing CVD so high? The American Heart Association says it is because too many of us have the risk factors associated with CVD. These include diabetes, high blood pressure, high cholesterol, obesity, and a cluster of risk factors called metabolic syndrome.

Among those 20 and older, 11% have diabetes and 37% are prediabetic. **1 in 3** of adults 20 or older have high blood pressure and **1 in 3.1** have high cholesterol. **1 in 3.7** adults 18 or older are obese, which is asscociated with 13% of cardiovascular deaths.

A person has metabolic syndrome if he or she has three of the following risk factors: elevated blood glucose, low HDL cholesterol, high triglyceride levels, being overweight or obese, and high blood pressure. **1 in 2.9** adults are considered to have metabolic syndrome.

SOURCE: Book of Odds estimates based on data in RL Veronique, AS Go, DM Lloyd-Jones, RJ Adams, JD Berry, et al., on behalf of the American Heart Association Statistics Committee and Stroke Statistics Subcommittee, "Heart Disease and Stroke Statistics—2011 Update: A Report from the American Heart Association," *Circulation* 123, 2011: e18–e209.

Cardiovascular Disease
by Race, Ethnicity, and Gender

The odds a man 20 or older has cardiovascular disease are **1 in 2.7**.

The odds a woman 20 or older has cardiovascular disease are **1 in 2.9**.

The odds a non-Hispanic white man 20 or older has cardiovascular disease are **1 in 2.7**.

The odds a non-Hispanic white woman 20 or older has cardiovascular disease are **1 in 3**.

The odds a non-Hispanic black man 20 or older has cardiovascular disease are **1 in 2.2**.

The odds a non-Hispanic black woman 20 or older has cardiovascular disease are **1 in 2.1**.

The odds a Mexican American man 20 or older has cardiovascular disease are **1 in 3.3**.

The odds a Mexican American woman 20 or older has cardiovascular disease are **1 in 3.2**.

Demographic Group	%
Men	37
Women	35
Non-Hispanic white men	37
Non-Hispanic white women	34
Non-Hispanic black men	45
Non-Hispanic black women	47
Mexican American men	31
Mexican American women	31

SOURCE: Book of Odds estimates based on data in RL Veronique, AS Go, DM Lloyd-Jones, RJ Adams, JD Berry, et al., on behalf of the American Heart Association Statistics Committee and Stroke Statistics Subcommittee, "Heart Disease and Stroke Statistics—2011 Update: A Report from the American Heart Association," *Circulation* 123, 2011: e18–e209.

Selected Heart Attack Odds

Demographic Group	%
Men 20 or older	4
Women 20 or older	2
Non-Hispanic white men 20 or older	4
Non-Hispanic white women 20 or older	2
Non-Hispanic black men 20 or older	4
Non-Hispanic black women 20 or older	2
Mexican American men 20 or older	3
Mexican American women 20 or older	1

SOURCE: Book of Odds estimate based on data in RL Veronique, AS Go, DM Lloyd-Jones, RJ Adams, JD Berry, et al., on behalf of the American Heart Association Statistics Committee and Stroke Statistics Subcommittee, "Heart Disease and Stroke Statistics—2011 Update: A Report from the American Heart Association," *Circulation* 123, 2011: e18–e209.

Use of Dietary Supplements

The odds an adult over 20 took supplements:

2003–2006: **1 in 1.9**

1988–1994: **1 in 1.9**

The odds an adult over 20 took multivitamins/multiminerals:

2003–2006: **1 in 2.6**

1988–1994: **1 in 3.3**

The odds a woman over 60 took supplemental calcium:

2003–2006: **1 in 1.6**

1988–1994: **1 in 3.5**

The odds a woman 20–39 took folic acid dietary supplements:

2003–2006: **1 in 2.9**

1988–1994: **1 in 3.1**

The odds a man 20–39 took vitamin D supplements:

2003–2006: **1 in 3.8**

The odds a man 40–59 took vitamin D supplements:

2003–2006: **1 in 2.6**

The odds a man 60 and over took vitamin D supplements:

2003–2006: **1 in 2.3**

SOURCE: J Gahche, R Bailey, V Burt, J Hughes, E Yetley, J Dwyer, MF Picciano, M McDowell, C Sempos, "Dietary Supplement Use Among U.S. Adults Has Increased Since NHANES III (1988–1994)," *National Center for Health Statistics Data Brief* 61, April 2011.

The State in the Worst Condition?

Mississippi

According to the "State of the Heart Report," 7 out of 8 Mississippi adults older than 45 have at least one major risk factor for developing cardiovascular disease. America's Health Rankings has placed Mississippi among the bottom three states every year since 1990, when the rankings began, and the

bottom state every year from 2002 to 2010, thanks to an obesity rate at 35% and a lifetime mortality rate among people with CVD at 373.7 deaths per 100,000. The odds a person in Mississippi will die from cardiovascular disease in a year are **1 in 287**, much higher than the odds for the entire US population.

Other states with a high percentage of deaths from CVD include Alabama (**1 in 302**), Oklahoma (**1 in 311**), West Virginia (**1 in 323**), and Tennessee (**1 in 325**). The District of Columbia also has an especially high CVD death rate (**1 in 307**). The common thread among DC and these four states is that all rank in the bottom quintile in America's Health Rankings' "overall state rankings," which considers twenty-two measures covering "determinants of health" and "health outcomes," as well as prevalence of smoking and obesity.

SOURCES: Mississippi Department of Health, *Mississippi State of the Heart Report 2005.* ✔ United Health Foundation, American Public Health Association, Partnership for Prevention, *America's Health Rankings—2010 Edition.* ✔ Book of Odds estimates based on National Health and Nutrition Examination Survey 2006 state death rate data, http://www.cdc.gov/nchs/nhanes.htm. ✔ KD Kochanek, J Xu, SL Murphy, AM Miniño, HC Kung, "Deaths: Preliminary Data for 2009," *National Vital Statistics Reports* 59(4), March 16, 2011.

 ODDS COUPLE

AKA: Heart Attack

The odds a person will die from acute myocardial infarction in a year: **1 in 265**

The odds an NFL kickoff will be returned for a touchdown: **1 in 270**

SOURCES: KD Kochanek, J Xu, SL Murphy, AM Miniño, HC Kung, "Deaths: Preliminary Data for 2009," *National Vital Statistics Reports* 59(4), March 16, 2011. ✔ Book of Odds estimate based on data compiled from the 2006–2007 season of the National Football League.

Death Odds for
Major Cardiovascular Conditions or Events

The odds a person will die from:

cardiovascular disease in a year	1 in 427
coronary heart disease in a year	1 in 1,300
stroke in a year	1 in 2,571
heart failure in a year	1 in 5,917
hypertension in a year	1 in 12,987
aortic aneurysm and dissection in a year	1 in 30,303
atherosclerosis in a year	1 in 45,465

SOURCE: KD Kochanek, J Xu, SL Murphy, AM Miniño, HC Kung, "Deaths: Preliminary Data for 2009," *National Vital Statistics Reports* 59(4), March 16, 2011.

 ODDS COUPLE

The Telltale Heart

The odds a death will be due to heart disease: **1 in 4.2**

The odds a music listener will download 11–20 songs in a month: **1 in 4.2**

SOURCES: DL Hoyert, JQ Xu, "Deaths: Preliminary Data for 2011," *National Vital Statistics Reports* 61(6), October 10, 2012. ✔ Lab 42, "Survey of Music Listening and Sharing Habits of Social Media Users," http://blog.lab42.com/socialmusicsoundbytes.

Selected Heart Failure Odds

The odds an adult 20 or older has heart failure . . . . **1 in 41.7**

The odds a man 20 or older has heart failure . . . . **1 in 33.3**

The odds a woman 20 or older has heart failure . . . . **1 in 50**

The odds a non-Hispanic white man 20 or older has heart failure . . . . **1 in 37**

The odds a non-Hispanic white woman 20 or older has heart failure . . . **1 in 55.6**

The odds a non-Hispanic black man 20 or older has heart failure . . . . . . **1 in 22.2**

The odds a non-Hispanic black woman 20 or older has heart failure . . . . **1 in 26.3**

The odds a Mexican American man 20 or older has heart failure . . . . . . **1 in 43.5**

The odds a Mexican American woman 20 or older has heart failure . . . . **1 in 76.9**

The odds a man 20–39 has heart failure . . . . **1 in 500**

The odds a woman 20–39 has heart failure . . . . **1 in 333**

The odds a man 40–59 has heart failure . . . . **1 in 52.6**

The odds a woman 40–59 has heart failure . . . . **1 in 125**

The odds a man 60–79 has heart failure . . . . **1 in 11.1**

The odds a woman 60–79 has heart failure . . . . **1 in 18.5**

The odds a man 80 or older has heart failure . . . . **1 in 8.7**

The odds a woman 80 or older has heart failure . . . . **1 in 8.5**

Demographic group	%
Adult 20 or older	2
Men 20 or older	3
Women 20 or older	2
Non-Hispanic white men 20 or older	3
Non-Hispanic white women 20 or older	2
Non-Hispanic black men 20 or older	5
Non-Hispanic black women 20 or older	4
Mexican American men 20 or older	2
Mexican American women 20 or older	1
Men 20–39	0.2
Women 20–39	0.3
Men 40–59	2
Women 40–59	1
Men 60–79	9
Women 60–79	5
Men 80 or older	12
Women 80 or older	12

SOURCE: Book of Odds estimate based on National Health and Nutrition Examination Survey data in RL Veronique, AS Go, DM Lloyd-Jones, RJ Adams, JD Berry, et al., on behalf of the American Heart Association Statistics Committee and Stroke Statistics Subcommittee, "Heart Disease and Stroke Statistics—2011 Update: A Report from the American Heart Association," *Circulation* 123, 2011: e18–e209.

Some **Procedures** Are **Much Riskier** Than Others

The odds a person will die during mitral valve surgery: **1 in 16.7**

The odds a person will die during aortic valve surgery: **1 in 32.3**

The odds a person will die during coronary artery bypass surgery: **1 in 52.6**

SOURCE: Book of Odds estimate based on National Health and Nutrition Examination Survey 2008 data, http://www.cdc.gov/nchs/nhanes.htm.

Lifesavers

The odds a person who has out-of-hospital cardiac arrest will receive CPR from a bystander: **1 in 3.1**

The odds a person who has out-of-hospital cardiac arrest will receive defibrillation from a bystander: **1 in 47.6**

The odds a person who has out-of-hospital cardiac arrest will be discharged alive: **1 in 14.3**

SOURCE: Book of Odds estimates based on data in RL Veronique, AS Go, DM Lloyd-Jones, RJ Adams, JD Berry, et al., on behalf of the American Heart Association Statistics Committee and Stroke Statistics Subcommittee, "Heart Disease and Stroke Statistics—2011 Update: A Report from the American Heart Association," *Circulation* 123, 2011: e18–e209.

Have 1 in 10,000 People
Misplaced Their Hearts?

A small percentage of people—in the United States, about **0.01%**, or **1 in 10,000**—has a congenital condition known as "situs inversus" (SI), in which his or her internal organs are a mirror image of the typical organ layout: thus, the liver and gallbladder lie on the left, and the stomach, spleen, and heart on the right. Because SI presents few symptoms, many people do not discover their organs are inverted until later in life, often after a medical procedure.

Despite its orientation, the heart itself is generally unaffected. People with situs inversus are only slightly more at risk for heart disease. It does come with a predisposition to sinus infections and chest colds, which manifest themselves in approximately **20%** of people with SI. This symptom, known as Kartagener syndrome, occurs when the body's cilia (the tiny, moving hairs that flush foreign objects out of the respiratory tract) are immobile from birth. Because half of people with Kartagener syndrome have situs inversus, too, a sort of ongoing chicken-and-egg debate has arisen over which causes which.

Organ reversion does not typically affect a person's lifespan, but—prior to being diagnosed—he or she is at risk for some disquieting mix-ups. For example, a seemingly benign pain in the lower left of the abdomen can end up being appendicitis; a tingling right arm, a heart attack. Often, people who know they have SI wear bracelets to indicate their dextrocardia, so that in a medical emergency doctors know where their heart lies.

SOURCES: DN Kennedy, KM O'Craven, BS Ticho, AM Goldstein, N Makris, JW Henson, "Structural and Functional Brain Asymmetries in Human Situs Inversus Totalis," *Neurology* 53(6), October 12, 1999: 1260–1265. ✍ Office of Rare Disease Research, National Institutes of Health, Situs Inversus, Genetic and Rare Disease Information Center, http://rarediseases.info.nih.gov/GARD/Condition/4883/Situs_inversus.aspx.

 **GENDER WARS**

The odds a woman 45 or older who survives her first heart attack will die within one year of the event are **1 in 3.8** vs. **1 in 5.3** for a man.

SOURCE: Book of Odds estimate based on data in RL Veronique, AS Go, DM Lloyd-Jones, RJ Adams, JD Berry, et al., on behalf of the American Heart Association Statistics Committee and Stroke Statistics Subcommittee, "Heart Disease and Stroke Statistics—2011 Update: A Report from the American Heart Association," *Circulation* 123, 2011: e18–e209.

Heart Attacks Come in Packs

Of the 935,000 heart attacks in a year, **35%** or 325,000 are not first-time events.

The odds a woman 45 or older will have another heart attack or fatal coronary heart disease within five years are **1 in 4.5**. Men 45–64 face better odds: **1 in 6.7**. For a man 65 or older, however, the odds are **1 in 4.5**.

SOURCE: Book of Odds estimates based on pooled data from the Atherosclerosis Risk in Communities Study, the Cardiovascular Health Study, and Framingham Heart Study published in "Heart Disease and Stroke Statistics—2011 Update: A Report from the American Heart Association," *Circulation* 123, 2011: e18–e209.

More Than We Can Bear

You really can die from a broken heart.

A decade ago, Japanese cardiologists noticed something odd about several victims of cardiac arrest. A typical heart attack results from deterioration of the heart and arteries, cholesterol buildup, embolism, or some other factor. But these patients showed little or no sign of cardiovascular disease. EKG imaging revealed an unusual problem: a partial malfunction of the left ventricle caused the tip of that heart chamber to bulge instead of contracting. On the EKG, the ventricle resembled, to the Japanese doctors' eyes, a *tako-tsubo*—an octopus trap. Hence the syndrome's first name: takotsubo cardiomyopathy, or as it is more commonly called, "Broken Heart Syndrome."

Broken Heart Syndrome most often occurs in the face of overwhelming shock or loss. A heart reacts adversely to the release of stress hormones and stops pumping correctly—Dr. Scott Sharkey of the Minneapolis Heart Institute refers to it as a "concussion" of the heart.

The odds a person will experience Broken Heart Syndrome in a year are **1 in 25,010**. Those are slightly lower than the odds a person in the United States will be murdered in a year (**1 in 24,605**). The odds a person will die of it in a year are only **1 in 2,345,000**. With proper treatment, almost all patients make a full recovery.

The odds a person will survive Broken Heart Syndrome are **1 in 1.01**. Only a heartbreaking few will die from it.

SOURCES: D Derrick, "The 'Broken Heart Syndrome': Understanding Takotsubo Cardiomyopathy," *Clinical Care Nurse* 29, February 2009: 49–57. ✔ Book of Odds estimates based on data in US Census Bureau, Population Division, "Table 1. Annual Estimates of the Population for the United States, Regions, States, and Puerto Rico: April 1, 2010 to July 1, 2011" (NST-EST2011-01), December 2011. ✔ US Department of Justice, Federal Bureau of Investigation, *Crime in the United States, 2011*, September 2012.

Selected Stroke Odds by Age, Race, and Gender

Group	Men Odds (1 in)	Women Odds (1 in)
Person 20 or older	37.0	30.3
Non-Hispanic white 20 or older	41.7	30.3
Non-Hispanic black 20 or older	22.2	22.7
Mexican American 20 or older	50.0	50.0
20–39	333.0	200.0
40–59	62.5	41.7
60–79	13.9	12.2
80+	6.9	6.8

SOURCE: Book of Odds estimates based on National Health and Nutrition Examination Survey data in RL Veronique, AS Go, DM Lloyd-Jones, RJ Adams, JD Berry, et al., on behalf of the American Heart Association Statistics Committee and Stroke Statistics Subcommittee, "Heart Disease and Stroke Statistics—2011 Update: A Report from the American Heart Association," *Circulation* 123, 2011: e18–e209.

Cancer

Racial Disparities: Lifetime Cancer Risk

The odds a person will ever be diagnosed with cancer:

White
1 in 2.4

Black
1 in 2.6

Hispanic
1 in 2.7

Asian or Pacific Islander
1 in 2.8

American Indian or Native Alaskan
1 in 3.5

SOURCE: N Howlader, AM Noone, M Krapcho, N Neyman, R Aminou, SF Altekruse, et al., eds., *SEER Cancer Statistics Review, 1975–2009 (Vintage 2009 Populations)*. Bethesda, MD: National Cancer Institute, http://seer.cancer.gov/csr/1975_2009_pops09/, based on November 2011 SEER data submission, posted to the SEER website, April 2012.

⚕ GENDER WARS

The odds a woman will ever be **diagnosed with cancer** are **1 in 2.6** vs. **1 in 2.2** for a man.

SOURCE: N Howlader, AM Noone, M Krapcho, N Neyman, R Aminou, SF Altekruse, et al., eds., *SEER Cancer Statistics Review, 1975–2009 (Vintage 2009 Populations)*. Bethesda, MD: National Cancer Institute, http://seer.cancer.gov/csr/1975_2009_pops09/, based on November 2011 SEER data submission, posted to the SEER website, April 2012.

Lifetime Odds of Cancer
(most likely to least likely)

Cancer Type	All People (1 in)	Males (1 in)	Females (1 in)
All sites	2.4	2.2	2.6
Lung	14.3	12.9	15.7
Breast	15.6	769.0	8.1
Colorectal	20.2	19.3	20.9
Bladder	41.8	26.2	87.0
Non-Hodgkin lymphoma	47.2	42.7	51.8
Melanoma	50.3	40.2	63.3
Kidney	62.5	49.0	83.3
Pancreas	68.0	67.6	69.0
Leukemia	74.1	62.9	87.7
Oral	92.6	66.7	147.0
Thyroid	97.1	192.0	65.4
Stomach	116.0	91.7	152
Liver	120.0	84.7	204.0
Myeloma	149.0	130.0	175.0
Brain	161.0	143.0	182.0
Esophagus	196.0	123.0	435.0
Larynx	278.0	167.0	714.0
Hodgkin lymphoma	435.0	400.0	476.0
Mesothelioma	769.0	476.0	2,000.0
Karposi sarcoma	2,000.0	1,250.0	10,000.0

SOURCE: N Howlader, AM Noone, M Krapcho, N Neyman, R Aminou, SF Altekruse, er al., eds., *SEER Cancer Statistics Review, 1975–2009 (Vintage 2009 Populations)*. Bethesda, MD: National Cancer Institute, http://seer.cancer.gov/csr/1975_2009_pops09/, based on November 2011 SEER data submission, posted to the SEER website, April 2012.

As the Smoke Drifts

Part, but not all, of the changing likelihood of **lung cancer** can be traced back to smoking habits. The increasing odds a woman will die of lung cancer in a year can be explained by the increase in smoking by women in the fififtes and sixties, for example . . .

Here is an overview: In 1965, the prevalence of smoking among men was 52% versus 34% for women. By 1979, the prevalence had dropped to 38% for men and 30% for women, and in 1998, 26% for men and 22% for women. By 2011 the smoking prevalence dropped to 22% for men and 17% for women, so lung cancer death rates will continue to decline going in the future.

The odds a woman/man will die of lung cancer in a year (by year):

1975	1980	1985	1990	1995	2000	2005	2009
woman	woman	woman	woman	woman	woman	woman	woman
1 in 5,695	1 in 4,144	1 in 3,288	1 in 2,714	1 in 2,484	1 in 2,432	1 in 2,461	1 in 2,593
man	man	man	man	man	man	man	man
1 in 1,309	1 in 1,180	1 in 1,128	1 in 1,104	1 in 1,185	1 in 1,308	1 in 1,436	1 in 1,614

Dying of Lung Cancer	Men		Women	
Year	%	Rate/100,000	%	Rate/100,000
1975	.08	76.4	.02	17.6
1980	.08	84.7	.02	24.1
1985	.09	88.6	.03	30.4
1990	.09	90.6	.04	36.9
1995	.08	84.4	.04	40.3
2000	.08	76.5	.04	41.1
2005	.07	69.7	.04	40.6
2009	.06	62.0	.04	38.6
1975–2009	.08	79.8	.04	35.1

SOURCES: Office on Smoking and Health, *Women and Smoking: A Report of the Surgeon General*, Atlanta, GA: Centers for Disease Control and Prevention, March 2001, http://www.ncbi.nlm.nih.gov/books/NBK44303/ ✔ Office on Smoking and Health, "Trends in Current Cigarette Smoking Among High School Students and Adults, United States, 1965–2009," Centers for Disease Control and Prevention, http://www.cdc.gov/tobacco/osh/index.htm. ✔ Centers for Disease Control and Prevention/ National Center for Health Statistics, "Summary Health Statistics for U.S. Adults: National Health Interview Survey, 2011," *Vital and Health Statistics Report* 10(256), December 2012. ✔ N Howlader, AM Noone, M Krapcho, N Neyman, R Aminou, SF Altekruse, et al., eds., *SEER Cancer Statistics Review, 1975–2009 (Vintage 2009 Populations)*. Bethesda, MD: National Cancer Institute, http://seer.cancer.gov/csr/1975_2009_pops09/, based on November 2011 SEER data submission, posted to the SEER website, April 2012.

GENDER WARS
But What if One Never Smoked?

The odds a woman 40–79 who never smoked will be diagnosed with lung cancer in a year are **1 in 6,579** vs. **1 in 8,929** for a man 40–79.

SOURCE: US Department of Health and Human Services, *SEER Cancer Statistics Review, 1975–2007.*

Breast Cancer

The odds are **1 in 8.1** a woman will receive a diagnosis of breast cancer in her lifetime, about the odds a person lives in California, the most populous state. For men the odds are **1 in 769**, about the same odds a Major League Baseball game will be a no-hitter.

Young women are less likely to get the disease. For those under age 50, the odds of being diagnosed with breast cancer in a year are only **1 in 6,959**; for women older than 50, the odds shoot up to **1 in 1,037**. Peak incidence occurs between the ages of 75 and 79.

Thanks to the widespread adoption of regular mammography screenings, more and more women are being diagnosed with breast cancer before it's too late. In 1975, the odds a woman would be diagnosed with breast cancer in a year were **1 in 952** compared to **1 in 802** in 2007, an increase of 16%. Early detection has lowered the odds a woman will die of the disease in a year from **1 in 3,185** in 1975 to **1 in 4,348** in 2005–2009.

Depending on the type of breast cancer and what stage it was when discovered, treatment can involve chemotherapy, radiation therapy, surgery, or a combination of the three. With early detection and proper treatment, the outlook is good and getting better. During the period of 1985 to 1989, the odds a living woman had survived five years or longer after diagnosis were **1 in 1.2**; for those diagnosed in 2004, those odds had increased 9% to **1 in 1.1**. And as of 2009, the odds of having survived for at least twenty years were **1 in 1.5**—the fifth-best survival odds among leading cancers affecting women.

SOURCE: N Howlader, AM Noone, M Krapcho, N Neyman, R Aminou, SF Altekruse, et al., eds., *SEER Cancer Statistics Review, 1975–2009 (Vintage 2009 Populations)*. Bethesda, MD: National Cancer Institute, http://seer.cancer.gov/csr/1975_2009_pops09/, based on November 2011 SEER data submission, posted to the SEER website, April 2012.

Breast Biopsy Results by Age

The odds a woman who has a biopsy as a result of a mammogram will be diagnosed with **invasive breast cancer:**

Age 40–49	**1 in 7**
Age 50–59	**1 in 4**
Age 60–69	**1 in 3**
Age 70–79	**1 in 2.3**
Age 80–89	**1 in 1.8**

The odds a woman who has a biopsy as a result of a mammogram will have **benign findings:**

Age 40–49	**1 in 1.2**
Age 50–59	**1 in 1.5**
Age 60–69	**1 in 1.7**
Age 70–79	**1 in 2.1**
Age 80–89	**1 in 2.7**

Result of a **Suspicious Lesion** on a Mammogram by Age:

Invasive Breast Cancer

Age	%
40–49	14
50–59	25
60–69	33
70–79	44
80–89	55

Benign

Age	%
40–49	81
50–59	69
60–69	59
70–79	48
80–89	37

SOURCE: DL Weaver, RD Rosenberg, WE Barlow, L Ichikawa, PA Carney, K Kerlikowske, et al., "Cancer: Pathologic Findings from the Breast Cancer Surveillance Consortium," *Cancer* 106, 2006: 732–742.

Breast Cancer Treatment Odds

The odds a woman 20 or older diagnosed with invasive breast cancer at a stage less than IIIA:

will receive multiagent chemotherapy treatment . . . . 1 in 1.4

will have breast-conserving surgery with radiation . . . . 1 in 2.4

will have a mastectomy . . . . 1 in 2.9

will have breast-conserving surgery without radiation . . . . 1 in 4.7

will not require surgery . . . . 1 in 56.7

Treatment	%
Multiagent chemotherapy treatment	74
Breast-conserving surgery with radiation	43
A mastectomy	35
Breast-conserving surgery without radiation	21
No surgery	2

SOURCE: National Cancer Institute, National Institutes of Health, Department of Health and Human Services, *Cancer Trends Progress Report—2009/2010 Update*, April 2010, http://progressreport.cancer.gov.

Prostate and Breast Cancer
Increase in Incidence or Result of Increased/New Testing?

Both prostate cancer and breast cancer exhibited an apparent increase in incidence in the early 1990s. In those years, the PSA (prostate-specific antigen) test became widely used as part of routine medical exams for men. In 1987, 29% of women reported having a mammogram in the past two years and that increased to 70% by 2000. Thus the increase in incidence of prostate cancer and breast cancer in the 1990s was earlier detection of those cancers due to changes in the number of women receiving mammograms and to the introduction of the PSA test. Incidence rates of both are returning to 1980s levels.

Incidence of Prostate and Breast Cancer by Year

Year	Prostate Cancer			Female Breast Cancer		
	%	Rates/100,000	Odds (1 in)	%	Rates/100,000	Odds (1 in)
1975	0.1	94.0	1,064	0.1	105.1	952
1980	0.1	106.0	943	0.1	102.2	979
1985	0.1	115.6	866	0.1	124.2	806
1990	0.2	171.1	586	0.1	131.8	759
1995	0.2	169.3	593	0.1	132.6	755
2000	0.2	183.2	552	0.1	136.4	736
2005	0.2	157.0	658	0.1	126.0	806
2009	0.2	155.6	603	0.1	130.1	769
1975–2009	0.2	153.1	653	0.1	125.3	798

SOURCES: N Howlader, AM Noone, M Krapcho, N Neyman, R Aminou, SF Altekruse, et al., eds., *SEER Cancer Statistics Review, 1975–2009 (Vintage 2009 Populations)*. Bethesda, MD: National Cancer Institute, http://seer.cancer.gov/csr/1975_2009_pops09/, based on November 2011 SEER data submission, posted to the SEER website, April 2012. ↗ American Cancer Society, *Breast Cancer Facts and Figures, 2011–2012*. Atlanta, GA: American Cancer Society.

A Frightening Diagnosis

Every year, more than 42,000 people in the United States are diagnosed with pancreatic cancer. As shown previously men and women have a similar lifetime risk (about **1 in 70**). It is the eighth most commonly diagnosed cancer. Based on the latest available data, the odds a person diagnosed with pancreatic cancer will survive at least one year are only **1 in 3.3**.

Pancreatic cancer has been notoriously hard to treat because of an outer coating that surrounds the cancerous cells, protecting them from being destroyed by traditional chemotherapy. Groundbreaking new treatments target this tough layer, enabling a second drug to reach the cancer cells, and there is real hope that survival odds may increase.

SOURCE: N Howlader, AM Noone, M Krapcho, N Neyman, R Aminou, SF Altekruse, et al., eds., *SEER Cancer Statistics Review, 1975–2009 (Vintage 2009 Populations)*. Bethesda, MD: National Cancer Institute, http://seer.cancer.gov/csr/1975_2009_pops09/, based on November 2011 SEER data submission, posted to the SEER website, April 2012.

The Odds of
Beating Colorectal Cancer

1 in 51.5 people will die from colorectal cancer.

The odds of surviving:

1 year: **1 in 1.2**   5 years: **1 in 1.5**   10 years: **1 in 1.7**

The best way to prevent colorectal cancer is to have routine colonoscopies.

The odds a routine colonoscopy will find:

diverticulosis: **1 in 2.2**

a polyp: **1 in 2.7**

hemorrhoids: **1 in 2.9**

nothing abnormal: **1 in 4.8**

multiple polyps: **1 in 13.9**

suspected malignant tumor: **1 in 15.6**

a tumor: **1 in 250**

SOURCES: N Howlader, AM Noone, M Krapcho, N Neyman, R Aminou, SF Altekruse, et al., eds., *SEER Cancer Statistics Review, 1975–2009 (Vintage 2009 Populations)*. Bethesda, MD: National Cancer Institute, http://seer.cancer.gov/csr/1975_2009_pops09/, based on November 2011 SEER data submission, posted to the SEER website, April 2012. ✔ JE Everhart, ed., *The Burden of Digestive Diseases in the United States* (NIH Publication No. 09-6443). Washington, DC: Government Printing Office, 2008.

Gender-Specific Cancers
Prostate Cancer

The surge in prostate cancer detection shown on the previous page is largely attributable to the development of the prostate-specific antigen blood tests for men. The odds of receiving a diagnosis of prostate cancer in a given year also rise with advancing age: for a male 65 or older the odds are **1 in 126,** compared to **1 in 1,577** for males younger than 65. For reasons that are not fully understood, both the incidence and the death rate are roughly double in black men compared to white men.

Luckily, prostate cancer is widely considered to be one of the most treatable forms of cancer, especially when it is detected early. The odds a man will die of prostate cancer in a year declined from **1 in 3,229** in 1975 to **1 in 4,548** in 2009—a reduction of 28%.

SOURCE: N Howlader, AM Noone, M Krapcho, N Neyman, R Aminou, SF Altekruse, et al., eds., *SEER Cancer Statistics Review, 1975–2009 (Vintage 2009 Populations)*. Bethesda, MD: National Cancer Institute, http://seer.cancer.gov/csr/1975_2009_pops09/, based on November 2011 SEER data submission, posted to the SEER website, April 2012.

Average Emergency Room Wait Times by State

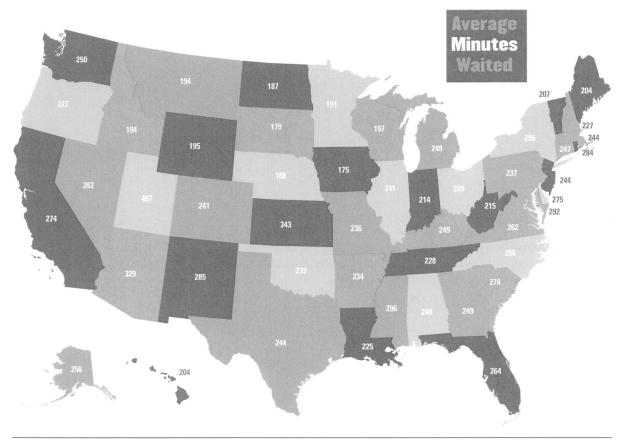

Average Minutes Waited

SOURCE: Press Ganey, *2010 Emergency Department Pulse Report.*

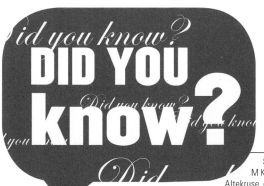

The Odds a
Man
Has:

Testicular cancer:
1 in 1,425

SOURCE: N Howlader, AM Noone, M Krapcho, N Neyman, R Aminou, SF Altekruse, et al., eds., *SEER Cancer Statistics Review, 1975–2009 (Vintage 2009 Populations).* Bethesda, MD: National Cancer Institute, http://seer.cancer.gov/csr/1975_2009_pops09/, based on November 2011 SEER data submission, posted to the SEER website, April 2012.

The Odds a
Woman
Has:

Uterine cancer: **1 in 500**
Cervical cancer: **1 in 1,324**
Ovarian cancer: **1 in 1,570**

SOURCE: N Howlader, AM Noone, M Krapcho, N Neyman, R Aminou, SF Altekruse, et al., eds., *SEER Cancer Statistics Review, 1975–2009 (Vintage 2009 Populations).* Bethesda, MD: National Cancer Institute, http://seer.cancer.gov/csr/1975_2009_pops09/, based on November 2011 SEER data submission, posted to the SEER website, April 2012.

Chronic Conditions
Hypertension

Hypertension, or high blood pressure, is the measure of the force against the walls of arteries as blood is pumped through the body by the heart. Blood pressure is measured as two readings, in millimeters of mercury—for example, 120/80. The first number is the systolic pressure (the measure of force when the heart is contracting), considered high for a person if it is more than 140 most of the time and normal if it is below 120 most of the time. The bottom number is the diastolic pressure (measure of the force when the heart is relaxing), considered high for a person if more than 90 most of the time and normal if below 80 most of the time. People are more likely to be diagnosed with high blood pressure as they get older because blood vessels become stiffer as people age.

A person has a higher risk of hypertension if he/she:

- is African American
- is obese
- eats too much salt
- has a family history of high blood pressure
- has diabetes
- smokes

High blood pressure is a risk factor for several other conditions or events, such as atherosclerosis (buildup of plaque on the arterial walls), congestive heart failure, chronic kidney disease, heart attack, and stroke.

SOURCES: PubMed Health, Hypertension, http://www.ncbi.nlm.nih.gov/pubmedhealth/PMH0001502/. ✔ Book of Odds estimates based on National Health and Nutrition Examination Survey data in RL Veronique, AS Go, DM Lloyd-Jones, RJ Adams, JD Berry, et al., on behalf of the American Heart Association Statistics Committee and Stroke Statistics Subcommittee, "Heart Disease and Stroke Statistics—2011 Update: A Report from the American Heart Association," *Circulation* 123, 2011: e18–e209.

Hypertension:
Odds by Gender and Race

The odds a person 20 or older has high blood pressure:

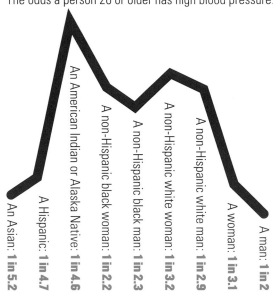

An Asian: **1 in 5.2**
A Hispanic: **1 in 4.7**
An American Indian or Alaska Native: **1 in 4.6**
A non-Hispanic black woman: **1 in 2.2**
A non-Hispanic black man: **1 in 2.3**
A non-Hispanic white woman: **1 in 3.2**
A non-Hispanic white man: **1 in 2.9**
A woman: **1 in 3.1**
A man: **1 in 2**

At younger ages, more men than women have hypertension but the odds equalize at midlife and women have a higher prevalence after age 65.

Age Group	Men Odds (1 in)	Women Odds (1 in)
20–34	9.0	14.7
35–44	4.0	5.3
45–54	2.7	2.8
55–64	1.9	1.9
65–74	1.6	1.4
75+	1.5	1.3

SOURCES: PubMed Health, "Hypertension," http://www.ncbi.nlm.nih.gov/pubmedhealth/PMH0001502/. ✔ Book of Odds estimates based on NHANES data in RL Veronique, AS Go, DM Lloyd-Jones, RJ Adams, JD Berry et al., on behalf of the American Heart Association Statistics Committee and Stroke Statistics Subcommittee, "Heart Disease and Stroke Statistics—2011 Update: A Report from the American Heart Association," *Circulation* 123, 2011: e18–e209.

When the Scale Is Scary: The Odds an 18-Year-Old Will Develop Diabetes

The odds an underweight man age 18 will be diagnosed with diabetes in his lifetime . . . . **1 in 13.2**

The odds a normal-weight man age 18 will be diagnosed with diabetes in his lifetime. . . . . **1 in 5.1**

The odds an overweight man age 18 will be diagnosed with diabetes in his lifetime . . . . **1 in 3.4**

The odds an obese man age 18 will be diagnosed with diabetes in his lifetime. . . . . **1 in 1.8**

The odds a very obese man age 18 will be diagnosed with diabetes in his lifetime. . . . . **1 in 1.4**

The odds an underweight woman age 18 will be diagnosed with diabetes in her lifetime . . . . **1 in 8.2**

The odds a normal-weight woman age 18 will be diagnosed with diabetes in her lifetime . . . . **1 in 5.9**

The odds an overweight woman age 18 will be diagnosed with diabetes in her lifetime. **1 in 2.8**

The odds an obese woman age 18 will be diagnosed with diabetes in her lifetime . . . . **1 in 1.8**

The odds a very obese woman age 18 will be diagnosed with diabetes in her lifetime . . . . **1 in 1.3**

	Men	Women
Weight	**%**	**%**
Underweight (BMI<18.5)	8	12
Normal weight (BMI 18.5–<25)	20	17
Overweight (BMI 25–<30)	30	35
Obese (BMI 30–<35)	57	55
Very obese (BMI 35+)	70	74

SOURCE: JP Boyle, EW Gregg, KMV Narayan, TJ Thompson, DF Williamson, "Effect of BMI on Lifetime Risk for Diabetes in the U.S.," *Diabetes Care* 30(6), 2007: 1562–1566.

1 in 44.4

The odds a person has **undiagnosed** diabetes.

SOURCE: Book of Odds estimate based on data in National Center for Chronic Disease Prevention and Health Promotion, Division of Diabetes Translation, *National Diabetes Fact Sheet, 2011.*

Diabetes

The odds a person has been **diagnosed** with diabetes:

1 in 16.1

A man: **1 in 15.2**

A woman: **1 in 20**

A black person: **1 in 11.1**

A Hispanic person: **1 in 11.9**

A white person: **1 in 17.2**

An Asian person: **1 in 16.9**

SOURCE: Centers for Disease Control and Prevention, National Diabetes Surveillance System, http://apps.nccd .cdc.gov/DDTSTRS/NationalSurvData .aspx.

The Odds a Person Has Prediabetes

Prediabetes is defined as having blood glucose levels, as measured by A1C levels, higher than normal but not high enough to be classified as diabetes.

20–64: **1 in 2.9**

65 or older: **1 in 2**

SOURCE: National Center for Chronic Disease Prevention and Health Promotion, Division of Diabetes Translation, *National Diabetes Fact Sheet, 2011.*

The Odds an Adult Diagnosed with Diabetes:

Takes any medication: **1 in 1.3**

Takes pills only: **1 in 2.1**

Takes insulin only: **1 in 6.5**

Takes pills and insulin: **1 in 8.1**

SOURCE: National Center for Chronic Disease Prevention and Health Promotion, Division of Diabetes Translation, *National Diabetes Fact Sheet, 2011.*

Unwanted Kidneys

A human kidney, if properly refrigerated, will keep for up to forty-eight hours. After it is harvested from a donor, the kidney is chilled in an ice bath, flushed with a preservative solution, and placed in a carefully labeled picnic cooler to await transplantation. Of the 117,793 people awaiting organs on April 6, 2013, 95,835 (81.4%) needed new kidneys. As of year-end 2011, the percentage of transplant patients on the waiting list for a kidney had increased by 86% compared with year-end 2001—while the number of transplants performed in 2011 was 16,055 or only 18% higher than 2001 levels.

According to the Organ Procurement and Transplantation Network and the Scientific Registry of Transplant Recipients' annual report, the rate at which kidneys recovered for transplant are discarded has increased steadily from 12.7% in 2002 to 17.9% in 2011. The most common reason for rejection was biopsy results (37% in 2011). According to the report, "this result may be somewhat biased, since biopsies are more likely to be obtained when the donor kidney for some reason is suspected to be suboptimal." Since biopsies have been shown to be poor predictors of graft outcomes, the report suggests they should be used less often.

According to a study by Juanjuan Zhang of MIT's Sloan School of Management, just 2.9% of the kidney offers made are accepted. The reason, Zhang suggests, lies in herd behavior. If a kidney is offered to the first person on the waiting list and rejected for any reason, patients further down the list assume there is something wrong with it. The organ cascades down the list, becoming like a house that has been sitting on the market too long. No one wants to claim something that many others have pronounced lacking.

In Zhang's sample, the average kidney was not accepted until it reached the thirty-fourth patient. That patient had previously declined fifteen other kidneys and spent 209 days on the waiting list.

Every minute an organ spends in storage causes incremental cell damage. Repeated rejection by patients means that each year, scores of kidneys available for transplant reach and then surpass their two-day expiration date.

The odds someone on the kidney waiting list will die in a year are **1 in 16.7**.

SOURCES: US Department of Health and Human Services, Health Resources and Services Administration, OPTN/SRTR Annual Data Report, 2011, December 2012. ✗ The Organ Procurement and Transplantation Network Database, http://www.usrds.org/adr.htm. ✗ Health Resources and Services Administration, Organ Procurement and Transplantation Network data as of April 6, 2013, http://optn.transplant.hrsa.gov/data/. ✗ J Zhang, "The Sound of Silence: Observational Learning in the US Kidney Market," Marketing Science Journal 29(2), 2010: 31–35. ✗ US Department of Health and Human Services, Organ Procurement and Transplantation Network, http://www.ustransplant.org/csr/current/nationalViewer.aspx?o=KI.

Going in the Wrong Direction

As the rate of diabetes has increased, so has the incidence of end-stage renal disease. The odds a person will be diagnosed with end-stage renal disease in a year:

2010:	1 in 2,874
2008:	1 in 2,759
2005:	1 in 2,835
2000:	1 in 2,932
1995:	1 in 3,570
1990:	1 in 4,543
1985:	1 in 7,080
1980:	1 in 11,620

SOURCE: US Renal Data System, USRDS 2012 Annual Data Report: Atlas of Chronic Kidney Disease and End-Stage Renal Disease in the United States, National Institutes of Health, National Institute of Diabetes and Digestive and Kidney Diseases, 2012.

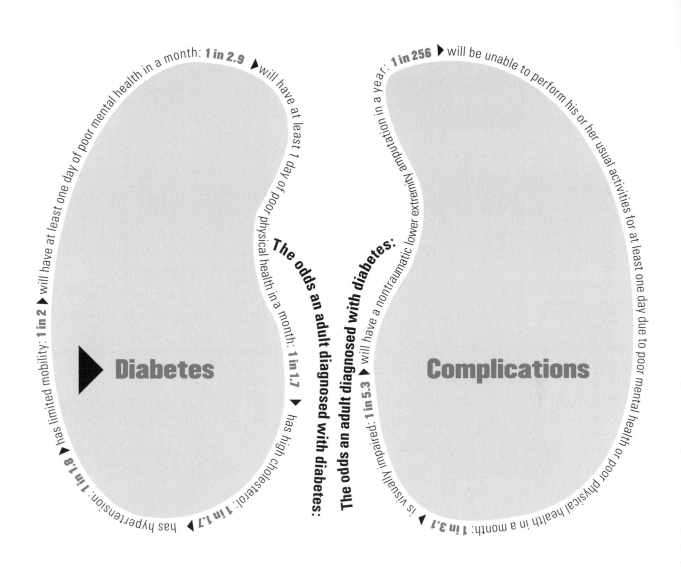

The odds an adult diagnosed with diabetes:

The odds an adult diagnosed with diabetes:

Diabetes

- will have at least one day of poor mental health in a month: **1 in 2.9** ▶
- ▶ will have at least 1 day of poor physical health in a month: **1 in 1.7**
- has high cholesterol: **1 in 1.7** ◀
- has hypertension: **1 in 1.8** ◀
- ▶ has limited mobility: **1 in 2**

Complications

- amputation in a year: **1 in 256** ▶ will be unable to perform his or her usual activities for at least one day due to poor mental health or poor physical health in a month: **1 in 3.1** ◀
- will have a nontraumatic lower extremity
- **1 in 5.3** ▶ is visually impaired:

Complications for Adults Diagnosed with Diabetes	%
One day of poor physical health a month	58
High cholesterol	57
Hypertension	56
Limited mobility	49
One day of poor mental health a month	35
Inability to perform his or her usual activities for at least one day a month due to poor mental health or poor physical health	33
Visual impairment	19
Nontraumatic lower extremity amputation	0.4

SOURCES: Centers for Disease Control and Prevention, National Diabetes Surveillance System, http://apps.nccd.cdc.gov/DDTSTRS/NationalSurvData .aspx. ✎ Centers for Disease Control and Prevention/National Center for Health Statistics, "Summary Health Statistics for U.S. Adults: National Health Interview Survey, 2008," *Vital and Health Statistics Report* 10(242), December 2009.

Autoimmune Diseases
and Other Miseries

GENDER WARS

The odds a woman will be diagnosed with an autoimmune disease in a year are **1 in 769** vs. **1 in 2,000** for a man.

SOURCE: Autoimmune Disease Coordinating Committee, National Institutes of Health, *Progress in Autoimmune Disease Research*, report to Congress, March 2005.

Psoriasis Racial Disparities

The odds a white adult will report having psoriasis are **1 in 40** vs. **1 in 76.9** for a black adult.

SOURCE: JM Gelfand, RS Stem, T Nijsten, SR Feldman, J Thomas, J Kist, et al., "The Prevalence of Psoriasis in African Americans: Results from a Population-Based Study," *Journal of the American Academy of Dermatology* 52, 2005: 23–26.

Sickle Cell Anemia

Sickle cell anemia is a genetic, lifelong disease. People inherit two genes for sickle hemoglobin—one from each parent.

According to the National Heart, Lung, and Blood Institute, sickle cell anemia is common in people whose families come from Africa, South or Central America (Panama, in particular), Caribbean islands, India, Saudi Arabia, and Mediterranean countries.

Racial Disparities

The odds a black person has sickle cell anemia: **1 in 500**

The odds a Hispanic person has sickle cell anemia: **1 in 36,000**

The odds a person is a sickle cell carrier: **1 in 152**

The odds a black person is a sickle cell carrier: **1 in 12**

SOURCE: National Heart, Lung, and Blood Institute, "Who Is at Risk for Sickle Cell Anemia," http://www.nhlbi.nih.gov/health/health-topics/topics/sca/atrisk.html.

 The odds a person will report at least one symptom of eczema: **1 in 5.9**

SOURCE: JM Hanifin, ML Reed, "A Population-Based Survey of Eczema Prevalence in the United States," *Dermatitis* 18(2), 2007: 82–91.

The Odds an Adult Has Ever Had an
Ulcer:

18–44	1 in 21.1
45–64	1 in 10.3
65–74	1 in 7.7
75 or older	1 in 8.5

SOURCE: Centers for Disease Control and Prevention/National Center for Health Statistics, "Summary Health Statistics for U.S. Adults: National Health Interview Survey, 2009," *Vital and Health Statistics Report* 10(249), December 2010.

Fibromyalgia

The odds an adult will go to the doctor in a year for treatment of fibromyalgia: **1 in 50.8**

SOURCE: United States Bone and Joint Initiative, *The Burden of Musculoskeletal Diseases in the United States*, 1st ed., Rosemont, IL: American Academy of Orthopaedic Surgeons, 2008.

The Odds a Person Has:

multiple sclerosis: **1 in 746**

Tourette's syndrome: **1 in 1,493**

Huntington's disease: **1 in 9,767**

amyotrophic lateral sclerosis (Lou Gehrig's disease): **1 in 9,956**

SOURCES: Patient Education Institute, X-Plain Patient Education. ✗ National Tourette Syndrome Association, TS Fact Sheet. ✗ http://www.alsa.org/als/who.cfm. ✗ About.com, Huntington's Disease.

 The odds a person will die from chronic constipation: **1 in 2,215,900**

SOURCE: Book of Odds estimate based on Centers for Disease Control and Prevention, *Wonder Database Compressed Mortality File*.

The odds an upper endoscopy will find a foreign body or retained food: **1 in 47.6**

SOURCE: JE Everhart, ed., *The Burden of Digestive Diseases in the United States* (NIH Publication No. 09-6443). Washington, DC: Government Printing Office, 2008.

Emphysema
Racial Disparities
The odds an adult has emphysema:

White . . . . **1 in 42.2**   Hispanic. . . . . **1 in 157**

Black . . . . **1 in 76**   Asian . . . . **1 in 182**

SOURCE: Centers for Disease Control and Prevention/National Center for Health Statistics, "Summary Health Statistics for U.S. Adults: National Health Interview Survey, 2009," *Vital and Health Statistics Report* 10(249), December 2010.

The odds a person will visit an ambulatory care facility for hemorrhoids in a year: **1 in 144**

SOURCE: JE Everhart, ed., *The Burden of Digestive Diseases in the United States* (NIH Publication No. 09-6443). Washington, DC: Government Printing Office, 2008.

GENDER WARS

The odds a man will have chronic bronchitis in a year are **1 in 34.4** vs. **1 in 17.5** for a woman.

SOURCE: Centers for Disease Control and Prevention/National Center for Health Statistics, "Summary Health Statistics for U.S. Adults: National Health Interview Survey, 2009," *Vital and Health Statistics Report* 10(249), December 2010.

Liver Disease
Racial/Ethnic Disparities

The odds an adult will be diagnosed with liver disease in a year:

White: 1 in 65.5   Hispanic: 1 in 96.22

Asian: 1 in 91.2   Black: 1 in 109.5

SOURCE: Centers for Disease Control and Prevention/National Center for Health Statistics, "Summary Health Statistics for U.S. Adults: National Health Interview Survey, 2009," *Vital and Health Statistics Report* 10(249), December 2010.

Giving Blood

Only about **4.3%**, **1 in 23.4** Americans, will donate blood in a year.

A quick way to remember who can receive what: add "O" to a blood type, and you will have every possible type that blood can receive. For instance: type A. Add an O, to make AO—A can receive A or O blood. Or AB—add an O to make ABO—AB can receive A, B, AB, or O. O, you'll notice, can only receive O blood but (according to the rule) may be donated to anyone.

The Rh factor complicates donation a little, in that blood with the Rh factor present (or Rh+) can only be given to other positive blood. Rh negative blood may be given to a + or − recipient, as long as the ABO group is a match, too.

O− is the universal donor. With very few exceptions, anyone can receive O− blood. AB+ is the universal receiver, on the other hand, and can receive blood of any type. While neither is the most common type, they aren't the least common, either. Here is a breakdown of the odds on blood types, from common to rare.

O+	**1 in 2.6**
A+	**1 in 2.9**
B+	**1 in 11.1**
O−	**1 in 14.3**
A−	**1 in 16.7**
AB+	**1 in 33.3**
B−	**1 in 50**
AB−	**1 in 100**

SOURCES:

Hay Fever

Make a lot of hay? You probably have the fever.

The odds an adult with a family income of $100,000 or more will suffer from hay fever in a year are **1 in 10.4,** or a little under 10%. The odds an adult with a family income below the poverty line will experience the allergy are significantly lower—**1 in 14**.

An estimated 50 million Americans a year complain of allergic rhinitis, otherwise known as hay fever. Hay fever results from an overly sensitive immune system reaction, one that in this case treats pollen as a dangerous invader. And like other allergies, it has been growing in prevalence, especially in developed nations.

For reasons that aren't entirely clear, hay fever disproportionately plagues the wealthy. One possible explanation for this phenomenon, according to epidemiologist David P. Strachan, is the hygiene hypothesis, which states that allergies are prevented by infections in early childhood. Put simply, a dirty child will yield a healthy adult. Though Strachan's hypothesis has not been proven, there is compelling evidence to back it up. Studies have shown that owning a dog, having multiple siblings, and living on a farm—all obvious sources of germs and infection—reduce the chance of developing skin allergies. The same could be true for respiratory ones.

SOURCES: Centers for Disease Control and Prevention/National Center for Health Statistics, "Summary Health Statistics for U.S. Adults: National Health Interview Survey, 2009," *Vital and Health Statistics Report* 10(249), December 2010. ✒ DP Strachan, "Family Size, Infection, and Atopy: The First Decade of the 'Hygiene Hypothesis,'" *Thorax: An International Journal of Respiratory Medicine* 55(Suppl 1): S2–S10. ✒ J Hurst, "The 'Hygiene Hypothesis' Revisited," *Thorax: An International Journal of Respiratory Medicine* 59(8), August 2004: 698.

But Asthma Afflicts the Poor

For adults, the odds of having asthma at any time in life are **1 in 7.7**. However, in families living below the poverty level, the odds of this for an adult are greater: **1 in 6**. In children, the odds of ever having had asthma are **1 in 7.3,** but for children in families living below the poverty level, the odds are **1 in 5.6**.

SOURCE: Centers for Disease Control and Prevention/National Center for Health Statistics, "Summary Health Statistics for U.S. Adults: National Health Interview Survey, 2009," *Vital and Health Statistics Report* 10(249), December 2010.

Vision Problems

The odds an adult has vision problems:

18–44: **1 in 18.7**	65–74: **1 in 9.7**
45–64: **1 in 9.2**	75 or older: **1 in 6.1**

SOURCE: Centers for Disease Control and Prevention/National Center for Health Statistics, "Summary Health Statistics for U.S. Adults: National Health Interview Survey, 2009," *Vital and Health Statistics Report* 10(249), December 2010.

The odds a person 40 or over has a specific vision problem: **1 in 34**

Blindness: **1 in 111**	Cataracts: **1 in 5.8**
Low vision*: **1 in 49.1**	Diabetic retinopathy: **1 in 18.6**
Myopia[†]: **1 in 4.2**	
Hyperopia[††]: **1 in 10.1**	Glaucoma: **1 in 52.5**

*Low vision is defined as the best-corrected visual acuity less than 6/12 (‹20/40) in the better-seeing eye (excluding those who were categorized as being blind by the US definition).

[†]nearsightedness   [††]farsightedness

SOURCE: National Eye Institute, "Prevalence of Adult Vision Impairment and Age-Related Eye Diseases in America," http://www.nei.nih.gov/eyedata/adultvision_usa.asp.

Hearing Problems

The odds an adult 18–44 has hearing problems: **1 in 15.6**.

The odds for an adult 75 or older: **1 in 2.2**.

White: **1 in 6.1**	Black: **1 in 10.6**
American Indian or Native Alaskan: **1 in 6.7**	Asian: **1 in 10.6**
	Hispanic: **1 in 12.9**

SOURCE: Centers for Disease Control and Prevention/National Center for Health Statistics, "Summary Health Statistics for U.S. Adults: National Health Interview Survey, 2009," *Vital and Health Statistics Report* 10(249), December 2010.

Anatomy of Aches and Breaks
Sprains, Strains, Fractures, Contusions, and Dislocations
by Gender and Age

The odds a **man 18–44** will suffer a:
sprain or strain in a year: **1 in 16.4**
fracture in a year: **1 in 24.4**
contusion in a year: **1 in 40**
dislocation in a year: **1 in 55.6**

The odds a **man 45–64** will suffer a:
sprain or strain in a year: **1 in 19.2**
fracture in a year: **1 in 25.6**
contusion in a year: **1 in 52.6**
dislocation in a year: **1 in 41.7**

The odds a **man 65 or older** will suffer a:
sprain or strain in a year: **1 in 32.3**
fracture in a year: **1 in 18.5**
contusion in a year: **1 in 29.4**
dislocation in a year: **1 in 83.3**

The odds a **woman 18–44** will suffer a:
sprain or strain in a year: **1 in 16.7**
fracture in a year: **1 in 37**
contusion in a year: **1 in 40**
dislocation in a year: **1 in 100**

The odds a **woman 45–64** will suffer a:
sprain or strain in a year: **1 in 13.9**
fracture in a year: **1 in 17.5**
contusion in a year: **1 in 34.5**
dislocation in a year: **1 in 29.4**

The odds a **woman 65 or older** will suffer a:
sprain or strain in a year: **1 in 16.4**
fracture in a year: **1 in 5.7**
contusion in a year: **1 in 12.8**
dislocation in a year: **1 in 25.6**

Gender, Age	Sprain/Strain %	Fracture %	Contusion %	Dislocation %
Men 18–44	6	4	3	2
Men 45–64	5	4	2	2
Men 65+	3	5	3	1
Women 18–44	6	3	3	1
Women 45–64	7	6	3	3
Women 65+	6	18	8	4

SOURCE: United States Bone and Joint Initiative, *The Burden of Musculoskeletal Diseases in the United States*, 1st ed., Rosemont, IL: American Academy of Orthopaedic Surgeons, 2008.

DID YOU know?

The odds an adult wears premade drugstore reading glasses:
1 in 7.1

SOURCE: All About Vision, "Statistics on Eyeglasses and Contact Lenses," http//www.allaboutvision.com/resources/statistics-eyewear.htm.

Of Time and the River:
The Indignities of Bladder Control
as One Ages

The odds a man 60 or older reports having had difficulty controlling his bladder in the last year:
1 in 5.8

The odds a woman 60 or older reports having had difficulty controlling her bladder in the last year:
1 in 2.6

SOURCE: L Stothers, D Thom, E Calhoun, "Urologic Diseases in America Project: Urinary Incontinence in Males—Demographics and Economic Burden," *Journal of Urology* 173, 2005: 1302–1308.

GENDER WARS

The odds a woman wears contacts are **1 in 3.9** vs. **1 in 7.1** for a man.

SOURCE: All About Vision, "Statistics on Eyeglasses and Contact Lenses," http://www.allaboutvision.com/resources/statistics-eyewear.htm.

GENDER WARS

The odds a woman 50 or older has macular degeneration are **1 in 50.5** vs. **1 in 86.3** for a man.

SOURCE: Prevent Blindness America, Vision Problems in the U.S., http://visionproblemsus.org/.

Conditions That Land You
in the Hospital

The odds a person will be hospitalized for pancreatitis in a year: **1 in 1,060**

SOURCE: JE Everhart, ed., *The Burden of Digestive Diseases in the United States* (NIH Publication No. 09-6443). Washington, DC: Government Printing Office, 2008.

Appendicitis

More men than women are stricken with appendicitis. In a year, the odds that a man will be hospitalized for appendicitis are **1 in 971** compared to **1 in 1,316** for a woman—a difference of 36%.

The odds a bellyache is actually appendicitis go up and down with age. Under the age of 15, the odds are **1 in 5,000**. Those age 15–44 are at the highest risk, **1 in 901**. After that the odds fall to **1 in 1,370** for those 45–64 and **1 in 1,639** for those 65 or older.

Appendicitis can turn deadly if the swollen appendix bursts, releasing pus and bacteria into the abdominal cavity. The odds that a person will die of appendicitis in a year are **1 in 887,121**. You are more than twice as likely to choke to death on food (**1 in 343,300**).

SOURCES: US Centers for Disease Control and Prevention/National Center for Health Statistics, "Average Length of Stay for Discharges from Short-Stay Hospitals, by First-Listed Diagnosis and Age," *National Hospital Discharge Survey, 2010,* http://www.cdc.gov/nchs/data/nhds/2average/2010ave2_dischargesage .pdf. ✗ Book of Odds estimates based on Centers for Disease Control and Prevention, *Wonder Database Compressed Mortality File.*

Kidney Stones

Kidney stones have long been regarded as something that afflicts unsuspecting adults, but physicians are increasingly diagnosing them in children. The increase is so dramatic that some hospitals have opened kidney stone clinics as part of their pediatric care centers. The reason for the increased incidence in children is not fully understood, although dietary changes may be to blame. Kidney stones are often caused by an imbalance in the salts in the urine, arising in people who consume too much salt and drink too few fluids. Metabolic problems like obesity and diabetes may also play a part.

But it's still true that far more adults are afflicted than children.

The odds a person will be hospitalized for kidney stones in a year:

Under 5: **1 in 70,840**	15–44: **1 in 2,218**
6–10: **1 in 38,150**	45–64: **1 in 1,266**
11–15: **1 in 20,270**	65 or older: **1 in 1,190**

SOURCES: http://www.childrenshospital.org/az/Site1642/mainpageS1642P0.html. ✗ TE Novak, Y Lakshamanan, BJ Trock, JP Gearhart, BR Matlage, "Sex Prevalence of Pediatric Kidney Stone Disease in the United States: An Epidemilogic Investigation," *Urology* 74(1), July 2009: 104. ✗ US Centers for Disease Control and Prevention/National Center for Health Statistics, "Average Length of Stay for Discharges from Short-Stay Hospitals, by First-Listed Diagnosis and Age," *National Hospital Discharge Survey, 2010,* http:// www.cdc.gov/nchs/data/nhds/2average/2010ave2_dischargesage.pdf.

The odds a person 65 or older has Alzheimer's disease: **1 in 6.9**

The odds a person 85 or older has Alzheimer's disease: **1 in 1.6**

SOURCE: Alzheimer's Association, 2010 Alzheimer's Disease Facts and Figures.

Older Adults and Hip Fractures

The odds an adult has ever broken or fractured a hip:

45–64: **1 in 125**

65–74: **1 in 50**

75–84: **1 in 28.6**

85 or older: **1 in 9.4**

SOURCE: Centers for Disease Control and Prevention/National Center for Health Statistics, "Summary Health Statistics for U.S. Adults: National Health Interview Survey, 2009," *Vital and Health Statistics Report* 10(249), December 2010.

The odds a woman will have her tonsils removed in a year: **1 in 353**

SOURCE: Centers for Disease Control and Prevention, *National Ambulatory Surgery in the US.*

Numbers Tell the Story

"I Got More than Flowers During My Hospital Stay."

The odds a hospitalized patient:

will be diagnosed with a hospital-acquired infection . . . . 1 in 22.1

will be diagnosed with a hospital-acquired urinary tract infection . . . . 1 in 88.4

will be diagnosed with a hospital-acquired surgical site infection . . . . 1 in 137

will be diagnosed with a hospital-acquired bloodstream infection . . . . 1 in 281

will be diagnosed with hospital-acquired pneumonia . . . . 1 in 290

will die as a result of a hospital-acquired infection . . . . 1 in 17.2

The Moral: **Stay out of the hospital.**

SOURCE: RM Klevens, JR Edwards, CL Richards, TC Horan, RP Gaynes, DA Polock, "Estimating Health Care–Associated Infections and Deaths in U.S. Hospitals," *Public Health Reports* 122, March–April 2007: 160–166.

Dental Problems
Odds on Visiting a Dentist

The odds an adult has never visited the dentist: **1 in 127**

The odds an adult last visited the dentist more than 5 years ago: **1 in 7.9**

The odds an adult last visited the dentist 3–5 years ago: **1 in 8.8**

The odds an adult last visited the dentist 1–2 years ago: **1 in 7.6**

The odds an adult last visited the dentist 6 months–1 year ago: **1 in 5.9**

The odds an adult last visited the dentist less than 6 months ago: **1 in 2.3**

Last Visit	%
Never	1
5+ years	13
3–5 years	11
1–2 years	13
6 months–1 year	17
<6 months	44

SOURCE: Centers for Disease Control and Prevention/National Center for Health Statistics, "Summary Health Statistics for U.S. Adults: National Health Interview Survey, 2009," *Vital and Health Statistics Report* 10(249), December 2010.

The odds an adult 35–49 has lost all of his or her teeth: **1 in 38.0**

The odds an adult 50–64 has lost all of his or her teeth: **1 in 9.9**

SOURCE: BA Dye, S Tan, V Smith, BG Lewis, K Barker, G Thornton-Evans, et al., "Trends in Oral Health Status: United States, 1988–1994 and 1999–2004," *Vital and Health Statistics* 11(248), April 2007.

Parkinson's Disease
Racial/Ethnic Disparities

The odds of dying from Parkinson's disease in a year:

White:
1 in 12,850

Asian or Pacific Islander:
1 in 43,969

Black:
1 in 50,875

American Indian or Native Alaskan:
1 in 58,831

Hispanic:
1 in 61,620

SOURCE: Book of Odds estimates based on data from Centers for Disease Control and Prevention, *Wonder Database Compressed Mortality File.*

GENDER WARS

The odds a woman 65 or older has osteoporosis are **1 in 3.9** vs. **1 in 27** for a man.

SOURCE: Centers for Disease Control and Prevention/National Center for Health Statistics, "Summary Health Statistics for U.S. Adults: National Health Interview Survey, 2009," *Vital and Health Statistics Report* 10(249), December 2010.

Infectious Diseases
Infectious Disease Incidence—Bacterial and Viral

The odds a person will be diagnosed with:

gonorrhea	**1 in 1004**
salmonellosis	**1 in 6,369**
whooping cough	**1 in 7,498**
Lyme disease	**1 in 11,357**
coccidioidomycosis	**1 in 18,402**
shigellosis	**1 in 22,967**
giardiasis	**1 in 23,815**
invasive streptococcus pneumoniae	**1 in 25,095**
chicken pox	**1 in 26,515**
tuberculosis	**1 in 29,355**
cryptosporidiosis	**1 in 44,381**
West Nile virus disease	**1 in 55,623**
Shiga toxin-producing E. coli	**1 in 55,872**
spotted fever rickettsiosis*	**1 in 83,157**
animal rabies	**1 in 87,685**
Legionellosis	**1 in 98,346**
invasive haemophilus influenzae disease . .	**1 in 100,207**
acute viral hepatitis B	**1 in 106,441**
acute viral hepatitis C	**1 in 208,499**
acute viral hepatitis A	**1 in 223,966**
malaria	**1 in 266,716**
listeriosis	**1 in 472,892**
invasive meningococcal disease	**1 in 625,498**
typhoid fever	**1 in 1,129,496**
mumps	**1 in 1,577,889**
brucellosis	**1 in 2,552,846**
botulism	**1 in 2,661,017**
streptococcal toxic shock syndrome	**1 in 2,795,584**
measles	**1 in 5,709,091**
tetanus	**1 in 8,722,222**
chancroid	**1 in 13,652,174**
hantavirus pulmonary syndrome	**1 in 14,952,381**
trichinellosis	**1 in 20,933,333**
Eastern equine virus	**1 in 25,160,256**
rubella	**1 in 37,740,385**
cholera	**1 in 78,500,000**
plague	**1 in 104,666,667**

*Includes Rocky Mountain spotted fever.

SOURCE: J Kriseman, DA Adams, WJ Anderson, L Blanton, R Dhara, DH Onweh, AW Schley, "Notifiable Diseases and Mortality, United States, 2008," *Morbidity and Mortality Weekly Report*, 57(54), June 25, 2010.

DID YOU know?

The odds a person will contract a flesh-eating disease in a year:

1 in 302,900

SOURCE: B Sarani, M Strong, J Pascual, W Schwab, "Necrotizing Fasciitis: Current Concepts and Review of the Literature," *Journal of the American College of Surgeons* 10(32), 2008.

If You Are Lying About Washing, Raise Your Hands

More people report they wash their hands than actually are observed doing so. Researchers secreted in locations such as the restrooms at New York's Grand Central Terminal tally who washes and who doesn't, which is compared to what people report.

	Men		Women	
	%	Odds (1 in)	%	Odds (1 in)
Report washing	91	1.1	99	1.01
Washed	77	1.3	91	1.1
Didn't wash	23	4.4	7	14.3

SOURCE: Harris Interactive, *A Survey of Handwashing Behavior (Trended),* prepared for the American Microbiology Society and the American Cleaning Institute, August 2010.

Pneumonia Deaths

The odds an infant will die of pneumonia . . . **1 in 20,868**

The odds a child

1–4 will die of pneumonia in a year . . . . **1 in 185,024**

5–14 will die of pneumonia in a year . . . . **1 in 590,646**

The odds a person

15–24 will die of pneumonia in a year . . . . **1 in 277,818**

25–34 will die of pneumonia in a year . . . . . . **1 in 126,847**

35–44 will die of pneumonia in a year . . . . . . **1 in 56,286**

45–54 will die of pneumonia in a year . . . . . . **1 in 23,362**

55–64 will die of pneumonia in a year . . . . . . **1 in 10,563**

65–74 will die of pneumonia in a year . . . . **1 in 3,520**

75–84 will die of pneumonia in a year . . . . . . **1 in 679**

85 or older will die of pneumonia in a year . . . . **1 in 219**

SOURCE: Book of Odds estimates based on Centers for Disease Control and Prevention, *Wonder Database Compressed Mortality File*, 2007 deaths.

GENDER WARS

The odds a woman has been diagnosed with arthritis are

1 in 4.1

vs.

1 in 5.5

for a man.

SOURCE: Centers for Disease Control and Prevention/National Center for Health Statistics, "Summary Health Statistics for U.S. Adults: National Health Interview Survey, 2009," *Vital and Health Statistics Report* 10(249), December 2010.

"Don't Forget! Flu Shot Tomorrow."

The odds a person will die of the flu in a year:

1 in 733,871

SOURCE: Book of Odds estimate based on Centers for Disease Control and Prevention, *Wonder Database Compressed Mortality File*, 2007 deaths.

What Are the Odds Your Temperature Is Normal?

98.6 degrees Fahrenheit is an overestimate of average body temperature. A German doctor named Carl Reinhold August Wunderlich came up with it by sticking a foot-long mercury thermometer into 25,000 people's armpits for fifteen minutes each. It was the mid-nineteenth century, so he averaged the readings by hand. This average became the medical standard for normal body temperature. And Wunderlich's thermometer wasn't even calibrated correctly—it read a good three degrees too low.

So what *is* normal? A team of researchers at the University of Maryland School of Medicine tried to answer this in 1992. They used digital thermometers, oral temperatures, and a mere 148 patients. Average body temperature, they decided, was 98.2 degrees.

But that's not the end of it, because "average" isn't "normal." "Normal" is a spread, defined as the range in which 95% of temperature readings of healthy people fall: between 97.5 and 98.9 degrees. That means there's a **1 in 20** chance your body temperature—your normal body temperature—is higher or lower than the average.

It's getting harder and harder to stay home from school.

SOURCE: PA Mackowiak, SS Wasserman, MM Levine, "A Critical Appraisal of 98.6°F," *Journal of the American Medical Association* 268(12), 1992: 1578–1580.

Sick Day Beliefs

Belief	Yes %	Yes Odds (1 in)	No %	No Odds (1 in)
Staying home sick will jeopardize his or her job.	31	**3.2**	69	**1.5**
Choosing to take a sick day will affect his or her performance review.	33	**3.0**	67	**1.5**
He or she cannot afford to stay home sick.	38	**2.6**	62	**1.6**
If he or she could find a comparable job that had more paid sick time he or she would take it.	32	**3.1**	68	**1.5**
His or her employer offers enough sick time for their employees.	77	**1.3**	23	**4.4**

SOURCE: Harris Interactive, "Most U.S. Adults Support Paid Sick Time Requirements," for the *Wall Street Journal Online*, March 7, 2007.

The odds an adult will fake being sick to miss work in a year: **1 in 3.5**

SOURCE: CareerBuilder.com, "CareerBuilder Releases Annual List of the Most Unusual Excuses for Calling in Sick, According to US Employers," press release, October 27, 2010.

ODDS COUPLE

Postscripts

The odds an adult does not have a living will: **1 in 1.5**.

These are about the same odds an adult does not believe in ghosts.

SOURCES: PEW Research Center and the People and the Press, "More Americans Discussing and Planning End-of-Life Treatment, Strong Public Support for Right to Die," press release, January 5, 2006. ⚹ Ipsos Public Affairs, *The Associated Press Poll: Ghost Study* (Project #81-5681-64), interview dates: October 16–18, 2007.

Solipsists

The odds a death will be due to intentional self-harm (suicide): **1 in 65.6**

The odds a person has a unique last name: **1 in 66.76**

SOURCES: DL Hoyert, JQ Xu, "Deaths: Preliminary Data for 2011," *National Vital Statistics Reports* 61(6), October 10, 2012. ⚹ Book of Odds calculation from US Census 2000 genealogy data.

When the End Is Near
Views on End-of-Life Care

The odds an adult approves of laws that let patients decide whether to be kept alive through medical treatment: **1 in 1.2**

The odds an adult disapproves of laws that let patients decide whether to be kept alive through medical treatment: **1 in 10**

The odds an adult believes "doctors and nurses should allow patients to die under certain circumstances": **1 in 1.4**

The odds a man believes a person suffering great pain with no hope of improvement has a moral right to end his or her life: **1 in 1.5**

The odds an adult approves of laws that allow doctors to prescribe lethal doses of drugs that a terminally ill patient could use to commit suicide: **1 in 2.2**

The odds an adult disapproves of laws that allow doctors to prescribe lethal doses of drugs that a terminally ill patient could use to commit suicide: **1 in 2.2**

The odds an adult believes that if a patient with a terminal disease is unable to communicate and has not made his or her wishes known in advance, the closest family member should be allowed to decide whether to continue medical treatment: **1 in 1.4**

The odds an adult believes that if a patient with a terminal disease is unable to communicate and has not made his or her wishes known in advance, the closest family member should not be allowed to decide whether to continue medical treatment: **1 in 6.7**

The odds a woman believes a person suffering great pain with no hope of improvement has a moral right to end his or her life: **1 in 1.9**

The odds a man believes a person with an incurable disease has a moral right to end his or her life: **1 in 1.8**

The odds a woman believes a person with an incurable disease has a moral right to end his or her life: **1 in 2**

The odds an adult will tell a doctor to stop treatment if he or she has a disease with no hope of improvement and is suffering a great deal of physical pain: **1 in 1.9**

The odds a man believes a person who is an extremely heavy burden on family has a moral right to end his or her life: **1 in 2.9**

The odds a woman believes a person who is an extremely heavy burden on family has a moral right to end his or her life: **1 in 4**

The odds an adult believes "doctors and nurses should do everything possible to save a person's life": **1 in 4.6**

The odds an adult believes a person is justified helping a spouse suffering terrible pain from a terminal disease commit suicide:

{
Always justified: **1 in 7.1**

Sometimes justified: **1 in 1.9**

Never justified: **1 in 4**
}

SOURCE: Book of Odds estimates based on PEW Research Center and the People and the Press, "More Americans Discussing and Planning End-of-Life Treatment, Strong Public Support for Right to Die," press release, January 5, 2006.

CHAPTER 8

LOOKING GOOD AND FEELING FINE

HAIR

1 in 6.3 women prefers a man to shave all of his pubic hair. **1 in 2.4** women prefers that he keep it all.

SOURCE: Remington, "Survey: Women Want Men to Do More Body Hair Grooming, Especially Below the Neck," press release, November 12, 2009.

Rise and Shine

The odds an adult brushes his or her teeth:

Once a day . . . . 1 in 3.1

Twice a day or after every meal. . . . . 1 in 1.3

During the day at work. . . . . 1 in 7.1

The odds an adult flosses daily . . . . 1 in 2

SOURCES: Mentadent, "New Survey Reveals Americans Need to Polish Up Their Dental Habits: Tooth Alert," press release, May 30, 2002. ✒ American Dental Association, "Survey Results Reveal Oral Hygiene Habits of Men Lag Behind Women," press release, May 11, 2004.

The odds an adult showers less than once a week.

Things as likely:

1 in 100

A person considers beef to be his or her favorite Thanksgiving dish

An adult has eleven siblings

An adult considers track and field to be his or her favorite sport

An adult believes couples with healthy sex lives have sex once a month

SOURCES: Moen, "Who's Sloppier in the Bathroom, Men or Women? Both According to a New Survey by Moen, Inc.," press release, September 11, 2006. ✒ J Carroll, "Pass the Turkey, Say Americans," press release, Gallup News Service, November 24, 2004. ✒ Book of Odds estimates based on: JA Davis, TW Smith, PV Marsden, *General Social Surveys, 1972–2008* [CUMULATIVE FILE] [Computer file]. ICPSR04697, v. 1., Chicago: National Opinion Research Center [producer], 2009. Storrs, CT: Roper Center for Public Opinion Research, University of Connecticut/Ann Arbor, MI: Inter-university Consortium for Political and Social Research [distributors]. ✒ Harris Interactive, "Football Expands Lead over Baseball as America's Favorite Sport," Harris Poll #15, press release, February 1, 2010. ✒ AskMen.com, "Part I: Dating & Sex," *The Great Female Survey, 2009 Edition*, www.askmen.com/specials/yahoo_shine_great_female_survey/part1.html. ✒ AskMen.com, "Part I: Dating & Sex," *The Great Male Survey, 2010 Edition*, http://www.askmen.com/specials/2010_great_male_survey.

⚔ GENDER WARS
Don't Use Up the Hot Water

Men are more likely than women to shower at least once a day: **1 in 1.4** vs. **1 in 1.8**

SOURCE: Moen, "Who's Sloppier in the Bathroom, Men or Women? Both According to a New Survey by Moen, Inc.," press release, September 11, 2006.

Take Care of Your Fingers and Toes

The odds a person who gets a manicure or pedicure is:

A female 20 or younger . **1 in 11.9**

A woman 21–25 . . . . . . **1 in 7.5**

A woman 26–35 . . . . . . **1 in 4.8**

A woman 36–45 . . . . . . **1 in 3.9**

A woman 46 or older . . **1 in 3.7**

A man . . . . **1 in 23.3**

SOURCE: 2010 Industry Statistics, *Nails Magazine*, http://files.nailsmag.com/Market-Research/bb2010-11stats-reprints.pdf.

DID YOU know?

The odds an adult usually showers in the morning: **1 in 1.6**

The odds an adult usually showers in the evening: **1 in 3.6**

SOURCE: Moen, "Who's Sloppier in the Bathroom, Men or Women? Both According to a New Survey by Moen, Inc.," press release, September 11, 2006.

Ever Hear of Deodorant?

The odds a woman will report that she has dumped a man because of his body odor: **1 in 7.1**

SOURCE: "What Are the Rules of Attraction?" *Elle/MSNBC.com Sex and Beauty Survey, Elle* magazine, 2004.

It's Not All for Show

The odds a woman believes wearing makeup makes her feel more self-confident: **1 in 1.2**

The odds a woman does not like being caught without makeup on: **1 in 3.3**

SOURCES: "L'Oreal 100th Anniversary Cosmetic Usage Survey," press release, August 27, 2009. ✒ J Weaver, "What Are Our Dating Pet Peeves?," *Elle/MSNBC.com Sex and Beauty Survey*, MSNBC.com, May 5, 2005, http://www.nbcnews.com/id/7736649.

Breakfast
Time for Caffeine

The odds an adult will
drink coffee in a day:

1 in 1.8

SOURCE: National Coffee Association Drinking
Trends Study, March 2007.

The Odds an Adult
Regularly Eats Breakfast:

1 in 1.6

What's Usually for
Breakfast?

1 in 3.3:	Cold cereal
1 in 9.1:	Bacon and eggs
1 in 11.1	Hot cereal
1 in 11.1:	Eggs, no bacon or ham
1 in 20:	Toast
1 in 25:	Bagel
1 in 33.3:	French toast
1 in 50:	Muffin
1 in 100:	Pancakes

SOURCE: G Langer, "What's for Breakfast? Liver
and Grits!," *ABC News Poll,* press release,
May 15, 2005.

The odds a dollar spent
on food eaten at home will be for
fruits and vegetables: **1 in 6.3**

SOURCE: US Bureau of Labor Statistics, US
Department of Labor, *Consumer Expenditures in
2009,* Report 1029, May 2011.

What Type of
Restaurant Food
Do Adults Prefer? Odds Are:

1 in 3.6: American	**1 in 14.3:** Japanese
1 in 4.5: Italian	**1 in 50:** Indian
1 in 5.9: Mexican	**1 in 100:** French
1 in 6.3: Chinese	**1 in 100:** Middle Eastern

SOURCE: Harris Interactive, "American Food Top Choice for People When Dining Out," 2007.

ODDS COUPLE
Who Took the Last Slice?

The odds an adult has eaten cold pizza for breakfast. . . . . **1 in 2.6**

The odds an adult usually skips breakfast. . . . . **1 in 2.6**

SOURCE: G Langer, "What's for Breakfast? Liver and Grits!," ABC News Poll, press release, May 15, 2005.

The Lowdown on Organic Food

1 in 1.3: The odds an adult believes organic food is safer for the environment.

1 in 1.3: The odds an adult believes organic food is healthier.

1 in 2.7: The odds an adult believes organic food tastes better.

1 in 1.1: The odds an adult thinks organic food is more expensive.

1 in 3: The odds an adult rarely purchases organic food.

1 in 100: The odds an adult purchases organic food all the time.

SOURCE: Harris Interactive, "Large Majorities See Organic Food as Safer, Better for the Environment and Healthier—But More Expensive," Harris Poll #97, press release, October 8, 2007.

Staying Fit

To achieve substantial health benefits, the US Department of Health and Human Services recommends, adults should do the equivalent of 150 minutes of moderate-intensity exercise or 75 minutes of vigorous-intensity aerobic exercise a week in episodes of 10 minutes or more.

The odds an adult will get the recommended amount of exercise in a week, by age:

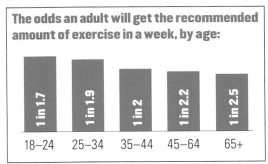

18–24	25–34	35–44	45–64	65+
1 in 1.7	1 in 1.9	1 in 2	1 in 2.2	1 in 2.5

SOURCES: US Department of Health and Human Services, *2008 Physical Activity Guidelines for Americans.* ✗ Book of Odds Estimates based on Centers for Disease Control and Prevention, U.S. Physical Activity Statistics [Internet database], http://apps.nccd.cdc.gov/PASurveillance/DemoComparev.asp.

GENDER WARS

The odds a man will take a multivitamin at least once a week are **1 in 1.9** vs. **1 in 1.6** for a woman.

SOURCE: JE Kimmons, HM Blanck, BC Tohill, J Zhang, LK Khan, "Multivitamin Use in Relation to Self-Reported Body Mass Index and Weight Loss Attempts," *Medscape Journal of Medicine* 8(3), July 6, 2006: 3.

Since 2009, the odds an adult is vegetarian have stayed roughly the same: **1 in 31.4**. The odds of being vegan? **1 in 229** in 2009; **1 in 100** in 2012.

SOURCES: *Vegetarian Times* study, "Vegetarianism in America," http://www.vegetariantimes.com/features/archive_of_editorial/667. ✗ C Stahler, "How Often Do Americans Eat Vegetarian Meals? And How Many Adults in the US Are Vegetarians? The Vegetarian Resource Group Asks in a 2012 National Harris Poll," Vegetarian Resource Group Blog, May 18, 2012.

GENDER WARS
At the Gym

The odds a man/woman will at least once a year:

walk for fitness
man: **1 in 3**   woman: **1 in 2.2**

use free weights
man: **1 in 4.1**   woman: **1 in 5.2**

use weight or resistance machines
man: **1 in 4.9**   woman: **1 in 8.8**

run or jog for fitness
man: **1 in 5.5**   woman: **1 in 7.6**

use a treadmill
man: **1 in 5.8**   woman: **1 in 5.2**

use a stationary bike
man: **1 in 8.2**   woman: **1 in 8.1**

use an abdominal machines
man: **1 in 12.8**   woman: **1 in 16.7**

stretch
man: **1 in 10.1**   woman: **1 in 6.4**

do home gym exercises
man: **1 in 10.2**   woman: **1 in 12.8**

use an elliptical motion trainer
man: **1 in 11.2**   woman: **1 in 10.1**

do aerobics
man: **1 in 15.8**   woman: **1 in 5.8**

swim
man: **1 in 15.8**   woman: **1 in 16.5**

use a stair-climbing machine
man: **1 in 22.1**   woman: **1 in 21.1**

use a rowing machine
man: **1 in 26.2**   woman: **1 in 36.8**

do yoga
man: **1 in 28.4**   woman: **1 in 9.5**

calisthenics
man: **1 in 25.7**   woman: **1 in 38.8**

do aquatic exercises
man: **1 in 49.6**   woman: **1 in 24.3**

do Pilates training
man: **1 in 107**   woman: **1 in 19.7**

do cardio kickboxing
man: **1 in 69.5**   woman: **1 in 35.9**

do tai chi
man: **1 in 99.3**   woman: **1 in 75.6**

Activity	Men %	Women %
Walk for fitness	37	45
Free weights	25	19
Weight/resistance machines	21	11
Jog for fitness	18	13
Treadmill	17	19
Stationary bike	12	12
Abdominal machines	8	6
Stretch	10	16
Home gym exercises	10	8
Elliptical	9	10
Aerobics	6	17
Swim	6	6
Stair-climbing machine	5	5
Rowing machine	4	3
Yoga	4	11
Calisthenics	4	2
Aquatic exercises	2	4
Pilates	1	5
Cardio kickboxing	1	3
Tai chi	1	1

SOURCE: Sporting Goods Manufacturers Association, *Tracking the Fitness Movement 2009*, 2010.

⚔ GENDER WARS

A person is considered inactive if he/she does not participate in any physical activity beyond the usual light or sedentary activities of daily living.

The odds a woman is inactive are **1 in 7** vs. **1 in 7.9** for a man.

SOURCES: US Department of Health and Human Services, *2008 Physical Activity Guidelines for Americans*. ↗ Centers for Disease Control and Prevention, U.S. Physical Activity Statistics [Internet database], http://apps .nccd.cdc.gov/PASurveillance/DemoComparev.asp.

Numbers Tell the Story

Resolving to do better, an adult makes a New Year's resolution to:

Exercise more frequently:
1 in 4.4

Lose weight:
1 in 4.6

Eat a healthier diet or less food:
1 in 4.8

The odds the resolution will be kept throughout the year:

Exercise more frequently:
1 in 2.2

Lose weight:
1 in 2.3

Eat a healthier diet or less food:
1 in 1.8

SOURCE: "Fewer U.S. Adults Are Making New Year's Resolutions, According to the Latest WSJ.com/ Harris Interactive Study," *Wall Street Journal Online*, February 12, 2008.

ODDS COUPLE

Love Those Greens?

The odds an adult is vegetarian or vegan:

1 in 25

The odds an adult's favorite sport is golf:

1 in 25

SOURCES: C Stahler, "How Often Do Americans Eat Vegetarian Meals? And How Many Adults in the US Are Vegetarians? The Vegetarian Resource Group Asks in a 2012 National Harris Poll," Vegetarian Resource Group Blog, May 18, 2012. ↗ Sporting Goods Manufacturers Association, *Tracking the Fitness Movement* 2009, 2010.

Be Careful with Those Weights!

The odds a person will wind up in the ER due to an accident involving exercise or exercise equipment:

1 in 808

SOURCE: US Consumer Product Safety Commission, *2010 NEISS Data Highlights*, June 2011.

Fitness Levels by State

The odds a man/woman will get the recommended amount of exercise in a week:

State	Gender	%	Odds (1 in)
Alabama	Men	45	2.2
	Women	39	2.6
Alaska	Men	64	1.6
	Women	56	1.8
Arizona	Men	54	1.9
	Women	51	2.0
Arkansas	Men	51	2.0
	Women	41	2.4
California	Men	51	2.0
	Women	49	2.0
Colorado	Men	55	1.8
	Women	54	1.9
Connecticut	Men	55	1.8
	Women	51	2.0
Delaware	Men	52	1.9
	Women	45	2.2
District of Columbia	Men	59	1.7
	Women	49	2.0
Florida	Men	49	2.0
	Women	48	2.1
Georgia	Men	51	2.0
	Women	46	2.2
Hawaii	Men	55	1.8
	Women	48	2.1
Idaho	Men	59	1.7
	Women	53	1.9
Illinois	Men	50	2.0
	Women	48	2.1
Indiana	Men	52	1.9
	Women	44	2.3
Iowa	Men	51	2.0
	Women	46	2.2
Kansas	Men	50	2.0
	Women	47	2.1

State	Gender	%	Odds (1 in)
Kentucky	Men	48	2.1
	Women	42	2.4
Louisiana	Men	41	2.5
	Women	38	2.7
Maine	Men	58	1.7
	Women	55	1.8
Maryland	Men	50	2.0
	Women	47	2.2
Massachusetts	Men	52	1.9
	Women	52	1.9
Michigan	Men	52	1.9
	Women	50	2.0
Minnesota	Men	49	2.0
	Women	49	2.1
Mississippi	Men	44	2.3
	Women	36	2.8
Missouri	Men	50	2.0
	Women	48	2.1
Montana	Men	61	1.7
	Women	56	1.8
Nebraska	Men	54	1.9
	Women	52	1.9
Nevada	Men	50	2.0
	Women	47	2.1
New Hampshire	Men	56	1.8
	Women	52	1.9
New Jersey	Men	51	2.0
	Women	46	2.2
New Mexico	Men	56	1.8
	Women	50	2.0
New York	Men	51	2.0
	Women	47	2.1
North Carolina	Men	46	2.2
	Women	42	2.4

State	Gender	%	Odds (1 in)
North Dakota	Men	52	1.9
	Women	54	1.9
Ohio	Men	54	1.9
	Women	47	2.1
Oklahoma	Men	47	2.1
	Women	45	2.2
Oregon	Men	58	1.7
	Women	55	1.8
Pennsylvania	Men	54	1.9
	Women	49	2.0
Rhode Island	Men	50	2.0
	Women	51	2.0
South Carolina	Men	52	1.9
	Women	42	2.4
South Dakota	Men	50	2.0
	Women	47	2.1
Tennessee	Men	45	2.2
	Women	35	2.8
Texas	Men	48	2.1
	Women	46	2.2
Utah	Men	56	1.8
	Women	55	1.8
Vermont	Men	59	1.7
	Women	57	1.8
Virginia	Men	50	2.0
	Women	49	2.0
Washington	Men	55	1.8
	Women	53	1.9
West Virginia	Men	51	2.0
	Women	44	2.3
Wisconsin	Men	57	1.8
	Women	54	1.9
Wyoming	Men	58	1.7
	Women	56	1.8

SOURCE: Centers for Disease Control and Prevention, U.S. Physical Activity Statistics [Internet database], http://apps.nccd.cdc.gov/PASurveillance/ DemoComparev.asp.

Height

5 foot 2, Eyes of Blue: The Odds of a Given Height

The odds a man 20–79 is:

5 feet 4 inches tall or less	1 in 23.7
5 feet 5 inches tall	1 in 32
5 feet 6 inches tall	1 in 18.1
5 feet 7 inches tall	1 in 12
5 feet 8 inches tall	1 in 8.2
5 feet 9 inches tall	1 in 9
5 feet 10 inches tall	1 in 7
5 feet 11 inches tall	1 in 7.8
6 feet tall	1 in 10.7
6 feet 1 inch tall	1 in 11
6 feet 2 inches tall	1 in 23.3
6 feet 3 inches tall	1 in 31.1
6 feet 4 inches tall	1 in 65.4
6 feet 5 inches tall	1 in 222
6 feet 6 inches tall or taller	1 in 513

The odds a woman 20–79 is:

4 feet 11 inches tall or less	1 in 32.7
5 feet tall	1 in 23.1
5 feet 1 inch tall	1 in 14.6
5 feet 2 inches tall	1 in 12
5 feet 3 inches tall	1 in 8.3
5 feet 4 inches tall	1 in 6.7
5 feet 5 inches tall	1 in 7.3
5 feet 6 inches tall	1 in 7.2
5 feet 7 inches tall	1 in 10.3
5 feet 8 inches tall	1 in 15.1
5 feet 9 inches tall	1 in 34.9
5 feet 10 inches tall	1 in 41.7
5 feet 11 inches tall	1 in 101
6 feet tall	1 in 517
6 feet 1 inch tall	1 in 1,140
6 feet 2 inches tall	1 in 2,686
6 feet 3 inches tall or taller	1 in 1,101

SOURCE: Book of Odds estimate based on height by age from National Health and Nutrition Examination Survey data published in the *Statistical Abstract of the United States, 2012,* 131st ed., Washington, DC, 2010, http://www .census.gov/compendia/statab/, and also US Census Bureau, *2008 National Population Projections,* August 2008.

Obesity by State

State	%	Odds (1 in)
Alabama	32	3.1
Alaska	27	3.6
Arizona	25	4.0
Arkansas	31	3.2
California	24	4.2
Colorado	21	4.8
Connecticut	25	4.1
Delaware	29	3.5
District of Columbia	24	4.2
Florida	27	3.8
Georgia	28	3.6
Hawaii	22	4.6
Idaho	27	3.7
Illinois	27	3.7
Indiana	31	3.2
Iowa	29	3.4
Kansas	30	3.4
Kentucky	30	3.2
Louisiana	33	3.0
Maine	28	3.6
Maryland	28	3.5
Massachusetts	23	4.4
Michigan	31	3.2
Minnesota	26	3.9
Mississippi	35	2.9
Missouri	33	3.3
Montana	25	4.1

State	%	Odds (1 in)
Nebraska	28	3.5
Nevada	25	4.1
New Hampshire	26	3.8
New Jersey	24	4.2
New Mexico	26	3.8
New York	25	4.1
North Carolina	29	3.4
North Dakota	28	3.6
Ohio	30	3.4
Oklahoma	31	3.2
Oregon	27	3.7
Pennsylvania	29	3.5
Rhode Island	25	3.9
South Carolina	31	3.2
South Dakota	28	3.6
Tennessee	29	3.4
Texas	30	3.3
Utah	24	4.1
Vermont	25	3.9
Virginia	29	3.4
Washington	27	3.8
West Virginia	32	3.1
Wisconsin	28	3.6
Wyoming	25	4.0

SOURCE: "Prevalence of Self-Reported Obesity Among US Adults," *Behavioral Risk Factor Surveillance System*, Overweight and Obesity, Centers for Disease Control and Prevention, 2011, http://www.cdc.gov/obesity/data/adult.html#Prevalence/.

Junk

The odds an adult often overeats junk food: **1 in 5.3**

SOURCE: P Taylor, C Funk, P Craighill, *Eating More; Enjoying Less, a Social Trends Report.* Washington, DC: Pew Research Center, April 19, 2006.

GENDER WARS

The odds a man reports he is seriously trying to lose weight: **1 in 4.8** vs. **1 in 3.1** for a woman.

SOURCE: E Mendes, "In U.S., 62% Exceed Ideal Weight, 19% at Their Goal," Gallup Health and Healthcare Survey, November 24, 2010, http://www.gallup.com/poll/144941/Exceed-Ideal-Weight-Goal.aspx.

Growing
in the Wrong Direction

The odds an adult 20–74 is obese:

1960–1962: **1 in 7.5**	2001–2002: **1 in 3.2**
1971–1974: **1 in 6.9**	2003–2004: **1 in 3**
1976–1980: **1 in 6.7**	2005–2006: **1 in 2.9**
1988–1994: **1 in 4.4**	2007–2008: **1 in 2.9**
1999–2000: **1 in 3.2**	2009–2010: **1 in 2.8**

SOURCES: CL Ogden, MD Carroll, "Prevalence of Overweight, Obesity, and Extreme Obesity Among Adults: United States, Trends 1960–1962 Through 2007–2008," *National Center for Health Statistics Health E-Stats,* June 2010. ✗ CL Ogden, MD Carroll, BK Kit, KM Flegal, "Prevalence of Obesity in the United States, 2009–2010," *NCHS Data Brief* 82, January 2012.

What We Think About Ourselves
The Odds of What Adults Think of Their Weight

The average man reports he weighs 195 but would like to weigh 183, while the average woman reports she weighs 159 but would like to weigh 140.

The odds a man believes he is underweight: **1 in 20**

The odds a man believes he is about the right weight: **1 in 1.6**

The odds a man believes he is overweight: **1 in 3.3**

The odds a woman believes she is underweight: **1 in 25**

The odds a woman believes she is about the right weight: **1 in 2**

The odds a woman believes she is overweight: **1 in 2.2**

Belief About Weight	Men %	Women %
Underweight	5	4
About the right weight	64	50
Overweight	30	45

SOURCE: E Mendes, "In U.S., 62% Exceed Ideal Weight, 19% at Their Goal," Gallup Health and Healthcare Survey, November 24, 2010, http://www.gallup.com/poll/144941/Exceed-Ideal-Weight-Goal.aspx.

Weight
Tipping the Scales: The Odds of a Given Weight

The odds a man 20–79 weighs:

<130 lbs: **1 in 34.9**	
130–139 lbs: **1 in 25.3**	
140–149 lbs: **1 in 19.5**	
150–159 lbs: **1 in 12.7**	
160–169 lbs: **1 in 11**	
170–179 lbs: **1 in 8.9**	
180–189 lbs: **1 in 10**	
190–199 lbs: **1 in 8.8**	
200–209 lbs: **1 in 12.1**	
210–219 lbs: **1 in 13.2**	
220–229 lbs: **1 in 17.6**	
230–239 lbs: **1 in 23.8**	
240–249 lbs: **1 in 33.9**	
250–259 lbs: **1 in 39.2**	
260–269 lbs: **1 in 60.3**	
270–279 lbs: **1 in 85.6**	
280–289 lbs: **1 in 77.3**	
290–299 lbs: **1 in 85.1**	
300–319 lbs: **1 in 127**	
320–339 lbs: **1 in 187**	
340–359 lbs: **1 in 283**	
360–379 lbs: **1 in 649**	
380–399 lbs: **1 in 1,401**	
400–419 lbs: **1 in 5,205**	
420–440 lbs: **1 in 1,676**	

The odds a woman 20–79 weighs:

<110 lbs: **1 in 21.9**

110–119 lbs: **1 in 17.5**

120–129 lbs: **1 in 11.2**

130–139 lbs: **1 in 9.1**

140–149 lbs: **1 in 9.1**

150–159 lbs: **1 in 9.8**

160–169 lbs: **1 in 11.3**

170–179 lbs: **1 in 11.5**

180–189 lbs: **1 in 15.6**

190–199 lbs: **1 in 19.9**

200–209 lbs: **1 in 25**

210–219 lbs: **1 in 27.2**

220–229 lbs: **1 in 31.8**

230–239 lbs: **1 in 51**

240–249 lbs: **1 in 58.2**

250–259 lbs: **1 in 71.7**

260–269 lbs: **1 in 107**

270–279 lbs: **1 in 116**

280–289 lbs: **1 in 304**

290–299 lbs: **1 in 219**

300–319 lbs: **1 in 171**

320–339 lbs: **1 in 270**

340–359 lbs: **1 in 730**

360–379 lbs: **1 in 1,418**

380–399 lbs: **1 in 5,407**

400–419 lbs: **1 in 4,973**

420–439 lbs: **1 in 4,973**

SOURCE: Book of Odds estimate based on weight by age from National Health and Nutrition Examination Survey data published in the *Statistical Abstract of the United States, 2012,* 131st ed., Washington, DC: 2010. http://www.census.gov/compendia/statab, and also U.S. Census Bureau, *2008 National Population Projections,* August 2008.

When It Comes to the Perfect Size, Can We Believe Our Eyes?

Several magazine editors have admitted to engaging in a practice dubbed "reverse retouching": using computer techniques to erase signs of malnutrition, like jutting bones, sunken eyes, and acne, from their models.

What makes the practice particularly insidious is that women who are too thin to be judged attractive are airbrushed to look beautiful—all by having the markers of good health artificially applied. The final product is the image of a woman who looks both extremely thin (yet without the skeletal look of a starvation victim) and glowing (dry hair, sallow complexion, and pimples are all fixed through computer magic). Too bad the millions of women who unfavorably compare themselves to this brand of artificial perfection are often unaware of the depth of deception.

SOURCES: L Hardy, "A Big Fat (and Very Dangerous) Lie: A Former *Cosmo* Editor Lifts the Lid on Airbrushing Skinny Models to Look Healthy," *Daily Mail*, May 20, 2010, http://www.dailymail .co.uk/femail/article-1279766/Former-Cosmo-editor-LEAH-HARDY -airbrushing-skinny-models-look-healthy-big-fat-dangerous-lie .html. ✒ S Coates, "Don't Airbrush Advertisements Aimed at Teens, Say Lib Dems," *The Times*, August 2, 2009.

You Can Be Too Thin

The odds a man has ever been diagnosed with:

binge-eating disorder	**1 in 50**
bulimia nervosa.	**1 in 200**
anorexia nervosa	**1 in 333**

The odds a woman has ever been diagnosed with:

binge-eating disorder	**1 in 28.6**
bulimia nervosa.	**1 in 66.7**
anorexia nervosa	**1 in 111**

Everyone knows that eating disorders are dangerous, but just how risky they are may surprise some of us. According to the National Institute of Mental Health, people with anorexia are up to ten times more likely to die as a result of the illness compared to people without it.

SOURCES: E Hiripi, JI Hudson, RC Kessler, HG Pope, "The Prevalence and Correlates of Eating Disorders in the National Comorbidity Survey Replication," *Biological Psychiatry* 61, 2007: 348–358. ✒ National Institute of Mental Health, *Eating Disorders,* http://www .nimh.nih.gov/health/publications/eating-disorders/index.shtml.

The odds a man will report he feels unattractive when he is out of shape: **1 in 2.3**

SOURCE: "What Are the Rules of Attraction?" *Elle/MSNBC.com Sex and Beauty Survey, Elle* magazine, 2004.

The odds a woman will undress in front of her partner: **1 in 1.2**

SOURCE: DA Frederick, A Peplau, J Lever, "The Barbie Mystique," *International Journal of Sexual Health* 20(3), March 2008: 200–212.

GENDER WARS
Cosmetic Procedure Odds

The odds a surgical cosmetic procedure will be performed on a:

female 13 and over in a year: **1 in 1.2**

male 13 and over in a year: **1 in 7.5**

Distribution by gender of surgical cosmetic procedures performed in a year on people 13 and over:

Procedure	For People %	For People Odds (1 in)	For Females %	For Females Odds (1 in)	For Males %	For Males Odds (1 in)
Liposuction (lipoplasty)	19	**5.3**	19	**5.3**	18	**5.6**
Breast augmentation			21	**4.8**	Does not apply	
Eyelid surgery (blepharoplasty)	8	**11.8**	8	**12.1**	10	**10.1**
Tummy tuck (abdominoplasty)	8	**12.4**	10	**10.1**	3	**34.3**
Breast reduction or gynecomastia treatment	8	**13.3**	7	**13.3**	8	**13.1**
Breast lift	7	**13.7**	8	**11.9**	Does not apply	
Nose reshaping (rhinoplasty)	7	**13.8**	7	**14.8**	11	**9.3**
Facelift	7	**15.0**	7	**14,3**	4	**22.3**
Hair transplantation	6	**17.2**	1	**106**	38	**2.7**
Autologous fat implant	4	**24.9**	5	**21.6**	2	**66.6**
Forehead lift	2	**61.7**	2	**60,2**	1	**73.3**
Upper arm lift	1	**93.0**	1	**81,8**	<0.5	**811**
Thigh lift	1	**124.5**	1	**113**	<0.5	**459**
Chin augmentation	1	**156**	1	**175**	1	**89.7**
Lower-body lift	1	**190**	1	**186**	<0.5	**218**
Buttock augmentation	<0.5	**236**	<0.5	**208**	<0.5	**1633**
Buttock lift	<0.5	**463**	<0.5	**438**	<0.5	**725**
Vaginal rejuvenation	<0.5	**812**	<0.5	**704**	Does not apply	

SOURCES: Book of Odds estimates based on American Society of Plastic Surgeons, *Report of the 2011 Plastic Surgery Statistics,* ASPS Public Relations, 2012, and International Society of Hair Restoration Surgery, *2011 Practice Census Results,* conducted by Relevant Research, July 2011.

The Odds an Obese Person Who Has
Weight-Loss Surgery
Will Have:

Gastric bypass: **1 in 1.1**

Malabsorptive surgery: **1 in 9.6**

Gastroplasty: **1 in 13.4**

Gastrectomy: **1 in 23.4**

SOURCE: HP Santry, DL Gillen, DS Lauderdale, "Trends in Bariatric Surgical Procedures," *Journal of the American Medical Association* 294(15), October 19, 2005:1909–1917.

GENDER WARS

The odds a nonsurgical cosmetic procedure will be performed on a female 13 and over in a year are **1 in 1.1**, versus **1 in 11.6** for a male 13 and over.

SOURCE: Book of Odds estimates based on American Society of Plastic Surgeons, *Report of the 2011 Plastic Surgery Statistics,* ASPS Public Relations, 2012.

The odds a person who has weight-loss surgery is a male are **1 in 6.3** vs. **1 in 1.2** a female.

SOURCE: HP Santry, DL Gillen, DS Lauderdale, "Trends in Bariatric Surgical Procedures," *Journal of the American Medical Association* 294(15), October 19, 2005:1909–1917.

The Odds on Cosmetic Surgery
"If Money Were No Object"

The odds a person reports he or she would have a surgical or nonsurgical cosmetic procedure if money were not an issue:

woman: 1 in 1.3

If money were not an issue
the odds a woman reports she would have:

a teeth-whitening procedure: **1 in 2.8**

a tummy tuck: **1 in 3.2**

vision correction surgery: **1 in 3.7**

a hair removal procedure: **1 in 3.7**

liposuction: **1 in 4.9**

a breast lift: **1 in 4.9**

cellulite treatment: **1 in 6.1**

vein treatment: **1 in 7.1**

a facelift: **1 in 7.5**

injectible wrinkle filler: **1 in 8.5**

microdermabrasion: **1 in 9.2**

laser skin treatment: **1 in 11.7**

a scar removed: **1 in 11.7**

breast augmentation surgery: **1 in 12.8**

a chemical face peel: **1 in 14.3**

Botox: **1 in 14.3**

a breast reduction: **1 in 16**

hair replacement: **1 in 25.6**

rhinoplasty: **1 in 25.6**

lip augmentation (by any method): **1 in 64.1**

man: 1 in 1.7

If money were not an issue
the odds a man reports he would have:

a teeth-whitening procedure: **1 in 3.3**

vision correction surgery: **1 in 3.8**

a hair removal procedure: **1 in 9.3**

liposuction: **1 in 9.3**

hair replacement: **1 in 10.4**

a tummy tuck: **1 in 11.1**

a scar removed: **1 in 16.7**

a facelift: **1 in 20.8**

injectible wrinkle filler: **1 in 23.8**

laser skin treatment: **1 in 23.8**

vein treatment: **1 in 27.8**

a chemical face peel: **1 in 33.3**

microdermabrasion: **1 in 41.7**

Botox: **1 in 41.7**

rhinoplasty: **1 in 41.7**

lip augmentation (any method): **1 in 41.7**

cellulite treatment: **1 in 55.6**

breast augmentation surgery: **1 in 83.3**

a breast reduction: **1 in 83.3**

a breast lift: **1 in 167**

SOURCE: Book of Odds estimate based on RealSelf.com survey conducted by Harris Interactive, reported in National Clearinghouse of Plastic Surgery Statistics, American Society of Plastic Surgeons, *2010 Report of the 2009 Statistics*, June 2010.

What Women Think of Their Bodies

The odds a woman 18–65 believes her body is:

Perceived Body	%	Odds (1 in)
Great	5	**20.0**
Good	38	**2.6**
Okay	36	**2.8**
Unattractive	21	**4.8**

SOURCE: DA Frederick, A Peplau, J Lever, "The Barbie Mystique," *International Journal of Sexual Health* 20(3), March 2008: 200–212.

Appearance Important?

The odds a man will report that . . .

The odds a man reports that his appearance is very important to him: **1 in 2.9**

his "shopping style" is to buy what he stumbles across that suits him: **1 in 2.3**

his "shopping style" is to buy clothes in big batches once or twice a year: **1 in 3.5**

his "shopping style" is to go out looking for new clothes regularly: **1 in 4.2**

his partner buys his clothes for him: **1 in 33.3**

he is a compulsive buyer: **1 in 18.2**

style is the most important factor governing his clothes purchases: **1 in 1.5**

comfort is the most important factor governing his clothes purchases: **1 in 5.6**

uniqueness is the most important factor governing his clothes purchases: **1 in 25**

trendiness is the most important factor governing his clothes purchases: **1 in 33.3**

price is the most important factor governing his clothes purchases: **1 in 20**

ODDS COUPLE

All He Has to Do Is Be

The odds a person is male: **1 in 2.04**

The odds a man thinks he is sexy: **1 in 2.04**

SOURCES: Book of Odds estimate based on US Census Bureau, Population Estimates Program, http://www.census.gov/popest/estimates.php. ✗ Synovate, "Synovate Global Male Beauty Survey Uncovers Attitudes and Perceptions Towards Appearances and Male Beauty Products," press release, December 1, 2008.

The Odds a Man Owns:

1–3 pairs of shoes: **1 in 6.7**

4–6 pairs of shoes: **1 in 2.5**

7–9 pairs of shoes: **1 in 4.2**

10 or more pairs of shoes: **1 in 6.7**

1–3 suits: **1 in 4.8**

4–6 suits: **1 in 13**

7 or more suits: **1 in 6.7**

1 in 20

The Odds a Man Does NOT Own:

a T-shirt: **1 in 14.3**

a pair of blue jeans: **1 in 10**

a button-down shirt: **1 in 4.0**

a sport coat or blazer: **1 in 2.9**

a tuxedo: **1 in 1.2**

What's in His Closet?
Men and Clothes

SOURCES: Book of Odds estimate based on Karlyn Bowman's Poll-Pourri, "We Are What We Wear," Independent Women's Forum, *Woman's Quarterly*, Spring 2001. ✗ LM Korin, RJ Faber, E Aboujaoude, MD Large, RT Serpe, "Estimated Prevalence of Compulsive Buying Behavior in the United States," *American Journal of Psychiatry* 163(10), October 2000:1806–1812.

Really Bad Hair

In case you haven't noticed, body hair is out. Way out. And none is more out than back hair.

Body hair has been a part of humanity for as long as humans have been humans. Early hominids sported thick, dark hair over almost their entire bodies, males and females alike. Apes and monkeys retained it; we, for the most part, lost it.

No one knows exactly why humans evolved out of fur suits and into birthday suits; a leading theory is that vigorous hunting in hot climates saw our ancestors trade panting for sweating as a means of cooling ourselves—and sweating is carried out far more efficiently on a body that is covered only with the vestige of our ancestral selves: the tiny, nearly transparent fuzz covering our bodies, called vellus hair.

"Body hair" is something different. The dark, shaveable stuff is called androgenic hair or terminal hair, and it grows on the legs, pubis, arms, and armpits of nearly everyone, and the chests and faces of men. And for more than a few, on their backs and shoulders, too.

Since the dawn of metrosexuality, men have been urged to "manscape"—shave, pluck, thread, electrolyze, laser, or wax the hair away, especially that stuff that creeps up over the back of their shirt collars. So have they taken the hint?

Nah. The odds a male does not groom his back hair are 1 in 1.3. Odds a female would prefer that he do so are almost as high: 1 in 1.4. The majority of men (1 in 1.2) also do not trim their chest hair or pubic hair (1 in 1.6). However, 1 in 2.5 women prefers he trim his chest hair and 1 in 5.6 prefers he shave all his chest hair, while 1 in 2.4 prefers a man trim his pubic hair and 1 in 6.3 prefers he shave it off.

SOURCES: Remington, "Survey: Women Want Men to Do More Body Hair Grooming, Especially Below the Neck," press release, November 12, 2009. ✒ "The Average Woman, Woman's Health Poll," Women's Health 8(5), May 2011.

Women and Bad Hair Days

The Odds a Woman:	%	Odds (1 in)
Cried after a haircut	26	3.9
Had mood affected by a bad hair day	44	2.3
Loves her hair	19	5.3
Likes her hair	41	2.4
Dislikes her hair	5	20.0
Hates her hair	4	25.0
Has naturally straight hair	49	2.0
Has naturally curly hair	23	4.4
With straight hair styles it curly	10	10.0
With naturally curly hair styles it straight	19	5.3
Colors her hair	53	1.9
Would rather have great hair for the rest of her life than gain IQ points	57	1.8
Would give up social networking websites to have good hair	39	2.6
Would stop texting forever to have good hair	32	3.1
Would give up chocolate to have good hair	28	3.7
Will report her hair has ever made her mad	93	1.1
Will report her hair made her mad in the last week	56	1.8

SOURCES: ShopSmart magazine, "ShopSmart Hair Poll Gets to the Roots: 60% Like It or Love It, 4% Hate It," press release, April 2010. ✒ Pantene, "Pantene Pro-V Survey Finds Women Are Dissatisfied with Their Hair," press release, March 2010.

Take It All Off

The odds a woman 18–34 describes a man with a shaved head as sexy: **1 in 2.8**

The odds a woman finds baldness sexy: **1 in 12.5**

SOURCES: NOP World's Roper Public Affairs, "Bald Is Beautiful, Says Roper Study," press release, March 14, 2005. ✒ "The Average Woman, Woman's Health Poll," *Women's Health* 8(5), May 2011.

The odds a man does not groom his eyebrow, ear, and nose hair.

1 in 4.2

SOURCE: Remington, "Survey: Women Want Men to Do More Body Hair Grooming, Especially Below the Neck," press release, November 12, 2009.

How Do They Match Up?

The odds . . .

a man 15–30 is clean-shaven .... **1 in 2.2**

a woman 15–30 finds him sexiest that way .... **1 in 2.1**

a man 15–30 has facial stubble .... **1 in 8.3**

a woman 15–30 finds him sexiest that way .... **1 in 33.3**

a man 15–30 has a mustache .... **1 in 9.1**

a woman 15–30 finds him sexiest that way .... **1 in 33.3**

SOURCE: Gilette Company, "Clean Shave Gets the Rave: Survey of Attitudes About Facial Hair Reveals That 'Less Is More,'" press release, September 24, 2003, http://www.esquire.com/women/women-issue/survey-of-american-women-0510.

The odds a woman does not own a pair of high heels: **1 in 2.6**

SOURCE: Book of Odds estimate based on Karlyn Bowman's Poll-Pourri, "We Are What We Wear," Independent Women's Forum, *Woman's Quarterly,* Spring 2001.

Whose Men Dress Best?

The odds a man believes it is:

Italy
1 in 2.8

United States
1 in 3.1

United Kingdom
1 in 7.7

France
1 in 14.3

Spain
1 in 25

Germany
1 in 33.3

Japan
1 in 33.3

Australia
1 in 50

Brazil
1 in 100

SOURCE: Askmen.com, "Part II: Lifestyle," The Great Male Survey, 2010 Edition, http://www.askmen.com/specials/2010_great_male_survey/.

How **People with Tattoos** Feel Compared to **People Without Tattoos**

The odds an adult with a tattoo feels:

more rebellious: **1 in 2.8**   less rebellious: **1 in 50**

sexier: **1 in 3.2**   less sexy: **1 in 100**

more attractive: **1 in 5.3**   less attractive: **1 in 33.3**

stronger: **1 in 5.3**   less strong: **1 in 200**

more spiritual: **1 in 7.7**   less spiritual: **1 in 20**

more intelligent: **1 in 20**   less intelligent: **1 in 50**

more athletic: **1 in 20**   less athletic: **1 in 100**

healthier: **1 in 25**   less healthy: **1 in 33.3**

The odds an adult without a tattoo believes people with tattoos are:

more rebellious: **1 in 1.9**   less rebellious: **1 in 33.3**

sexier: **1 in 16.7**   less sexy: **1 in 2.6**

more attractive: **1 in 25**   less attractive: **1 in 2.1**

stronger: **1 in 12.5**   less strong: **1 in 10**

more spiritual: **1 in 20**   less spiritual: **1 in 4**

more intelligent: **1 in 100**   less intelligent: **1 in 3.7**

more athletic: **1 in 20**   less athletic: **1 in 7.7**

healthier: **1 in 50**   less healthy: **1 in 4**

SOURCE: Harris Interactive, "Three in Ten Americans with a Tattoo Say Having One Makes Them Feel Sexier," Harris Poll #15, press release, February 12, 2008.

DID YOU know?

The odds a person 24 or older with less than a high school diploma has a tattoo are **1 in 2.5** vs. **1 in 7.1** for a person 24 or older with a bachelor's degree.

SOURCE: AE Laumann, AJ Derick, "Tattoos and Body Piercings in the United States: A National Data Set," *Journal of the American Academy of Dermatology* 55(3), March 26, 2006: 413–421.

Tattoos by Age

Age	%	Odds (1 in)
18–24	9	**11.1**
25–29	32	**3.1**
30–39	25	**4.0**
40–49	12	**8.3**
50–64	8	**12.5**
65+	9	**11.1**

SOURCE: Harris Interactive, "Three in Ten Americans with a Tattoo Say Having One Makes Them Feel Sexier," Harris Poll #15, press release, February 12, 2008.

 GENDER WARS

The odds a man 18–50 has ever had both a tattoo and body piercing are **1 in 14.3** vs. **1 in 10** for a woman 18–50.

SOURCE: AE Laumann, AJ Derick, "Tattoos and Body Piercings in the United States: A National Data Set," *Journal of the American Academy of Dermatology* 55(3), March 26, 2006: 413–421.

Tattoo Regrets

The odds an adult with a tattoo **does not regret** getting it: **1 in 1.2**

The odds an adult with a tattoo **regrets** getting it: **1 in 6.3**

Regret	%	Odds (1 in)
Never	84	**1.2**
Ever	16	**6.3**
Regret Reason		
Too young at the time	20	**5.0**
It's permanent	19	**5.3**
Does not like it anymore	18	**5.6**
It fades over time	16	**6.3**
Bad location	12	**8.3**
Picked a bad tattoo	11	**9.1**
Feels it was stupid to get one	10	**10.0**
Poorly done	9	**11.1**
Cost too much	7	**14.3**
Does not look good	7	**14.3**
Does not fit his or her present lifestyle	3	**33.3**

SOURCE: Harris Interactive, "Three in Ten Americans with a Tattoo Say Having One Makes Them Feel Sexier," Harris Poll #15, press release, February 12, 2008.

ODDS COUPLE

I Betcha Think These Odds Are About You

The odds an adult has ever met the American Psychiatric Association's criteria for narcissistic personality disorder are **1 in 16.1**.

The odds are about the same that a divorced man is 30–34 years old.

SOURCES: FS Stinson, DA Dawson, RB Goldstein, SP Chou, B Huang, SM Smith, et al., "Prevalence, Correlates, Disability, and Comorbidity of DSM-IV Narcissistic Personality Disorder: Results from the Wave 2 National Epidemiologic Survey on Alcohol and Related Conditions," *Journal of Clinical Psychiatry* 69(7), July 2008: 1033–1045. ✔ US Census Bureau, Age and Sex in the United States: 2009, http://www.census.gov/population/www/socdemo/age/age_sex_2009.html.

Characteristics of People Who Meet Criteria for
Narcissistic Personality Disorder

The odds a man has ever met *DSM-IV* criteria for narcissistic personality disorder . . . . **1 in 13**

The odds a woman has ever met *DSM-IV* criteria for narcissistic personality disorder . . . . **1 in 20.8**

The odds a never-married adult has ever met *DSM-IV* criteria for narcissistic personality disorder . . . . **1 in 10.5**

The odds a separated, widowed, or divorced adult has ever met *DSM-IV* criteria for narcissistic personality disorder. . . .**1 in 13.7**

The odds a married or cohabiting adult has ever met *DSM-IV* criteria for narcissistic personality disorder . . . . . **1 in 20**

The odds an adult 20–29 has ever met *DSM-IV* criteria for narcissistic personality disorder . . . . **1 in 10.6**

The odds an adult 30–44 has ever met *DSM-IV* criteria for narcissistic personality disorder . . . . **1 in 14.1**

The odds an adult 45–64 has ever met *DSM-IV* criteria for narcissistic personality disorder . . . . **1 in 17.9**

The odds an adult 65 or older has ever met *DSM-IV* criteria for narcissistic personality disorder . . . . **1 in 31.3**

SOURCE: FS Stinson, DA Dawson, RB Goldstein, SP Chou, B Huang, SM Smith, et al., "Prevalence, Correlates, Disability, and Comorbidity of DSM-IV Narcissistic Personality Disorder: Results from the Wave 2 National Epidemiologic Survey on Alcohol and Related Conditions," *Journal of Clinical Psychiatry* 69(7), July 2008: 1033–1045.

Ouch,
Don't Touch!

The odds a person 25–29 has had a major sunburn:

No major sunburns: **1 in 15.9**

1–2 major sunburns: **1 in 5**

3–5 major sunburns: **1 in 5.1**

5 or more major sunburns: **1 in 1.9**

SOURCE: D Lazovich, RI Vogel, M Berwick, MA Weinstock, KE Anderson, EM Warshaw, "Indoor Tanning and Risk of Melanoma: A Case-Control Study in a Highly Exposed Population," *Cancer Epidemiology, Biomarkers, & Prevention* 19(6), May 26, 2010: 1557–1568.

The odds a tanning facility operator would let a child age 10–12 use the facility:
1 in 1.5

SOURCE: B Balaraman, LK Biesbroeck, SH Lickerman, LA Cornelius, DB Jeffe, "Practices of Unregulated Tanning Facilities in Missouri: Implications for Statewide Legislation," *Pediatrics* 131(3), March 1, 2013.

Going—and Going Back—
for That Healthy Glow

The odds a person has ever used a sunless tanning bed:
1 in 2

The odds a person has used a sunless tanning booth:

10 times or fewer: **1 in 7.8**

11–24 times: **1 in 11**

25–100 times: **1 in 7.5**

100 or more times: **1 in 7.1**

The odds of using a sunless tanning booth in a year:

Age 14–17: **1 in 18.1**

Age 18–24: **1 in 4.6**

Age 25 or older: **1 in 7**

SOURCES: D Lazovich, RI Vogel, M Berwick, MA Weinstock, KE Anderson, EM Warshaw, "Indoor Tanning and Risk of Melanoma: A Case-Control Study in a Highly Exposed Population," *Cancer Epidemiology, Biomarkers, & Prevention* 19(6), May 26, 2010: 1557–1568. ✗ National Cancer Institute, National Institutes of Health, Department of Health and Human Services, *Cancer Trends Progress Report—2009/2010 Update*, April 2010, http://progressreport.cancer.gov.

Sunless Tanning Booths and Skin Cancer

The odds a person diagnosed with skin cancer has used a sunless tanning booth 10 times or fewer. . . . . **1 in 7.8**

The odds a person diagnosed with skin cancer has used a sunless tanning booth 11–24 times . . . . **1 in 9**

The odds a person diagnosed with skin cancer has used a sunless tanning booth 25–100 times. . . . . **1 in 6.8**

The odds a person diagnosed with skin cancer has used a sunless tanning booth 100 times or more . . . . **1 in 4.2**

SOURCE: D Lazovich, RI Vogel, M Berwick, MA Weinstock, KE Anderson, EM Warshaw, "Indoor Tanning and Risk of Melanoma: A Case-Control Study in a Highly Exposed Population," *Cancer Epidemiology, Biomarkers, & Prevention* 19(6), May 26, 2010: 1557–1568.

 **GENDER WARS**

The odds a woman will use an indoor tanning device in a year are **1 in 5.5** compared to **1 in 8.3** for a man.

SOURCE: "Sun Protection" in National Cancer Institute, National Institutes of Health, Department of Health and Human Services, *Cancer Trends Progress Report—2009/2010 Update*, April 2010, http://progressreport.cancer.gov.

Acne by Age
"It's Not Just a Teen Problem"

Age	Men %	Men Odds (1 in)	Women %	Women Odds (1 in)
20s	43	**2.4**	51	**2.0**
30s	20	**5.0**	35	**2.8**
40s	12	**8.3**	26	**3.8**

SOURCE: CN Collier, JC Harper, WC Cantrell, W Wang, KW Foster, BE Elewski, "The Prevalence of Acne in Adults 20 Years and Older," *Journal of the American Academy of Dermatology* 58(1), October 18, 2007: 56–59.

The odds a person 12–54 believes popping pimples causes more acne: **1 in 2**

SOURCE: American Acne and Rosacea Society, "'Popping the Myth' Survey," press release, October 2, 2007.

CHAPTER 9

MIND, PSYCHE, AND ADDICTION

HAPPY

The odds a person will report being pretty happy:

1 in 2

SOURCE: P Taylor, C Funk, P Craighill, *Are We Happy Yet?*, A Social Trends Report. Washington, DC: Pew Research Center, February 2006.

How Smart Are We?

Since IQ tests are fitted to a normal distribution, our intelligence is graded "on the curve." This means that 95% of us are of "normal" intelligence, two standard deviations above and below 100.

What intelligence tests really measure—latent abilities or manifest skills, innate gifts or learned ones—is a subject of ongoing controversy. Since 1904 some have searched  for the general or "g factor," the psychometric holy grail, and others for evidence of cultural factors muddling the very idea of an intellectual g-spot. These folks may have noticed that there is a "g" in eugenics.

The target moves, too. Scores worldwide tend to rise over time and those taking older versions of the tests tend to do better. This is generally called the Flynn Effect, after James Flynn, who called this effect reason for a "crisis in confidence" in what is being measured.

Whatever it is we are really measuring and summarizing in a number, it is fascinating that we have been doing it diligently for more than a century and assigning to ourselves based on these numbers titles such as genius or natural-born fool.

SOURCE: JR Flynn, "The Mean IQ of Americans: Massive Gains 1932 to 1978," *Psychological Bulletin* 95(1), 1984: 29–51.

ODDS COUPLE

Giants Upon the Earth

The odds a person will have an IQ of 202 or higher, **1 in 200,000,000,000,** are a million times higher than the odds a person will be diagnosed with acromegaly in a year, **1 in 200,000**.

SOURCES: http://www.iqcomparisonsite.com/IQtable.aspx. ⚡ S Melmed, "Acromegaly Pathogenesis and Treatment," *Journal of Clinical Investigation* 119, 2009: 3189–3202.

The odds a person will meet the membership criteria for Mensa: **1 in 50**

The odds a person will meet the membership criteria for the Pi Society: **1 in 1,000,000**

SOURCES: 2011 Mensa International Limited, http://www.mensa.org/. ⚡ The Pi Society, http://www.lygeros.org/PI.

Even if You Aren't Smart, Can You Buy a Little Happiness?

We know it can't buy us love—but can money buy happiness?

Research suggests that money does make people happier, but only to a certain point. In the United States, the odds a person with a family income under $30,000 reports being very happy are **1 in 4.2**, compared to **1 in 3** for those with family incomes between $30,000 and $74,999. Beyond that, money continues to have an effect on happiness, but with diminishing returns. The odds are **1 in 2.6** that a person with a family income between $75,000 and $99,999 will report being very happy, and **1 in 2** for a person whose family income is $100,000 or higher.

SOURCE: P Taylor, C Funk, P Craighill, *Are We Happy Yet?*, A Social Trends Report. Washington, DC: Pew Research Center, February 2006.

Mental Illness

The odds a person will ever be diagnosed with a mental disorder:

1 in 1.7

Things as likely...

A person has employment-based health insurance.

An adult plans to celebrate Valentine's Day.

An adult regularly tries to eat a healthy breakfast.

SOURCES: "Lifetime Prevalence of DSM-IV/ WMH-CIDI Disorders by Sex and Cohort," *National Comorbidity Survey,* 2007. ✔ US Census Bureau, "Historical Health Insurance Tables: 1999 to 2007," Current Population Survey Annual Social and Economic Supplement, http://www.census.gov/ hhes/www/hlthins/usernote/schedule.html. ✔ National Retail Federation, *NRF Valentine's Day 2010,* February 2010. ✔ Harris Interactive, "Two-Thirds of U.S. Adults Consider Themselves to Be Healthy Eaters," March 2006: 1–6.

Is There a Happiness Gene?

The latest development in the growing field of happiness studies purports to have nailed down a specific gene that, according to researchers, "predicts subjective well-being." It's a serotonin transporter gene with the name 5-HTT*, and it exists in several forms. The more efficient your form of 5-HTT, the more likely you will be to report a higher degree of satisfaction with your life.

The 5-HTT gene has several other names, including HTT, SLC6A4, and SERT.

SOURCE: J-E De Neve, JH Fowler, BS Frey, "Genes, Economics, and Happiness," *CESIFO* Working Paper No. 2946, Category 12: Empirical and Theoretical Methods, February 2010.

Navigating Life

The odds an adult visited a psychiatrist in the past year: **1 in 22.2**

Of those, the odds they made...

1 visit: **1 in 5.4**

2–4 visits: **1 in 2.5**

5–9 visits: **1 in 5.8**

10–19 visits: **1 in 6.2**

20–49 visits: **1 in 16.4**

50 visits or more: **1 in 62.5**

SOURCE: PS Wang, M Land, M Olfson, HA Pincus, KB Wells, RC Kessler, "Twelve-Month Use of Mental Health Services in the United States: Results from the National Comorbidity Survey Replication," *Archives of General Psychiatry* 62, June 2005.

GENDER WARS

The Odds an Adult Has Been Diagnosed with:

Major Depressive Disorder
Women: **1 in 5** . . . . Men: **1 in 7.6**

Obsessive-Compulsive Disorder
Women: **1 in 32.3** . . . . Men: **1 in 62.5**

A Specific Phobia
Women: **1 in 6.3** . . . . Men: **1 in 11.2**

Social Phobia
Women: **1 in 7.7** . . . . Men: **1 in 9**

SOURCES: Harvard School of Medicine, "National Comorbidity Survey (NCS-R) Appendix Tables," July 19, 2007. ✔ *Health, United States, 2007: With Chartbook on Trends in the Health of Americans,* Hyattsville, MD: National Center for Health Statistics, 2008.

ODDS COUPLE

Maybe There Is Something to Worry About

The odds an adult has an anxiety disorder: **1 in 5.2**

The odds a man 18–24 will visit a pornographic website once or twice in a month: **1 in 5.2**

SOURCES: Harvard School of Medicine, "National Comorbidity Survey (NCS-R) Appendix Tables," July 19, 2007. ✔ Book of Odds estimates based on JA Davis, TW Smith, PV Marsden, *General Social Surveys, 1972–2008,* [CUMULATIVE FILE] [Computer file] ICPSR04691, v. 1., Chicago: National Opinion Research Center, 2009 [producer]; Storrs, CT: Roper Center for Public Opinion Research, University of Connecticut/ Ann Arbor, MI: Inter-university Consortium for Political and Social Research [distributors].

Panic Disorder

Panic disorder is an anxiety disorder characterized by repeated, unexpected panic attacks with a range of somatic and cognitive symptoms. The criteria for a *DSM-IV* diagnosis of panic disorder include "discrete periods of fear or discomfort accompanied by at least four somatic or cognitive symptoms."

The odds:

A person will ever meet the *DSM-IV* criteria for panic disorder: **1 in 21.3**

A woman will ever meet the *DSM-IV* criteria for panic disorder: **1 in 16.1**

A man will ever meet the *DSM-IV* criteria for panic disorder: **1 in 32.3**

A person will ever experience panic attacks but will not meet the criteria for panic disorder: **1 in 17.4**

A woman will ever experience panic attacks but will not meet the criteria for panic disorder: **1 in 14**

A man will ever experience panic attacks but will not meet the criteria for panic disorder: **1 in 23.2**

SOURCE: Book of Odds estimates based on data in Harvard School of Medicine, "National Comorbidity Survey (NCS-R) Appendix Tables," July 19, 2007, and JI Sheikh, GA Leskin, DF Klein, "Gender Differences in Panic Disorder: Findings from the National Comorbidity Survey," *American Journal of Psychiatry* 159, 2002: 55–58.

Type of cognitive or somatic symptom a person 15–54 with panic disorder experiences during a panic attack:

Panic Attack Symptoms

Heart pounding: **1 in 1.04**
Time seems slow or quick: **1 in 1.3**
Sweating: **1 in 1.3**
Trembling or shaking: **1 in 1.3**
Pain in the chest: **1 in 1.4**
Shortness of breath: **1 in 1.5**
Dizziness or lightheadedness: **1 in 1.6**
Hot flashes or chills: **1 in 1.6**
Things seem unreal: **1 in 1.7**
Dry mouth: **1 in 1.8**
Feeling faint: **1 in 1.8**
Feeling smothered: **1 in 1.8**
Fear of acting crazy: **1 in 1.9**
Pain in the stomach: **1 in 1.9**
Fear of dying: **1 in 2.0**
Feet tingling or numbness: **1 in 2.4**
Nausea: **1 in 2.4**
Choking or difficulty swallowing: **1 in 2.4**

Panic Disorder Symptom	%
Heart pounding	96
Time seems slow or quick	78
Sweating	78
Trembling or shaking	78
Pain in the chest	74
Shortness of breath	65
Dizziness or lightheadedness	64
Hot flashes or chills	62
Things seem unreal	59
Dry mouth	56
Feeling faint	55
Feeling smothered	55
Fear of acting crazy	53
Pain in the stomach	52
Fear of dying	49
Feet tingling or numbness	42
Nausea	42
Choking or difficulty swallowing	42

SOURCE: Book of Odds estimates based on JI Sheikh, GA Leskin, DF Klein, "Gender Differences in Panic Disorder: Findings from the National Comorbidity Survey," *American Journal of Psychiatry* 159, 2002: 55–58.

The Odds a Person Who Will Ever Be Diagnosed with a **Panic Disorder First Experienced It:**

Before age 7: **1 in 20**

Before age 17: **1 in 4**

Before age 11: **1 in 10**

Before age 25: **1 in 2**

SOURCE: RC Kessler, P Burglund, O Demler, R Jin, KR Merikangas, EE Walters, "Lifetime Prevalence and Age-of-Onset Distribution of DSM-IV Disorders in the National Comorbidity Survey Replication," *Archives of General Psychiatry* 62, June 2005.

The Odds an Adult Has Ever Been Diagnosed With **Major Depressive Disorder:**

Age 18–29: **1 in 6.3**

Age: 45–59: **1 in 5**

Age 30–44: **1 in 5.2**

Age 60 or older: **1 in 9.4**

SOURCE: Harvard School of Medicine, "National Comorbidity Survey (NCS-R) Appendix Tables," July 19, 2007.

Bipolar Diagnosis by Age

The odds an adult 18–29 has ever been diagnosed with bipolar disorder: **1 in 14.3**

The odds an adult 30–44 has ever been diagnosed with bipolar disorder: **1 in 18.9**

The odds an adult 45–59 has ever been diagnosed with bipolar disorder: **1 in 27**

The odds an adult 60 or older has ever been diagnosed with bipolar disorder: **1 in 76.9**

Age	%
18–29	7
30–44	5
45–59	4
60+	1

SOURCE: Harvard School of Medicine, "National Comorbidity Survey (NCS-R) Appendix Tables," July 19, 2007.

Depression and Other Disorders

The odds a person with major depression also has:

Comorbidity	%	Odds (1 in)
A substance use disorder	19	**5.2**
A substance abuse disorder	7	**15.1**
A substance dependency	13	**7.9**
An alcohol use disorder	16	**6.1**
An alcohol abuse disorder	5	**18.6**
An alcohol dependency	11	**9.1**
A drug use disorder	7	**15.1**
A drug abuse disorder	3	**32.6**
A drug dependency	4	**28.3**

SOURCE: BF Grant, FS Stinson, DA Dawson, SP Chou, MC Dufour, W Compton, RP Pickering, "Prevalence and Co-occurrence of Substance Use Disorders and Independent Mood and Anxiety Disorders," *Archives of General Psychiatry* 61, 2004: 807–816.

GENDER WARS

The Odds an Adult Will Report Using **Antidepressants in a Month**

Women: **1 in 9.4**

Men: **1 in 19.2**

SOURCE: *Health, United States, 2007: With Chartbook on Trends in the Health of Americans,* Hyattsville, MD: National Center for Health Statistics, 2008.

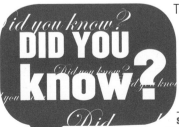

The odds an adult who has diagnosed bipolar disorder will not receive mental health services in a year:

1 in 2.3

SOURCE: PS Wang, M Land, M Olfson, HA Pincus, KB Wells, RC Kessler, "Twelve-Month Use of Mental Health Services in the United States: Results from the National Comorbidity Survey Replication," *Archives of General Psychiatry* 62, June 2005.

Suicide

A Sluggish Economy Takes a Toll

There were 263 workplace suicides in 2009—equalling the highest annual total ever recorded, set in 2008, when suicides in the workplace shot up 34% from the prior year's 196. From 1992 through 2007, workplace suicides averaged 211 per year, and annual levels were within 15% lower and 9% higher of that average. An analysis of the 2008 data by Catherine Rampel, New York Times blogger, found that employees who killed themselves on the job tended to be male, 45–54, white, and in management occupations. Interestingly, while white workers accounted for 78% of suicides but only 69% of job hours, males and people age 45–54 who committed suicide tended to work less than the general population:

- Males accounted for 94% of suicides but only 57% of job hours.

- People age 45–54 accounted for 35% of suicides but only 25% of job hours.

SOURCES: Bureau of Labor Statistics, *Census of Fatal Occupational Injuries in 2009*, revised data, May 4, 2011, http://www.bls.gov/iif/oshwc/cfoi/cfoi_revised09.pdf. ✔ Bureau of Labor Statistics, *Census of Fatal Occupational Injuries in 2008*, revised data, April 22, 2010, http://www.bls.gov/iif/oshwc/cfoi/cfoi_revised08.pdf. ✔ C Rampel, "More on Workplace Suicides," Economix blog, *New York Times*, August 31, 2009.

Racial/Ethnic Differences

The odds a person will commit suicide in a year: 1 in 7,521

White	**1 in 8,259**
American Indian or Native Alaskan	**1 in 8,878**
Asian or Pacific Islander	**1 in 18,260**
Black	**1 in 19,450**
Hispanic	**1 in 19,620**

SOURCES: Book of Odds estimate based on data from Centers for Disease Control and Prevention, National Center for Health Statistics, *Compressed Mortality File 1999–2007*, Series 20, No. 2M, 2010, CDC WONDER online database, http://wonder.cdc.gov/cmf-icd10.html. ✔ Book of Odds estimate based on data from Centers for Disease Control and Prevention, National Center for Injury Prevention and Control, *Suicide Facts at a Glance 2012*, and US Census Bureau, *US Census 2012*.

DID YOU know? More suicides are committed on Monday than any other day of the week, **1 in 6.3**, and the fewest on Saturday, **1 in 7.7**.

SOURCE: Book of Odds estimate based on data from Centers for Disease Control and Prevention, National Center for Health Statistics, *Compressed Mortality File 1999–2007*, Series 20, No. 2M, 2010, CDC WONDER online database, http://wonder.cdc.gov/cmf-icd10.html.

Age and Suicide

The odds a person who committed suicide was:

5–9: **1 in 7,695**	25–34: **1 in 6.3**	65–74: **1 in 13.3**
10–14: **1 in 125**	35–44: **1 in 4.8**	75–84: **1 in 14.6**
15–19: **1 in 20.1**	45–54: **1 in 4.9**	85 or older: **1 in 38.6**
20–24: **1 in 12.7**	55–64: **1 in 8.3**	

Age	%
5–9	0.0
10–14	0.8
15–19	5
20–24	8
25–34	16
35–44	21
45–54	20
55–64	12
65–74	8
75–84	7
85+	3

SOURCE: Book of Odds estimate based on data from Centers for Disease Control and Prevention, National Center for Health Statistics, *Compressed Mortality File 1999–2007*, Series 20, No. 2M, 2010, CDC WONDER online database, http://wonder.cdc.gov/cmf-icd10.html.

The Suicide Rate Varies by State

Above US Average

Average US Rate

Below US Average

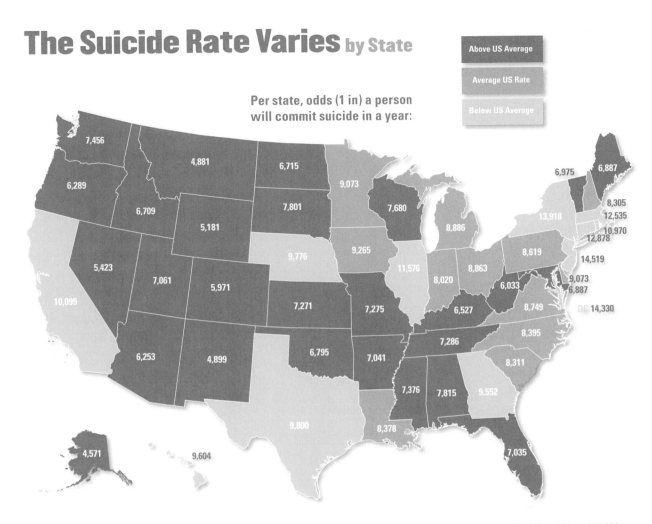

Per state, odds (1 in) a person will commit suicide in a year:

7,456
4,881
6,715
9,073
6,289
6,709
7,801
7,680
6,975
6,887
5,181
8,886
13,918
8,305
12,535
9,776
9,265
8,619
10,970
12,878
5,423
7,061
5,971
11,576
8,020
8,863
6,033
14,519
9,073
6,887
10,099
7,271
7,275
6,527
8,749
DC 14,330
6,253
4,899
6,795
7,041
7,286
8,395
7,376
7,815
9,552
8,311
9,800
8,378
4,571
9,604
7,035

Note: The overall US suicide rate is 11.5 per 100,000 and the 95% confidence interval for variation among the states is 11.0 per 100,000 to 12.0 per 100,000.

SOURCE: Book of Odds estimate based on data from Centers for Disease Control and Prevention, National Center for Health Statistics, *Compressed Mortality File 1999–2007*, Series 20, No. 2M, 2010, CDC WONDER online database, http://wonder.cdc.gov/cmf-icd10.html.

GENDER WARS

The odds a man will commit suicide in a year are
1 in 4,680 vs. **1 in 18,208** for a woman

SOURCE: Book of Odds estimate based on data from Centers for Disease Control and Prevention, National Center for Injury Prevention and Control, *Suicide Facts at a Glance 2012*, and US Census Bureau, *US Census 2012*.

GENDER WARS

The means used to commit suicide vary between the genders.

Men most frequently use **guns**. **Women** most often choose **poison**.

The odds a male suicide used a firearm are **1 in 1.8**.

The odds a female suicide used poison are **1 in 2.7**.

SOURCE: Book of Odds estimate based on data from Centers for Disease Control and Prevention, National Center for Injury Prevention and Control, *Suicide Facts at a Glance 2012*, and *Web-based Injury Statistics Query and Reporting Systems* (WISQARS 2010 data), http://www.cdc.gov/injury/wisqars/index.html.

Military Suicides:
Almost One a Day, Almost One an Hour

Military suicides have passed milestones of late—or perhaps headstones. A report released by the Pentagon revealed that the rate of suicide among members of the army from October 1, 2008, to September 30, 2009, exceeded the civilian rate for the first time since the Vietnam War. The rate for soldiers was approximately 20 per 100,000, compared to a demographically adjusted civilian rate of approximately 19 per 100,000. There were 160 active-duty suicides in this twelve-month period.

By 2012 there were 349 active-duty suicides, almost one a day, according to the US military.

What about veterans? This is a larger base, with twenty-three million veterans. The latest study by the US Department of Veterans' Affairs reported that veterans were committing suicide at a rate of 22 a day, almost one an hour. These suicides are mostly among older people: the odds a veteran who commits suicide will be fifty or older are **1 in 1.5**.

SOURCES: L Alvarez, "Suicides of Soldiers Reach High of Nearly 3 Decades," *New York Times*, January 29, 2009. ✗ Book of Odds Estimate based on T Watkins, M Schneider, "325 Army Suicides in 2012 a Record," CNN, and US Army, Deployment Health Assessment Program Update, Army Reserve Conference, September 20, 2012, Defense Manpower Data Center, August 17, 2012. ✗ J Kemp, R Bossarte, "Suicide Data Report, 2012," Department of Veterans Affairs, Mental Health Services, Suicide Prevention Program ✗ Reuters, "US Military Suicides Rise, One Dies Every 65 Minutes," February 1, 2013.

Post-Traumatic Stress Disorder

About 60% of men and 50% of women will experience a traumatic event in their lifetime. A trauma is defined by the Department of Veterans Affairs as something horrible and scary that you see or that happens to you whereby "you think that your life or others' lives are in danger." Traumatic events affecting women are most likely to be sexual assault and childhood sexual abuse, while traumatic events affecting men are more likely to be accidents, physical assault, combat, disaster, or witnessing death or injury. Women who experience a traumatic event are more likely to develop PTSD—**1 in 5** vs. **1 in 12.5** for men.

It wasn't until the Vietnam War—a conflict that left many veterans vulnerable to flashbacks, panic attacks, sleep disturbances, substance abuse, and/or other problems—that the therapeutic community formally recognized PTSD. Veterans experts think PTSD occurs:

- In about 30% of Vietnam veterans or **1 in 3.3**.

- In about 10% of Gulf War (Desert Storm) veterans or **1 in 10**.

- In about 6% to 11% of Afghanistan war (Enduring Freedom) veterans or **1 in 9** to **1 in 16**.

- In about 12% to 20% of Iraq war (Iraqi Freedom) veterans or **1 in 5** to **1 in 8**.

SOURCE: National Center for PTSD, US Department of Veterans Affairs, "How Common Is PTSD?," http://ncptsd.va.gov/ncmain/ncdocs/fact_shts/fs_how_common_is_ptsd.html.

We're All Stressed Out

ODDS COUPLE
Doing Damage

The odds a man will experience a traumatic event during his life: **1 in 1.7**

The odds an NFL pass will be a completion: **1 in 1.7**

SOURCES: National Center for PTSD, US Department of Veterans Affairs, "How Common Is PTSD?," http://ncptsd.va.gov/ncmain/ncdocs/fact_shts/fs_how_common_is_ptsd.html. ✗ Book of Odds estimate based on Pro-Football-Reference.com, 2010 NFL Passing, http://www.pro-football-reference.com/years/2010/passing.htm.

ODDS COUPLE
Smoldering...

The odds an adult has intermittent explosive disorder: **1 in 24.4**

These are about the same odds that a white man is a nondaily smoker (**1 in 24**).

SOURCES: Harvard School of Medicine, "National Comorbidity Survey (NCS-R) Appendix Tables," July 19, 2007. ✗ JR Pleis, BW Ward, JW Lucas, "Summary Health Statistics for U.S. Adults: National Health Interview Survey, 2009," *Vital and Health Statistics* 10 (249), 2010.

Greatest Stress Factors

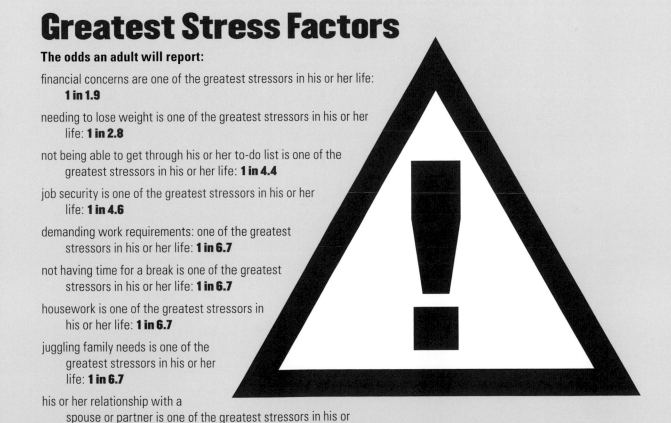

The odds an adult will report:

financial concerns are one of the greatest stressors in his or her life: **1 in 1.9**

needing to lose weight is one of the greatest stressors in his or her life: **1 in 2.8**

not being able to get through his or her to-do list is one of the greatest stressors in his or her life: **1 in 4.4**

job security is one of the greatest stressors in his or her life: **1 in 4.6**

demanding work requirements: one of the greatest stressors in his or her life: **1 in 6.7**

not having time for a break is one of the greatest stressors in his or her life: **1 in 6.7**

housework is one of the greatest stressors in his or her life: **1 in 6.7**

juggling family needs is one of the greatest stressors in his or her life: **1 in 6.7**

his or her relationship with a spouse or partner is one of the greatest stressors in his or her life: **1 in 7.7**

information overload is one of the greatest stressors in his or her life: **1 in 14.3**

the relationship with his or her children is one of the greatest stressors in his or her life: **1 in 16.7**

SOURCE: Princess Cruises, "Chicago Tops List of America's Most Stressed Out Cities; Miami Is Most Laid Back," press release, October 21, 2009.

What People Would Like to Do, if Only They Had the Time

The odds an adult will report he or she, in a typical week, would like to but does not have time to:

exercise: **1 in 4.2**

volunteer: **1 in 4.2**

work on hobbies: **1 in 4.4**

take a break: **1 in 4.8**

spend time with friends: **1 in 6.3**

read: **1 in 9.1**

be spiritual: **1 in 10**

spend time with siblings: **1 in 11.1**

garden: **1 in 12.5**

spend more time with his or her parents: **1 in 14.3**

work more: **1 in 14.3**

cook: **1 in 20**

spend more time with his or her children: **1 in 20**

spend more time with his or her significant other: **1 in 25**

watch more TV: **1 in 33.3**

sleep more: **1 in 33.3**

do more housework: **1 in 50**

Activity	%
Exercise	24
Volunteer	24
Work on hobbies	23
Take a break	21
Spend time with friends	16
Read	11
Be spiritual	10
Spend time with siblings	9
Garden	8

Activity	%
Spend more time with parents	7
Work more	7
Cook	5
Spend more time with children	5
Spend more time with significant other	4
Watch more TV	3
Sleep more	3
Do more housework	2

SOURCE: Princess Cruises, "Chicago Tops List of America's Most Stressed Out Cities; Miami Is Most Laid Back," press release, October 21, 2009.

One of These Days, I Will Find Peace

The odds an adult believes lack of support from his or her spouse, family, friends, or work prevents him or her from achieving a balanced life: **1 in 5.9**

SOURCE: Princess Cruises, "Chicago Tops List of America's Most Stressed Out Cities; Miami Is Most Laid Back," press release, October 21, 2009.

When Adults Believe They Will Achieve a Balanced Life

The odds an adult believes he or she:

will be able to achieve a balanced life when he or she becomes more financially successful: **1 in 2.5**

will be able to achieve a balanced life when the economy improves: **1 in 2.8**

will be able to achieve a balanced life when he or she retires: **1 in 6.7**

will be able to achieve a balanced life when he or she switches jobs: **1 in 10**

will be able to achieve a balanced life when his or her spouse gets a better job: **1 in 14.3**

will be able to achieve a balanced life when his or her children grow up: **1 in 16.7**

Balance Will Arrive When	%
He or she becomes more financially successful	40
The economy improves	36
He or she retires	15
He or she switches jobs	10
His or her spouse gets a better job	7
His or her children grow up	6

SOURCE: Princess Cruises, "Chicago Tops List of America's Most Stressed Out Cities; Miami Is Most Laid Back," press release, October 21, 2009.

The Odds an Adult Will Unwind at the End of the Day by:

Changing clothes: **1 in 2.8**

Lying down: **1 in 2.9**

Reading a book or magazine: **1 in 3.1**

Kissing his or her spouse or partner: **1 in 3.1**

Playing with a pet: **1 in 3.1**

Going on Facebook: **1 in 3.5**

Listening to or playing music: **1 in 3.6**

Working on a hobby: **1 in 5.6**

Exercising: **1 in 5.9**

Enjoying an alcoholic beverage: **1 in 5.9**

Reading the newspaper: **1 in 5.9**

Discussing the day's events: **1 in 6.7**

Calling a friend: **1 in 7.7**

Hugging his or her children: **1 in 7.7**

SOURCE: Princess Cruises, "Chicago Tops List of America's Most Stressed Out Cities; Miami Is Most Laid Back," press release, October 21, 2009.

Crying Styles
by Gender

The folks who help you dry your tears with their tissues funded this study on how people describe their own crying styles. Whether we have only one "crying style" is open to debate. The British psychoanalyst John Bowlby proposed "Attachment Theory" in the last century. This theory views crying as a two-way act between people, such as mother and child or a married couple, a cry and response. The analogy to imprinting and bonding behaviors in animals is persuasive and suggests an evolutionary value to crying. Later theorists, such as Judith Kay Nelson, have posited multiple styles of crying and even refer to the fourth option in the survey as either "inhibited or prohibited" crying.

The odds a man will describe his crying as real sobbing and bawling are **1 in 33.3**.

The odds a man will describe his crying as slight sobbing and shaking are **1 in 6.7**.

The odds a man will describe his crying as red eyes and a couple of tears are **1 in 2.1**.

The odds a man will describe his crying as getting a lump in his throat or welling up but no actual tears are **1 in 3.5**.

The odds a woman will describe her crying as real sobbing and bawling are **1 in 14.3**.

The odds a woman will describe her crying as slight sobbing and shaking are **1 in 2.9**.

The odds a woman will describe her crying as red eyes and a couple of tears are **1 in 2.2**.

The odds a woman will describe her crying as getting a lump in her throat or welling up but no actual tears are **1 in 11.1**.

SOURCES: Social Issues Research Centre, *The Kleenex for Men Crying Report: A Study of Men and Crying*, September 30, 2004. ✗ JK Nelson, *Seeing Through Tears: Crying and Attachment*, New York: Brunner-Routledge, 2005. ✗ I Bretherton, "The Origins of Attachment Theory: John Bowlby and Mary Ainsworth," *Developmental Psychology* 28(5), 1992: 159. ✗ J Bowlby, *Attachment and Loss*, vol. 1., *Attachment*, 2nd ed., New York: Basic Books, 1999.

Male Attitudes Toward Crying

The odds a man believes real men cry but only in response to tragedies like the death of a loved one: **1 in 2.5**

The odds a man believes real men cry and aren't afraid to show their emotions: **1 in 3.2**

The odds a man believes real men cry but not in public: **1 in 3.4**

The odds a man believes real men never cry: **1 in 20**

Real Men Cry...	%
Only in response to tragedies	35
Are not afraid to show their emotions	31
Not in public	29
Never	5

SOURCE: AskMen.com, "Part II: Lifestyle," *The Great Male Survey, 2011 Edition*, http://www.askmen.com/specials/2011_great_male_survey/.

GENDER WARS

1 in 1.7
men have never seen their fathers cry vs.

1 in 2
women.

SOURCE: Social Issues Research Centre, *The Kleenex for Men Crying Report: A Study of Men and Crying*, September 30, 2004

Reasons for Crying

The odds a man has cried:

over the death of someone close: 1 in 1.4

over a sad moment in a movie, TV show, or book: 1 in 2.3

over the breakup of a relationship: 1 in 2.6

over someone close to him getting hurt: 1 in 4

over an argument with a loved one: 1 in 4.2

over feelings of loneliness: 1 in 4.6

over a happy moment in a movie, TV show, or book: 1 in 4.8

when listening to music: 1 in 5.6

out of self-pity: 1 in 5.9

over an injury: 1 in 6.3

over his feelings getting hurt: 1 in 7.7

over feelings of anger: 1 in 9.1

at a wedding: 1 in 11.1

The odds a woman has cried:

over the death of someone close: 1 in 1.1

over a sad moment in a movie, TV show, or book: 1 in 1.3

over the breakup of a relationship: 1 in 1.8

over someone close to her getting hurt: 1 in 1.7

over an argument with a loved one: 1 in 1.6

over feelings of loneliness: 1 in 2.2

over a happy moment in a movie, TV show, or book: 1 in 2.1

when listening to music: 1 in 3.2

out of self-pity: 1 in 2.9

over an injury: 1 in 2

over her feelings getting hurt: 1 in 2

over feelings of anger: 1 in 2.3

at a wedding: 1 in 2.5

Situation	Men %	Women %
The death of someone close	74	91
A sad moment in a movie, TV show, or book	44	80
The breakup of a relationship	39	57
Someone close getting hurt	25	58
An argument with a loved one	24	63
Feelings of loneliness	22	45
A happy moment in a movie, TV show, or book	21	47
When listening to music	18	31
Self-pity	17	34
An injury	16	49
Feelings getting hurt	13	50
Feelings of anger	11	43
A wedding	9	40

SOURCE: Social Issues Research Centre, *The Kleenex for Men Crying Report: A Study of Men and Crying*, September 30, 2004.

BAD HABITS AND ADDICTION
Some Stress Relievers Are Bad for Us

Tobacco

The Age of Mad Men

The mid-1960s were the height of American smoking. In 1965, the peak year, **1 in 2** men smoked and **1 in 3** women smoked, more people per capita than at any other time in US history. Cigarette ads

were everywhere: magazines, newspapers, television, even baseball cards.

But things were about to change. Just the year before, *Smoking and Health: Report of the Advisory Committee of the Surgeon General of the Public Health Service* for the first time publicly linked smoking with cancer and other health risks—leading to the Surgeon General's warning labels that are now slapped on every pack.

SOURCE: *Health, United States, 2008: With Special Feature on the Health of Young Adults,* Hyattsville, MD: National Center for Health Statistics, March 2009.

DID YOU know? The odds an adult has ever been diagnosed with nicotine dependence disorder: **1 in 3.4**

SOURCE: Harvard School of Medicine, "National Comorbidity Survey (NCS-R) Appendix Tables," July 19, 2007.

Cigarette Smoking Over Time
The odds an adult smokes:

Year	%	Odds (1 in)
1965	42	2.4
1974	37	2.7
1979	33	3.0
1983	32	3.1
1985	30	3.3
1987	29	3.5
1988	28	3.6
1990	25	4.0
1991	26	3.9
1992	26	3.8
1993	25	4.0
1994	25	4.0
1995	25	4.1
1996	unavailable	unavailable
1997	25	4.1
1998	24	4.2
1999	23	4.3
2000	23	4.3
2001	23	4.4
2002	22	4.5
2003	22	4.7
2004	21	4.8
2005	21	4.8
2006	21	4.8
2007	20	5.1
2008	20	4.9
2009	20	4.9

Going Down

SOURCES: *Health, United States, 2008: With Special Feature on the Health of Young Adults,* Hyattsville, MD: National Center for Health Statistics, March 2009. ✗ *Health, United States, 2008: With Special Feature on Death and Dying,* Hyattsville, MD: National Center for Health Statistics, February 2011.

The odds an adult smoker tried to quit in the past year: **1 in 2.4**

SOURCE: Data from the National Health Interview Survey, National Center for Health Statistics, Hyattsville, MD, March 2010, in "Health Behaviors of Adults: United States, 2005–2007," *Vital and Health Statistics* 10(245).

Smoking by Age, Gender, Region, Education

The odds a man 18–24 is a smoker: **1 in 3.6**

The odds a man 25–34 is a smoker: **1 in 3.6**

The odds a man 35–44 is a smoker: **1 in 3.9**

The odds a man 45–64 is a smoker: **1 in 4.1**

The odds a man 65 or older is a smoker: **1 in 10.5**

The odds a woman 18–24 is a smoker: **1 in 6.4**

The odds a woman 25–34 is a smoker: **1 in 4.6**

The odds a woman 35–44 is a smoker: **1 in 4.7**

The odds a woman 45–64 is a smoker: **1 in 5.1**

The odds a woman 65 or older is a smoker: **1 in 10.5**

The odds an adult with less than a high school diploma is a smoker: **1 in 3.4**

The odds an adult with a high school diploma or GED is a smoker: **1 in 3.4**

The odds an adult with some college education is a smoker: **1 in 4.6**

The odds an adult with a bachelor's degree or higher is a smoker: **1 in 11.1**

The odds an adult in the Northeast is a smoker: **1 in 5**

The odds an adult in the Midwest is a smoker: **1 in 4.3**

The odds an adult in the South is a smoker: **1 in 4.6**

The odds an adult in the West is a smoker: **1 in 6.2**

Group	%
Men 18–24	28
Men 25–34	28
Men 35–44	25
Men 45–64	25
Men 65+	10
Women 18–24	16
Women 25–34	22
Women 35–44	21
Women 45–64	20
Women 65+	10
Less than a high school diploma	30
High school diploma or GED	30
Some college education	22
Bachelor's degree or higher	9
Northeast	20
Midwest	23
South	22
West	16

1 in 3.9

The odds a high school student will use smokeless tobacco, cigarettes, or cigars in a month.

SOURCE: DK Eaton, L Kann, S Kinchen, S Shanklin, J Ross, J Hawkins, et al., "Youth Risk Behavior Surveillance—United States, 2009," Surveillance Summaries, *Morbidity and Mortality Weekly Report* 59(SS-5), 2010.

 **GENDER WARS**

The odds a woman is a former smoker are **1 in 5.6** vs. **1 in 3.9** for a man.

SOURCE: JR Pleis, BW Ward, JW Lucas, "Summary Health Statistics for U.S. Adults: National Health Interview Survey, 2009," *Vital and Health Statistics* 10(249), 2010.

SOURCES: *Health, United States, 2008: With Special Feature on Death and Dying,* Hyattsville, MD: National Center for Health Statistics, February 2011. ✎ JR Pleis, BW Ward, JW Lucas, "Summary Health Statistics for U.S. Adults: National Health Interview Survey, 2009," *Vital and Health Statistics* 10(249), 2010.

The Toll

Cigarette smoking causes 443,000 premature deaths in the United States each year and about twenty times that number suffer from a serious smoking-caused illness.

This means that about **1 in 5** premature deaths each year are caused by smoking. These are about the same odds as an NFL field goal attempt will be unsuccessful. There is no safe level of exposure to cigarette smoke.

SOURCES: Centers for Disease Control and Prevention, "Tobacco-Related Mortality," *Smoking & Tobacco Use Fact Sheet*, http://www.cdc.gov/tobacco/data_ statistics/fact_sheets/health_effects/ tobacco_related_mortality/index.htm. ⚊ US Department of Health and Human Services, *How Tobacco Smoke Causes Disease: The Biology and Behavioral Basis for Smoking-Attributable Disease: A Report of the Surgeon General*, Atlanta, GA: US Department of Health and Human Services, Centers for Disease Control and Prevention, National Center for Chronic Disease Prevention and Health Promotion, Office on Smoking and Health, 2010. ⚊ Book of Odds estimate based on ESPN NFL Player Kicking Statistics—2010, http://espn.go.com/nfl/statistics/player/_/ stat/kicking/sort/fieldGoalPct/qualified/ false/count/41.

Cancer Deaths Due to Smoking

The US Surgeon General and US Department of Health and Human Services have determined that "the evidence is sufficient to infer a causal relationship between smoking and [the following types of cancer]":

Bladder	Kidney and renal	Lung and bronchus	Stomach
Cervical	Laryngeal	Oral	
Esophageal	Leukemia	Pancreatic	

The following table shows the lifetime odds of getting a given cancer and the odds that a death from it was caused by smoking.

Cancer Type	Lifetime Risk of Cancer %	Lifetime Risk of Cancer Odds (1 in)	Cancer Death Due to Smoking %	Cancer Death Due to Smoking Odds (1 in)
Lung and bronchus	6.5	15.4		
Men			90	1.1
Women			80	1.3
Kidney and renal	1.5	67.1		
Upper bound			40	2.5
Lower bound			30	3.3
Pancreas	1.4	70.9		
Men			29	3.4
Women			34	2.9
Esophagus	0.5	200.0		
Men			78	1.3
Women			75	1.3

SOURCES: N Howlader, AM Noone, M Krapcho, N Neyman, R Aminou, SF Altekruse, et al., eds., *SEER Cancer Statistics Review, 1975–2008*, Bethesda, MD: National Cancer Institute, http://seer.cancer.gov/csr/1975_2008/, based on November 2010 SEER data submission, posted to the SEER website, 2011. ⚊ US Department of Health and Human Services, *The Health Consequences of Smoking: A Report of the Surgeon General*, Washington, DC: Government Printing Office, 2004.

Or Did You Think It Was Zero?

The odds a person 18 or older will die of lung cancer caused by secondhand smoke: **1 in 62,900**

SOURCE: B Adhikari, J Kahende, A Malarcher, T Pechacek, V Tong, "Smoking-Attributable Mortality, Years of Potential Life Lost, and Productivity Losses—United States, 2000–2004," *Morbidity and Mortality Weekly Report* 57(45), 2008.

The Odds a Current Smoker Will Be
Diagnosed with Disease

The odds a current smoker 18 or older will:

be diagnosed with a smoking-attributable disease in a year: **1 in 9**

be diagnosed with chronic bronchitis in a year: **1 in 18.5**

be diagnosed with emphysema in a year: **1 in 38.2**

have a heart attack in a year: **1 in 67.6**

have a stroke in a year: **1 in 127**

be diagnosed with any cancer except lung cancer in a year: **1 in 136**

be diagnosed with lung cancer in a year: **1 in 1,056**

Disease	%
A smoking-attributable disease	11
Chronic bronchitis	5
Emphysema	3
Heart attack	1
Stroke	1
Any cancer except lung cancer	1
Lung cancer	0.09

SOURCE: A Hyland, C Vena, J Bauer, Q Li, GA Giovino, J Yang, et al., "Cigarette Smoking–Attributable Morbidity—United States, 2000," *Morbidity and Mortality Weekly Report* 52(35), 2003.

Number of Cigarettes Smoked in a Day
The odds a smoker 18 or older has:

fewer than 15 cigarettes a day: **1 in 1.9**   25–34 cigarettes a day: **1 in 14.7**

15–24 cigarettes a day: **1 in 2.8**   35 or more cigarettes a day: **1 in 19.6**

Number of Cigarettes Smoked in a Day	%
Fewer than 15	53
15–24	35
25–34	7
35+	5

SOURCE: Data from the National Health Interview Survey, National Center for Health Statistics, Hyattsville, MD, March 2010, in "Health Behaviors of Adults: United States, 2005–2007," *Vital and Health Statistics* 10(245).

Alcohol
The Odds of Being a **Teetotaler**

The odds an adult is a **lifetime abstainer** from alcohol: **1 in 5**

THE ODDS:

a Pacific Island adult is a lifetime abstainer from alcohol: **1 in 2.1**

an Asian adult is a lifetime abstainer from alcohol: **1 in 2.3**

a Hispanic adult is a lifetime abstainer from alcohol: **1 in 3.3**

a black adult is a lifetime abstainer from alcohol: **1 in 3.4**

an American Indian or Native Alaskan adult is a lifetime abstainer from alcohol: **1 in 4.1**

a non-Hispanic adult is a lifetime abstainer from alcohol: **1 in 5.4**

a white adult is a lifetime abstainer from alcohol: **1 in 5.7**

an adult with less than a high school diploma is a lifetime abstainer from alcohol: **1 in 3.3**

an adult with a high school diploma or GED is a lifetime abstainer from alcohol: **1 in 5**

an adult with some college education is a lifetime abstainer from alcohol: **1 in 6.8**

an adult with a bachelor's degree or more is a lifetime abstainer from alcohol: **1 in 7.5**

an adult with a family income less than 1 times the poverty level is a lifetime abstainer from alcohol: **1 in 3.2**

an adult with a family income 1–2 times the poverty level is a lifetime abstainer from alcohol: **1 in 3.8**

an adult with a family income 2 or more times the poverty level is a lifetime abstainer from alcohol: **1 in 6.3**

a widowed adult is a lifetime abstainer from alcohol: **1 in 3.3**

a never-married adult is a lifetime abstainer from alcohol: **1 in 3.8**

a married adult is a lifetime abstainer from alcohol: **1 in 5.4**

a separated or divorced adult is a lifetime abstainer from alcohol: **1 in 6.8**

a cohabitating adult is a lifetime abstainer from alcohol: **1 in 9.3**

an adult in the Northeast is a lifetime abstainer from alcohol: **1 in 5.4**

an adult in the Midwest is a lifetime abstainer from alcohol: **1 in 6.1**

an adult in the South is a lifetime abstainer from alcohol: **1 in 4.3**

an adult in the West is a lifetime abstainer from alcohol: **1 in 4.7**

Characteristics of Adult Lifetime Abstainers from Alcohol	%
All adults	20
Pacific Island	47
Asian	43
Hispanic	30
Black	29
American Indian or Native Alaskan	24
Non-Hispanic	19
White	18
Less than a high school diploma	30
A high school diploma or GED	20
Some college education	15
Bachelor's degree or higher	13
Family income less than 1 times the poverty level	31
Family income 1–2 times the poverty level	27
Family income 2 or more times the poverty level	16
Widowed	30
Never married	27
Married	18
Separated or divorced	15
Cohabitating	11
Northeast	18
Midwest	16
South	23
West	22

SOURCE: JR Pleis, BW Ward, JW Lucas, "Summary Health Statistics for U.S. Adults: National Health Interview Survey, 2009," *Vital and Health Statistics* 10(249), 2010.

The Odds of Being a Current, Binge, or Heavy Drinker by Age

Age	Current Drinker (Not Binge or Heavy)		Binge Drinker (Not Heavy)		Heavy Drinker		Current Drinker	
	%	Odds (1 in)	%	Odds (1 in)	%	Odds (1 in)	%	Odds (1 in)
12–13	1.8	55.6	1.4	71.4	0.2	500	3.4	28.6
14–15	6	16.7	6	17.9	1	71.4	13	7.7
16–17	9	10.8	13	8.0	4	22.2	26	3.8
18–20	15	6.7	23	4.3	11	8.8	50	2.0
21–25	24	4.2	31	3.2	15	6.5	70	1.4
26–29	28	3.6	28	3.6	11	9.3	66	1.5
30–34	28	3.5	25	4.0	10	10.5	63	1.6
35–39	32	3.1	20	5.0	7	13.5	60	1.7
40–44	34	2.9	20	5.0	7	14.7	61	1.6
45–49	35	2.9	18	5.7	7	14.9	59	1.7
50–54	35	2.9	14	7.1	6	15.6	55	1.7
55–59	37	2.7	13	7.5	6	16.9	56	1.8
60–64	38	2.6	9	11.5	4	26.3	50	2.0
65+	29	3.4	8	13.3	2	45.5	39	2.6

SOURCE: Substance Abuse and Mental Health Services Administration, *Results from the 2009 National Survey on Drug Use and Health,* vol. 1, *Summary of National Findings,* Office of Applied Studies, NSDUH Series H-38A, HHS Publication No. SMA 10-4586 Findings, 2010.

The odds a man thinks that the type of drink a man orders at a bar reflects his masculinity: **1 in 1.9**

SOURCE: AskMen.com, "Part II: Lifestyle," *The Great Male Survey, 2011 Edition,* http://askmen.com/specials/2011_great_male_survey/

The odds an adult has ever been diagnosed with alcohol abuse disorder: **1 in 7.6**

SOURCE: Harvard School of Medicine, "National Comorbidity Survey (NCS-R) Appendix Tables," July 19, 2007.

 **GENDER WARS**

The odds a man is a lifetime abstainer from alcohol are **1 in 7.2** vs. **1 in 3.9** for a woman.

The odds a man is a regular drinker are **1 in 1.6** vs. **1 in 2.3** for a woman.

Note: A current drinker had at least 12 drinks in his/her lifetime or in any one year and had a drink between 1 to 365 times in the past year. A regular drinker had at least 12 drinks in the past year.

SOURCE: JR Pleis, BW Ward, JW Lucas, "Summary Health Statistics for U.S. Adults: National Health Interview Survey, 2009," *Vital and Health Statistics* 10(249), 2010.

Badass Boomers

Baby boomers, those born from 1946 to 1964, have changed societal norms at every age group they have passed through. This generation created Woodstock, free love, and student protests that shut down many universities after the Kent State shooting in 1970.

Baby boomers are middle-aged, but some continue the habits they began in their youth. The odds a baby boomer is a binge drinker or a heavy drinker are each **1 in 16.7**. The odds a baby boomer uses illicit drugs are **1 in 17.5**.

SOURCES: Substance Abuse and Mental Health Services Administration, *Results from the 2010 National Survey on Drug Use and Health,* vol. 1, *Summary of National Findings,* Office of Applied Studies, NSDUH Series H-38A, HHS Publication No. SMA 10-4586 Findings, 2011. ✎ LM Howden, JA Meyer, "Age and Sex Composition: 2010," *2010 Census Briefs,* US Census Bureau, May 2011.

The Odds of Going to a Bar

The odds a man never goes to a bar: **1 in 2.1**

The odds a man will go to a bar several times a week: **1 in 10.1**

The odds a man will go to a bar almost daily: **1 in 100**

The odds a woman never goes to a bar: **1 in 2**

The odds a woman will go to a bar several times a week: **1 in 21.3**

The odds a woman will go to a bar almost daily: **1 in 333**

The odds an adult 18–29:
never goes to a bar: **1 in 2.9**

will go to a bar several times a week: **1 in 5.8**

will go to a bar almost daily: **1 in 111**

The odds an adult 30–49:

never goes to a bar: **1 in 2.6**

will go to a bar several times a week: **1 in 17.9**

will go to a bar almost daily: **1 in 250**

The odds an adult 50–64:

never goes to a bar: **1 in 1.8**

will go to a bar several times a week: **1 in 19.6**

will go to a bar almost daily: **1 in 250**

The odds an adult 65 or older:

never goes to a bar: **1 in 1.2**

will go to a bar several times a week: **1 in 76.9**

will go to a bar almost daily approaches **1 in 6,000,000**

Going to a Bar	Never	Several Times a Week	Almost Daily
Group	**%**	**%**	**%**
Men	47	10	1
Women	51	5	0.3
Adults 18–29	35	17	1
Adults 30–49	39	6	0.4
Adults 50–64	57	5	0.4
Adults 65+	80	1	~0

SOURCE: Book of Odds estimates based on JA Davis, TW Smith, PV Marsden, *General Social Surveys, 1972–2008,* [CUMULATIVE FILE] [Computer file] ICPSR04691, v. 1., Chicago: National Opinion Research Center, 2009 [producer]; Storrs, CT: Roper Center for Public Opinion Research, University of Connecticut/Ann Arbor, MI: Inter-university Consortium for Political and Social Research [distributors].

The Odds of Alcohol-Attributed Deaths by Gender

Alcohol-Attributable Cause of Death	Men %	Men Odds (1 in)	Women %	Women Odds (1 in)
Motor vehicle traffic crash	16	**6.4**	11	**9.4**
Alcoholic liver disease	13	**7.7**	12	**8.6**
Homicide	9	**11.2**	6	**17.5**
Suicide	8	**12.0**	5	**19.4**
Hemorrhagic stroke	8	**12.7**	11	**8.9**
Liver cirrhosis	6	**16.8**	10	**9.7**
Poisoning (not alcohol)	5	**19.0**	6	**16.2**
Esophageal cancer	5	**19.6**	2	**48.4**
Alcohol dependence syndrome	4	**22.8**	3	**34.5**
Fall injury	4	**24.0**	9	**10.7**
Liver cancer	4	**27.8**	3	**35.9**
Alcohol abuse	3	**37.1**	2	**55.0**
Laryngeal cancer	2	**56.9**	1	**151.0**
Prostate cancer	2	**67.9**		
Breast cancer			6	**16.1**
Hypertension	1	**72.1**	1	**73.9**
Supraventricular cardiac arrhythmia	1	**84.4**	3	**30.1**
Drowning	1	**96.7**	0.5	**186.0**
Fire injury	1	**100.0**	2	**60.7**
Alcohol psychosis	1	**122.0**	1	**155.0**
Alcoholic cardiomyopathy	1	**178.0**	0.2	**480.0**
Acute pancreatitis	1	**189.0**	1	**86.0**
Ischemic stroke	1	**193.0**	0.5	**218.0**
Chronic pancreatitis	0.5	**209.0**	0.3	**296.0**
Alcohol poisoning	0.4	**237.0**	0.3	**363.0**
Hypothermia	0.3	**381.0**	0.3	**325.0**
Motor vehicle non-traffic crash	0.2	**471.0**	0.1	**786.0**
Occupational and machine injury	0.2	**533.0**	0.02	**4,042.0**
Aspiration	0.2	**636.0**	0.3	**298.0**
Firearm injury	0.2	**641.0**	0.05	**1,886.0**
Air-space transport	0.2	**666.0**	0.07	**1,347.0**
Epilepsy	0.1	**679.0**	0.3	**322.0**
Child maltreatment	0.1	**722.0**	0.3	**393.0**
Water transport	0.1	**796.0**	0.04	**2,572.0**
Low birth weight resulting from a premature birth	0.1	**845.0**	0.1	**726.0**
Degeneration of the nervous system	0.1	**900.0**	0.05	**2,021.0**

SOURCE: Book of Odds estimate based on data in Centers for Disease Control and Prevention, Alcohol Related Disease Impact (ARDI) application, 2008, http://apps.nccd.cdc.gov/DACH_ARDI/Default.aspx.

GENDER WARS

The odds a man will die from an alcohol-attributable cause are **1 in 17.2** vs. **1 in 43.7** for a woman. For an alcohol-attributable acute cause, the odds are **1 in 37.2** for a man but only **1 in 107** for a woman. For an alcohol-attributable chronic cause, the odds are **1 in 32.2** for a man and **1 in 73.9** for a woman.

SOURCE: Book of Odds estimate based on data in Centers for Disease Control and Prevention, Alcohol Related Disease Impact (ARDI) application, 2008, http://apps.nccd.cdc.gov/DACH_ARDI/Default.aspx.

DRIVING UNDER THE INFLUENCE

The odds an arrest for driving under the influence will be of a man are **1 in 1.3** vs. **1 in 4.6** for a woman. The odds a driver involved in a fatal motor vehicle accident with a blood alcohol level of 0.08 or higher will be a man are **1 in 1.2** vs. **1 in 6.2** for a woman.

SOURCES: Federal Bureau of Investigation, *Crime in the United States, 2009*, http://www2.fbi.gov/ucr/cius2009/index.html. ⤢ National Center for Statistics and Analysis, National Highway Traffic Safety Administration, "Alcohol-Impaired Driving," *Traffic Safety Facts, 2009 Data* (DOT HS 811 385).

Drugs

The Odds of Illicit Drug Use
in the Past Month by Age

The odds an adolescent 12–13 used illicit drugs. . . . . . **1 in 25**

The odds a teenager 14–15 used illicit drugs . . . . **1 in 10.8**

The odds a teenager 16–17 used illicit drugs . . . . **1 in 6**

The odds an adult 18–20 used illicit drugs . . . . **1 in 4.3**

The odds an adult 21–25 used illicit drugs . . . . **1 in 4.9**

The odds an adult 26–29 used illicit drugs . . . . **1 in 6.8**

The odds an adult 30–34 used illicit drugs . . . . **1 in 7.8**

The odds an adult 35–39 used illicit drugs . . . . **1 in 12.3**

The odds an adult 40–44 used illicit drugs . . . . **1 in 14.5**

The odds an adult 45–49 used illicit drugs . . . . **1 in 13.9**

The odds an adult 50–54 used illicit drugs . . . . **1 in 13.9**

The odds an adult 55–59 used illicit drugs . . . . **1 in 24.4**

The odds an adult 60–64 used illicit drugs . . . . **1 in 37**

The odds an adult 65 or older used illicit drugs. . . . . **1 in 90.9**

Note: Illicit drugs include marijuana/hashish, cocaine (including crack), heroin, hallucinogens, inhalants, or prescription-type psychotherapeutics used nonmedically.

Age	%
12–13	4
14–15	9
16–17	17
18–20	23
21–25	21
26–29	15
30–34	13
35–39	8
40–44	7
45–49	7
50–54	7
55–59	4
60–64	3
65+	1

SOURCE: Substance Abuse and Mental Health Services Administration, *Results from the 2010 National Survey on Drug Use and Health*, vol. 1, *Summary of National Findings*, Office of Applied Studies, NSDUH Series H-38A, HHS Publication No. SMA 10-4586 Findings, 2011.

Racial/Ethnic Differences in
Illicit Drug Use
in the Last Month

The odds a white person 12 or older used illicit drugs: **1 in 11**

The odds an African American person 12 or older used illicit drugs: **1 in 9.3**

The odds an Asian person 12 or older used illicit drugs: **1 in 9.3**

The odds a Hispanic person 12 or older used illicit drugs: **1 in 12.3**

SOURCE: Substance Abuse and Mental Health Services Administration, *Results from the 2010 National Survey on Drug Use and Health*, vol. 1, *Summary of National Findings*, Office of Applied Studies, NSDUH Series H-38A, HHS Publication No. SMA 10-4586 Findings, 2011.

The Odds of Illicit Drug Use in the Last Month by Type Among Persons 12 or Older

Marijuana and hashish: **1 in 14.5**

Any prescription-type psychotherapeutic drugs used nonmedically: **1 in 37:**

Pain relievers, including OxyContin: **1 in 50**

Tranquilizers: **1 in 111**

Stimulants, including methamphetamine: **1 in 250**

Sedatives: **1 in 1,000**

Cocaine, including crack cocaine: **1 in 167**

Hallucinogens, including LSD, PCP, and ecstasy: **1 in 200**

SOURCE: Substance Abuse and Mental Health Services Administration, *Results from the 2010 National Survey on Drug Use and Health*, vol. 1, *Summary of National Findings*, Office of Applied Studies, NSDUH Series H-38A, HHS Publication No. SMA 10-4586 Findings, 2011.

Marijuana

ODDS COUPLE
Seeing Double?

The split between the legalizers and those opposed is quite close:

1 in 2.2 believes in legalizing the possession of small amounts of marijuana for personal use.

1 in 1.9 Americans does not believe in legalizing the possession of small amounts of marijuana for personal use.

SOURCE: Gary Langer, "Changing Views on Social Issues: Allemande Left. Allemande Right," *ABC News/Washington Post Polls: Hot Button Issues,* April 24, 2009.

GENDER WARS

The Odds of Marijuana Use in the Last Month

The odds a man used marijuana are **1 in 12** vs. **1 in 15.6** for a woman.

SOURCE: Substance Abuse and Mental Health Services Administration, 2011. *Results from the 2010 National Survey on Drug Use and Health,* vol. 1, *Summary of National Findings,* Office of Applied Studies, NSDUH Series H-38A, HHS Publication No. SMA 10-4586 Findings, 2011.

The odds a US banknote contains traces of cocaine:

1 in 1.1

SOURCE: D. Biello, "Cocaine Contaminates Majority of US Currency," *Scientific American,* August 16, 2009, http://www.scientificamerican.com/article.cfm?id=cocaine-contaminates.

I Get High with a Little Help

How do nonmedical users of prescription-type pain relievers 12 or older obtain them?

Given by friend or relative: **1 in 1.8**

Through a prescription from a single doctor: **1 in 5.8**

Purchased from a friend or relative: **1 in 8.8**

Stolen from a friend or relative: **1 in 20.8**

Purchased from a drug dealer or stranger: **1 in 22.7**

Purchased on the Internet: **1 in 250**

Source of Recreational Pain Relievers	%
Given by friend or relative	55
Through a prescription from a single doctor	17
Purchased from a friend or relative	11
Stolen from a friend or relative	5
Purchased from a drug dealer or stranger	4
Purchased on the Internet	0.4

SOURCE: Substance Abuse and Mental Health Services Administration, *Results from the 2010 National Survey on Drug Use and Health,* vol. 1, *Summary of National Findings,* Office of Applied Studies, NSDUH Series H-38A, HHS Publication No. SMA 10-4586 Findings, 2011.

Fatal Overdoses

The odds a person will die from taking too many drugs—both legal and illegal—have more than doubled from **1 in 25,010** in 1999 to **1 in 10,870** in 2007, the latest year for which data are available. Many deaths are attributed to the mixing of drugs.

Mortality rates are highest among middle-aged adults. New Mexico has the highest rate of unintentional poisonings (**1 in 6,691**) and Maryland has the lowest (**1 in 99,020**).

SOURCE: Book of Odds estimates based on Centers for Disease Control and Prevention, *Compressed Mortality File,* 1999 and 2006 data.

CHAPTER 10

BELIEFS AND FEARS

REALLY?

The odds an adult believes the government staged or faked the Apollo moon landing:

1 in 16.7

SOURCE: Gallup News Service, "Did Men Really Land on the Moon?," Time/CNN/ Yankelovich Partners Poll, February 15, 2001.

Changes in Religious Denominations, 1990 vs. 2008

The Institute for the Study of Secularism in Society and Culture conducts periodic studies on the religious affiliation of people in the United States. Between 1990 and 2008 (the most recent year for which data are available) the most startling changes were in the percentages of the adult population who:

- do not affiliate with any religion (from **8%** in 1990 to **15%** in 2008).

- consider themselves mainline Christians (from **19%** in 1990 to **13%** in 2008).

The percentage who consider themselves Christian but do not affiliate with any denomination has remained about the same at **14%** of the adult population. In 2008 that group was fourth overall, displacing mainline Christians.

SOURCE: BA Kosmin, A Keysar, *American Religious Identification Survey, Summary Report,* Institute for the Study of Secularism in Society and Culture, Trinity College, March 2009.

1990

The odds an adult is Catholic: **1 in 3.8**

The odds an adult is Baptist: **1 in 5.2**

The odds an adult is mainline Christian: **1 in 5.4**

The odds an adult is Methodist: **1 in 12.4**

The odds an adult is Lutheran: **1 in 19.3**

The odds an adult is Presbyterian: **1 in 35.2**

The odds an adult is **Atheist** in 2008: **1 in 140.8**

The odds an adult is Episcopalian or Anglican: **1 in 57.7**

The odds an adult is a member of the United Church of Christ: **1 in 401**

The odds an adult is a Christian (generic): **1 in 6.8**

The odds an adult is a Christian but not a specific denomination: **1 in 21.2**

The odds an adult is a Protestant but not a specific denomination: **1 in 10.2**

The odds an adult is an Evangelical or born-again Christian: **1 in 321**

The odds an adult has no religion: **1 in 12.2**

The odds an adult is Pentecostal or Charismatic: **1 in 31.1**

The odds an adult is Pentecostal: **1 in 56.3**

The odds an adult is a member of the Assemblies of God: **1 in 284**

The odds an adult is a member of the Church of God: **1 in 297**

The odds an adult is a Protestant denomination: **1 in 10.2**

The odds an adult is a member of the Churches of Christ: **1 in 99.2**

The odds an adult is a Jehovah's Witness: **1 in 127**

The odds an adult is a Seventh-day Adventist: **1 in 263**

The odds an adult is Jewish: **1 in 55.9**

The odds an adult is a Mormon or Latter-Day Saint: **1 in 70.5**

The odds an adult is a part of a new religious movement: **1 in 135**

The odds an adult is a member of an Eastern religion: **1 in 255**

The odds an adult is Buddhist: **1 in 434**

The odds an adult is Muslim: **1 in 333**

2008

The odds an adult is Catholic: **1 in 4**

The odds an adult is Baptist: **1 in 6.3**

The odds an adult is mainline Christian: **1 in 7.8**

The odds an adult is Methodist: **1 in 20.1**

The odds an adult is Lutheran: **1 in 26**

The odds an adult is Presbyterian: **1 in 48.3**

The odds an adult is
Agnostic in 2008:
1 in 115

The odds an adult is Episcopalian or Anglican: **1 in 94.9**

The odds an adult is a member of the United Church of Christ: **1 in 310**

The odds an adult is a Christian (generic): **1 in 6.8**

The odds an adult is a Christian but not a specific denomination: **1 in 28.4**

The odds an adult is a Protestant but not a specific denomination: **1 in 43.5**

The odds an adult is an Evangelical or born-again Christian: **1 in 106**

The odds an adult has no religion: **1 in 6.7**

The odds an adult is Pentecostal or Charismatic: **1 in 28.7**

The odds an adult is Pentecostal: **1 in 42.1**

The odds an adult is a member of the Assemblies of God: **1 in 281**

The odds an adult is a member of the Church of God: **1 in 344**

The odds an adult is a member of a Protestant denomination: **1 in 32.3**

The odds an adult is a member of the Churches of Christ: **1 in 119**

The odds an adult is a Jehovah's Witness: **1 in 119**

The odds an adult is a Seventh-day Adventist: **1 in 243**

The odds an adult is Jewish: **1 in 85.1**

The odds an adult is a Mormon or Latter-Day Saint: **1 in 72.3**

The odds an adult is a part of a new religious movement: **1 in 81.4**

The odds an adult is a member of an Eastern religion: **1 in 116**

The odds an adult is Buddhist: **1 in 192**

The odds an adult is Muslim: **1 in 169**

Spiritual Beliefs
Belief in God

The odds an adult believes:

There is definitely a personal God: **1 in 1.4**

There is a higher power but not a personal God: **1 in 8.3**

There is no such thing as God: **1 in 43.5**

There's no way to know for sure: **1 in 23.3**

Not sure what to think: **1 in 17.5**

SOURCE: BA Kosmin, A Keysar, *American Religious Identification Survey, Summary Report*, Institute for the Study of Secularism in Society and Culture, Trinity College, March 2009.

Racial and Religious Differences

Race makes very little difference in whether people report being sure there's a God. A large—and comparable—proportion of whites (**1 in 1.4**), blacks (**1 in 1.3**), and Hispanics (**1 in 1.3**) report being "certain there is a God." Jews and Catholics are more likely to doubt the existence of God than are Protestants and born-again Christians. The odds a born-again Christian is not sure whether there is a God are **1 in 50**. The odds for a practicing Jew: **1 in 4.4**.

SOURCE: H Taylor, "Three in Five Adults Are Absolutely Certain There Is a God," Harris Poll #142, December 17, 2009, http://news.harrisinteractive.com.

Is God Male or Female?

The odds an adult believes God is neither male nor female:
1 in 2.9

The odds an adult believes God is both male and female:
1 in 9.1

SOURCE: H Taylor, "Three in Five Adults Are Absolutely Certain There Is a God," Harris Poll #142, December 17, 2009, http://news.harrisinteractive.com.

 GENDER WARS

The odds a man believes God is male: **1 in 3.1**

The odds a woman believes God is male: **1 in 2.3**

SOURCE: H Taylor, "Three in Five Adults Are Absolutely Certain There Is a God," Harris Poll #142, December 17, 2009, http://news.harrisinteractive.com.

Omniscience and Destiny

The odds a Catholic believes God observes but does not control what happens on Earth: **1 in 1.6**

The odds for a Protestant: **1 in 2.5**

The odds a Catholic believes God controls what happens on Earth: **1 in 5.3**

The odds for a Protestant: **1 in 2.3**

SOURCE: H Taylor, "Three in Five Adults Are Absolutely Certain There Is a God," Harris Poll #142, December 17, 2009, http://news.harrisinteractive.com.

ODDS COUPLE
Who Walks the Talk?

The odds an adult owns a Bible are **1 in 1.1**.

These are the same odds an adult has never had revenge sex.

SOURCES: Barna Group, "Americans Draw Theological Beliefs from Diverse Points of View," October 8, 2002, http://www.barna.org/. ✗ Book of Odds estimate based on "The American Sex Survey: A Peek Beneath the Sheets," *ABC News Primetime Live Poll*, October 21, 2004, http://abcnews.go.com/images/Politics/959a1AmericanSex Survey.pdf.

 No, we didn't get this from Pew.

The odds a person's last name is Church: **1 in 7,791**

SOURCE: US Census Bureau, *Top 1000 Names*, 2000.

Religious Ceremonies

The odds an adult has had a religious initiation ceremony:
1 in 1.4

The odds an ever-married adult was married in a religious ceremony:
1 in 1.5

The odds an adult expects to have a religious funeral: **1 in 1.5**

SOURCE: BA Kosmin, A Keysar, *American Religious Identification Survey, Summary Report*, Institute for the Study of Secularism in Society and Culture, Trinity College, March 2009.

1 in 1.8 adults will plan to go to church on Christmas Eve or Christmas Day.

SOURCE: Rasmussen Reports, "67% Prefer Merry Christmas While 26% Opt for Happy Holidays," press release, national survey of 1,000 adults, November 18–19, 2007.

⚨ GENDER WARS
Equal Opportunities Believers

The odds an adult who follows a new religious movement is male: **1 in 1.9**

The odds an adult who follows a new religious movement is female: **1 in 2.1**

SOURCE: BA Kosmin, A Keysar, *American Religious Identification Survey, Summary Report*, Institute for the Study of Secularism in Society and Culture, Trinity College, March 2009.

They Say Confession Is Good for the Soul
The Odds a Catholic Adult Will Go to Confession:

Never. . . . . **1 in 2.2**

Less than once a year. . . . . **1 in 3.3**

Once a year. . . . . **1 in 8.3**

Several times a year. . . . . **1 in 8.3**

At least once a month . . . . **1 in 50**

SOURCE: Center for Applied Research in the Apostolate, *The Sacrament of Reconciliation*, January 10, 2009.

Practicing What's Preached
The Odds a Catholic Adult Attends Mass:

Rarely or never other than for weddings or funerals: **1 in 3.1**

Almost every week: **1 in 9.1**

Every week: **1 in 5**

More than once a week: **1 in 33.3**

SOURCE: Center for Applied Research in the Apostolate, *Demographic and Background Characteristics*, 2008.

New Century, Old Debate

The odds a person believes in Darwin's theory of evolution: **1 in 1.9**

The odds a person does not believe in Darwin's theory of evolution: **1 in 4.8**

The odds an adult believes only Darwin's theory of evolution should be taught in schools: **1 in 4.4**

The odds an adult believes only creationism should be taught in schools: **1 in 5.9**

The odds an adult believes both Darwin's theory of evolution and creationism should be taught in schools: **1 in 2.5**

The odds an adult believes neither Darwin's theory of evolution nor creationism should be taught in schools: **1 in 9.1**

SOURCE: Harris Interactive, "No Consensus, and Much Confusion, on Evolution and the Origin of Species," *BBC America/The Harris Poll*, press release, February 18, 2009.

Belief in
Clairvoyance, ESP, Telepathy, Fortune Tellers, Astrologers

The odds an adult believes a person can have extrasensory perception (ESP):

1 in 2.1

The odds an adult believes in mental telepathy:

1 in 3.2

The odds an adult believes in astrology:

1 in 3.9

The odds an adult believes in clairvoyance:

1 in 3.9

The odds an adult agrees that astrologers, palm readers, tarot card readers, fortune tellers, and psychics can foresee the future:

1 in 7.8

Belief	%
Extrasensory perception (ESP)	48
Mental telepathy	31
Astrology	26
Clairvoyance	26
Astrologers, palm readers, tarot card readers, fortune tellers, and psychics can foresee the future	13

SOURCES: Ipsos Public Affairs, "The Associated Press Poll Conducted by Ipsos Public Affairs: Project #81-5681-64, Ghost Study," press release, October 2007. ✔ DW Moore, "Three in Four Americans Believe in Paranormal," Gallup News Service, press release, June 16, 2005. ✔ Baylor Institute for Studies of Religion, *American Piety in the 21st Century: Selected Findings from the Baylor Religion Survey*, September 2006.

GENDER WARS
"Practical Magic"

The odds a woman has used a Ouija board to contact the dead: **1 in 9.4** vs. **1 in 25** for a man.

SOURCE: Baylor Institute for Studies of Religion, *American Piety in the 21st Century: Selected Findings from the Baylor Religion Survey*, September 2006.

Where Do You Come Down?
The Odds an Adult Believes:

It's possible for some people to "channel" a spirit:
1 in 11.1 believe vs. **1 in 1.4** don't believe.

Some people can communicate with the dead:
1 in 4.8 believe vs. in **1 in 1.8** don't believe.

In psychic or spiritual healing:
1 in 1.8 believe vs. **1 in 3.9** don't believe.

A person can be possessed by the devil:
1 in 2.4 believe vs. **1 in 2.3** don't believe.

SOURCE: Baylor Institute for Studies of Religion, *American Piety in the 21st Century: Selected Findings from the Baylor Religion Survey*, September 2006.

The World's Getting Scarier

In 2005, the odds an adult believed in ghosts were **1 in 3.1**.

By 2009, the odds had increased to **1 in 2.4**.

SOURCES: DW Moore, "Three in Four Americans Believe in Paranormal," Gallup News Service, press release, June 16, 2005. ✔ Harris Interactive, "What People Do and Do Not Believe In," Harris Poll #140, press release, December 15, 2009, http://www.harrisinteractive.com/vault/Harris_Poll_2009_12_15.pdf.

The Odds an Adult
Does Not Believe in Witches: 1 in 1.7

The odds are the same that...

- An adult who believed in Santa Claus as a child stopped believing between ages 7 and 10.
- A woman believes homosexuality is okay.
- An adult has a mostly favorable opinion of black people.
- A person 65 or older believes public libraries should not remove books advocating doing away with elections and letting the military run the country.

SOURCES: Harris Interactive, "What People Do and Do Not Believe In," Harris Poll #140, press release, December 15, 2009, http://www.harrisinteractive.com/vault/Harris_Poll_2009_12_15.pdf. ✗ Ipsos, AP-AOL News Poll on Angels, December 12–14, 2006, Associated Press, press release, December 23, 2006. ✗ "The American Sex Survey: A Peek Beneath the Sheets," *ABC News Primetime Live Poll*, October 21, 2004, http://abcnews.go.com/images/Politics/959a1AmericanSex Survey.pdf. ✗ A Kohut, R Suro, S Keeter, C Doherty, G Escobar, *America's Immigration Quandry: No Consensus on Immigration Problem or Proposed Fixes*, Washington, DC: Pew Research Center for the People and Press, March 30, 2006. ✗ Book of Odds estimates based on JA Davis, TW Smith, PV Marsden, *General Social Surveys, 1972–2008* [CUMULATIVE FILE] [Computer file] ICPSR04691 v. 1., Chicago: National Opinion Research Center, 2009 [producer]; Storrs, CT: Roper Center for Public Opinion Research, University of Connecticut/Ann Arbor, MI: Inter-university Consortium for Political and Social Research [distributors].

Dream On

The odds an adult agrees that "dreams can sometimes foretell the future or reveal hidden truths" are 1 in 1.9.

The odds an adult reports having had a dream that later came true are 1 in 2.3.

SOURCE: Baylor Institute for Studies of Religion, *American Piety in the 21st Century: Selected Findings from the Baylor Religion Survey*, 2005.

 ODDS COUPLE
"I Am Napoleon Bigfoot"

The odds an adult agrees that "creatures such as Bigfoot and the Loch Ness Monster will one day be discovered by science" are 1 in 5.6, the same odds that an adult will receive mental health services in a year.

SOURCES: Baylor Institute for Studies of Religion, *American Piety in the 21st Century: Selected Findings from the Baylor Religion Survey*, September 2006. ✗ RC Kessler, P Burglund, O Demler, R Jin, KR Merikangas, EE Walters, "Lifetime Prevalence and Age-of-Onset Distribution of DSM-IV Disorders in the National Comorbidity Survey Replication," *Archives of General Psychiatry* 62, June 2005.

The Odds of
Zombification?

You see them in movies, parades, and shopping malls. They are bruised and decomposed. They move slow as nightmare horrors, hunting for human flesh. These are zombies, of course, the reanimated dead and, no, they don't want your money; they want *you*! In a consumerist culture, what could be finer cultural sabotage than to consume the consumer?

Should we be worried? Depends on the odds, of course. If a zombie bites a non-zombie, the bitten becomes a zombie, too. Sound familiar? Let the mosquito transmit the transforming bite and this is the way malaria works. So does the flu and anything else that grows virally. If nothing stops a zombie or cures the zombified, eventually *everyone* becomes one. In fact, it can happen rather quickly.

But let's say the outbreak starts and we learn how to nullify some zombies after only five days. What are the odds then? It turns out that with pestilence that spreads virally, the difference between good odds of cure and great ones is all the difference in the world.

Here's a model that tells the tale. Suppose on the first day of the outbreak there is just one zombie. Let's say that each zombie creates a new zombie a day by biting a regular human and that we start working off the zombie backlog on day five.

Suppose the odds of the Zombie Cure working are **1 in 1.05** or 95%. This is great but even so, after 100 days there will be 865 zombies, about the number of languages spoken by 100,000 or more. But what if the the odds of the Zombie Cure working were just a bit worse, say, **1 in 1.1** or 90%? One hundred days pass and there are 75,299 zombies! This is more people than fit in Green Bay's Lambeau Field or Berlin's Olympic Stadium!

Okay, now suppose the odds of the Zombie Cure working is **1 in 1.25**, or 80%. That is pretty effective, about the rate that a household owns an outdoor barbecue grill. What happens at this level? In 100 days we would have almost 320 million zombies, more than the population of the United States.

(Thanks for this go to Munz et al. and Lakeland, whose work we simplified, and whom we regard as the inventors of "Zombie Modeling," a mathematical and not a fashion runway term.)

SOURCES: W Davis, *Passage of Darkness: The Ethnobiology of the Haitian Zombie*, Chapel Hill: University of North Carolina Press, 1988. ✏ K Thomas, "Haitian Zombie, Myth, and Modern Identity," *Comparative Literature and Culture* 12(2), 2010, http://docs.lib.purdue.edu/cgi/viewcontent.cgi?article=1602&context=clcweb. ✏ M Murtaugh, "Constructing the Haitian Zombie: An Anthropological Study Beyond Madness," 2009, Benedict Award–winning paper. ✏ A Gelman, G Romero, "'How Many Zombies Do You Know?' Using Indirect Survey Methods to Measure Alien Attacks and Outbreaks of the Undead," March 31, 2010. ✏ MP Lewis, ed., *Ethnologue: Languages of the World*, 16th ed., Dallas: SIL International, 2009. ✏ P Munz, I Hudea, J Imad, RJ Smith, "When Zombies Attack! Mathematical Modelling of an Outbreak of Zombie Infection," *Infectious Disease Modelling Research Progress*, Nova Science, 2009: 133–150. ✏ D Lakeland, "Improved Zombie Dynamics," *Models of Reality, Engineering, Science and Society*, March 1, 2010, http://models.street-artists.org/2010/03/01/improved-zombie-dynamics/.

They Walk Among Us

1 in 3.1 American adults believes in UFOs. The odds an American adult reports actually having seen a UFO are **1 in 5.8**. And a Reuters News poll reveals that when people all over the globe were asked, "Do you believe that aliens have come down to Earth, and live in our communities, disguised as humans?," **1 in 5** answered yes.

More than 23,000 people in twenty-three countries were surveyed.
China and India have the highest percentages of believers. 45% of Indian respondents, and 42% of Chinese, believe in incognito ETs. The believers come from all economic brackets, tend to be men (22% vs. 17% of women), and are generally 35 or younger.

On the other end of the spectrum, northern European countries like Belgium, Sweden, and the Netherlands contain the fewest believers: only 8% each. The poll was conducted for Reuters by Ipsos, a survey-based research company, whose senior vice president, John Wright, speculates that "in a less populated country, you are more likely to know your next door neighbor better"—and thus have a certain confidence that he or she has not been body-snatched.

SOURCES: Harris Interactive, "What People Do and Do Not Believe In," Harris Poll #140, press release, December 15, 2009, http://www.harrisinteractive.com/vault/Harris_Poll_2009_12_15.pdf. ✏ Baylor Institute for Studies of Religion, *American Piety in the 21st Century: Selected Findings from the Baylor Religion Survey*, September 2006. ✏ Reuters Ipsos poll, "They Walk Among Us: 1 in 5 Believe in Aliens?," press release, April 8, 2010.

Conspiracy Theories

- The odds an adult believes it is very likely that the Pentagon was not struck by an airliner captured by terrorists on 9/11 but was instead hit by a cruise missile fired by the US military: **1 in 16.4**

- The odds an adult believes there is a chance that Elvis Presley is still alive: **1 in 12.5**

- The odds an adult believes it is very likely that officials in the federal government were directly responsible for the assassination of President Kennedy: **1 in 8.3**

- The odds an adult believes it is very likely that the federal government is withholding proof of the existence of intelligent life on other planets: **1 in 6.3**

- The odds an adult believes it is very likely that people in the federal government either assisted in the 9/11 attacks or took no action to stop the attacks because they wanted the United States to go to war in the Middle East: **1 in 6.2**

- The odds an adult believes the crash that killed Princess Diana was probably planned: **1 in 3.9**

- The odds an adult believes it is likely that the CIA allowed drug dealers from Central America to sell crack cocaine to black people in US inner cities: **1 in 1.9**

SOURCES: C Stempel, T Hargrove, GH Stempel III, "Media Use, Social Structure and Belief in 9/11 Conspiracy Theories," *Journalism and Mass Communication Quarterly* 84(2), Summer 2007. ✔ D Blanton, "Poll: For a Few True Believers Elvis Lives," Fox News Poll, August 14, 2002. ✔ "The Death of Princess Diana," press release, *CBS News/48 Hours Poll*, April 21, 2004. ✔ C DiLouie, "Most Americans Believe in Conspiracy Theories," *Disinformation Archive*, December 13, 2001.

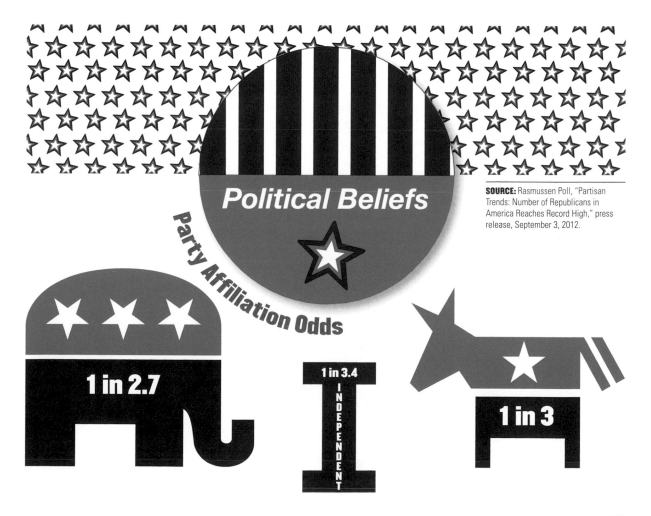

Political Beliefs

Party Affiliation Odds

1 in 2.7

1 in 3.4 INDEPENDENT

1 in 3

SOURCE: Rasmussen Poll, "Partisan Trends: Number of Republicans in America Reaches Record High," press release, September 3, 2012.

Political Trending, 1969–2011

The Odds an Adult Will Report He or She Is a/an:

SOURCES: Rasmussen Poll, "Partisan Trends: Number of Republicans in America Reaches Record High," press release, September 3, 2012. ✔ Pew Research Center for the People and the Press, *Independents Take Center Stage in Obama Era: Trends in Political Values and Core Attitudes, 1987–2009*, press release, May 21, 2009. ✔ Harris Interactive, "Democratic Lead in Party Identification at Highest Point in 25 Years," press release, March 3, 2009.

"I Could Date a Moderate"

The odds a woman considers political views as the most important characteristic when searching for a significant other:

1 in 100

SOURCE: Yahoo! Personals and TheKnot .com, "Dating Survey: Women on Finding 'The One,'" September 13, 2009.

	Republican		Democrat		Independent
2011	1 in 2.9	2011	1 in 2.9	2011	1 in 3.2
2010	1 in 3.1	2010	1 in 2.8	2010	1 in 3.1
2009	1 in 3.1	2009	1 in 2.6	2009	1 in 3.4
2008	1 in 3.2	2008	1 in 2.5	2008	1 in 3.5
2007	1 in 3.2	2007	1 in 2.8	2007	1 in 4.4
2006	1 in 3	2006	1 in 2.7	2006	1 in 3.3
2005	1 in 2.8	2005	1 in 2.8	2005	1 in 3.5
2004	1 in 2.8	2004	1 in 2.6	2004	1 in 3.7
2003	1 in 3.3	2003	1 in 3.2	2003	1 in 3.2
2002	1 in 3.3	2002	1 in 3.2	2002	1 in 3.3
2001	1 in 3.4	2001	1 in 2.9	2001	1 in 3.4
2000	1 in 3.6	2000	1 in 3	2000	1 in 3.3
1999	1 in 3.7	1999	1 in 2.9	1999	1 in 2.9
1998	1 in 3.6	1998	1 in 3	1998	1 in 3.1
1997	1 in 3.6	1997	1 in 3	1997	1 in 3.1
1996	1 in 3.4	1996	1 in 3	1996	1 in 3.2
1995	1 in 3.2	1995	1 in 3.3	1995	1 in 3
1994	1 in 3.3	1994	1 in 3.1	1994	1 in 2.9
1993	1 in 3.7	1993	1 in 2.9	1993	1 in 2.9
1992	1 in 3.6	1992	1 in 3	1992	1 in 2.8
1991	1 in 3.2	1991	1 in 3.2	1991	1 in 3
1990	1 in 3.2	1990	1 in 3	1990	1 in 2.9
1989	1 in 3.1	1989	1 in 2.9	1989	1 in 3.3
1988	1 in 3.3	1988	1 in 2.9	1988	1 in 3.2
1987	1 in 3.3	1987	1 in 2.9	1987	1 in 3.2
1986	1 in 3.2	1986	1 in 2.8	1986	1 in 3.3
1985	1 in 3.1	1985	1 in 2.9	1985	1 in 3.4
1984	1 in 3.4	1984	1 in 2.6	1984	1 in 3.4
1983	1 in 4.2	1983	1 in 2.3	1983	1 in 3.3
1982	1 in 4	1982	1 in 2.3	1982	1 in 3.7
1981	1 in 3.7	1981	1 in 2.4	1981	1 in 3.3
1980	1 in 4.3	1980	1 in 2.2	1980	1 in 3.4
1979	1 in 4.8	1979	1 in 2.3	1979	1 in 3.1
1978	1 in 4.5	1978	1 in 2.2	1978	1 in 3.6
1977	1 in 4.8	1977	1 in 2.2	1977	1 in 3.3
1976	1 in 4.5	1976	1 in 2.2	1976	1 in 3.4
1975	1 in 4.8	1975	1 in 2.3	1975	1 in 3
1974	1 in 4.3	1974	1 in 2.3	1974	1 in 3.2
1973	1 in 4.2	1973	1 in 2.4	1973	1 in 3.2
1972	1 in 3.8	1972	1 in 2.4	1972	1 in 3.3
1971	1 in 4	1971	1 in 2.3	1971	1 in 3.4
1970	1 in 3.7	1970	1 in 2.3	1970	1 in 3.6
1969	1 in 3.7	1969	1 in 2.4	1969	1 in 3.4

Political Leanings

(Liberal vs. Conservative)

The odds an adult is a conservative . . . . 1 in 2.4

The odds an adult is a moderate . . . . 1 in 2.7

The odds an adult is a liberal . . . . 1 in 4.8

	Conservative	Moderate	Liberal
	%	%	%
Adults	42	37	21

SOURCE: F. Newport, JM Jones, L Saad, "Democrats More Liberal, Less White than 2008," Gallup, press release, November 7, 2011, http://www.gallup.com.

Means of Political Expression

The odds an adult 26 or older will express him- or herself politically by:

engaging in a boycott in a year . . . . **1 in 2.6**

engaging in a buycott in a year . . . . **1 in 3**

signing a paper petition in a year. . . . . **1 in 3.9**

signing an email petition in a year . . . . **1 in 4.8**

contacting a public official in a year . . . . **1 in 4.6**

protesting in a year. . . . . **1 in 20**

contacting broadcast media in a year . . . . **1 in 12.5**

contacting print media in a year . . . . **1 in 9.1**

canvassing in a year . . . . **1 in 50**

Political Expression	Age 15–25 %	Age 15–25 Odds (1 in)	Age 26+ %
Engaging in a boycott	30	**3.3**	38
Engaging in a buycott	29	**3.5**	33
Signing a paper petition	18	**5.6**	26
Signing an email petition	16	**6.3**	21
Contacting a public official	11	**9.1**	22
Protesting	11	**9.1**	5
Contacting broadcast media	9	**11.1**	8
Contacting print media	7	**14.3**	11
Canvassing	3	**33.3**	2

SOURCE: MH Lopez, P Levine, *The 2006 Civic and Political Health of the Nation: A Detailed Look at How Youth Participate in Politics and Communities*, Center for Information and Research on Civic Learning and Engagement, October 2006.

Partisan Nation

The odds an adult agrees that "it is the responsibility of the government to take care of people who can't take care of themselves":
1 in 1.6

The odds an adult agrees that "the federal government controls too much of our daily lives":
1 in 1.8

The odds an adult 26 or older believes "politics is a way for the powerful to keep power for themselves":
1 in 1.9

The odds an adult 26 or older believes "it is his or her responsibility to get involved and make things better for society":
1 in 2.4

SOURCES: Pew Research Center for the People and the Press, *Independents Take Center Stage in Obama Era: Trends in Political Values and Core Attitudes, 1987–2009*, press release, May 21, 2009. ⤢ MH Lopez, P Levine, *The 2006 Civic and Political Health of the Nation: A Detailed Look at How Youth Participate in Politics and Communities*, Center for Information and Research on Civic Learning and Engagement, October 2006.

The Odds on Being
Proud to Be an American
by Age

The odds an adult 18–24 is very proud to be an American citizen: **1 in 1.5**

The odds an adult 18–24 is somewhat proud to be an American citizen: **1 in 3.7**

The odds an adult 18–24 is not very proud to be an American citizen: **1 in 16.7**

The odds an adult 18–24 is not at all proud to be an American citizen: **1 in 50**

The odds an adult 25–29 is very proud to be an American citizen: **1 in 1.6**

The odds an adult 25–29 is somewhat proud to be an American citizen: **1 in 4.2**

The odds an adult 25–29 is not very proud to be an American citizen: **1 in 12.5**

The odds an adult 25–29 is not at all proud to be an American citizen: **1 in 100**

The odds an adult 30–39 is very proud to be an American citizen: **1 in 1.3**

The odds an adult 30–39 is somewhat proud to be an American citizen: **1 in 4.8**

The odds an adult 30–39 is not very proud to be an American citizen: **1 in 50**

The odds an adult 30–39 is not at all proud to be an American citizen: **1 in 100**

The odds an adult 40–49 is very proud to be an American citizen: **1 in 1.3**

The odds an adult 40–49 is somewhat proud to be an American citizen: **1 in 5.6**

The odds an adult 40–49 is not very proud to be an American citizen: **1 in 25**

The odds an adult 40–49 is not at all proud to be an American citizen: **1 in 100**

The odds an adult 50–64 is very proud to be an American citizen: **1 in 1.2**

The odds an adult 50–64 is somewhat proud to be an American citizen: **1 in 7.1**

The odds an adult 50–64 is not very proud to be an American citizen: **1 in 33.3**

The odds an adult 65 or older is very proud to be an American citizen: **1 in 1.1**

The odds an adult 65 or older is somewhat proud to be an American citizen: **1 in 11.1**

The odds an adult 65 or older is not very proud to be an American citizen: **1 in 100**

Age	Very Proud %	Somewhat Proud %	Not Very Proud %	Not at All Proud %
18–24	65	27	6	2
25–29	63	24	8	1
30–39	75	21	2	1
40–49	77	18	4	1
50–64	83	14	3	0
65+	90	9	1	0

SOURCE: Harris Interactive, "Americans Just as Proud to Be an American Citizen Now as After 9/11," press release, September 10, 2009.

Priorities in the United States

The odds a likely voter thinks:

the economy should be a very important issue this year: **1 in 1.3**

health care should be a very important issue this year: **1 in 1.5**

government ethics and corruption should be a very important issue this year: **1 in 1.5**

education should be a very important issue this year: **1 in 1.6**

taxes should be a very important issue this year: **1 in 1.7**

Social Security should be a very important issue this year: **1 in 1.7**

energy policy should be a very important issue this year: **1 in 1.9**

national security/the war on terror should be a very important issue this year: **1 in 1.9**

immigration should be a very important issue this year: **1 in 2.2**

SOURCE: Rasmussen Reports, "Importance of Issues, Economy Continues to Top List of Most Important Issues, Election 2012," September 21, 2012.

 **1 in 2.6** adults believes a communist college professor should be fired.

SOURCE: Book of Odds estimates based on JA Davis, TW Smith, PV Marsden, *General Social Surveys, 1972–2008* [CUMULATIVE FILE] [Computer file] ICPSR04691 v. 1., Chicago: National Opinion Research Center, 2009 [producer]; Storrs, CT: Roper Center for Public Opinion Research, University of Connecticut/Ann Arbor, MI: Inter-university Consortium for Political and Social Research [distributors].

A Limit to Free Speech?

The odds a person believes public libraries should remove books:

saying that black people are genetically inferior: **1 in 2.9**

written by communists: **1 in 3.3**

advocating doing away with elections and letting the military run the country: **1 in 3.5**

against churches or religion: **1 in 3.7**

in favor of homosexuality, written by homosexual men: **1 in 4.4**

The odds a person believes in banning public speeches:

claiming black people are genetically inferior: **1 in 2.5**

by militarists: **1 in 3**

by communists: **1 in 3.1**

against churches or religion: **1 in 4.3**

by homosexual men: **1 in 5.9**

SOURCE: Book of Odds estimates based on JA Davis, TW Smith, PV Marsden, *General Social Surveys, 1972–2008* [CUMULATIVE FILE] [Computer file] ICPSR04691 v. 1., Chicago: National Opinion Research Center, 2009 [producer]; Storrs, CT: Roper Center for Public Opinion Research, University of Connecticut/Ann Arbor, MI: Inter-university Consortium for Political and Social Research [distributors].

HOT BUTTONS Stem Cell Research

1 in 1.7
The odds an adult believes embryonic stem cell research is morally acceptable.

1 in 2.9
The odds an adult "is worried that science is going too far and is hurting society rather than helping it."

1 in 3.1
The odds an adult believes embryonic stem cell research is morally wrong.

1 in 5.3
The odds an adult believes the federal government should not fund stem cell research.

1 in 7.1
The odds an adult believes the federal government should not have funding restrictions on stem cell research.

SOURCES: F Newport, "Americans and Embryonic Stem Cells," Polling Matters, Gallup, August 24, 2010. ✎ Pew Research Center for the People and the Press, *Independents Take Center Stage in Obama Era: Trends in Political Values and Core Attitudes, 1987–2009,* press release, May 21, 2009. ✎ L Morales, "Majority of Americans Likely Support Stem Cell Decision, Analysis of Stem Cell Research Poll Results," Gallup, March 9, 2009.

Racial Profiling

Driving While Black" is an expression African Americans use for racial profiling, black humor suggesting that one has as much choice about race as intoxication. In many parts of the country it's been replaced with "Driving While Hispanic."

The odds a black adult believes that traffic patrols use racial profiling are **1 in 5**, less than those of Hispanic adults: **1 in 1.5**. By contrast, the odds a white driver believes police use racial profiling as a basis for stopping drivers are **1 in 2**.

What the numbers show depends upon whom you ask and when. Studies in the 1990s showed large disparities on the New Jersey Turnpike, and in Maryland and Ohio. An observational study Dr. John Lamberth performed on the "pike" showed that 73.2% of those stopped and arrested were black, while only 13.5% of the cars on the road had a black driver or passenger; patrol and radio logs showed a similar but somewhat smaller disparity. In either accounting, chance couldn't account for this disparity. Consent decrees, sensitivity training, and further polemics followed.

More recent statistics of the Bureau of Justice Statistics (using national data from law enforcement) show no evidence of a dramatic difference in the likelihood of a driver being pulled over: the odds a white driver will be stopped by the police in a year are **1 in 11.4**; for a Hispanic driver they are **1 in 11.7**; for black drivers **1 in 10.9**—about a 4% greater likelihood a black driver will be pulled over than a white or Hispanic driver.

The big difference comes in what happens next. The odds a white driver stopped by the police was not given a reason for getting pulled over are **1 in 56.4**. The odds for a black driver are more than double: **1 in 22.3**. The odds for a Hispanic driver are in between the two.

In some jurisdictions, Hispanic drivers may be more likely than other drivers to end up with a ticket. A January 2012 *New York Times* article revealed that more than half of the tickets issued along two main thoroughfares in East Haven, Connecticut, were given to Hispanic drivers—although the local population has fewer than 6% Hispanic residents.

SOURCES: DA Harris, "The Stories, the Statistics, and the Law: Why 'Driving While Black' Matters, II: The Statistical Analysis," *Minnesota Law Review* 84, 1999: 265–326. ✔ DK Carlson, "Racial Profiling Seen as Pervasive, Unjust," Gallup, press release, July 20, 2004. ✔ Bureau of Justice Statistics, "Characteristics of Drivers Stopped by Police, 2002," June 1, 2006. ✔ "East Haven Police Ticket More Hispanics," *New York Times*, January 31, 2012.

Racial Disparities

The odds a white adult believes most Americans are not racist: **1 in 1.7**

The odds a black adult believes most Americans are not racist: **1 in 2.3**

SOURCE: Rasmussen Reports, "82% Have Favorable Opinion of Martin Luther King, Jr.," January 17, 2011.

GENDER WARS
Family Values?

1 in 3.1 women vs. **1 in 2.6** men agree that it's much better if the man is the achiever outside the home and the woman takes care of the home and family.

SOURCE: Book of Odds estimates based on JA Davis, TW Smith, PV Marsden, *General Social Surveys, 1972–2008* [CUMULATIVE FILE] [Computer file] ICPSR04691, v. 1., Chicago: National Opinion Research Center, 2009 [producer]; Storrs, CT: Roper Center for Public Opinion Research, University of Connecticut. Ann Arbor, MI: Inter-university Consortium for Political and Social Research [distributors].

1 in 8.1: The odds an adult believes life achievement depends only on family background.

1 in 1.9: The odds an adult believes life achievement depends only on abilities and hard work.

SOURCE: Campbell Public Affairs Institute, "Inequality and the American Public, Results of the Fourth Annual Maxwell School Survey," September 2007.

Attitudes Toward Gay Marriage by Demographic

The odds an adult favors same-sex marriage: **} 1 in 2.9**

Do You Favor or Oppose Same-Sex Marriage?

Demographic	Favors %	Favors Odds (1 in)	Opposes %	Opposes Odds (1 in)
Adults	35	**2.9**	54	**1.9**
Republicans	17	**5.9**	77	**1.3**
Democrats	50	**2.0**	41	**2.4**
Independents	34	**2.9**	55	**1.8**
Men	30	**3.3**	57	**1.8**
Women	39	**2.6**	52	**1.9**
Bachelor's degree or higher	49	**2.0**	44	**2.3**
Some college	37	**2.7**	51	**2.0**
High school or less	25	**4.0**	62	**1.6**
Northeast	52	**1.9**	38	**2.6**
Midwest	33	**3.0**	56	**1.8**
South	26	**3.9**	64	**1.6**
West	36	**2.8**	52	**1.9**
Protestants	24	**4.2**	67	**1.5**
Catholics	39	**2.6**	45	**2.2**
18–29	43	**2.3**	45	**2.2**
30–49	38	**2.6**	51	**2.0**
50–64	29	**3.5**	61	**1.6**
65+	24	**4.2**	64	**1.6**

SOURCES: "Americans' Opposition to Gay Marriage Eases Slightly," Gallup, press release, May 24, 2010. ⚞ Pew Research Center for the People and the Press, *Independents Take Center Stage in Obama Era: Trends in Political Values and Core Attitudes, 1987–2009*, press release, May 21, 2009.

Divided We Stand

The odds an adult believes abortion should be legal in most/all cases: 1 in 2

The odds an adult believes abortion should be illegal in most/all cases: 1 in 2.3

The odds an adult believes "we should all be willing to fight for our country, whether it is right or wrong": 1 in 1.9

The odds an adult does not believe "we should all be willing to fight for our country, whether it is right or wrong": 1 in 2.4

SOURCE: Pew Research Center for the People and the Press, *The Generation Gap and the 2012 Election,* November 3, 2011.

Immigration

According to a June 2010 Pew poll, **1 in 1.5** people favors some sort of illegal immigrant forgiveness program that would allow illegal immigrants in the United States to gain citizenship if they meet a set of conditions, namely that they undergo background checks, pay some sort of fine, and have steady work. **1 in 3.3** opposes such a measure.

Immigration restriction has been a US legislative matter since 1882, when President Chester A. Arthur enacted the Chinese Exclusion Act, in response to fears that Chinese immigrants would overwhelm the job market. It was repealed sixty-one years later.

Even then, the issue was tightly bound to others, like employment, race, health care, and crime rates. Today, **1 in 1.7** adults believes immigrants take jobs that Americans do not want, while **1 in 3.3** believes immigrants take jobs away from Americans. In time those people whom anti-immigration laws are meant to exclude become political forces in their own right and these positions become impolitic, as the political aftermath of the Republican loss of the Hispanic vote in the 2012 elections demonstrates yet again. Gentler immigration policies are now on the agenda of both parties.

SOURCES: Pew Research Center for the People and the Press, *Obama's Ratings Little Affected by Recent Turmoil*, June 24, 2010. ✔ Harvard University Library Open Collections Program, *Aspiration, Acculturation, and Impact: Immigration to the United States, 1789–1930*, http://ocp .hul.harvard.edu/immigration/.

Going in the Wrong Direction

The odds an adult is satisfied with the way things are going in the United States: **1 in 4.4**

The odds an adult is dissatisfied with the way things are going in the United States: **1 in 1.4**

SOURCE: Pew Research Center for the People and the Press, *Independents Take Center Stage in Obama Era: Trends in Political Values and Core Attitudes, 1987–2009*, press release, May 21, 2009.

Death Penalty

1 in 1.6: The odds an adult favors the death penalty for persons convicted of murder.

1 in 3.5: The odds an adult opposes the death penalty for persons convicted of murder.

SOURCE: F Newport, "In U.S., 64% Support Death Penalty in Cases of Murder," Gallup, press release, November 8, 2010.

Gun Control Laws

1 in 9.1: The odds an adult believes gun control laws should be less strict.

1 in 2.3: The odds an adult believes gun control laws should be kept as they are now.

1 in 2.3: The odds an adult believes gun control laws should be more strict.

SOURCE: JM Jones, "Record-Low 26% in U.S. Favor Handgun Ban," Gallup, press release, October 26, 2011.

The odds a woman has a specific phobia . . . . **1 in 8.2**

The odds a man has a specific phobia . . . . **1 in 17.2**

SOURCE: Harvard School of Medicine, "National Comorbidity Survey (NCS-R) Appendix Tables," July 19, 2007.

GENDER WARS

The odds a man owns a firearm . . . . **1 in 2.2**

The odds a woman owns a firearm . . . . **1 in 4.3**

SOURCE: L Saad, "Self-reported Gun Ownership in the US Is Highest Since 1993," Gallup, press release, October 26, 2011.

Our Most Common **Phobia**

Few sights strike fear in the heart as surely as the sight of a snake headed in our direction. The odds that an adult is afraid of snakes are **1 in 2**; the odds he or she is *very afraid* are **1 in 2.8**.

The chances that a person will die from contact with a venomous snake or lizard in a year are just **1 in 37,420,000**. But the odds an adult has ever been bitten by a snake or witnessed someone who has are **1 in 14.3**.

SOURCES: G Brewer, "Snakes Top List of Americans' Fears," Gallup, press release, March 19, 2001. ✎ Harris Interactive, "What We Are Afraid Of," Harris Poll #49, press release, August 18, 1999. ✎ Book of Odds estimate based on Centers for Disease Control and Prevention, WONDER online database, *Compressed Mortality File.* ✎ American Red Cross, *Summer Safety March 2010 Polling.*

Creepy Crawlies and the Creeps

The odds an adult is afraid of mice: **1 in 5**

The odds an adult is very afraid: **1 in 10**

The odds an adult is afraid of spiders or insects: **1 in 3.7**

The odds an adult is very afraid: **1 in 8.3**

The odds an adult is afraid of being home alone at night: **1 in 7.1**

The odds an adult is very afraid: **1 in 33.3**

SOURCES: L Saad, "Two in Three Americans Worry About Identity Theft," Gallup, press release, October 6, 2009. ✎ Harris Interactive, "What We Are Afraid Of," Harris Poll #49, press release, August 18, 1999.

Crime Worries

The odds an adult worries about being a victim of identity theft . . . . **1 in 1.5**

The odds an adult worries about having his or her car stolen or broken into . . . . **1 in 2.1**

The odds an adult worries about having his or her home burglarized when he or she is not there . . . . **1 in 2.2**

The odds an adult worries about being a victim of terrorism . . . . **1 in 2.9**

The odds an adult worries about having his or her home burglarized when he or she is there . . . . **1 in 3**

The odds an adult worries about being mugged . . . . **1 in 3.2**

The odds an adult worries about being attacked while driving . . . . **1 in 4.4**

The odds an adult worries about being murdered . . . . **1 in 5.3**

The odds an adult worries about being sexually assaulted . . . . **1 in 5.3**

The odds an adult worries about being a victim of a hate crime . . . . **1 in 5.9**

Worry	%
Being a victim of identity theft	66
Having car stolen or broken into	47
Having home burglarized when he or she is not there	46
Being a victim of terrorism	35
Having home burglarized when he or she is there	33
Being mugged	31
Being attacked while driving	23
Being murdered	19
Being sexually assaulted	19
Being a victim of a hate crime	17

SOURCE: L Saad, "Two in Three Americans Worry About Identity Theft," Gallup, press release, October 6, 2009.

Fear of Flying

The odds an airline passenger will be involved in a plane crash in a year are a slim **1 in 3,128,000**. You're more likely to die in a year because of measles (**1 in 2,448,000**), or being electrocuted (**1,439,000**). Arnold Barnett, the MIT statistician who follows aviation, has struggled for years to find a way to convey the relative safety of flights in the "first world." He points out that passengers in the United States faced a death risk of **1 in 45,000,000** from 2008 to 2012. Barnett points out that a flyer could fly every day for an average of 123,000 years before experiencing a fatal crash. But reality often has little to do with what makes us nervous. For the **1 in 5.6** adults who fear flying (**1 in 4.6** women, **1 in 7.1** men), here are some numbers:

Why so fearful?

1 in 3.7 says it's because flying is inherently dangerous.

1 in 3.9 hates to hand over control.

What brings it on?

1 in 1.4 gets spooked by media coverage of crashes.

1 in 2.6 has had a bad experience on a plane.

The symptoms

1 in 1.2 feels the fear in his or her chest or heart.

1 in 1.3 feels the fear in his or her stomach.

1 in 1.3 breaks out in a sweat.

1 in 1.3 has thoughts of crashing.

1 in 1.5 has trouble focusing.

1 in 1.5 panics.

1 in 1.7 can't stop thinking about dying.

What makes it worse?

1 in 1.03: A rough flight

1 in 1.04: Poor weather

1 in 1.11: Takeoff

1 in 1.19: Hearing plane noises

1 in 1.23: A flight with more than one leg

1 in 1.30: A long flight

1 in 1.41: Hectic preflight conditions

1 in 1.45: Flying alone

1 in 1.45: Landing

1 in 1.56: Night flights

1 in 1.72: Boarding time

1 in 1.79: A crowded cabin

1 in 1.82: Cabin announcements

1 in 1.85: Flight delays

What helps?

1 in 1.22: A friendly cabin attendant

1 in 1.25: Knowing more about planes

1 in 1.25: Seeing or talking to the pilot

1 in 1.30: A tranquilizer

1 in 1.39: Movies or music

1 in 1.54: Meditation or breathing exercises

1 in 1.69: Talking to people

1 in 1.75: Interesting reading material

Hope on the horizon?

1 in 1.3 believes the fear can be overcome.

1 in 1.8 believes the fear is irrational.

SOURCES: PlaneCrashInfo.com, Accident Database. ✔ Book of Odds estimate based on Centers for Disease Control and Prevention, WONDER online database, *Compressed Mortality File.* ✔ KD Kochanek, J Xu, SL Murphy, AM Miniño, HC Kung, "Death: Preliminary Data for 2009," *National Vital Statistics Report* 59(4), March 16, 2011. ✔ StruckbyLightning.org/resources/statistics, 2008–2012. ✔ J Mouawad, C Drew, "Airline Industry at Its Safest Since the Dawn of the Jet Age," *New York Times, Business Day,* February 11, 2013.

What Scares Us?

Fears
by Gender

SOURCE: G Brewer, "Gallup Fear Survey-Snakes Top List of Americans' Fears," Gallup, press release, March 19, 2001.

Fear	Women Odds (1 in)	Men Odds (1 in)
Snakes	1.6	2.6
Public speaking	2.3	2.7
Enclosed space	2.4	4.0
Heights	2.4	3.2
Spiders or insects	2.6	6.7
Mice	3.0	16.7

Fear	Women Odds (1 in)	Men Odds (1 in)
Needles or shots	4.8	5.0
Thunder or lightning	6.3	16.7
Dogs	7.1	14.3
Crowds	8.3	10
The dark	12.5	50
Going to the doctor	12.5	9.1

CHAPTER 11

ACCIDENTS AND DEATH

R.I.P.

The odds a
person will die
from a vending
machine accident
in a year:
1 in 112,000,000

SOURCE: US Consumer
Product Safety Commission,
Vending Machine Accidents,
1975–2005 data.

Deaths by Month

The Odds, by Month, a Death Will Occur:

January
1 in 10.9

February
1 in 11.8

March
1 in 10.9

April
1 in 12.1

May
1 in 12.1

June
1 in 13

July
1 in 12.7

August
1 in 12.7

September
1 in 13

October
1 in 12

November
1 in 12.4

December
1 in 11.4

SOURCE: National Center for Health Statistics, "Provisional Monthly and 12-Month Ending Number of Live Births, Deaths, and Infant Deaths and Rates: United States, January 2009–December 2010," *National Vital Statistics Report* 58(25), 2010.

The Odds of Dying in an Accident in a Year
by Age Group

The odds for:

infant . . . . **1 in 3,571**
1–4 . . . . **1 in 11,765**
5–14 . . . . **1 in 24,390**
15–24 . . . . **1 in 3,484**
25–44 . . . . **1 in 2,882**
45–64 . . . . **1 in 2,451**
65 or older . . . . **1 in 1,006**
person . . . . **1 in 2,618**

Age	%	Per 100,000
Infant	.028	28.0
1–4	.009	8.5
5–14	.004	4.1
15–24	.029	28.7
25–44	.035	34.7
45–64	.041	40.8
65+	.099	99.4
Person	.038	38.2

SOURCE: KD Kochanek, J Xu, SL Murphy, AM Miniño, HC Kung, "Death: Preliminary Data for 2009," *National Vital Statistics Report* 59(4), March 16, 2011.

GENDER WARS

The odds a woman's death will be accidental: **1 in 2.8**

The odds for a man: **1 in 1.5**

SOURCE: Book of Odds estimates based on Centers for Disease Control and Prevention, WONDER online database, *Compressed Mortality File*, 1999–2006 data.

Falls
Are a Leading Cause of Accidental Deaths

The odds an accidental death will be due to a fall involving

falling down stairs: **1 in 69.1**

tripping or slipping: **1 in 175**

falling out of or off a building: **1 in 190**

tumbling out of bed: **1 in 203**

falling off a ladder: **1 in 294**

a wheelchair: **1 in 421**

furniture other than a bed: **1 in 444**

falling from a tree: **1 in 1,144**

ice or snow: **1 in 1,270**

falling off a cliff: **1 in 1,458**

falling off scaffolding: **1 in 1,965**

being dropped while carried by other people: **1 in 7,933**

colliding with another person: **1 in 8,562**

playground equipment: **1 in 48,040**

SOURCE: Book of Odds estimates based on Centers for Disease Control and Prevention, WONDER online database, *Compressed Mortality File*, 1999–2006 data.

Fatal Accidental Falls by Age Group

The odds a fatal accidental fall will occur to:

an infant	1 in 994	an adult 35–44	1 in 26.4
a child 1–4	1 in 403	an adult 45–54	1 in 15.9
a child 5–9	1 in 907	an adult 55–64	1 in 14
an adolescent 10–14	1 in 665	an adult 65–74	1 in 8.3
a teenager 15–19	1 in 187	an adult 75–84	1 in 3.4
an adult 20–24	1 in 111	an adult 85+	1 in 2.7
an adult 25–34	1 in 53.5		

SOURCE: Book of Odds estimates based on Centers for Disease Control and Prevention, WONDER online database, *Compressed Mortality File*, 1999–2006 data.

Some People Fall
into a Very Big Hole

The odds a person visiting the Grand Canyon will die during the trip } **1 in 232,100**

The odds a person visiting the Grand Canyon will:

fall to his or her death: **1 in 1,586,000**

drown: **1 in 2,447,000**

commit suicide: **1 in 3,059,000**

be murdered: **1 in 8,156,000**

die in a flash flood: **1 in 14,270,000**

...or Drive Their Car into It

On July 14, 2009, a man drove off the South Rim behind Thunderbird Lodge, falling 600 feet to his death.

Amazingly, another man drove off the South Rim on April 27, 2011, falling this time 200 feet, the length of two basketball courts and then some, but survived.

There is no way to calculate the odds of survival when an event is this rare, but it is good to be reminded that black swans fly, to use the memorable term Nassim Nicholas Taleb made popular for unpredictable events of major import. This black swan did not change the world as, say, the Internet has, but for the driver its import could not have been much greater; let's call it a black cygnet.

SOURCES: Books of Odds estimates based on data in MP Ghiglieri, TM Meyers, *Over the Edge: Death in Grand Canyon*, 1st ed., 13th rev., Flagstaff, AZ: Puma Press, 2006. ⤳ Nicholas Taleb Nassim, *The Black Swan: The Impact of the Highly Improbable*, 2nd ed., New York: Random House, 2010.

Drowning Deaths by Sex, Age, Race, and Type of Incident

The odds an accidental
death will be due
to drowning: } **1 in 31.4**

Drowning Accidental Death	%	Rate per 100,000	Odds (1 in)
Drowning	3.18	3,181.8	**31.4**
Natural water	1.21	1,214.0	**82.4**
Swimming pool	0.55	552.1	**181.0**
Fall into water	0.35	346.6	**289.0**
Bathtub	0.33	326.8	**306.0**

The odds the victim of a fatal drowning accident will be:

male. . . . . **1 in 1.3**

female . . . . **1 in 4.7**

a white person . . . . **1 in 1.3**

a black person. . . . . **1 in 6.1**

an infant . . . . **1 in 54.1**

a child 1–4 . . . . **1 in 7.4**

a child 5–9 . . . . **1 in 22.2**

an adolescent 10–14 . . **1 in 22.9**

a teenager 15–19 . . . . . **1 in 10.7**

an adult 20–24 . . . . **1 in 11.7**

an adult 25–34 . . . . . . **1 in 8.5**

an adult 35–44 . . . . **1 in 7.2**

an adult 45–54 . . . . **1 in 8.4**

an adult 55–64 . . . . **1 in 14**

an adult 65–74 . . . . **1 in 18.4**

an adult 75–84 . . . . **1 in 20.7**

an adult 85 or older. . . . **1 in 45**

SOURCE: Book of Odds estimates based on Centers for Disease Control and Prevention, WONDER online database, *Compressed Mortality File*, 1999–2006 data.

Keep Your Eye on the Kids

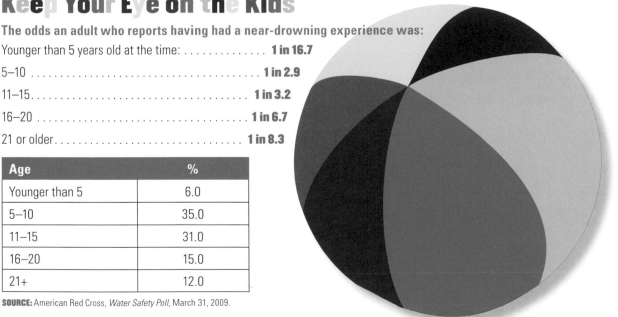

The odds an adult who reports having had a near-drowning experience was:

Younger than 5 years old at the time: . . . . **1 in 16.7**

5–10 . . . . **1 in 2.9**

11–15. . . . . **1 in 3.2**

16–20 . . . . **1 in 6.7**

21 or older. . . . . **1 in 8.3**

Age	%
Younger than 5	6.0
5–10	35.0
11–15	31.0
16–20	15.0
21+	12.0

SOURCE: American Red Cross, *Water Safety Poll*, March 31, 2009.

Traffic Fatalities by Age Group

The odds a child younger than 5 will be killed in a motor vehicle accident in a year:
------------------------------**1 in 47,915**

The odds a child 5–9 will be killed in a motor vehicle accident in a year:
------------------------------**1 in 53,176**

The odds an adolescent 10–15 will be killed in a motor vehicle accident in a year:
------------------------------**1 in 33,774**

The odds a person 16–20 will be killed in a motor vehicle accident in a year:
------------------------------**1 in 5,558**

The odds a person 21–24 will be killed in a motor vehicle accident in a year:
------------------------------**1 in 5,112**

The odds a person 25–34 will be killed in a motor vehicle accident in a year:
------------------------------**1 in 7,169**

The odds a person 35–44 will be killed in a motor vehicle accident in a year:
------------------------------**1 in 8,632**

The odds a person 45–54 will be killed in a motor vehicle accident in a year:
------------------------------**1 in 8,275**

The odds a person 55–64 will be killed in a motor vehicle accident in a year:
------------------------------**1 in 9,278**

The odds a person 65–74 will be killed in a motor vehicle accident in a year:
------------------------------**1 in 8,811**

The odds a person 75 or older will be killed in a motor vehicle accident in a year:
------------------------------**1 in 6,400**

Age Killed	%	Rate per 100,000
Younger than 5	.0021	2.09
5–9	.0019	1.88
10–15	.0029	2.96
16–20	.0180	17.99
21–24	.0196	19.56
25–34	.0139	13.95
35–44	.0116	11.58
45–54	.0121	12.08
55–64	.0108	10.78
65–74	.0113	11.35
75+	.0156	15.62

SOURCES: National Center for Statistics and Analysis, National Highway Traffic Safety Administration, *Traffic Safety Facts, 2009 Data* (DOT HS 811 402). ✔ US Census Bureau, 2010 Census, Summary Data File 1, P2.

Driving Can Be a Hazardous Pursuit

The odds a licensed driver will be involved in a motor vehicle accident in a year:

16–20 . . . . **1 in 9.7**
21–24 . . . . **1 in 12.3**
25–34 . . . . **1 in 19**
35–44 . . . . **1 in 22.5**
45–54 . . . . **1 in 26**
55–64 . . . . **1 in 33.4**
65–74 . . . . **1 in 39.8**
75 or older . . . . **1 in 43.8**

Age	%
16–20	10.3
21–24	8.2
25–34	5.3
35–44	4.4
45–54	3.8
55–64	3.0
65–74	2.3
75+	4.6

SOURCE: National Center for Statistics and Analysis, National Highway Traffic Safety Administration, *Traffic Safety Facts, 2009 Data* (DOT HS 811 402).

 The odds a person will visit an emergency room due to an accident involving nursery equipment in a year: **1 in 2,898**

The odds a person will visit an emergency room due to an accident involving toys in a year: **1 in 1,280**

SOURCE: US Consumer Product Safety Commission, *National Electronic Injury Surveillance System (NEISS) Data Highlights—2010,* http://www.cpsc.gov/LIBRARY/neiss.html.

Is Grandpa Really the Worst Driver?

There are more and more people carrying AARP (American Association of Retired Persons) cards navigating our roads. The percentage of the population 65 or older with driver's licenses rose from **63%** in 1982 to around **85%** in 2008. Currently, the odds are **1 in 1.1** a person 70–74 has a valid driver's license; for those 75–79, the odds are **1 in 1.3**; **1 in 1.7** for adults 85 and up.

2008 was the first year in which there were more female drivers licensed than males, but among the older age groups, male drivers still outnumber female.

But when it comes to accidents, the most dangerous drivers are between the ages of 16 and 20, followed by those 21–34. Drivers aged 65 and older are the third-highest risk group, followed by drivers 35–54 and 55–64.

What gives? Are the results skewed by the fact that younger drivers log more miles? No. A 2005 Dutch study comparing drivers who drove similar distances in a year found that those age 75 and up were safer drivers than all other drivers. Only seniors who drove fewer than about 1,900 miles a year—just over 10% of all older drivers in the survey—had elevated crash rates. Despite being better drivers, older drivers are more prone to injury. When car crashes do occur, older drivers are more likely to suffer serious injuries or die than younger people.

Older drivers are also less likely to be inebriated, according to the US National Highway Traffic Safety Administration. In 2008, only **5%** of drivers over 65 in fatal crashes had blood alcohol content of .08 or higher, compared to **17%** of drivers age 16–20 and **32%** of drivers age 21–34. Two studies suggest that the critical factor when it comes to aging and driving is the "useful field of view"—basically the area in which you notice things without moving your eyes or turning your head. Among older drivers, those whose field of view had decreased were six times as likely to be involved in crashes; a separate 2009 study also found reduced field of view correlated with a high likelihood of running red lights. Other factors, such as advancing age and cognitive status, had very little effect on the chances of being in accidents.

SOURCES: Federal Highway Administration, *Highway Statistics 2008*, http://www.fhwa.dot.gov/policyinformation/statistics/2008/. ✔ J Ebarhard, "Older Drivers' 'High Per-Mile Crash Involvement': The Implications for Licensing Authorities," *Traffic Injury Prevention* 9(4), August 2008: 284–290. ✔ J Langford, M Methorst, L Hakamies-Blomquist, "Older Drivers Do Not Have a High Crash Risk: A Replication of Low Mileage Bias," *Accident Analysis and Prevention* 38(3), May 2006: 574–578. ✔ K Ball, C Owsley, ME Sloan, DE Roenker, JR Bruni, "Visual Attention Problems as a Predictor of Vehicle Crashes in Older Drivers," *Investigative Journal of Ophthalmology and Visual Science* 34, 1993: 3110–3123. ✔ SK West, DV Hahn, C Baldwin, T Dunkin, BE Munoz, KA Turano, et al., "Older Drivers and Failure to Stop at Red Lights," *Journal of Gerontology* 65A(2), 2010: 179–183. ✔ National Center for Statistics and Analysis, National Highway Traffic Safety Administration, *Traffic Safety Facts, 2008 Data* (DOT HS 811 170).

The odds a driver 18 or older has ever nodded off or fallen asleep while driving: **1 in 3.6**

The odds a driver 18 or older will have an accident or near accident due to driving while he or she is drowsy in a year: **1 in 100**

SOURCE: National Sleep Foundation, *2009 Sleep in America Poll*, March 2009.

 **GENDER WARS**

Women Drivers vs. Men Drivers

The odds a female licensed driver will be involved in a motor vehicle accident in a year are **1 in 25.3**, compared to **1 in 19.1** for a male. The odds a licensed driver involved in a fatal motor vehicle accident is female are **1 in 3.8**; odds for male **1 in 1.4**.

SOURCE: National Center for Statistics and Analysis, National Highway Traffic Safety Administration, *Traffic Safety Facts, 2009 Data* (DOT HS 811 402).

👁 Numbers Tell the Story

The odds a driver involved in a motor vehicle accident resulting in injury was wearing a seat belt: **1 in 1.1**

The odds a driver involved in a motor vehicle accident resulting in injury was not wearing a seat belt: **1 in 27.8**

The odds a passenger vehicle occupant killed in an accident was wearing a seat belt: **1 in 2.3**

The odds a passenger vehicle occupant killed in an accident was not wearing a seat belt: **1 in 2**

The odds a passenger vehicle driver killed in an accident was wearing a seat belt: **1 in 2**

The odds a passenger vehicle driver killed in an accident was not wearing a seat belt: **1 in 2.4**

SOURCE: National Center for Statistics and Analysis, National Highway Traffic Safety Administration, *Traffic Safety Facts, 2009 Data* (DOT HS 811 402).

Drinkers Aren't the Only
Dangerous Drivers on the Road

A driver who is sending text messages is twenty-three times more likely to be involved in a car accident, according to a simulation by the Virginia Tech Transportation Institute.

The Virginia Tech study tracked truck drivers over an eighteen-month period using video cameras installed in their cabs. When drivers who  were texting crashed, a review of the footage revealed their attention had been diverted from the road for an average of five seconds. A similar study done at the University of Utah used a sophisticated driving simulator to track college-aged drivers and found they were eight times more likely to get into an accident if they were texting. Those students were also distracted for approximately five seconds prior to the crash.

The odds an adult who uses text messaging has sent or read a text message while driving are **1 in 2.1**.

SOURCES: Virginia Tech Transportation Institute, "New Data VTTI Provides Insight into Cell Phone Use and Driving Distraction." ✎ M Maden, L Rainie, *Adults and Cell Phone Distractions*, Pew Research Center, June 18, 2010.

Roadkill

The odds a collision on the roads of Michigan will involve a deer are **1 in 5.3**. The odds such a collision will result in a human fatality are **1 in 5,630**. It is more than five times as likely that an accidental death was caused by a fall from a tree (**1 in 1,101**) than it is that a collision with a deer in Michigan proved fatal to a human.

Though states like Michigan carefully document deer-related crashes, none tracks how many animals are killed or injured on the roads of America every year. This is where Brewster Bartlett, also known as Dr. Splatt, comes in. Since 1992, Splatt and his colleagues have maintained the RoadKill database, a repository of information about flattened animals. Added to annually by students and adult enthusiasts, it represents one of the few concerted efforts to gather knowledge about nonhuman traffic deaths. They've found that **50%** of animals killed on the road are gray squirrels. There is also a category for unidentifiable blobs.

SOURCES: Michigan State Police, Traffic Crash Statistics, http://www.michigan.gov/msp/0,4643,7-123-1645_3501_4626---,00.html. ✎ B Bartlett et al., *RoadKill 2012*, Edutel Technology, http://roadkill.edutel.com/.

Horse vs. Hog

A horse may be more likely to land you in a hospital than a Harley.

The odds a person will visit an emergency room due to a horseback riding accident in a year are **1 in 4,492**. Most of these accidents are caused when a horse bucks or bolts, throwing the rider, and female injury rates are typically higher.

Trying to figure out which activity is more likely to *kill* you is hard because numbers associated with being killed while riding a horse aren't fully tallied. Many horse accidents occur on private property and tend not to generate police reports.

Statistics on motorcycle deaths, however, are readily available and the numbers are stark. In 2009, 4,462 motorcyclists died in accidents, and 90,000 were injured out of a total of 7,929,724 registered motorcycles. Compare that to 2,116 killed and 53,000 injured out of a total of 3,826,373 registered motorcycles in 1997—in one decade, the number of injuries almost doubled, and deaths more than doubled. The odds a motorcyclist will be injured in an accident in a year are **1 in 88.1**. The odds a motorcyclist will be killed in an accident in a year are **1 in 1,777**. The odds a rider killed in a motorcycle accident in a year was not wearing a helmet are **1 in 2.3**.

History bears out just how risky both motorcycling and horseback riding can be. Horseback riding is thought to have resulted in the deaths of historical figures such as Mongol emperor Genghis Khan, and injuries from it are known to have resulted in the death of Ellen Church (the first airline stewardess). Motorcycle accidents have claimed the lives of astronaut Pete Conrad (the third man to walk on the moon) and British military officer T. E. Lawrence "of Arabia."

After treating T. E. Lawrence's fatal head wounds, neurosurgeon Hugh Cairns pioneered research that ultimately led to the widespread use of motorcycle helmets.

SOURCES: US Consumer Product Safety Commission, *National Electronic Injury Surveillance System (NEISS) Data Highlights—2010*, http://www.cpsc.gov/LIBRARY/neiss.html. ✎ C Floyd, P Evans, "Helmets, Heads and Health for Horse Enthusiasts," *4H/Equine/2009-04pr*, Utah State University, August 2009. ✎ DJ Caine, *Equestrian Injuries: Sports Injuries, Mechanisms, Prevention and Treatment.* ✎ National Center for Statistics and Analysis, National Highway Traffic Safety Administration, *Traffic Safety Facts, 2009 Data* (DOT HS 811 402).

DID YOU know?

You can learn a lot from horses, such as not to walk behind them.

What the French mathematician Siméon Denis Poisson learned from the randomness of people being kicked by horses in nineteenth-century Paris was a distribution in active use in statistics today, called the Poisson distribution.

SOURCE: Z Turpin, "Behind the Numbers: Who's Going Through a Toll Booth First?," Ask Poisson, http://www.bookofodds.com/Daily-Life-Activities/Transportation/Articles/A0278-Behind-the-Numbers-Who-s-Going-Through-a-Toll-Booth-First-Ask-Poisson.

The odds a licensed driver will not pass a written driver's test: **1 in 5**

SOURCE: General Motors Acceptance Corporation, "Executive Summary," *2009 GMAC Insurance National Drivers Test.*

More Danger Behind the Wheel

According to the Center for Injury Research and Policy in Columbus, Ohio, the number of Americans injured by golf carts has skyrocketed in recent years, from 5,772 in 1990 to 13,411 in 2006—an increase of 132% over this period. In 2010, the odds of being injured in a golf cart incident were **1 in 22,355**. But only half of those injuries took place on a golf course.

SOURCES: Center for Injury Research and Policy, Nationwide Children's Hospital, "First National Study to Examine Golf Cart–Related Injuries," press release, June 10, 2008. ✕ Book of Odds estimate based on a query of 2010 data in the US Consumer Product Safety Commission *National Electronic Injury Surveillance System (NEISS)* database.

Some Travel Is Vertical

The odds an adult is afraid of being alone in an elevator: **1 in 10**

The odds a person will visit an emergency room due to an injury involving elevators in a year: **1 in 12,928**

SOURCES: National Center for Statistics and Analysis, National Highway Traffic Safety Administration, *Traffic Safety Facts, 2009 Data* (DOT HS 811 402). ✕ Harris Interactive, "What We Are Afraid Of," Harris Poll #49, press release, August 18, 1999.

The Most Vertical Spaceflight
Is Downright Dangerous

1 in 3 { The odds a manned spaceflight will suffer a problem that threatens completion of the mission and the lives of the astronauts.

1 in 49.3 { The odds an astronaut will be killed during a mission.

SOURCE: *Encyclopedia Astronautica*, http://www.astronautix.com/index.html.

The odds a fatal motor vehicle crash will involve street racing: **1 in 475**

SOURCE: S Knight, LJ Cook, LM Olson, "The Fast and the Fatal: Street Racing Fatal Crashes in the United States," *Injury Prevention* 10, 2004: 53–55.

Is It Safer to Take the Subway?

It crosses the mind of every subway rider: what if some lunatic shoves me in front of an oncoming train?

It's such a common fear that 80% of New York City subway passengers admit to taking precautions against being pushed, even though it is extremely uncommon—a New York subway rider's odds of being fatally pushed in front of a train in a year are less than **1 in 2,211,000,000**.

You're likelier to accidentally fall on the tracks, or to jump on purpose.

Out of 668 New York subway-related deaths between 1990 and 2003, 343 were suicides, 315 accidents, and 10 homicides, including those involving weapons. Injuries for those who survive subway-related trauma can be life-changing. According to a study of 208 subway-related injuries treated at Bellevue Hospital, **1 in 4.7** people injured in subway incidents in New York City will undergo an amputation, typically a major one. **1 in 5.5** will lose one or more limbs and **1 in 34.7** will undergo a minor amputation.

1 in 5.1 people injured in subway incidents in New York City is female; the odds a person injured is male are **1 in 1.3**.

SOURCES: T Diflo, AA Guth, A O'Neill, HL Pachter, "Public Health Lessons Learned in Analysis of New York City Subway Injuries," *American Journal of Public Health* 96(4), April 2006: 631–633. ✕ RR Gershon, JM Pearson, V Nandi, D Vlahov, A Bucciarelli-Prann, M Tracy, et al., "Epidemiology of Subway-Related Fatalities in New York City, 1990–2003," *Journal of Safety Research* 39(6), 2008: 583–588.

Daring Pursuits

Jumping from a plane or a high place would qualify as daring but the odds of dying varies significantly depending on what you jump from. Skydiving is done from an aircraft, and if done from sufficient altitude allows time for free fall, control, and several minutes of drifting down with the parachute open.

The odds skydiving will result in the death of the jumper are **1 in 101,100.** This is about the odds a person will visit an emergency room in a year due to an accident involving a drinking straw.

BASE jumping is done from a fixed base. The acronym BASE stands for "Buildings, Antennas, Spans, Earth." Parachuting from a bridge or a cliff is much more dangerous since the altitude is generally lower and the object jumped from is nearby.

According to a British study of 106 deaths from 1981 to 2006, the odds of a person who BASE jumps dying are **1 in 60.** This is about the odds a teenager will be diagnosed with chlamydia in a year.

SOURCES: Bandolier, "Risk of Dying and Sporting Activities," http://www.medicine.ox.ac.uk/bandolier/booth/Risk/sports.html. ✗ US Consumer Product Safety Commission, *National Electronic Injury Surveillance System (NEISS) Data Highlights—2010,* http://www.cpsc.gov/LIBRARY/neiss.html. ✗ Centers for Disease Control and Prevention, *Sexually Transmitted Disease Surveillance, 2006,* Atlanta, GA: US Department of Health and Human Services, November 2007.

What Causes Skydiving Fatalities?

The odds a skydiving fatality worldwide will be caused by:

a bad or hard landing . . . . **1 in 3.2**

a malfunction . . . . **1 in 6**

a collision . . . . **1 in 6.2**

"other causes" . . . . **1 in 7**

no pull or suicide . . . . **1 in 11.5**

reserve problems . . . . **1 in 20.5**

Cause of Fatality	%
Bad/hard landing	31
Malfunction	17
Collision	14
"Other causes"	13
No pull or suicide	9
Reserve problems	5

SOURCE: Book of Odds estimate based on data from Dropzone.com, "Fatalities by Year," Dropzone.com Skydiving Fatalities Database.

The odds a person who died in a BASE jumping accident was American are **1 in 3.1**. No other nationality comes close. Australians and Russians come next with the odds being **1 in 10.3** for each.

Overall the odds a person who died in a BASE jumping accident was *not* American are **1 in 1.5**.

Nationality	%	Odds (1 in)
American	32.3	**3.1**
Australian	9.7	**10.3**
Russian	9.7	**10.3**
French	6.5	**15.5**
English	5.8	**17.2**
Norwegian	4.5	**22.1**
Italian	3.9	**25.8**
German	3.2	**31.0**
Swiss	3.2	**31.0**
Austrian	2.6	**38.8**
Not American	67.7	**1.5**

SOURCE: "Base Fatalities Statistics," *BLiNC Magazine,* http://www.blincmagazine.com/forum/wiki/Fatality_Statistics, 1981–2010 data.

Air Is More Dangerous than Water

The odds a whitewater rafter 6 or older will die in a rafting accident in a year: 1 in 76,250

The odds a scuba diver 6 or older will die in a diving accident: 1 in 34,480

The odds a mountaineer 6 or older will die in a climbing accident: 1 in 179

SOURCES: AmericanWhitewater.org, Search Results Found 2009, *Accident Database, Completed Safety Committee Reports.* ✗ JJ Windsor, "Mountain Mortality: A Review of Deaths That Occur During Recreational Activities in the Mountains," *Postgrad Medical Journal* 85, March 2009: 316–321.

TAMER PURSUITS
Odds of Injury by Sport

The odds a:

football player will be injured while playing football in a year: 1 in 19.7

basketball player will be injured while playing basketball in a year: 1 in 48.7

skateboarder will be injured while skateboarding in a year: 1 in 58.2

soccer player will be injured while playing soccer in a year: 1 in 65.3

baseball player will be injured while playing baseball in a year: 1 in 69.3

bicyclist will be injured while riding a bicycle in a year: 1 in 71.2

cheerleader will be injured while cheerleading in a year: 1 in 92.2

softball player will be injured while playing softball in a year: 1 in 97.4

snowboarder will be injured while snowboarding in a year: 1 in 114

ice hockey player will be injured while playing ice hockey in a year: 1 in 163

volleyball player will be injured while playing volleyball in a year: 1 in 178

weightlifter will be injured while lifting weights in a year: 1 in 400

fisherman will be injured while fishing in a year: 1 in 436

tennis player will be injured while playing tennis in a year: 1 in 457

golfer will be injured while playing golf in a year: 1 in 544

water-skier will be injured while water-skiing in a year: 1 in 739

mountain biker will be injured while mountain biking in a year: 1 in 873

bowler will be injured while bowling in a year: 1 in 2,155

billiards player will be injured while playing billiards in a year: 1 in 5,352

SOURCE: National Safety Council, *Injury Facts 2011 Edition.*

Want to Improve Your Odds of Making It Back Down from Everest's Summit?

Be a Sherpa.

The odds a climber who attempts to climb Mount Everest and ascends above base camp will not survive the expedition: **1 in 62.5**

The odds a mountaineer who attempts to climb Mount Everest and ascends above base camp will not survive the expedition: **1 in 76.9**

The odds a Sherpa who attempts to climb Mount Everest and ascends above base camp will not survive the expedition: **1 in 90.9**

The odds a climber who reaches the summit of Mount Everest will not survive the descent: **1 in 37**

The odds a mountaineer who reaches the summit of Mount Everest will not survive the descent: **1 in 52.6**

The odds a Sherpa who reaches the summit of Mount Everest will not survive the descent: **1 in 250**

SOURCE: PG Firth, H Zheng, JS Windsor, AJ Sutherland, CH Imray, GWK Moore, et al., "Mortality on Mount Everest, 1921–2006: Descriptive Study," *British Medical Journal* 337, 2008: a2654.

Watch Out for
Mother Nature

Struck by Lightning

One lightning bolt can reach over 50,000 degrees Fahrenheit—five to six times hotter than the surface of the sun—and contain 100 million volts of electricity. Every year there are approximately 25 million cloud-to-ground lightning strikes. Only **1 in 1,101,000** people is struck by lightning in a year, and incredibly **1 in 1.1** victims survive.

You are somewhat likelier to be killed by heat prostration (**1 in 1,356,000**) than to be struck by lightning.

SOURCES: Book of Odds estimates based on Centers for Disease Control and Prevention, WONDER online database, *Compressed Mortality File*, 1999–2006 data. ✔ StruckbyLightning.org, Resources, Strike Statistics, 2008–2012. ✔ US Census Bureau, Population Estimates Program, http://www.census.gov/popest/estimates.php.

Odds on Being Hurt in the Wild

Type of Death Event	Per 100,000	Odds (1 in)
Natural heat	0.0738	1,356,000
Stung by a bee, wasp, or hornet	0.0204	5,585,577
Bitten or struck by a dog	0.0107	6,769,710
High winds	0.0096	10,436,000
Natural cold	0.0090	11,110,000
An avalanche	0.0045	22,460,000
Venomous arthropod	0.0023	27,420,105
Contact with a venomous spider	0.0027	43,088,737
A mudslide	0.0011	94,670,000
Bitten or struck by an alligator	0.0007	149,700,000
Bitten by a rat	0.0003	299,400,000
Stung by a scorpion	0.0003	299,400,000
Contact with a marine animal	0.0003	299,400,000
A dust storm	0.0002	497,000,000
Hail	0.0003	662,700,000
A dust devil	0.0003	1,238,000,000
A waterspout	0.0001	1,988,000,000

SOURCES: National Weather Service, "Summary of Natural Hazard Fatalities in the United States," individual years from 1995 through 2009; US Census Bureau, "Table 1: Annual Estimates of the Resident Population for the United States, Regions, States, and Puerto Rico, 1995 Through 2008," Population Estimates Program. ✔ Book of Odds estimates based on Centers for Disease Control and Prevention, WONDER online database, *Compressed Mortality File*, 1999–2006 data.

Get Out of the Water!

The odds a person will die from a shark attack in a year: **1 in 251,800,000**

Things likelier to happen to a person in a year:

- Die of food poisoning: **1 in 103,864**
- Diagnosed with the plague: **1 in 69,695,398**
- Die from an escalator accident: **1 in 90,470,000**
- Die from contact with hot air: **1 in 99,800,000**
- Die from exposure to excessive cold of man-made origin: **1 in 148,200,000**

Shark deaths are rare and so are deaths from vending machines, but the latter is the more common event in the United States. Of course we are exposed to vending machines more frequently than sharks, even in the typical aquarium.

SOURCES: Book of Odds estimate based on US Food and Drug Administration, US Department of Health and Human Services, Foodborne Illness Statistics, February 2011, and US Census Bureau Population Division, "Table 1. Annual Estimates of the Resident Population for the United States, Regions, States, and Puerto Rico: April 1, 2000, to July 1, 2009" (NST-EST2009-01), December 2009. ✔ Book of Odds estimate based on US Census Bureau Population Division, "Table 1. Annual Estimates of the Resident Population for the United States, Regions, States, and Puerto Rico: April 1, 2000, to July 1, 2009" (NST-EST2009-01), December 2009, and "Table 1. Provisional Cases of Infrequently Reported Notifiable Diseases, United States" in "Notifiable Diseases and Mortality Tables," *Morbidity and Mortality Weekly Report* 61(09), March 9, 2012. ✔ Center for Construction Research and Training, *Deaths and Injuries Involving Elevators and Escalators: A Report to the Center to Protect Workers' Rights*, 2006 [1992–2003 data]. ✔ Book of Odds estimates based on Centers for Disease Control and Prevention, WONDER online database, *Compressed Mortality File*, 1999–2006 data. ✔ Z Turpin, "Behind the Numbers: The Sharks and the Vending Machines," http://www.bookofodds.com/Accidents-Death/Accidental-Deaths/Articles/A0273BO-Behind-the-Numbers-The-Sharks-and-the-Vending-Machines.

QUIZ: Match the Injury Odds to the Cause

Choosing from the letters listed below, match the item involved in accidental injury with its odds.

Odds (1 in) Highest to Lowest

a:	433	g:	2,030	m:	3,456	s:	7,591	y:	16,554	ae:	35,842
b:	524	h:	2,348	n:	4,235	t:	9,247	z:	23,216	af:	68,774
c:	865	i:	2,660	o:	5,361	u:	10,002	aa:	24,115	ag:	79,688
d:	874	j:	2,966	p:	6,219	v:	13,532	ab:	26,645	ah:	110,838
e:	1,019	k:	3,174	q:	7,042	w:	13,714	ac:	29,470	ai:	123,542
f:	2,006	l:	3,357	r:	7,054	x:	15,970	ad:	33,614	aj:	175,667

	Accidental Injury Cause	Odds			Accidental Injury Cause	Odds
1	Snowblower			19	Chain saw	
2	Pens and pencils			20	Grooming device	
3	Glass doors, windows, or panels			21	Batteries	
4	Trampoline			22	Paint, solvent, or lubricant	
5	Drinking straws			23	Manual workshop tools	
6	Hatchet or ax			24	Chair and sofa	
7	Clothing			25	Holiday or party supplies	
8	Jewelry			26	Washer or dryer	
9	Table			27	Hammock	
10	Electric lamp or fixture			28	Home power tools	
11	Television set or stand			29	Carpet or rug	
12	Lawn mower			30	Bunk beds	
13	Cooking range or oven			31	Pogo stick	
14	Soap or detergent			32	Electric outlet	
15	Fence			33	Sound recording equipment	
16	Go-cart			34	Clothing	
17	Bed, mattress, or pillow			35	Lightbulb	
18	Nonglass door			36	Horseshoes	

SOURCE: US Consumer Product Safety Commission, *National Electronic Injury Surveillance System (NEISS) Data Highlights—2010,* http://www.cpsc.gov/LIBRARY/neiss.html.

Answers:

Snowblower ... 1 in 33,614 (ad)
Pens or pencils ... 1 in 13,714 (w)
Glass doors, windows, or panels ... 1 in 2,030 (g)
Trampoline ... 1 in 3,357 (l)
Drinking straws ... 1 in 110,838 (ah)
Hatchet or ax ... 1 in 29,470 (ac)
Fireworks ... 1 in 35,842 (ae)
Jewelry ... 1 in 3,174 (k)
Table ... 1 in 865 (c)
Electric lamp or fixture ... 1 in 5,361 (o)
Television set or stand ... 1 in 4,235 (n)
Lawn mower ... 1 in 3,456 (m)

Cooking range oven ... 1 in 6,219 (p)
Soap or detergent ... 1 in 9,247 (t)
Fence ... 1 in 2,660 (i)
Go-cart ... 1 in 26,645 (ab)
Bed, mattress, or pillow ... 1 in 433 (a)
Nonglass door ... 1 in 874 (d)
Chain saw ... 1 in 10,002 (u)
Grooming device ... 1 in 7,054 (r)
Batteries ... 1 in 24,115 (aa)
Paint, solvent, or lubricant ... 1 in 15,970 (x)
Manual workshop tools ... 1 in 2,348 (n)
Chair and sofa ... 1 in 524 (b)

Holiday or party supplies ... 1 in 16,554 (y)
Washer or dryer ... 1 in 13,532 (v)
Home power tools ... 1 in 2,966 (j)
Carpet or rug ... 1 in 2,006 (f)
Bunk beds ... 1 in 7,591 (s)
Pogo stick ... 1 in 175,667 (aj)
Electric outlet ... 1 in 68,774 (af)
Sound recording equipment ... 1 in 7,042 (q)
Clothing ... 1 in 1,019 (e)
Lightbulb ... 1 in 23,216 (z)
Horseshoes ... 1 in 123,542 (ai)

But if It's the Fourth of July,
You Might Want to Put Off That Hospital Visit

Do you need another reason to put down that firecracker?

It turns out what has long been regarded as an urban myth is actually true. July is the most dangerous time to land in one of America's celebrated teaching hospitals. And things are probably at their worst over the Fourth of July weekend.

Every July 1, thousands of interns, straight out of medical school, report for duty at the nation's teaching hospitals—while at the same time many more experienced hands are headed out the door. Experienced interns who have finished their year are off to residency programs, and when the long holiday weekend rolls around, attending physicians and senior residents are often off to the beach or the golf course.

For years there have been rumors—disputed by several studies—that July was the worst month to get a hospital bracelet slapped on your wrist. A 2003 study of patients in intensive care units found no unusual spike in mortality. A 2009 study by researchers at the University of Tennessee Health Science Center in Memphis analyzing the surgical outcomes for 12,525 patients found no significant difference in recovery times or death rates for people who underwent procedures in July. However, it now appears that those results may have been skewed by the fact that both surgery and intensive care units are among the most supervised environments in a hospital.

No one hands a newly minted intern a scalpel and walks away. But there are other hospital settings where interns have a greater degree of autonomy, especially on a busy holiday weekend. A large and comprehensive new study published in the *Journal of General Internal Medicine*—examining all computerized death certificates (over 62 million) from 1979 to 2006—tested what researchers called the "New Resident Hypothesis" and found fatal medication errors rose 10% in teaching hospitals in July. There was no spike in counties with no teaching hospitals, and no similar uptick in any other month. The lethal mistakes included dispensing the wrong drug, overdoses, and accidents involving drugs or biological agents.

A separate study by Harvard Business School health care economists estimated that between 1,500 and 2,750 people each year die earlier than they normally would due to the "July phenomenon."

So keep a safe distance from the sparklers and Roman candles: in a year, the odds are **1 in 34,810** a person will end up in the ER thanks to fireworks.

SOURCES: DP Phillips, GEC Barker, "A July Spike in Fatal Medication Errors: A Possible Effect of New Medical Residents," *Journal of General Internal Medicine* 25(8), August 2010: 774–779. ✒ R Huckman, J Barro, "Cohort Turnover and Productivity" (NBER Working Paper No. 11182), National Bureau of Economic Research.

In Fact, Be Careful Around All Holidays

The odds a person will visit an emergency room due to an accident involving Christmas tree lights in a year:

1 in 80,855

SOURCE: US Consumer Product Safety Commission, *National Electronic Injury Surveillance System (NEISS) Data Highlights—2010,* http://www.cpsc.gov/LIBRARY/neiss.html.

EVERYDAY HAZARDS
Duct Tape Can Hurt You

Believe it or not, the odds a person will visit an emergency room due to an accident involving masking, duct, or other adhesive tape in a year are **1 in 167,488**. You're about as likely to visit the emergency room for a tape-related injury as for one caused by a leaf blower (**1 in 161,204**).

SOURCE: US Consumer Product Safety Commission, *National Electronic Injury Surveillance System (NEISS) Data Highlights—2010,* http://www.cpsc.gov/LIBRARY/neiss.html.

STAYING ALIVE

 Numbers Tell the Story

Thanks, Dr. Heimlich!

The odds a person will die from choking on food in a year: **1 in 320,874**

The odds a person will die from choking on a nonfood object in a year: **1 in 97,644**

The odds an adult has ever needed help because he or she was choking: **1 in 11.1**

The odds an adult has ever seen someone choke: **1 in 3.6**

The odds an adult is confident he or she would know how to help someone who is choking: **1 in 1.3**

The odds a choking adult requiring emergency assistance was helped by:

- Family member: **1 in 1.8**
- Friend: **1 in 10**
- Stranger: **1 in 12.5**

SOURCES: Book of Odds estimates based on Centers for Disease Control and Prevention, WONDER online database, *Compressed Mortality File*, 1999–2006 data. ✗ American Red Cross, *Summer Safety*, March 2010 Polling.

I HAVE A PULSE!

The odds an adult has ever been in a situation where someone nearby collapsed and may have needed CPR: } **1 in 3.7**

Who's willing and able to help? The odds an adult:

has taken a class to learn CPR: **1 in 1.5**

has first-aid certification: **1 in 2.7**

has both first-aid and CPR or AED certification: **1 in 3**

The odds an adult is likely to administer CPR when needed by:

A family member: **1 in 1.2**

A friend: **1 in 1.4**

A coworker: **1 in 1.6**

A boss: **1 in 1.7**

A stranger: **1 in 2.2**

A pet: **1 in 3.6**

The odds an adult is prepared to rush someone in his or her family to the hospital during an unexpected event are **1 in 1.1**. Not prepared? **1 in 16.7**.

SOURCES: American Red Cross, *Summer Safety*, March 2010 Polling. ✗ American Red Cross, *Water Safety Poll*, March 31, 2009. ✗ Harris Interactive, "Majorities Say They Are Prepared for Certain Unexpected Events, but Less Than Half Have Actually Done Certain Preparedness Actions," Harris Poll #54, press release, June 12, 2007.

When We Don't Make It

The odds a person who died will be buried in a casket: **1 in 1.4**

The odds a person who died will be cremated: **1 in 2.9**

The odds a person's cremated remains will be scattered: **1 in 5.8**

The odds a person's cremated remains will be scattered on land: **1 in 14.5**

The odds a person's cremated remains will be scattered on water: **1 in 9.7**

The odds a person's cremated remains will be returned to the family: **1 in 1.3**

The odds a person's cremated remains will not be picked up: **1 in 58.8**

The odds a person's cremated remains will be kept at home: **1 in 3.3**

The odds a person's cremated remains will be buried in a cemetery: **1 in 3.4**

The odds a person who died will be cryogenically frozen at Alcor: **1 in 606,500**

SOURCES: Casket and Funeral Supply Association of America, http://www.cfsaa.org/about.php. ✗ Cremation Association of North America, Cremation Statistics, http://www.cremationassociation.org/Media/CremationStatistics/tabid/95/Default.aspx. ✗ M Kim, "How Cremation Works," howstuffworks.com, http://science.howstuffworks.com/cremation.htm. ✗ Alcor Life Extension Foundation, "Complete List of Alcor Crytopreservations," http://www.alcor.org/cases.html.

ACKNOWLEDGMENTS

Without the intelligence, vision, and labor of many people, this book would not have been possible.

First of all, it rests on the foundation of the Book of Odds project. Funded by farsighted and courageous investors, we spent three years and about fifty person-years of effort creating a database of more than 400,000 odds. These went onto a remarkable website, launched with a preannouncement by Stephen J. Dubner and the *New York Times* Freakonomics blog. We are grateful to him and to the Boston Museum of Science for hosting our launch event. But most of all we are grateful to the extraordinary team that made the project possible and created a groundbreaking website.

This book was a special labor of love. The editorial team, headed by Rosalind Wright, were the ones who figured out what people would like to know while researchers figured out how to get to real numbers. The efforts of Alison Caverly, Jon Sobel, and Zack Turpin were instrumental and invaluable.

On the research side, Jon Yale-Loehr and Carolina Morgan led the efforts for this book. Ian Stanczyk contributed invaluable advice, along with unique and fascinating new ways to consider probabilities. Eric Lawless, Benny Kriss, David Gassko, Greg Costa, Greg Goodwin, Nick Williams, and Andrea Chroniewicz all provided tremendous help. A nod of appreciation also goes to two great interns, Anthony Lydgate and Alyssa Demirjian. We would not be in a position to publish without the labor of Dan Riviello, who was head of permissions.

Carolina Morgan and Luca Shapiro, two very talented designers, were the first to bring new life to odds through innovative and creative visual representations, allowing us to fashion the book proposal. The design was superbly realized by Walter Zekanoski, whom we recommend to anyone in need of creativity and reliability. Jon Yale-Loehr worked tirelessly to create and proof our odds, building on the work of Cynthia Ramirez and others before him. Justin Refi and Matt Crawford worked on the semantic organization of the database. Donna Lanney and Beau Tremblay were essential to the working of the website and made substantial contributions to this book. And none of us could have functioned without the wise hand of George Campbell.

Steve Ross added zombie infestation modeling to his many talents and profound belief in the value of our efforts. Our thanks go to our agents, Andrew Wylie, Kristina Moore, and Rebecca Nagel, and to our persistent editor at HarperCollins, Julia Abramoff, and design director Leah Carlson-Stanisic. And finally we would like to give our heartfelt thanks to all the organizations and individuals who have generously allowed us to work with their data.

—*Amram Shapiro, founder and CEO; Louise Firth Campbell, COO; Rosalind Wright, editor in chief*

ABOUT BOOK OF ODDS

Book of Odds was founded in 2006 with the mission to create the missing dictionary of probabilities. Over four years we developed the first database of its kind as a proof of concept. We developed 500,000 odds, largely from North American data sources for a start, and put them into a rigorous format that made each one comparable to every other.

Book of Odds provides consulting and creative services to corporations, institutions, and nonprofits. For corporations and institutions we help make sense of data and provide decision support, ranging from discrete to major positioning decisions. We also collect data within the operations or the marketplace. Creative work focuses on the use of odds in public relations and marketing campaigns.

We offer similar services to nonprofits, which often must try to make the urgency and scale of their issue understood. Because we collect "the odds of everyday life," nonprofits are likely to be able to find something their target market can relate to personally. Some have operational needs such as surveys of volunteers. We modify our rates for nonprofits.

To reach us with inquiries:

Amram Shapiro, founder and CEO
ashapiro@bookofodds.com
Louise Firth Campbell, COO
lfirthcampbell@bookofodds.com